Korean Development
The Interplay of Politics and Economics

Written under the auspices of
The Center for International Affairs
Harvard University

Korean Development

The Interplay of Politics and Economics

David C. Cole
Princeton N. Lyman

Harvard University Press
Cambridge, Massachusetts
1971

Distributed in Great Britain by Oxford University Press, London

Library of Congress Catalog Card Number 75-131468

SBN 674-50563-8

Printed in the United States of America

Preface

This book was originally conceived in 1965, when we were both in South Korea, and when the directions of that country's politico-economic evolution were still quite uncertain. At that time, while the prevailing commentary on Korea was still emphasizing the weaknesses and the problems, we were optimistic that the trends were favorable and that the country was already well into a period of rapid progress. The first draft of the manuscript was written during the academic year 1967–1968, when we were both at the Center for International Affairs, Harvard University. By then our earlier expectations were widely shared, and we viewed our task as trying to describe and analyze the causes of a critical period of transformation.

Now as we somewhat painstakingly prepare these pages for publication, we again sense a divergence between popular conception and what we see as emerging reality. South Korea has been cited as one of the success stories of foreign aid and economic development by the Commission on International Development (the Pearson Commission) and many others. Admittedly, the economic growth indicators are all favorable; the final statistics for 1969, which have recently become available, show the highest rates of expansion so far attained in Korea. But there are structural distortions emerging in the economy that will need to be corrected if rapid growth is to continue, and there seems to be increasing inertia or resistance to taking corrective actions.

The fundamental problem that clouds the future, however, is in the political realm. South Korea, like so many other developing countries, has so far failed to devise a means for orderly change of government leadership. The national referendum of October 1969, which approved the possible continuation of the current administration for another term,

v

that is, until 1975, has, if anything, merely postponed the issue. The unwillingness of the president to step aside at the end of his second term, which repeats the pattern of Syngman Rhee, raises the possibility that he will try to remain in office indefinitely. The electoral process in Korea is probably not yet capable of removing an incumbent president from office.* Therefore he must either withdraw voluntarily or be forced out by some nonelectoral means. If the latter becomes the only likely prospect, it will generate forces that will tend to eat away at the political edifice which has recently been constructed. A scenario of possible developments based on the experience of a number of countries might proceed as follows. The president becomes increasingly surrounded and cut off from current problems by an expanded group of courtiers, who wield the effective power in the name of the president. They in turn exact a larger slice of graft from an expanded range of direct controls and special favors. In time public discontent reaches the boiling point, leading to popular demonstrations or coup attempts. These may be forestalled by increasingly repressive governmental actions and general economic accomplishments, but eventually a crisis will occur and the regime will be deposed. The amount of coercion, suffering, and mismanagement that will be experienced in the process is difficult to predict.

Such a sequence of developments could perhaps be avoided, especially if the existing administration would devote itself to creating conditions for an orderly transfer of power within a reasonable period of time. We sincerely hope that this will be done, but we have doubts about the realism of such a hope. For this reason our current assessment is that there will be some retrogression in the political sphere over the next few years and that this will probably affect Korea's economic progress as well. We are not necessarily suggesting that the deterioration has already begun or how far it may go; we say only that we do foresee some reversals in the future.

This may help to clarify the dimensions of our study. It is concerned primarily with the period of political and economic progress that was most marked: from roughly 1963 to 1967. Our analysis covers the preceding years to indicate the prior conditions, and the coverage has been carried out sufficiently through subsequent years to show the continuing pattern of growth and structural change. But we now see this critical 1963–1967 period not as one in which a transformation took place that put South Korea permanently on the smoothly ascending path of polit-

---

* This is an interesting contrast with the Philippines, where until recently it seemed that an incumbent president was unlikely to be reelected for a second term.

ical and economic development. Rather, it was a period of far-reaching rapid and interrelated improvement, which was preceded by one of politico-economic recession, and is likely to be followed by reversals of unpredictable dimension. We hope that the foundations which have been created or strengthened in recent years will prove strong enough to prevent serious difficulties, but the issues ahead are major ones and will place a heavy burden on those political institutions in Korea that seek to maintain a viable consensus within a democratic framework.

In presenting this volume, the authors are indebted to many who supported, criticized, commented, or just sympathized. Mr. Cole is indebted to the Harvard Development Advisory Service, and to the Agency for International Development under its contract with the Development Advisory Service, for support of his research during 1966–1968. Mr. Lyman is grateful to the Center for International Affairs, and to the Carnegie Corporation through its grant to the Center, for support of his research and writing during 1967–1968, and to the AID for granting him a year's leave of absence for this purpose. Many persons in the DAS Economic Development Seminar and the joint Harvard–MIT Seminar on Political Development provided advice and comment during this time.

As development specialists looking at Korea, rather than Korean specialists looking at development, we were aware of our limitations in being able to engage fully the sources in the Korean language. We are very grateful therefore to Korean and American scholars who have reviewed and discussed the themes of this book and who provided us with much useful material. Mr. Lyman is especially grateful to the project on Politics and Society in Korea, directed by Chong-Sik Lee and Sung-Chick Hong, which provided a stimulating atmosphere in Korea during 1967 for the development of some of the ideas for this book, and the papers produced there served as indispensable guides to the political development of South Korea.

An early summary of the main themes of this book, prepared in 1967, was read and commented on by many people, including Robert Scalapino, Sung-Chick Hong, Frank Baldwin, Joel Bernstein, Joan Nelson, and Chong-Sik Lee. The complete manuscript was read and commented on by Irma Adelman, Gregory Henderson, Walter Falcon, and Gustav Papanek, all of whom added immeasurably to our being able to improve both content and organization. Hahn-Been Lee provided continual counsel and the benefits of his store of knowledge, plus an advance manuscript of his excellent study of Korean administration, to guide us. Many persons in the Agency for International Development made data available and were helpful in locating sources. Finally, we wish to express appreciation to Samuel Huntington, Director of the program on Political Institutionalization and Social Change at the Center for International Affairs, who encouraged and assisted in this project from the outset, and who read and commented on the manuscript at several stages. Of course (and as one former and one present government employee, we insist), responsibility for all the views and any faults in this volume rest solely with us.

One final note on a point of style: after much deliberation we decided to forego the McCune-Reischauer system of spelling Korean names. We did so because we use only a few Korean names in our book and those of men with international reputations. It seemed odd and somewhat disrespectful to impose upon their names a spelling quite different from that which they have chosen and from that by which they are known outside of Korea. We therefore used the spelling they use; when in doubt we used that in the latest *Korea Annual,* published by the Hapdong News Agency in Seoul, which has also recently abandoned the McCune-Reischauer system. Similarly, in citing Korean authors who have published in English, we respected not only their choice of spelling but their reversal of family and surnames to match Western style.

No book is complete without the authors paying tribute to their wives and children, who lived through the process of writing, rewriting, editing, and publishing at no small sacrifice. Our families deserve such credit indeed, and we acknowledge it gratefully.

David C. Cole
Djakarta

Princeton N. Lyman
Washington, D.C.

May 1970

Contents

Tables

Appendix Tables

Korean Development

Korean developments

Introduction

Recent South Korean experience is an intriguing subject for study because it involves an astonishingly quick change from political and economic ill health to a condition of reasonable political stability and very rapid economic growth. Only a few years ago, in the period 1960–1961, there was a revolution, followed by a military coup; economic growth was slowing down; and the country was heavily dependent on economic and military assistance from the United States. In fact, there was some doubt as to whether South Korea could continue to exist even as a permanent American ward. By 1967, however, the economy was growing at a truly remarkable rate, the political system showed evidence of increasing strength and stability and of preserving a democratic character, and there was open discussion of ending United States aid in a few years. In foreign affairs, also, South Korea was beginning to assume a more independent role commensurate with its resources and population.

This study focuses on the transformation that took place in the middle 1960s, which basically altered South Korea's development situation. It was a transformation of political dynamics, national outlook, and economic structure—three factors bound up with one another. Our intention is to trace the relationship of these factors and to provide thereby some insight into the process of political and economic interaction in development.

South Korea is, of course, unique in many ways, not only in its culture and history but in the nature of external influence on recent development and on its political ideology. Nevertheless, it is an especially valuable laboratory in which to study development. Seldom in modern times has economic growth been so intensely rapid over several years to give us insight into the dynamics, as well as the strains, of economic change.

1

In few countries has so basic a transformation of economic structure taken place at the same time as pressures were brought to bear to reduce, rather than strengthen, the degree of authoritarianism in the political system. If continuing rapid economic development has not been completely assured nor democracy perfectly achieved, South Korea has nevertheless made a distinct contribution to pointing out ways in which these goals can be made complementary rather than competitive. But the Korean experience also points out how progress in these areas, once set into motion, is not likely to be constant. These then are the lessons of recent Korean experience for the theories of development.

In selecting the themes for study and in drawing our conclusions, we have inevitably been influenced by our special interests. Our focus is "development," the ambiguous but ubiquitous goal associated with two-thirds of the nations of the world. We prefer to treat that goal in economic and political terms, and in specific reference here to the needs of the economically poorer nations, those normally called "less developed."[1] We assume that economic structural change to provide long-term growth—economic development—is desirable for these nations, not only because it is necessary to provide growing populations with better living conditions but because it seems to be a goal of most of the peoples in these countries. It is not, however, a goal usually desired at any price and, in our opinion, not one worth pursuing if it benefits only a few, or if it destroys human dignity and all rights of individual choice in the process. Hence our interpretation of the political aspects of development is functionally related to economic modernization but also characterized by a value preference. We conceive of political development in these countries as movement toward that political situation which enables a country to modernize its economic structure while enlarging the access of the major elements of the population to the benefits of economic change and their continued influence over the major direction of national priorities and policies. Thus we define "development" as the mobilization of national resources for economic modernization by consensus rather than coercion, with all that such development requires of both economic and political institutions.[2]

This definition leaves much to be done in further definition and elaboration, and in sorting out the functional from the value-oriented. It also contains difficult problems of judgment, for example, about "more or less" coercion or consensus in any given case. But we think that, in the Korean case at least, the meaning of terms and the basis of judgment will be evident in the chapters that follow. We hope also to show, in this chapter and in the remainder of the book, that such an approach to development that involves both economic and political factors is essential to understanding fully either political or economic development in the "less developed" countries today.

Our particular analysis of South Korea's development emphasizes finally the "breakthrough" period of the mid-1960s when basic economic changes and, to a lesser degree, basic political changes were accomplished. We have thus selected those factors for analysis, both political and economic, that appeared to influence most the nature of that breakthrough. As a result we have given less attention to long-term historical, geographic, cultural, social, and family factors that have influenced underlying patterns of political and economic behavior in Korea and more to the makeup of, major influences on, and operations of the major contemporary forces and institutions in South Korea which manifest those patterns in the development context. Furthermore we have sought to point out the factors of the Korean experience that would help best to refine current theories of economic and political development.

ECONOMIC FACTORS

In our analysis of economic change, we have first compared Korean economic structure and its changes to the pattern of economic development for most countries. Economists (perhaps even more noneconomists) have often lamented the lack of a universally applicable theory or model of economic growth and development. But intensive study in the past 20 years has produced substantial agreement that, even though the process is complex, some normative patterns of economic growth and structural change of developing countries do exist.[3] Industrialization, involving rising shares of manufacturing and declining shares of agricultural output, is a universal element of growth. So, too, are urbanization and expansion of education, transportation, and communication. Because these transformations all require large amounts of capital, it is essential that increased shares of the total of available resources be freed from current consumption and allocated to capital formation if growth is to be accelerated. Overall, the correlation of these variables follows a pattern.

Along with the identification of normal patterns of growth and structural change, however, there has come a greater awareness of why individual countries or areas may be expected to deviate from the norms. While relative shares of agricultural and industrial production tend to move in opposite directions as per capita output rises, the absolute shares of agriculture and industry in each country are obviously influenced by national resource endowment and by human factors such as the degree or pattern of education. Similarly, the relative importance of foreign trade is associated with a country's size, its natural resource endowment, and the level of per capita income. It is possible, therefore, to say something about a particular country's growth performance and potential by investigating deviations from those norms.

We have chosen to compare South Korean structure and performance to universal norms, not because the Korean experience approximated the norms but because it deviated from them in so many ways. The Korean economic structure has at times been stretched far out of shape with overdevelopment in some sectors and extreme backwardness in others. The colonial heritage and the Korean war contributed to these imbalances; postwar recovery accentuated some of them. It was not until the 1960s that an appropriate configuration of demands and production evolved which took full advantage of Korea's productive capabilities. The new configuration, which is a result of both conscious policies and changing external conditions has demonstrated that Korea can achieve high rates of economic growth and that, given its human resources capabilities, it should probably be at a considerably higher level of development and real income than it is. This last factor particularly helps explain not only the sudden success that certain policy changes produced in the mid-1960s, but also some of the popular attitudes toward development and the political response that these policy changes produced.

A second major emphasis in the economic analysis is on economic policies and planning. One of the lessons of the last 20 years of study of economic development has been the variation in effectiveness of applying particular policies to different societies.[4] Policies to encourage private savings may be quite ineffective if political conditions are very unstable or if family responsibilities and loyalties siphon off any accumulation. It may also be unrealistic to try to create laissez-faire conditions in a setting where some degree of authoritarian treatment and guidance from the bureaucracy is customary. On the other hand, government attempts to regulate private enterprise, or manage major sectors of the economy, may be counterproductive if administrative capability is limited or if political conditions are such that much government-controlled resources will be diverted (through corruption, political payoffs, etc.) for nondevelopment uses.

South Korean experience in this regard seems especially instructive. In recent years there has been considerable experimentation with new policies that departed significantly not only from previous patterns in Korea but also from the policy prescriptions followed in the majority of less developed countries. These policies were surprisingly effective in inducing certain structural changes in savings, investment, and production that led to very rapid growth. Similarly, there were significant departures from past Korean experience in the seriousness and sophistication of long-term economic planning which also came to play a major role in the economic process. Equally important, both the policies and the planning seem also to have generated a positive political response by broadening both the awareness of, and participation in, the benefits derived from economic development.

POLITICAL FACTORS

In our analysis of South Korea's political development in this period, we have been especially sensitive to the requisites for economic modernization and the problems of achieving those requisites in a political system not marked primarily by coercion. The period under analysis in South Korea was one in which general concern over the problems of economic growth had become an important political factor. It was also a period in which a whole new generation of political leaders had been energized and recruited into politics by the revolution of 1960 and, even more, by the coup of 1961. This new leadership reflected a more determined and effective commitment to economic development than its predecessors, but there remained strong sympathies toward authoritarian methods of political control. Our focus has thus been on the gradual transition from military to civilian rule in this period and on the struggle between authoritarian and democratizing influences. We have given primary attention to those forces and institutions—the military, bureaucracy, parties, press, students, and intelligentsia—that shaped by their outlook and actions the nature of issues at stake and the political pattern by which a modernized Korea would be created. Finally, we have focused on the role of economic modernization, as an influence on the political attitudes of key groups and as a major factor in the resolution of key political issues.

Our judgment on the political trends is undoubtedly influenced by our concern with the need for economic modernization, especially in the South Korean setting of this period. If one were less concerned with economic modernization, one might well be more harsh than we have been on the absence of autonomous local government, the remaining restrictions on individual freedom after the compromises of 1965, and the extent of corruption, in deciding on the degree of progress in political development in this period. We have balanced these factors against the genuine degree of consensus achieved in support of economic modernization and of the political leadership that brought it about, the relatively broad, popular participation in economic development, plus the real compromises made by the leadership toward a more open political system in face of strong opposition to military-type rule.

POLITICAL AND ECONOMIC INTERACTION

Such trade-offs between politically desirable and economically desirable factors are very difficult to assess. The justification of one set of circumstances in one period can be easily perverted to justify another in a different period. Events in South Korea since 1967, for example, suggest that the delicate, mutually supporting relationship between economic modernization and political democratization of the mid-1960s has altered, with the former being used more and more as a means to justify retardation of the latter, and with possible adverse consequences for both. Country conditions vary greatly, also. Some developing countries, especially in Africa, have been more preoccupied with problems of political identity and national integration than major economic reorganization. Others, such as Pakistan, have pursued fairly successful policies of economic modernization but have been beset by political problems. The pressures for political and economic modernization also vary. In some countries, they are found, separately or combined, at the center of power, opposed by more traditional local elites. In others, the local level is the source of pressure for change, resisted by a traditionalist oligarchy at the center. Finally, of course, different analysts, and peoples, will accept different compromises with authoritarianism as the price for economic development.

Relating political to economic development in a general theory is thus quite difficult. Those theorists of modernization who have emphasized major economic transformations in discussing political development have relied heavily on historical models of Western experience in which the political problems arose more sequentially than in the less developed countries, or at least seem so in retrospect.[5] Much recent work on political development theory has meanwhile moved somewhat in the opposite direction, delineating a separate category of conditions, attributes, and goals for political development than necessarily associated with economic modernization. Many of the attributes so associated with political development per se are still functionally related, if not exclusively so, to the problems of a modern industrialized (or industrializing) economy: effective central authority, professionalized administrative capacity, greater structural differentiation, stability, and efficacy in international affairs.[6] Two of the conditions now commonly attributed to political development, while applicable to some preindustrial societies, become much more acute in an age of modern communications, mass education, and the social and physical mobility associated with modern economic development: the change among the population from "widespread subject status to mass participation" and greater sensitivity to equality.[7]

Nevertheless, much of the recent writing on political development reflects a sense of conflict between the requisites of political and economic development. This has been exacerbated by the hypotheses of some economists concerning the conditions associated with growth, e.g., that increased inequality of income is a necessary condition for mobilizing savings.[8] Political scientists have also pointed to the major emphasis on developing effective central authority and rationalized administration for support of economic modernization as possibly detrimental to the development of strong political parties and to more widespread political participation in general.[9] Economic growth itself has been frequently cited as politically destabilizing because it fosters social change, new aspirations, and insecurities which are often too burdensome for the still fragile political systems in the developing countries. Some theorists have thus concluded that political development should be seen and dealt with quite distinctly from economic development, or at least that the development of political institutions should be approached separately from the substance and issues of economic modernization.[10]

This separate attention to the attributes and goals of political development has been useful in two ways. It has clarified much of the previously less systematic thinking about how Western or Russian political institutions might take root in the less developed countries. It has also thrown more light on the choices—and possible costs—involved for political development in the emphasis on economic development in the developing countries. Yet, however one might separate out the factors of each and clarify the choices involved at different stages, in practice the processes are closely intertwined in nearly all the countries to which such theoretical analyses are directed. Economic modernization involves not only economic structural change but also changes in the basic structure of social and political relationships. The particular approach to economic development is critical to achieving, or deterring, progress toward the objective of greater equality stressed by political theorists. Finally, economic development is the goal of the articulate elite and of constantly increasing mass sections of the population in most of the developed countries. It is thus a major political factor, not only as a public issue but as a force in the development of political institutions.

It seems desirable, then, for theory to begin to focus more on the interaction of political and economic development, in order to derive useful concepts of how they might be made to interact more positively in terms of the goals of both. Emphasis should be placed on the phrase *made to interact*, for clearly pursuing one will not automatically produce the other. In fact it is likely that pursuing either one very much to the exclusion of the other could be detrimental to both in almost every case.

South Korea's experience is valuable in this regard because the two processes were made to interact. It is useful to contrast South Korea's experience in the 1960s to one of the typologies of transition to modernization described by David Apter, a political theorist who has emphasized the importance of such interaction.[11] South Korea in 1961 fit very closely the description of what Apter has called a "mobilization system": one in which new values are created from the top, modernization and industrialization become consummate values, centralized planning is emphasized, authority is hierarchical, and there is a great urgency of action. But South Korea also differed from the typology in certain important ways. The new regime did not have any clear ideology of modernization. Its early attempts to create even a vaguely defined nationalistic ideology gave way rather quickly to the more concrete objectives of economic growth and, through it, international prestige. Its economic and political policies thus reflected considerable pragmatism and flexibility. Second, the structure of authority was only imperfectly hierarchical. Neither the army, which in 1961 spawned the new regime, nor the government party that developed later, succeeded in creating complete national discipline and solidarity. The students, in particular, continued to espouse more democratic values and they, together with the intellectuals and, by circumstance, the older and more traditional elite formed a determined bloc of opposition to a more authoritarian and purely action-oriented regime.

Partly for these reasons, the transition to a more "conciliatory system," which Apter describes as a sequence to the stage of mobilization, came in South Korea during this same phase, even as the creation of new values and the emphasis on modernization was taking hold. It was thus during the critical period of major economic policy change and growth that the events suggested by Apter for a later phase took place:

> The leadership enlarges itself, authoritative decision-making is widened. Accountability groups are made more significant. The area of repressive law is reduced. The use of punishment as a political device declines. Resource determination and allocation take place more often on the local level, with new formulas being accepted. New consent groups emerge.[12]

Thus in many ways, the processes of economic and political development in South Korea were made mutually reinforcing in the 1960s. Widened participation in authority and decision-making improved rather than diminished economic efficiency and growth. Modernization of economic structures and high growth in turn provided goals around which were achieved a new national consensus and a basis for adapting the leadership's demands for government power and authority to the limitations imposed by the need for democratic consent and legitimization. The results were not perfect. And one can question the permanence of the accommodation between power and consent that was achieved. But the results were impressive in many ways and offer considerable promise for the future in South Korea. Also, they flowed not only from some of the special conditions extant in South Korea but from innovative policy decisions, energetic leadership, and national determination in the key areas for choice. As such, they perhaps provide clues by which other developing countries can escape some of the dilemmas of political and economic development.

Part I

1 / The Antecedents of
   Recent Development

This book concentrates on a relatively short if significant period in South Korean history and development. Obviously enough, the events of this period stemmed from a complicated amalgam of historical and modern influences. In dealing with them it is important to try to sort out to what degree the economic and political developments of this time reflected a continuing, thinly disguised historical pattern and to what degree they were the culmination of rapidly building forces of change.

Two recent works on Korean political development offer an interesting contrast in this regard. One, Gregory Henderson's *Korea: Politics of the Vortex*, is an extensively researched and revealing analysis, emphasizing long-standing historical and cultural influences on contemporary Korean political behavior.[1] The other, Hahn-Been Lee's *Time, Change, and Administration: Korea's Search for Modernization*, focuses instead on the period since liberation from Japan in 1945, and with great insight analyzes the forces of change and modernization in that time period alone that have shaped and altered recent political consciousness, ideology, action, and development.[2]

The two works aptly point up two significant factors in Korean development. On the one hand, Korea emerged from World War II with a long established, distinctive, and homogeneous culture that, despite economic changes during 35 years of Japanese rule, had not been greatly transformed in the colonial period. Many of the changes that followed tended to reinforce trends begun much earlier. It is nevertheless also true that, since 1945, in the space of just one generation, Korea has experienced a nearly unparalleled series of political, social, military, and economic upheavals—upheavals which in less than 20 years encompassed the first division of the country in 12 centuries, a major and extremely

13

destructive war, 4 very different governments in the South, a sharply altered economic structure and, finally, a confrontation between generations that would have been unbridgeable without a major revolution in thought and action. It was this combination of traditional outlook and experience of swift change that shaped the events of the 1960s.

TRADITIONAL ELEMENTS IN KOREAN CULTURE

In some very important ways, Korean culture has been molded by influences emanating from its neighbors. The Chinese imprint can be seen particularly in the Confucian ethics of Korean society, in civil service concepts, and in some significant religious influences; the Japanese, in administrative and organizational methods, in concepts of modernization, and in language. Nevertheless, Korea retained important distinguishing characteristics of its own that have differentiated Korean reaction to the influences of modernization from those of the Japanese and Chinese.

Significant in this connection is the fact of Korea's relative insularity. Having centuries ago closed its borders to other ethnic groups and its ports to outsiders, and discouraged commercial activity, Korea emerged into the twentieth century a remarkably homogeneous society. There were no significant minority groups and no important alien groups, such as a foreign merchant class. There also were no significant regional or separate political loyalties to compete seriously with the authority of the central regime.[3] Finally, unlike China and especially Japan, Korea lacked a strong warlord or military class,[4] which fact was to affect civil-military relations in the modern period. As a result of all these factors— ethnical and linguistical, and in the absence of strong religious groupings—Korea was unusually cohesive.

A second important characteristic was the fluidity of the class structure that did exist. As far back as the end of the seventeenth century the rigidities in the class system had begun to decline.[5] The leveling process was greatly accentuated by Japanese rule, which not only did away with opportunities for access to the top but also took over much of the land by which, through tax rights more than outright ownership, many of the aristocrats had maintained their position. By independence the lines of class division had been greatly blurred, so that even the landowning class was not composed as much of the older aristocracy as of former clerks (who had been able to use their local knowledge and technical ability to obtain title under Japanese registration procedures) and low-ranking aristocrats.[6]

Thus Korea had, within the general aegis of Chinese cultural influence, developed a distinct social and political system and a national character that was inward-looking and largely defensive. Unlike its neighbors, Japan and China, Korea did not respond very rapidly to the Western technological or intellectual influences that were by the end of the nineteenth century deeply affecting reformist elements in the two larger countries.[7] The establishment of a Japanese protectorate in Korea in 1905, followed by complete annexation in 1910, cut off the opportunities for further development of indigenous response and change.

With the onset of Japanese rule, external modernizing influences on Korean culture shifted into three channels. First was the Japanese influence, which came via the administrative process and the substantial changes Japanese capital and administrators made in Korea's economic structure. These changes involved both agricultural practices, such as the use of fertilizer, and the development of a fairly significant industrial base. However, the impact of Japanese influence was limited by discrimination against Korean participation in planning and management of either government or economy. The Japanese, however, did have a profound influence on the Korean legal-administrative structure (which the first independent Korean Government would copy largely without change), on the attitude of junior Korean bureaucrats who would later rise to important positions, and on the general structure of Korean economic development.

The second channel was the Christian missionary schools. These assumed great importance during the colonial period because they provided both the means of escaping Japanese cultural imperialism and a haven, under sympathetic Western missionaries, for Koreans with strong anti-Japanese nationalist feelings. But this channel was also limited, because Christians made up a very small percentage of the Korean population.[8] Moreover, especially in the thirties and forties, when the oppressiveness of Japanese rule increased, the educational activity of the missionaries was severely proscribed.[9] Nevertheless, because by then there was no longer any serious discrimination against this minority by Koreans themselves, and because of this nationalist association, Christians came to be highly regarded and were to play a role in post-liberation governments well beyond their numerical proportion. While numbering not more than 8 percent of the population, from 1952 to 1962 Christians provided 41 percent of the Cabinet members, Assemblymen, and other senior officials in South Korea.[10]

The third external influence was to become apparent later, though it owed its origin to the Japanese: this was the influence of the exiled nationalists and independence fighters. Many of them were to be prominent in postliberation Korea, but they spent the better part of the colonial period abroad—in Shanghai where the Korean Provisional Government provided a loose but rarely happy coalition of diverse nationalist groups, in Manchuria and China where various Korean military units harassed Japanese forces and served occasionally under Chinese command (both Kuomintang and Communist), in the United States where earnest figures lobbied for Western support for Korean independence, and elsewhere.[11] Even before 1945 the exile groups had divided fairly sharply into pro-Western and pro-Communist groups, absorbing the ideology of, as well as developing ties to, their preferred great power.[12] However, while individuals among them developed significant reputations and occasionally cliques on which to draw later, the exiled groups not only did not control events within Korea during the colonial period, but also were largely divorced from them.[13] This added to the difficulties of the political situation in 1945 when the revered but distant leaders returned to assume their roles in an independent country.

In sum, in the period of Japanese rule, the sources of external, and particularly modernizing, influences on Korean culture were significant but narrowly channeled. They were directed primarily to the elite, a situation that was to facilitate the immediate adoption of new values and norms in government, education, and the social structure when the elite group took command after liberation. This change was made easier by the fact that the old structure of king, court, and nobility had been swept away by the Japanese, leaving a major gap in the Confucian hierarchy to be filled by the new leaders. On the other hand, the mores and structure of Korean society as a whole had not been deeply affected during this period.

Nevertheless, even if in 1945 largely possessed of traditional values, Korean culture was not wholly in conflict with the demands of modernization that were to confront it. Korean "traditional" culture was more fluid in terms of class structure and in many other ways more adaptable to modernization than other traditional agricultural societies. Not all of these special characteristics have been cited as assets. Henderson sees the homogeneity of Korean culture and the fluidity of the class structure as having had detrimental effects on the Korean capacity for modern political organization. Historically, he believes, they prevented the development of strong intermediary institutions—whether based on class, region, or economic interest—thus forestalling the development of both the objective basis and organizational experience for a pluralistic society. Combined with a high degree of political centralism, they also contributed to a strong "upward draft" that drew political activists to the center of power and put them into a type of competition in which factions became common, while stable forms of group interest and countervailing influence were absent.[14] These characteristics, Henderson argues, have been transferred to modern political behavior.

Yet, in this same cultural setting one can readily also see advantages for a society that had to achieve difficult economic and social adjustments to meet the challenges of the twentieth century. As noted, unlike a host of other newly independent nations, South Korea did not have to overcome strong regional or religious differences in order to establish a viable political structure. It was able to take important economic steps, like the land reform of 1948–1950, more easily in part because there was a lack of class unity or even perceived common class interest on the part of those most adversely affected. Furthermore, the absence of deeply alienated minorities, and by 1945, of any historical class of oppressors, eliminated divisive and vindictive elements from the body politic. In short, if there were a strong "upward draft," it was one to which nearly all elements felt they might have access.

Another important characteristic was the absence of strong inhibitions against material gain. Confucian ethics, of course, were not oriented toward capitalism. Moreover, an environment characterized by scarcity and limited resources, as was traditional rural society in Korea, can tend to breed suspicion of anyone who gets ahead—presumably at the expense of others—and to reinforce the demands of the extended family on the individual's increased resources.[15] But none of these influences acted in Korea to create a serious antimaterialism as did some of the religions of South and Southeast Asia, which accentuated spiritual not only above but against material pleasures. Events in the postliberation period would confirm the responsiveness of the population to economic incentive.

Class fluidity also contributed to this adaptability to economic modernization. While there was disdain for merchant activity, and a consequent absence of any proud, entrepreneur, middle class in traditional society, the breakdown of class rigidity, especially at the top, and a long decline in the aristocratic privilege of dissociation from economic concerns made it easier for ambitious, respectable persons to move into entrepreneur activity after liberation. Many of Korea's modern entrepreneurs are thus descended from the former landlord class.[16] In fact, adjustments of this kind began under Japanese rule, which included the establishment of an industrial base in parts of Korea and the introduction even into the countryside of modern legal concepts and commercial activity. In spite of colonial discrimination, some Koreans were able to respond to their advantage.

To summarize, though concern over economic development, per se, in South Korea was only to become a critical political demand in the aftermath of the Korean War, postwar economic programs did not have to face any major obstacles of values.[17] Korean culture included many potentially favorable conditions for modernization. Nevertheless, this did not prevent some painful readjustments to the changes in economic and political conditions following independence.

OCCUPATION AND EARLY INDEPENDENCE
YEARS IN SOUTH KOREA: 1945–1949

The first years after 1945 were extraordinarily difficult ones for South Korea and clearly influenced the pattern of political and economic events thereafter. These years saw first of all the division of Korea into two states as a result of the inability of the USSR and the United States— who had accepted, respectively, Japanese surrender in the northern and southern parts of Korea—to agree on a program of mutual withdrawal and unification. Within the South, partly reflecting the ideological and political battle of the superpowers, there were increasingly bitter struggles for power. Finally, there was a general decline in economic, political, and social order, especially in the period 1946–1948, leading to increases in crime, gang warfare, political assassinations, violent strikes, and ultimately a communist-inspired military uprising in 1948 that in turn inspired a fierce rightist purge of nearly every political and social institution.

The division of the country was perhaps the most momentous factor. It meant the loss for South Korea of heavy industry, the major coal deposits, and almost all the developed power capacity. It also produced a heavy influx of refugees from the North.[18] Under these difficult circumstances, South Korea had to deal with its own drastically curtailed industrial production (which resulted partly from the repatriation of Japanese managers and technicians), an inflation that had by 1946 raised food prices a hundredfold over their prewar level, and the problem of disposing of Japanese industries and properties for which there was no plan and, indeed, no personnel. All of this also resulted in a consequence of great significance for Korea's future political as well as economic development: immediate heavy dependence on the United States. With Japan, for both political and economic considerations, out of the running, assistance could only come from the United States. The American government, with responsibility for postwar occupation, began responding to a constantly increasing need. In FY 1946, aid came to $6 million; in FY 1947 it rose to $93 million; and in FY 1948, the year of South Korean independence, it climbed to $113 million.[19]

Internally, there were grave, and for many Koreans, largely unexpected political difficulties. One of these was the widening and increasingly bitter split between left and right in South Korea, and especially between Communists and anti-Communists. The split was aggravated by the division of the country. This was a painful problem for nationalists of all political complexions. Despite differences over approach, none accepted the division with anything but dismay and a certainty that it could and should be overcome. Consequently, in the debates over various interim formulas proposed by the occupying powers—trusteeship, separate independence for the South, and so forth—feelings ran very high, and the bitterness became all the more intense.

Beyond the immediate issues, the dislodging of the Japanese had disclosed a severe lack of ready Korean political experience and organization. The gap was not overcome by the American military occupation authorities who arrived with virtually no preparation for civil administration and no knowledge of the Korean scene.[20] Further, American vacillation in this period regarding United States responsibilities for Korea and over its policy on reunification, plus fear of Communists and by implication leftists generally, led American authorities into occupation policies that had the effect of weakening the moderates and promoting predominantly conservative forces. The latter were backed strongly by Korean bureaucrats from the Japanese colonial period and by a growing and often ruthless police force. Belated American efforts, just prior to independence, to help restructure a moderate political force failed.

Thus the man who was able to rise successfully in this milieu was Syngman Rhee: unique, solitary, charismatic, conservative but with impeccable nationalist credentials going back to the late nineteenth century. Rhee fought the Americans on many issues in this period but he sided with them on two of crucial importance: the granting of separate independence to the South in 1948 when negotiations with the USSR on reunification were breaking down, and support of a strong anti-Communist position both internally and vis-à-vis the North.[21] Similarly, the first important postliberation political party in the South was the Korean Democratic party which was held together largely by anti-communism and was composed mainly of landlords, businessmen, and anti-Communist nationalists. It threw its support behind Rhee, who was elected South Korea's first president.

As noted, the conservative forces in this period were supported strongly by the bureaucracy and police. These groups had an important influence on events of the next decade. There was considerable feeling among most nationalist groups, though most strongly from the left, against Korean bureaucrats who had been trained by, and served under, the Japanese. However, in the interests of administrative efficiency and for convenience, Rhee, like the American occupation authorities, recruited his bureaucrats from their ranks despite political criticisms.[22] For a while after independence the bureaucracy grew rapidly, but then there followed a long period of relatively low new recruitment.[23] In this latter period the senior incumbents, often blocked from advancement to politically sensitive positions by lingering nationalist antagonisms (though this lessened in the mid-1950s) in turn protected themselves by exercising their influence on the tone of administrative personnel. They set highly legalistic, formal standards for admission to the bureaucracy unattuned to postliberation standards of education or to new concepts of development or administration. It would be a generation before the winds of change blowing in postliberation Korean society penetrated into the bureaucracy. The bureaucracy that took root was instead conservative, defensive, and closed.

As for the police they, too, were protecting themselves from anger at their role under the Japanese. The police had been the most visible, and surely the most disliked, Korean intermediary of Japanese rule. The police, nevertheless, expanded greatly in the turbulent postwar period, first under the American military occupation and later under Rhee. Like the bureaucracy, they were fearful of demands for expulsion of "collaborators." They thus became deeply involved in politics, supporting Rhee in his purge after 1948, and were often ruthless in their actions against opponents of the government.[24]

Under all these circumstances, the coming of independence still had a salutary and calming effect. An ebullience of spirit was kindled by the magic of the idea itself. With the more definite division of the country into North and South, and the establishment of the new government, internal political turmoil began to subside. With all his stubbornness, and later his narrow and short-sighted autocracy, Syngman Rhee in the first days of independence did provide a measure of suprapartisan unity and a symbol of strength. And the more or less experienced bureaucracy was able to provide a needed legal and rational framework for administrative efficiency which helped the recovery process. Thus notable progress was achieved in the first two years of the new republic. Increases in coal production (40 percent), electric power (33 percent), and industrial production (50 percent) were substantial. There was also an exceptionally good crop year. Thus, for South Koreans as a whole, 1949–1950 was probably the best year they had had in a decade.[25]

The conservative bias of the government and bureaucracy, furthermore, did not prevent an important and popular land reform from being enacted. It was the result of several forces that were, after 1945, acting upon both landlords and peasants in favor of redistribution.[26] The results of the land reform were tremendously significant. It was reasonably well implemented with about 70 percent of the land eligible actually being redistributed, and over one million of the total of two million rural households benefitting.[27] Before reform, 49 percent of the farm households had consisted wholly of tenant farmers and another 35 percent were part tenant; some 63 percent of the total cultivated land and 70 percent of the rice paddy land had been tenant-farmed. With the reform, tenancy as a major institution was virtually eliminated, and there was a three *chongbo* (a *chongbo* being approximately one hectare) limit on paddy holdings. To some degree, tenancy was later reestablished under different guises. Estimates have been made that as much as 20 percent of the new land received by farmers may have later been sold for debt or other reasons. Yet the overall effect was to create a basic rural structure of small—very small—owner-operated farms.[28] Compared to 1947, submarginal households, those having less than one *chongbo*, rose from 41 percent to 45 percent of the total. Close to 30 percent of farm households in 1953 owned no more than one *chongbo*. Hardly any households reached the legal limit on paddy land.

In terms of production, the reform was considered to have been somewhat detrimental, at least in the short run. But psychologically and politically it had very positive effects. Subsequent improvements in farm income, though probably resulting as much or more from other factors of production, were in the farmer's mind often connected with the land reform. Moreover, the reform eliminated the fundamental divisive issue in the countryside. Thereafter, the locus of serious political conflict shifted largely if not entirely to the urban centers. The reform similarly eliminated the last key issue on which the left wing could have hoped to develop substantial rural support in Korea. Finally, it changed the nature of government requirements in the countryside. The basic socio-political obstacle to rural development had been eliminated, but the problems of low productivity and low income remained. It was clear that further improvement in the rural sector would depend upon substantial and relatively sophisticated technical inputs and economic policy management.

These early years of independence thus saw the institutionalization of conservative political philosophy; the beginnings of a trend toward autocracy (but still checked by constitutional provisions and articulate forces in the legislature); a significant amount of economic recovery, balanced, however, by rather heavy dependence on United States aid; and the settlement of at least one basic social issue by the passage of land reform legislation.

THE KOREAN WAR AND ITS AFTERMATH

Korea had been spared any fighting on its soil during World War II. Now in 1950, when the North Koreans moved down the peninsula, they added the destruction of war to the burdens of South Korea. The main movements of the Korean War took less than a year, after which ground action was largely confined to the center of the country near the 38th parallel. But, in that one year, the destruction was enormous. The fighting had roamed over the whole country, except for the Pusan perimeter. Seoul changed hands four times and was almost totally destroyed in the process. Nearly one million South Korean civilians plus 320,000 hastily recruited South Korean soldiers had been killed. Property damage was estimated at $2 billion. Agricultural production dropped 27 percent from 1949 to 1952; the overall GNP dropped 14 percent in the same period. About five and a half million people, or 25 percent of the population, wandered the country as refugees during the war.[29]

By the time the war was over, all the dimensions of Korean development, its problems and requirements, had been altered. First of all, the war had changed South Korea from a small country with needs somewhat relevant to its size and capabilities into the defense bastion of the Far East. Korean forces had increased from 65,000 to over 700,000 men. Meeting the needs of such forces transformed the nature of the Korean economy. Quite apart from the military hardware that would also come from the United States, the domestic costs (salaries, food, etc.) for maintaining this force were well beyond the capacity of the economy and had to be met by economic aid. This created an import level far exceeding that of the past, giving to the trade sector a new importance that was itself almost revolutionary. The first annual United States economic aid bill after the armistice came to $200 million; it rose to a peak of $365 million in 1956, and never went below $200 million annually until nearly the mid-1960s.[30] The Korean government budget became dependent on such aid not only for defense, but for other expenditures as well.[31]

The dependence upon the United States, which had already been uncomfortable for both sides before the war, was now deepened, and developed into a semipermanent arrangement. The United Nations Command, under United States generals, took and maintained operational control of the Korean forces. American aid technicians entered the country by the hundreds, working in everything from public administration to the training of war widows as maids, from industrial development to social welfare.[32] From the earliest days of the war this relationship had not always been a happy arrangement, but it had seemed unavoidable.[33] However, the failure of the Korean government to do more later to overcome this dependence, by reducing the ratio of aid-generated revenue to domestic revenue or by raising domestic agricultural production in relation to United States food imports, was to become a serious charge against it.[34]

The impact of the war upon the structure of society was no less profound. Trends underway even before the twentieth century were given new impetus. One of these was the leveling of social distinctions and the loosening of old bonds. The effect has been most aptly described by Hahn-Been Lee:

> Life, physical and social, was never the same as before. Some families managed to hold together even in refuge but many became scattered and some were even divided and broken. The hold of the family, which had already begun to weaken before the tides of education, was further loosened drastically through the massive changes in human ecology. In this respect, the catastrophe of war was the most decisive factor in the levelling of traditional social structure. As a prominent thinker reflected with mixed feelings, "If there was any gain" out of this devastating war, "it was only that some trash of the old way of our society was rooted out."[35]

Two other important and interrelated social changes were also given impetus by the war, creating very new demands upon the political system in the process. One of these was urbanization, the other, increased education. The period of Japanese rule, with its industrialization, war-related activities, and—during the thirties and forties—real rural hunger, had already seen a rapid rise in the number and size of cities.[36] During and after the Korean War, however, the growth of urbanization in South Korea was accelerated, with the population in the largest cities (those over 100,000) nearly doubling between 1949 and 1960 to represent 23 percent of the total population. In all cities and towns of over 20,000 persons, the percentage of the population went up from 28 percent to 41 percent in this period. South Korea had become more urban than some of the industrialized countries of Europe.[37]

The growth of urban areas was accompanied by a virtual explosion in education. Here, too, the trend had begun earlier. But in both quality and quantity, postliberation changes in education were markedly different. Educational increases in the colonial period had been primarily at the lower levels. Though the number of students in Korea at all levels increased over 16 times from 1910 to 1941, only 5 percent of Korean children were by 1941 going beyond primary school. Only 304 Korean students were enrolled that year in Korea's one full-fledged university.[38] After 1945 the situation was very different. Primary education became universal, which was a tremendous advancement. But, proportionately, secondary and higher education grew even more rapidly. In the 20 years after liberation, the number of college students rose about 18 times; middle and high school students 14 times.[39] By 1960, in terms of its per capita income and production, the country had reached a level of educational development far advanced in relation to other countries.[40]

There was also a relationship between the increase in higher education especially and growing urbanization. By 1960, the percentage of persons with primary education living in small towns and villages was about the same as the latter's percentage of the total population. But 72 percent of those who had had college education lived in cities of more than 50,000 persons, though these cities contained only 28 percent of the total population.[41] Accompanying this trend, moreover, was the rise of newspapers and magazines. From 1945 to 1960, the circulation of leading newspapers went from 17,000 to 400,000—mostly in the capital city of Seoul. By 1960, 600 newspapers and periodicals were registered for publication.[42] There was thus developing not only an increasingly literate society, but an increasingly vocal urban population, stimulated by the concentration of intellectuals, students, and mass media.

In the years following the Korean War, this urban population came to be increasingly critical of both the economy and government under

Rhee. In part this was stimulated by the traditionally "opposition" attitude of the press. Moreover, the press as an institution served to bring together discontented intellectuals and journalists and to give the former a wide forum for their views.[43]

But the critical mood also had deeper roots. The Korean War had left "deep wounds in the internal consciousness," as a literary critic observed. It had destroyed the optimism and utopianism of the early period of independence. Urbanization, education, mass media, and the rapid introduction of foreign ideas and techniques into a once insulated culture were all creating a new self-consciousness. But it was one tinged with despair and frustration, and in time susceptible to revolution. The development and change of mood has been described by Hahn-Been Lee:

> Thus a period that began with an ideology—that of equal opportunity—was ending with a newly emerging ideology—that of a suffering and revolting self. This was the culmination of the cumulative change that occurred in the society during the fifteen year period since 1945. It was a qualitative change out of many mutually related quantitative changes.[44]

The mood was also aptly summed up in the popular slogan of the opposition party in the late 1950s: "We can't live like this any longer. Let's have a change."[45]

Criticism was also stimulated by the greater "visibility" of discouraging conditions in the postwar society. In the pre-Korean War period, economics had not been a major preoccupation of the society.[46] But the Korean War changed that. Inflation was hard to ignore; prices rose over 500 percent in 1951 and over 100 percent more in 1952,[47] and continued their upward spiral through 1957. There had been serious inflation in Korea before the war, but in a predominantly rural and only partially monetized economy, its effects had been limited. Now the problem was politically more serious. The war's destruction had also demonstrated the importance of productive facilities and the critical need to rebuild them in order to return the economy to normal operating condition. Furthermore, the massive levels of United States aid after 1953 increased economic consciousness. New fortunes were being made after the war in the cities, largely through the control of imports, while the economic prospects of the country as a whole seemed unsatisfactory. Aid, corruption, and poverty became intertwined in the view of urban critics. Finally there was the problem of jobs, especially for the burgeoning number of college graduates. In the 1950s, the bureaucracy still remained largely closed off to the new college graduate, while economic recovery, though substantial in overall terms, could not match the job demand created by the educational explosion. From 40 to 50 percent of college graduates were commonly believed to be unemployed and many more unsatisfactorily employed. The rumor of joblessness was as damaging to morale as any validity the statistics might have had.[48]

It is significant that the first years after the war did see a very substantial economic recovery. Growth in all sectors was considerable, if not remarkable, and the average rise in GNP was 5.5 percent from 1954 through 1958. Industrial production led the advance, growing by nearly 14 percent per year, despite continuing shortages of power and transportation. But the growth was not of a kind to quiet the swelling discontent in the country; in some ways it fed it. It was a period of rapid change, with new elite groups arising in business and the military—which was in itself disquieting for intellectuals and for politicians not in power. It was also marked by considerable corruption in the growth process, particularly in the sale of former Japanese properties, the distribution of bank loans, and the approval of import licenses. Much of this corruption was laid directly on the doorstep of the increasingly centralized regime.[49] Third, the pattern of industrialization in this period, emphasizing, as it did, the processing of imported raw materials and semifinished goods, was decried as not leading to a healthy and balanced economy. A fourth, related problem was that the growth was in step with an increasing and, to some, seemingly hopeless dependence on the United States, a dependence that appeared to be aggravated by government policies such as overvalued exchange rates and deliberately low crop estimates designed to help enlarge aid requirements.[50] Also, the mere fact of dependence itself, at this point when new self-consciousness was developing in the urban areas and a new search for identity was beginning, became offensive and disillusioning to nationalist sensitivities. Finally, there was a lack of planning and of sense of direction in the growth that was taking place. Although recovery was being pushed on many different fronts, the government seemed opposed to the whole idea of planning. In this atmosphere, factories were built that, because of lack of power, management, or even markets, ran at much less than full capacity. Imports of grain were believed to be providing disincentives to domestic agriculture. And, as already mentioned, inflation continued without adequate efforts to control it.

During this period of rapid change and growing social ferment, the politics of the country also changed. But, at least on the part of the regime in power, politics moved more to resist than to accommodate to the social changes taking place. Neither Rhee nor his lieutenants were oblivious of the changes wrought by the war. Indeed, perhaps earlier than many, Rhee saw the new attributes of economic and military power that South Korea would need to survive in the post-Korean War period.[51] But in common with many of his goals, he saw these attributes in grand terms, in broad strokes. He never faced the technical and administrative complexity that they demanded of the society.[52] Part of the problem was Rhee's age and his preoccupation with the past and with reunification. His goal was a very different Korea from the one he had inherited. In addition, his jealousy of associates as potential rivals and his reliance on personal, charismatic authority made it impossible for him to build the political, bureaucratic, and private institutions that could absorb and channel the new energies and resources in the country for purposes of modernization. At times, as in the period from 1954 to 1957, he did use technically competent and proficient ministers. But he used them, as he did contemporary political figures, "as mere instruments to be exploited."[53] Thus the tasks of reconstruction and development in the South, in Rhee's time, on which a new national identity might have been built, never gained the priority and attention they demanded.

It is important also that the overall leadership structure that had emerged at independence survived the war intact. In fact, through kidnapping, murder, and defection during North Korean occupation, the war served to destroy the final remnants of the moderate and Left-leaning leadership that had opposed Rhee before independence. It also delivered the final blow to the Left as a whole in South Korea—reconfirming the strictures of the official doctrine of anticommunism and also generating a popular revulsion against the communists in the wake of the cruel destructiveness of North Korean forces. Nevertheless, a growing split developed between Rhee and his original conservative backers, based largely on Rhee's independent and autocratic use of executive power. Thus, in 1952 Rhee found himself faced with a hostile Assembly, prepared either to refuse him reelection or to force compromises on him to achieve it. However, Rhee called upon the police to support him and, by arrests and physical threats, forced the Assembly to adopt a constitutional amendment providing for popular presidential election.[54] This was the first wholesale corruption of the democratic system of government that South Korea, under American tutelage and under the influence of long nationalist association with Western ideology, had adopted in its constitution. It set the stage for a steadily increasing corruption.

Rhee also took another very significant political step during the war when he formed his own Liberal party in 1951. Rhee personified what Gregory Henderson has said of all Koreans' approach to political parties: "Korean parties are formed grudgingly and precariously by individuals who would rather reach power by themselves."[55] Rhee had eschewed dependence on any one organized group of supporters, but his troubles with the Assembly after 1950 led him to believe he needed some formal organization to maintain his hold on both the electorate and the machinery of government. By 1954 the Liberal party apparatus had grown strong enough to produce the first party majority in the Assembly in the country's young history. Unfortunately, by this time Rhee was already 79 years old; he could not curb the party nor was it subjected to the review and limitations of the democratic process. Beginning in 1954 with amendments to the constitution strengthening party control over the bureaucracy, the party that had been built almost entirely around Rhee and his hold on the presidency began to develop an independent quest for control. The consequences were grave in face of the growing level of discontent following the war.

The growing popular opposition to the Rhee government manifested itself politically for the first time in the 1956 election. Whereas Rhee had received 72 percent of the popular vote in 1952, in 1956, in a virtually uncontested election, he received only 55 percent. More shocking to the Liberal party, the opposition—united in a new Democratic party—elected its vice-presidential candidate. Opposition to the government, at least overt opposition, centered in the urban areas. This was clear in the results of the Assembly elections in 1958, when 63 of the Democratic party's 79 successful candidates came from urban or semiurban areas; 43 of these from large cities. By contrast, the Liberal party elected 70 of its 126 members from rural constituencies and only 13 from large cities.[56]

In some ways 1956 marked a high point in Korean democracy under Syngman Rhee. To the Liberal party's discomfiture, the election of the Democratic party candidate for vice-president was allowed to stand. In the next two years, moreover, Rhee's government moved to tackle some of the most pressing of the nation's problems, giving promise of a more responsive administration. For the first time since independence, a meaningful stabilization program was put into effect. Prices, which had risen 81 percent in 1955 and 32 percent in 1956, rose only 16 percent in 1957 and actually declined by 7 percent in 1958. This achievement was helped considerably by the very large aid shipments from 1956 to 1958, but it also reflected a considerable government administrative effort. Within the administration, a small group of persons was also brought together in 1958 to begin work on a long-range economic plan.[57] This was thus a period of both political and economic promise.

But in 1958, the political situation changed again. Rhee was not in firm control of the Liberal party; the man under him, ostensibly in charge, was very ill. The party leadership, shaken by the results of the 1956 election, was seriously worried about the outcome of the next presidential election. Beginning in 1958, therefore, guided by the Liberal party apparatus, a shift in control and leadership began to take place within the administration. The incumbent cabinet leadership, which had since 1954 emphasized technical and professional specialists, began to be pushed aside. In its place, and throughout the party and bureaucracy, leadership moved to the group that was perhaps the most protected and most defensive one in the Rhee regime: it consisted of persons with legal and bureaucratic training, and a common experience of bureaucratic service under the Japanese, all fighting to retain their hold on power through the combination of Rhee and the Liberal party apparatus. Except for Rhee, the early nationalist figures who had dominated the first independence cabinets were gone; the professionals "drafted" from outside the party apparatus for ministerial positions after the Korean War were shunted aside.[58]

The changes in leadership were soon reflected on both the political and the administrative fronts. In December 1958, the Liberal party forced a new National Security Law through the Assembly; its opponents— carried from the floor by guards—were certain it would be used against them before and during the next elections. Police and gang terrorism began to increase again.[59] Within the executive group, an administrative contrariness and a lack of concern with development problems developed. The embryo Economic Development Plan was no longer given serious attention or guidance by the leaders, so that its potential contribution diminished. Incentives to assure full utilization of the recently reconstructed industrial facilities and, with stabilization goals achieved, to guide production and investment into new areas that would strengthen and balance the productive structure, were not forthcoming. Gross investment, which had risen in 1957 and 1958, began to fall off in 1959. Followed by a bad crop year in 1959–1960, it set in motion a recession that was to deepen in subsequent years. Finally, the bureaucracy as a whole became subservient to the demands of Liberal party machinery and guided by men sympathetic to this new leadership. In this atmosphere it retreated into the strictest kind of ritualism and routine. Innovations were not only rare but "viewed with suspicion."[60] The regime was now moving in the opposite direction from the forces of social change and of increasingly articulated dissent that had developed in the aftermath of the Korean War.

THE STUDENT REVOLUTION AND DEMOCRATIC GOVERNMENT

The trend of political repression begun in 1958 moved to a climax in 1960. One professor, recalling the atmosphere of early 1960, described it as "suffocating." The finale came in a series of bizarre political events connected with the election for vice-president in which the same candidates as in 1956 faced each other.[61] Perhaps no clearer indication of the loss of contact between the ruling oligarchy and the society could be found than in the results that were officially announced following election day in March. They showed the Liberal party candidate for vice-president defeating his opponent, the incumbent, by nearly 5 to 1. Few people would have found even a narrow victory credible.

Student demonstrations had already begun in the port city of Masan on election day. When one of the demonstrators was found dead a few days later, apparently from police brutality, this proved to be the final spark. Students rallied in Seoul on April 18. On the following day, when over 20,000 students returned, they were shot at by police; over 100 students were killed. The bonds of authority now disintegrated. The revolt spread to other major cities. The army was called in but, in action not soon to be forgotten, refused to take very strong action against the demonstrations. The revolution was no longer that of students alone. One observer of those events described it in this way:

> To those who witnessed it, the unanimity, the spontaneity, the utter conviction which swept Korea's cities in those days will remain unforgettable. . . It seemed as if the force of that consensus made up in a few hours for the hesitations, the paralysis of action, the frustration, of long years.[62]

After 12 years in power, the regime collapsed with amazing suddenness. Rhee resigned on April 26, 1960, and shortly thereafter left the country. An Interim Government arranged for a new constitutional system and new elections. In July of that year, the Democratic party—the heir apparent—was swept to an overwhelming victory.

Even before the election, the Interim Government had begun to make major changes in the governmental structure. Many senior bureaucrats were purged. The prerevolution Economic Development Plan that had been allowed to languish in the closing months of the Rhee regime was brought out for reworking. A parliamentary system of government was established to replace the presidential system wielded by Rhee into autocracy. The new government of the Democratic party continued these changes. For the first time, the bureaucracy was opened widely to postliberation college graduates. "Economic Development First" became the new government's slogan. It gave stronger backing to economic planning and initiated a number of key policy changes, such as the devaluation of early 1961. It permitted a greater degree of free expression, publication, and open political activity than the Republic had known before or has known since.[63]

But the Democratic regime was not the millenium for which many had hoped. For one thing, the Democratic party was not directly representative of the forces that had brought about the revolution. The party's leadership was of the same age and shared much of the same social and educational background as the Liberal elite.[64] The Democratic party, moreover, was only a diverse coalition of opponents to Rhee. One main segment identified closely with the growing urban community, but only a small part of that group had been concerned with new, alternative policies. The other main segment was made up of members of the original Korea Democratic party, and its later Assembly allies, who had backed Rhee in the preindependence period and then turned against him when he moved toward independent and highly autocratic rule.[65] Finally, while the Democratic party had become the parliamentary symbol of opposition during the late fifties, and the only constitutionally available alternative, it had not had a direct hand in the revolt. In fact, student action in 1960 arose partly out of the feeling that the responsibility had by default devolved upon student shoulders.[66]

Once in power, the Democratic party found the lack of cohesion among its membership too much to contain. After a factional struggle, the party selected as prime minister, from its more urban-oriented wing, Chang Myon, who had been the successful Democratic vice-presidential candidate in 1956 and whose failure to gain that office in 1960 had set off the storm that destroyed the old regime. His selection, however, led to a party split. The descendants of the Korea Democratic party, led by Yun Po-son, who had been elected to the largely ceremonial post of president in the new government, formed what they called the New Democratic party, which now became the party of the opposition. By

September the consensus of April 1960 was formally at an end. At first the new opposition deprived Chang of his parliamentary majority. But, as evidence of the fragility of political loyalties and factional alignments, Chang was able gradually to restore it, wooing some members of the opposition back. In the process, however, the new government became greatly weakened and discredited. So much persuasion and outright bribery had to be used to get bills through the Assembly that the Assembly and Democratic party developed a very bad image.[67]

The problems of the government were further complicated by events outside of the Democratic party. The April 1960 revolution had been especially liberating for the intellectuals and the press community. The Interim Government period has been described as "almost a period of government by a university-press nexus."[68] But the intellectuals, like many of the Democratic party politicians, had for years focused their energy on opposition to Rhee, not on development of constructive program alternatives. Like their political counterparts, they lacked the experience of administration and power. But unlike their counterparts, they were not anxious to undertake such responsibilities. They therefore formed a highly vocal but largely unconstructive critical group. As the Democratic regime split, foundered, and struggled, the press became almost universally critical of it. "Almost no newspapers had any thoughtful regard or sympathy for the problems which the Chang regime was struggling to solve in a democratic framework."[69]

A further difficulty came from students. After the revolution, students sought to be constructive and helpful in national development. But some elements became restless when the revolution failed to produce the more magic results it had seemed to promise. Moreover, after a long period of close control, the new freedom of ideas led to a burst of expression in directions once, and still, considered dangerous. Thus the Democratic regime was plagued with constant demonstrations— about 2,000 in the year following the revolution.[70] Most alarming to many critics, on several campuses a movement began for the peaceful reunification of Korea and for direct student debates with North Korean students. The extent of this movement was really not wide, nor were the other demonstrations usually large and significant. But there was a growing uneasiness about public order, and a growing doubt about the efficacy of the new political system.

In May 1961, just a little more than a year after the student uprising, the Chang Myon Government fell to the military, a group that was undergoing its own revolution, and one in which the Democratic party had sunk no roots.[71] The Chang Myon regime did not really have long enough to establish itself. It remains controversial within Korean political circles—the high point of democracy to some, the example of political immaturity and lack of readiness for complete democracy in South Korea to others. But the revolution that brought it about was not a "flash in the pan." It was a demand for "generational change," and despite the frustration and ambivalence of its originators, the revolution against the political-administrative elite of the pre-1960 period proved to be irreversible. The revolution reflected also a groping by these same groups for a new national identity, one that could be meaningful and satisfying for a South Korea cut off by force from the North and only beginning to face the long and difficult consequences of that division. Ideologically, the forces of revolution tied their banner to democracy and to economic development. In 1960 these were still largely generalized values drawn from the postliberation educational experience. As shown in later chapters, there was no full commitment on the part of the revolutionary forces themselves to these values and to the consequences, particularly, of economic development. Nevertheless, the values persisted. Meanwhile the search for national identity was given added momentum by the entrance into politics of an even more forceful and determined nationalist group: the military.

2 / The Change in Leadership: Transition from Military to Civilian Government, 1961-1964

Just before dawn on May 16, 1961, about 5,000 Korean Army, paratrooper, and Marine troops crossed the Han River Bridge into Seoul. They occupied quickly and with little resistance the key government and communications control points and by daybreak announced the formation of a Military Revolutionary Committee to take over the government. On May 18, when all hopes for some military or political counteraction had faded, the Chang Myon cabinet formally resigned. For the first time in seven centuries, Korea had come under an indigenous military rule. The military junta that ruled Korea for the next two years, gave way formally to a civilian form of government in 1963. The new government, however, represented the continuation in power of many of the revolutionary military leaders of the previous two years. But in the period from 1961 to 1964, a significant change took place within the new leadership itself. This change, more subtle but no less consequential than that of 1961, greatly affected the manner in which the new postwar ideas in South Korea were finally carried into Korean political and economic life. This change is the focus of this chapter. The broader implications of the transition to civilian government are discussed subsequently.

THE MILITARY OUTLOOK

The Korean coup of 1961 was not unique. It followed closely in time coups in Burma and Pakistan. Like some others in Asia and the Middle East, the coup was planned and led by junior officers without the support—and to a degree against—the senior officers of the armed forces as a whole. But the Korean military was a somewhat unique institution. It had no colonial roots, for the Japanese had destroyed the small Im-

34

perial Korean Army when annexing Korea and had never restored it during the colonial period. Even as a post-independence force, the Korean military was most of all a product of the Korean War. It was the Korean War that expanded the military from 100,000 men in 1950 to over 700,000 by 1956, from a small collection of units to the world's fourth (later fifth) largest military establishment, from a poorly organized and trained constabulary-like force to one of the very best equipped and trained military organizations in the developing countries.

The Korean War itself also had a very profound influence on officers' attitudes. There were some terrible, unnerving losses—44,000 Korean troops were killed, captured, or missing in the first week of the war— and some extremely heroic stands under conditions of minimal training and organization. The survivors were undoubtedly a hardened group, with strong convictions about their country and their own role in it.[1]

There were other important influences on the outlook and character that the military brought to government. The military, for one, had reasonably good relations with the populace. Lacking any unsavory colonial tradition, largely revered for its role in the Korean War, and remembered, too, for its standing by at the time of the student revolution of 1960, it possessed a relatively favorable image. Furthermore, the Korean Army, being largely conscript, had very wide roots, particularly in the rural areas where not only the bulk of the population lived, but where student deferments and the like were less possible. On the other hand, the Korean military, especially at the senior level, had been deeply involved in the corruption of the Rhee regime. As noted later, that gave added fuel to the coup leaders' cause.

The military in Korea, if less alienated, was nevertheless still not accepted in Korean culture as an honored group nor as an accepted source for the ruling class. Traditionally, as in most Confucian-influenced societies, the military occupied a relatively low role in the social hierarchy. The military establishment had never been either large or influential throughout most of Korean history and had been allowed to decline to extremely low levels of men and materials by the beginning of the twentieth century. After independence and even after the Korean War, when the general prestige of the military had risen, it continued to be a career opportunity for lesser privileged members of society. Officers rose primarily from families with the money to provide their children some education and assistance, but which lacked the entrée to the best schools and universities of Seoul, where elite careers were normally fashioned.[2]

In this light, a very important characteristic of the military establishment in Korea was the intense exposure to, and influence from, the outside, particularly the United States. While many of the army's first officers had had some experience in the Chinese and Japanese armies fighting in China and Manchuria during World War II, these were greatly outnumbered after 1948 by men who came into the military with no previous professional experience.[3] More than any other major Korean governmental institution, the military was thus organized, shaped, and trained on Western standards. The organization, training programs, and academies were modeled almost exactly on their American counterparts. By 1961, about 6,000 officers had received training at military schools in the United States. In certain characteristics, particularly time orientation, work habits, and managerial outlook, the military early became one of the most "modernized" institutions in Korea, out of balance in this respect with most government and educational institutions.[4]

The rapid growth of the military in these years, especially during the Korean War, created strains within its internal structure. The war had the initial effect of catapulting many young officers, some with minimal experience and training, into senior positions within a very short time. The promotion pattern of the much larger numbers who followed them, products of somewhat longer term and better training institutions, was considerably slower. The 8th Military Class of 1948–1949, for example—the largest class and the source of all the original plotters of the coup—bore much of the brunt of combat during the Korean War as platoon and company commanders. Half the class was estimated as having been lost. But after the war it found promotional opportunities limited by superiors, some of whom had reached senior rank in their twenties and thirties and had many years' active service ahead of them. Force reductions in 1957–1958 from 700,000 to 600,000 men further squeezed promotional potential.[5]

Another distinction developed as well in these layers of the officers corps. The group of officers just ahead of the 8th Class were in the most favorable position after the Korean War to take advantage of newly available advanced training opportunities, both in special new military schools in Korea and in the United States. There was therefore a greater concentration in this group of more senior officers of the managerial skills and attributes that perhaps most characterized the military as a "modernized" institution.[6] This was to be a distinction of some importance in the Military Government. At the very highest level of the military, by contrast, a different distinction developed after the war. The top positions came under firm political control and some of the senior staff became deeply involved in the corruption of the Rhee government. This added a moral and political fire to the other frustrations of those at lower levels, and provided a common bond between the 8th Class Members and those just ahead of them.

By 1961 the military was not part of or significantly tied, except at the very top, to the existing elite of Korea. Its development, training, and professional experiences were of the postliberation period in contrast to the patriots of the preindependence era who dominated the Rhee period and even the subsequent Democratic Government. Its schooling and professional standards were unusually influenced by outside Western sources, rather than traditional ideas and institutions. The military career, moreover, was built in an institution that lay outside the traditional route toward elite status, and attracted men who did not have access to that route. Finally, the rural base of the military leadership likely alienated them further from the somewhat Seoul-oriented background and activity of the established power structure. Significantly, an overwhelming percentage, 72 percent, of the military that participated in the coup and subsequent Military Government were born in rural areas.[7]

The military coup, therefore, planned by colonels and lieutenant colonels of the 8th Class and drawing support from slightly more senior officers, was not a counterreaction to the April 1960 student revolution or an attempt in any way to restore either the oligarchy or philosophy of the pre-1960 order. The leaders, in fact, saw the Military revolution as an extension of the earlier one and themselves as heirs of that revolutionary spirit. Their argument for the coup was that the political leaders and institutions of 1960–1961 had betrayed that spirit, that dangerous and radical elements were arising in the confusion, and perhaps, above all, that the revolutionary spirit and goals of 1960 needed a firm and competent hand to bring them about.[8]

The outlook of the new military leadership was thus revolutionary in tone and strongly nationalistic. But it was also pragmatic and managerial, rather than ideological in its emphasis. There was no deep concern with political or social theories, or particular systems, except for a preference for authoritarian controls. They shared with the students of 1960, though carried it forward more forcefully, a disdain of the negative dependence upon the United States and the emotional but frustrating harangues about reunification that characterized the Rhee period. They saw in economic development one of the keys to real national independence, and they expressed a strong "populist" outlook in the early period of the Military Government, particularly seeking to redress in rapid and dramatic fashion the distribution of wealth in favor of the farmers.

Some of the major steps energetically, if not always successfully, carried forward by the Military Government are illustrative of these attitudes and of the approach which the new leaders took.[9] In foreign affairs, an effort was made immediately after the coup to open up new, non-United States, sources of external financing, leading to important beginnings in this area that later bore much fruit. Diplomatic representation, confined under Rhee to the United States and its closest allies, was expanded from 23 to 76 countries, including a new emphasis on neutrals. Efforts were begun to put aside the emotional obstacles to a normalization of relations with Japan, thus to open up another major new source of aid and commercial credit. Though officially proclaiming a desire to strengthen relations with the United States, the Military Government defied United States opposition to the coup, twice reversed itself on its commitment to the United States regarding a return to civilian rule, and was at least suspected of instigating student demonstrations demanding a Status of Forces Agreement covering American soldiers in Korea.[10]

Internally, the new government moved rapidly in both the political and economic spheres. It undertook not only to unseat the previous elite but, in contrast to the period of the Democratic Government, to define a narrow range for permitted political activity. A Political Activities Purification Law was decreed in 1961, which banned initially over 4,000 persons from any future political activity. The list included almost all prominent politicians since independence. Over the next 20 months many of these persons were "cleared" or "pardoned," so that by January 1963, when open political activity was resumed, only 74 persons remained on the list. Nevertheless, these 74 included some of the principal leaders of the Democratic party and most of those leaders of "progressive" or "left" parties.[11] The process of clearance itself established the authority of the Military Government and was geared into the development of its own political party and base that emerged in 1963. In addition, in the period 1961–1962, the government through a special Revolutionary Court tried nearly 3,000 persons—mostly party activists, professors, students, and journalists—on charges of corruption or excessive radicalism. The net effect of these measures was to depose the former elite, to place in the hands of the new leadership the tasks of the revolution and national development, and to foreclose any political movements, even by those who shared some of the same goals, that might represent a "Left" or even a "quasi-Left" character. This narrowed range of political choices, continuing the earlier tradition of the Rhee government, was to continue as an important factor in the subsequent period of civilian government.

Equally dramatic actions were taken in the economic area, where the government sought to capture quickly the means of wealth in order to redirect them—first to such groups as the farmers but later to support the organization of a new political base for the regime. Agricultural credit at low interest was increased 30 times over the pre-1961 average. The government also offered to take over from the farmers their private high interest loans in order to relieve farmers of excessive debt. On the other side of the wealth equation, by heavy fines, the government attempted to recover the "illicit fortunes" made by big businessmen during the Rhee regime and to rechannel these funds into industrial investment. Finally, though with several objectives in mind, the government undertook in 1962 a coup-like reform of the currency, designed in part to capture the major elements of private wealth for state purposes. Few of the more dramatic economic measures were very successful in the long term and some, for example, the currency reform, backfired almost immediately. Moreover, those measures that became linked with scandal or the funding of progovernment political activities cost the government much of its reformist reputation. Nevertheless, they reflected some of the basic attitudes of the new leaders about economic problems and the early belief that basic economic relationships could be quickly reordered by administrative fiat.[12]

CHANGE WITHIN THE MILITARY LEADERSHIP

The new spirit of the military leaders, or more accurately the revolutionary spirit unleashed in April 1960 and given narrower political latitude but new administrative energy by the Military Revolution, would continue to shape policies and events for some years, even after the return to civilian government in 1963. The transformation from military to civilian government at the end of 1963, with General Park becoming president, has often been characterized as a changing from khaki to mufti of the Military Government.[13] Actually, however, the leaders had divided by 1963, and the power relationship that existed between the two main forces in the Military Government, that is, the colonels and the senior officers, was changing until it was eventually reversed in the subsequent government.

In the Military Government, the more senior generals were "drafted" into positions of prominence and of important managerial responsibility, but real power rested with the Colonels of the 8th Class. It was this latter group that drafted most of the initial political and economic measures described above and which gave the government much of its preemptive character. The Colonels' group controlled the Central Intelligence Agency (CIA), which was clearly the most powerful government body in all fields during this time. By contrast, the highest official organ of the Military Government, the Supreme Council for National Reconstruction, and the cabinet below it, consisted of the most prominent senior men in the regime but they lacked real control over policy or administration.[14] As the country prepared for a return to civilian rule, these two general categories of leaders moved in decisively different directions. Of those military who elected to stay in politics (many did not), there was a fairly clear division between the emphasis of the younger Colonels' group on the formation and control of the new Democratic Republican party (DRP) and the legislature, and that of the more senior officers on the executive. Thirty-nine persons prominent in the coup or in the Military Government went on to take prominent positions in the civilian government. Of these, 12 colonels but only 3 of the others (senior officers or civilians) became DRP assemblymen. On the other hand, 17 of the senior officers and civilians but only 7 of the colonels went into the executive.[15] The numbers alone, however, do not indicate the depth of the division. The leader of the Colonels and mastermind of the coup, Kim Chong-pil, while serving as director of the Central Intelligence Agency in the Military Government, developed the organizational structure, membership, and financial support for the DRP and then left the executive in 1963 to become the Democratic Republican party's first chairman. Three more members of the original 11 who had planned the coup joined him to become principal party leaders and assemblymen. By contrast only 1 member of the original group of 11 plotters became prominent in the executive—as director of the CIA—and only 2 of the other junior officers later prominent in planning and executing the coup became cabinet ministers, neither in critical policy-making posts.[16]

The division arose both by temperament and design. For the Colonels the critical factor in the transition to civilian rule was the maintenance of political power in their hands and the maintenance of revolutionary fervor. This they intended to achieve by forming a highly centralized and closely controlled political party to be the instrument of real power in the new government.[17] Critics have said that the party's structure and political role were patterned on those of communist parties. A more direct and likely model was that of the Kuomintang on Taiwan. It was to the development of such a party that the Colonels' group, principally through the CIA, began to turn its energies as early as 1962, and into which its leading members moved in 1963. On the other hand, those in the more senior group who continued in politics, maintaining a more managerial rather than revolutionary emphasis, chose to do so predominantly through the executive branch. There, allied with a new influx of civilian administrators, they were to assume firm control, increase their dominance over the DRP, and soon to achieve real direction of national policy.

CONSOLIDATION OF EXECUTIVE POWER

The growth of executive power owed very much to the attitudes and style of operations of the president, Park Chung-Hee. As a major general, Park had been the active head of the coup of 1961, even though the fire and drive had come from the colonels led by Kim Chong-pil. Taciturn and hard-boiled in manner and without much public appeal, Park lacked the revolutionary flair and outward zeal exhibited by leaders like Kim. (Park and Kim were, however, related by marriage, and the two men have remained close despite many strains on their relationship, quite a significant factor in later years.) Although Park's role as the head of the revolution, and later, of the government, was never challenged by the younger group, Park did come from that stratum of more senior officers, whose advanced training and experience gave it a decidedly managerial emphasis. He was thus the main link between the revolutionary leaders and the more senior officer group. In this role he continued to place emphasis on managerial skills and on the drafting of senior military men, as well as trained civilians into both the military and, later, into the civilian governments. Also, when he became president in 1963, he became head of the executive branch and, not surprisingly, turned his energies to strengthening this branch as the dominant part of the government vis-à-vis the party, which operated primarily through the Assembly. Thus both personality and training led Park to emphasize the executive. In addition, there were three rather specific considerations that also pointed in the same direction: the political situation surrounding the birth of the Democratic Republican party, the demands of the programs Park deemed essential to national recovery, and the exigencies of maintaining his own position among competing elements in and out of the government.

By the time it emerged officially in January 1963, the Democratic Republican party, as developed by Kim Chong-pil, had both created deep schisms within the Military Government and handed the opposition parties a valuable political issue at the outset of the resumption of political activities. The schism within the government was perhaps the more serious, for it threatened its solidarity just at the time that the government had to move into the uncertain clime of civilian politics. Opposition to Kim's plans came from those military who were opposed to a continuation of the military in politics, and particularly to a type of participation that smacked of the kind they had overthrown in 1961, and from those military and civilians who feared Kim's personal ambitions, which they saw embodied in the tightly centralized party structure.[18] The dispute became so serious and so threatening to the government's chances in any elections that Park had to intervene in February 1963. He arranged a compromise among the factions that involved modifying somewhat the highly centralized structure of the DRP and broadening the sources of leadership. Included in the compromise, moreover, was the temporary exile of Kim Chong-pil.

The February compromise did not end the party's internal problems. Nor was it even a clear victory for Kim's opponents, as many of them were arrested a month later on charges of conspiracy against the government. However, Park's intercession established the executive leader's role in party affairs and clearly gave that role real substance and authority, a precedent that would be continued thereafter. In the subsequent months of political maneuvering, jockeying, and struggle, leading up to national elections for the civilian government—which included Park's vacillation about running for president—the party became more dependent on Park's willingness to stand for office under its label than he was on the party. In fact Park's temporary flirtation with the formation of a new party in the summer of 1963 almost destroyed the DRP.[19]

The DRP reemerged a strong force in national affairs after the elections in October and November, holding the presidency, a very heavy majority of seats in the Assembly, and with Kim once more in the role of chairman. But factions within it continued to struggle; meanwhile the executive grew in stability and power, with Park remaining the principal arbitrating figure in the DRP as well as undisputed head of the executive. In the spring of 1965, commenting on an instance of cross-factional party revolt against one of the president's cabinet ministers, a prominent Korean daily noted that DRP members had discovered that while they had continued to fight over the factional issues of 1963–1964, real power had fallen to a "few Cabinet ministers."[20]

The comment was apt, for directly related to growing executive power was the growing strength and authority accorded to the cabinet after 1963 and, as a result, to the bureaucracy. The Military Government had itself carried forward the renovations in the bureaucracy begun with the 1960 revolution. Many senior officials of the Rhee period had been removed and younger persons promoted. As noted in Chapter 1, these changes opened new career opportunities to persons trained in Korean universities after 1945. They also gave encouragement to bureaucrats who had since 1954 received training abroad under American and other assistance programs, but who had been frustrated in carrying out new ideas or emphases by seniors whose bureaucratic roots extended back into the Japanese period.[21] There was also infusion of new managerial emphasis and organizational techniques, what one observer called "the Fort Leavenworth" style of charts, reports, and military-style briefings all the way down to the local level. But while these changes opened the door to new blood and gave the bureaucracy new methods and standards of performance, neither the Supreme Council for National Reconstruction, nor the cabinet gained real policy initiative in the Military Government.[22]

By the time of the inauguration of the civilian government, however, it had become clear that many of the Military Government reforms had gone awry and that the tasks of national development were more complex than early prognostication had indicated. Inflation became a serious problem as government spending increased, and the currency reform of 1962 brought the economy to a near standstill. Scandals in the development of certain industries and of the stock market had not only hurt the economy, but confidence in the new leadership's intentions and ability as well. Efforts to help the rural population had also not had the desired results on agricultural production or income. As the new government, which took office at the end of 1963, began to focus on these problems, the need for professionalism at both the cabinet level and in the bureaucracy became clearer to the president.

The first cabinet under the new government was still weak. It fell in May 1964 after only five months in office and under the pressure of student demonstrations against the government's policy toward Japan. The situation was, in fact, one in which the previous relationship of revolutionaries to administrators seemed to have been maintained; for,

Kim Chong-pil, though ostensibly not a member of the executive, was the most conspicuous government figure in the controversial negotiations with Japan in 1964, engaging in authoritative discussions with the Japanese government along with the foreign minister. Under student pressure, the president broke off these talks in March 1964 and, a short while later, again had Kim leave the country in order to maintain unity within the government and to quiet feelings generally. This second exile marked another turning point, as significant for the development of the cabinet, as the first had been for the party.

In the aftermath of the student protests, the president installed a new cabinet. With hindsight it is clear that it represented a most important set of appointments because, in spite of all expectations, this cabinet remained intact for over three years and in spite of the most serious and divisive political struggles. In fact, the prime minister was still in office in 1970. This record contrasts with an average of eight months in office for the six prime ministers who held the office from 1960 (when it was re-established) to 1964, and to the rather low percentage of cabinet ministers who remained in office for over a full year during the entire period since independence.[23]

Under such circumstances, this cabinet was to acquire a new function in Korean politics, changing from administrator and political scapegoat for policies largely initiated elsewhere, to a continuing source of both policy-formation and implementation in the executive. It was, moreover, specifically intended that it should remain in office long enough to obtain a firm grasp on the problems before it. Thus the president, for the next three years, resisted both public and, on more than one occasion, government and party pressure for a cabinet reshuffling.[24] The new cabinet's greater degree of independence from party control was further demonstrated by the president's refusal to ask its members to join the Democratic Republican party until late in 1964; in fact, one major member, the deputy prime minister and minister (concurrently) of economic planning, throughout his tenure in office refused to join, to the chagrin and anger of party leaders but without recrimination from the president, who even used him to carry out some delicate party functions.[25] The cabinet was thus seen as much as a technical and professional instrument as a political one. Its political role, moreover, was to give the president a source of power independent not only of party dictates, but of other special influences acting on the executive.

The cabinet of May 1964 deserves closer analysis, because it provides one of the clearest reflections of the type of leadership that had by then emerged and which was to characterize the pattern of executive leadership in the years to come. In fact, the changes in the original membership of 17 that did take place through the 1967 elections, made so little difference in the basic shape and outlook of the cabinet that it is useful to look at the 31 persons who served during this entire time.[26] In line with the aim of the original military coup to provide new and younger leadership, the mean age (as of 1966) of all the members was 47.4; this compares to 53.4 in a sample of all government leaders throughout the Liberal period of 1952–1960 (as of 1959), and 51.8 for the Democratic Government of 1960–1961. Five of the new cabinet members, or nearly a third, were in fact under 40 at the time of their appointment to posts that included Defense, Foreign Affairs, and Home Affairs. Only 2 of the 31 members who served in this cabinet reached 60 years of age during their tenure in office, and both did so as ministers without portfolio. This record compares to over 25 percent of the leaders in both the Liberal and Democratic regimes who were over 60.[27]

The cabinet also reflected the continuing influence of the military. Seven of the original 17 appointees, 9 of the total 31, were ex-military men, evidently chosen to meet critical administrative or specialized requirements. For example, the new prime minister, Chong Il-kwon, had at the age of 33 risen to the position of Army Chief of Staff during the Korean War, had gone on to become Chairman of the Joint Chiefs of Staff and then, after retirement from the army, had moved into ambassadorial appointments from 1959 to 1963. Chong brought to the cabinet close ties with, and the confidence of, the military as well as national recognition for his role in the war, experience abroad including familiarity with the United States, strong but relatively quiet and uncontroversial administrative leadership, and loyalty to the president. As much as any one person he symbolized the gradual nature of the transition from military to civilian rule, the emphasis of the president on infusing the government with the military's store of senior managerial skill, and the desire to give the cabinet a degree of both respect and vigor.

The other military appointees fell mainly into two categories: in those posts like Defense and Home Affairs, which seemed to carry a demand for military backgrounds, and in those like Communications and Government Administration, in which technical backgrounds were relevant. Not all these appointees, moreover, were really representative of the military per se. For example, in the appointment to the Ministry of Commerce and Industry, the choice was a man whose rather perfunctory military ties were secondary to his ability in promoting exports, handling sensitive economic matters efficiently (and without outward ambition), and dealing effectively with Americans in a post where that was deemed critical. He had begun work in this area in the Military Government, held his minister's portfolio in the new cabinet throughout the economic growth period of the next three years, and then rose to the post of deputy prime minister. In general, the military members of the cabinet were men who had demonstrated administrative or technical ability, as well as political loyalty to Park during the Military Government, and who were retained in their jobs in the following government on the basis of both performance and previous military ties.[28]

The nonmilitary members of the May 1964 cabinet represented a variety of professional skills and signaled the first real infusion of civilian personnel into policy-making positions since 1961. Bankers, bureaucrats, journalists, lawyers, professors, engineers, and physicians were represented. Some of the most important civilian members were the deputy prime minister, who was practically given *carte blanche* in shaping and directing economic policies over the next few years[29] and the foreign minister, who took the negotiations with Japan out of the hands of the original coup leaders and in 1965 brought them to a successful even if still stormy conclusion for the government.[30]

The new stability and authoritativeness of the cabinet led directly to a revitalization of the bureaucracy. The accent on achievement, technical proficiency, and Western methods of organization and administration that had been features of the Military Government Cabinet, were now backed by political support and by authority for the cabinet ministers; this gave new impetus to the better-trained bureaucrats. The reserve of talent and dedication that emerged in the next few years was testimony both to the educational build-up of the 1950s and to the conscientiousness of this younger group of civil servants.[31] They added the substance and detailed direction to the government's programs of development that were to become so critical in the next few years. By their achievements, moreover, they further encouraged the government in its support of professionally executed development efforts. In addition, the bureaucracy continued its traditional role as a source of political recruitment. Thus by 1967, vice-ministerial, presidential secretariat, and even Assembly ranks began to be filled by men who had come to the top of the bureaucracy under the new program-oriented emphasis of the administration and who served to institutionalize in the political-administrative structure the emphasis on development, professionalism, and program achievement. In the bureaucracy even more than in the cabinet, an important resurgence of civilian influence was emerging in the executive, and over national policies generally.

The final aspect of the growth of the executive power was in the extension beyond the cabinet of a wide variety of instruments dependent upon the president, which contributed to his independent political strength. It was not unusual in Korean politics for the president to be somewhat independent of his party. Syngman Rhee had not desired a government party at all, preferring to rely primarily on his own charisma as his principal and independent source of power; he had only reluctantly acceded to the necessity for a party in 1951. Park, on the other hand, lacked any measure of charisma. He even disliked appearing in public and was not considered terribly effective when he did. His strength lay in his firmness of will, his increasingly skillful administration, and his personal relationship with such key political figures as Kim Chong-pil. All these factors enabled him to take decisive and sometimes harsh actions against elements of his supporters without destroying the fabric of his political backing. Whereas Rhee had tended to weaken almost all institutional bases of power in order to retain his own position, even at the cost of program effectiveness, Park operated by permitting several instruments of power to develop, but always in careful balance: the party, cabinet and bureaucracy, as already discussed, and the military, CIA, and even public opinion. These provide clues to the personality of the president, as well as the realities of political life in Korea.

As described earlier, the military had by 1961 become one of the most powerful and best-organized institutions in Korea—and from the time of the coup, politically one of the most important. The new civilian government after 1963 continued to provide an outlet for the political interests of the military, as demonstrated in the makeup of the cabinet and the party leadership. But equally important, after 1963 the military institution as a whole largely withdrew from politics. Many of the prominent Military Government members returned to active service. While many retiring officers in the following years would receive positions in government-owned corporations, as provincial governors, and occasionally in the cabinet, they did so largely as part of a general effort by the new government to avoid the internal frustrations among the military that had in 1961 erupted in political action. Except perhaps in the case of the management of some of the government-owned corporations, moreover, the placing of ex-military personnel in key posts was not done at cost to policy and program objectives of the government or the institutions involved. The government thus fairly neatly balanced its military background with its official civilian posture.

The military, however, have not been without direct access to political activity. One of the most important continuing sources of this entrée is the Army Security Command (formerly the Counter-Intelligence Corps). If one were to draw a spectrum of influences in Korean politics ranging from totalitarian and police state approaches, on the one hand, to democratic practice on the other, the Security Command would fall at the former extreme of the spectrum. This organization has official functions relating to military security and antiespionage; but it maintains an interest, and is given some scope by the president, in internal political matters. In fact, it is probably the most active influence in favor of harsh action against antigovernment elements. In 1964 military groups were themselves involved in violence and in pushing for stronger government action against demonstrating students and the opposition press.[32] In 1965, military personnel were suspected of committing terrorist acts against some newspaper and broadcasting officials.[33] The "official channel" for this kind of thinking in the government is the Security Command, which serves as a check not only on the civilian forms of administration, but on other security forces as well.

The civilian and larger Central Intelligence Agency is only slightly different. The CIA was a creation of the Military Government, and for a time its authority extended nearly unchecked into all fields of government and politics. Since the end of 1963, with the departure of many of its founders into the Assembly as party leaders and with the emergence of stronger cabinet authority, the CIA has acquired a somewhat more restricted and institutionalized function. It nevertheless combines extensive internal and external intelligence activities, and while its official functions center on antistate, particularly Communist, activities, these areas offer direct access to internal politics and economics in Korea. In times of political crises, moreover, as in the dispute over the "third-term amendment" in 1969, its role undoubtedly expands to the detriment of the cabinet, bureaucracy, and other civilian government institutions. The Korean CIA thus represents a somewhat more subtle, more bureaucratized, but at the same time even more pervasive, force for state control than the Army Security Command. Given its origins, it is noteworthy that the CIA has developed into an organization loyal to the president's interests, rather than into an instrument for influence within the executive of its former leaders now in the Assembly. However, the CIA has unquestionably served overall party interests in its investigative and arrest functions, and was more than likely a source of valuable intelligence and operations during the 1967 elections.

The cabinet and bureaucracy, on the other hand, represent more overt sources of power, bodies more publicly responsible for their actions. Their strengthening in the new government therefore indicated a certain redressing of authoritarianism as it had developed in the Military Government. For example, the cabinet took over from the CIA many responsibilities in the economic and administrative areas that had for a while fallen almost exclusively to the latter organization. As pointed out earlier, they provided the means for the first major reentry of civilian influence into the power structure after 1961.

Finally, representing the other end of the spectrum from the Security Command and the CIA, public opinion has also become an element of power conducive to executive interests, though less intentionally so. Park was in no sense a popular leader and did not try to be one. He did not feel it necessary to cater to public opinion and on several occasions risked a public storm to push through programs he felt critical to his regime. But public outcry and political turmoil served in a significant way to stimulate Park in 1963 to curb the Democratic Republican party's original plans to exile Kim Chong-pil in 1964 in the aftermath of student protests, and in general to strengthen the largely civilian institutional bases of executive power within the new constitutional framework. As discussed in Chapter 4, later in his administration the development of a popular consensus behind the regime's programs was to become an even more central factor in Park's outlook and in his choice of administrative techniques.

By 1964 the president had thus emerged as the indisputable key source of power within the executive and within the DRP, and thus within the country. The policies, outlook, and operations of the executive bore his stamp. Park was not a democrat, sharing with certain elements among his supporters a preference for authoritarian controls. He maintained more than one secret police-type organization in positions of influence. Yet his approach to political development under the new constitution was predominantly pragmatic and program-oriented, aimed at securing maximum managerial effectiveness plus maximum political stability. Thus he found it increasingly advantageous to restrict to some extent the more authoritarian elements of the regime, to strengthen professional expertise within the government, to balance the several sources of government power, and in time to make some concessions to demands for a more democratic type of society. While many of these developments came gradually, the foundations had been laid by the spring of 1964. Thereafter, the executive moved with increasing confidence, authoritativeness, and overall effectiveness.

THE DEMOCRATIC REPUBLICAN PARTY

The consolidation of executive power understandably had a profound effect on the development of political parties, both government and opposition. With the growth of executive power and independence, the relationship between the executive and the Democratic Republican party came to resemble more the American system than that on Taiwan. The DRP, instead of being the principal power mechanism increasingly became the agent of the government in the hurly-burly of open party politics. It thus turned more and more to defense of the government program in the Assembly and to the particulars of politicking among, and between, diverse interests.

In its makeup, the DRP had set out to develop the image of a broad base; specifically, to overcome the leadership's "military" image as it approached the 1963 elections. At the same time it wished to stress new and younger leadership. The makeup of the party reflects both themes. Among the official list of founding members, there is a distribution of occupations across various civilian fields. There is also a reasonably wide age spread. However, among both the founding members and the DRP assemblymen elected in 1963, there is very heavy weighting in favor of persons who entered politics after 1961: of 70 founding members, only 9 had previous party affiliations; and of the 110 DRP assemblymen elected in 1963, more than half were recruited into political activity after 1961.[34]

In terms of national following and influence, the Democratic Republican party emerged in the new government in an ambiguous position. By numbers in the Assembly—110 out of 175 seats—and by access to government favors, it was immensely influential. Its popular base, however, and thus its real roots in the country, were more limited. Despite its superior organizational base, its access to funds, and the election of its presidential candidate a few weeks earlier, the Democratic Republican party polled only 34 percent of the vote in the Assembly elections of 1963. A proportional representation system adopted under the new constitution enabled the party to take advantage of opposition disunity and emerge nevertheless with an overwhelming majority in the

Assembly.[35] But the party's showing clearly reflected the fact that it had been organized from the top down, that its grass roots organization and constituency had to be manufactured, and that its programs and ambitions were still clearly reflections of the leaders rather than of a popular movement or even of acceptance. The Democratic Republican party was thus by 1964 the most effective political organization, but not necessarily the most popular party.

In terms of organization, as pointed out earlier, among the original intentions of the founders of the Democratic Republican party was the creation of a tightly centralized party hierarchy in which real policy direction would be limited to a select few. However, the internal struggles that began in January 1963 and continued through the following year forced considerable modification of that scheme. By the end of 1964 the party had developed a series of strong factions that competed for presidential favor and party power. Moreover, the factions shifted in membership and position, indicating that the party itself was changing as it operated under the new government. At first, the main factions appeared to be the "mainstreamers" from the coup plotters and junta, grouped around Kim Chong-pil, and the "nonmainstreamers" who entered the party later under different circumstances and who were opposed to Kim. But splits and realignments occurred, civilian and military lines were blurred, and new issues arose. The party thus became more diverse, in fact, than some of its founders had intended. Also, much of the antagonism of its early days shifted from intraparty struggle to struggles with the executive.[36]

Nevertheless, for all its factionalism and its frustration over executive power, the Democratic Republican party has been an exceptionally effective, stable, and reliable arm of executive policy. While there have been occasional feints of defection, the government's absolute and assured majority on nearly every vote taken in the Assembly since 1963 has become a major source of frustration for the opposition and a major problem for the operation of democratic politics. Those who have come into the DRP seem above all to be attracted to the source of power and, with all the various frustrations that might be present within the party, not inclined as in some past cases of Korean politics to carry their dissent to the point of a real break. The advantage of unity and of staying in the government party are, of course, obvious. But the fact that, in contrast to the extreme factionalism of the Democratic party in 1960–1961, unity has become a significant factor in the DRP testifies to the organizational efficiency and pragmatic emphasis within the DRP, as in the executive. It is not a coincidence that, on the one hand, the Democratic Republican party was organized by members of an entirely new generation of leaders and has attracted primarily new recruits into politics and that, on the other hand, it has been able to maintain an exceptionally effective working unity and organizational efficiency in the face of internal disputes, opposition assaults, and at times political unrest. In this sense, among others, it is a more "modernized" party than the opposition and many of its predecessors.

The result has been a much more effective control of policy by the government at both the executive and legislative levels. The cost, however, as discussed more fully in Part III, has been to the resiliency of the DRP as a political force independent of the president, and in the general weakening of the legislative function as an independent part of the governmental process.

OPPOSITION PARTIES

The parties in opposition to the Park government and the Democratic Republican party in 1963 together polled 53 percent of the presidential votes and 66 percent of the Assembly votes but ended up losing the presidency and being swamped in the Assembly. The outward reason, and the bane of opposition existence before and after 1963, was disunity. Four candidates ran against Park Chung-Hee; their presence showed the inability of precoup parties and factions to unite in face of the DRP challenge. Former President Yun Po-son thus lost to Park by only 156,000 votes, while the other three opposition candidates polled over 700,000 votes among them.[37] Over 800 candidates from 15 political parties competed for the 131 elective seats in the Assembly. Opposition votes split sufficiently to give the DRP victory in 88 electoral districts and, as a result, claim to 22 of the 44 proportional seats. There were charges of election fraud and government interference in the parties' attempts at organization. But the plight of the opposition was deeper than disunity—internal or instigated—or of voting irregularities. It went to the core of its representation.

The principal opposition leadership emerging in 1963 came from the former Democratic party of the late 1950s. As described in Chapter 1, the Democratic party had developed around opposition to Rhee and had drawn to itself the dissatisfaction felt throughout Korean society at the increasingly dictatorial and damaging policies of the Rhee regime. But the Democratic party itself had little specific program direction and its leadership was drawn not from the younger generation pushing for change but from leaders of Rhee's generation who had fallen out with him. When political activity resumed in 1963, it was Yun Po-son, former member of the conservative Korean Democratic party of early independence days, leader of the Old Faction in the intraparty dispute that plagued the Democratic party in 1960–1961, president of the Republic during the Democratic government, and 66 years old at this point, who assumed the leading position in opposition circles. Yun was a man of much appeal. His aristocratic family status, his role in opposition to Rhee, his dramatic resignation as president at the time of the coup, his scathing denunciation of military rule, his charges of dangerous Communist sympathies in the new military leadership, all made him an effective symbol not only of a lost democracy, but of a more traditional and accepted type of conservative civilian leadership.[38] He came within a hair's breadth of defeating Park in the election. But once the elections were over, his effectiveness declined.

It is a moot point, though it may well have influenced many voters, whether the military would have allowed a victory by Yun to stand; for, in the following period, the weaknesses of the opposition as a whole in the wake of the coup were revealed. Unable to unite to capitalize on popular sympathy in 1963, it failed afterward to enlist the new blood needed to meet the challenge of the DRP or to allow paths to the top to whatever newer recruits were available.[39] The various opposition parties and factions that were to merge and split and reemerge over the next several years were thus all led by politicians who had entered on the scene in a different era and who could not or would not relinquish leadership to a younger generation. Where much of the DRP membership came from recruits into politics after 1961, almost no prominent opposition figure emerged in this manner.[40] With regard to age, it is less in the average ages of the DRP and opposition Assemblymen, which are not so remarkably different, as all parties sought to give an impression of pan-national representation, but in the image and the actuality of overall leadership that this difference showed. The government featured men in their forties; the opposition featured men in their sixties.[41]

Another factor in the weakness of the opposition was that, although the opposition elements as a whole had obtained a very large popular vote in 1963, their sources of support were quite diverse and not readily amenable to organizational solidarity. Thus among its most articulate elements the opposition attracted politicians of various stripes who had been removed from influence by the coup; intellectuals concerned about democracy, as well as those dissillusioned at the unhappy outcome of an early cooperation with the military; ex-military who had broken with the Military Government; students moved by idealism and frustration but who had also been frustrated under the Chang Myon government, in which many opposition leaders had been prominent; and the press, traditionally in opposition to government but without loyalty to any specific institution or party.[42] Geographically, support was also widespread. There was solid urban support in Seoul and some other cities, influenced in part by the press and the intelligentsia; rural support in the northern provinces where charges of radicalism in the new government evidently had some effect, as well as the fact that Park was from the south; and despite some setbacks in 1963, potential support in the agriculturally rich Cholla provinces in the south, traditionally a source of opposition to the central government and formerly a strong source of support for the Democratic party.[43] In all this, however, there were no firm labor, business, or farm interests to give substance or direction to the opposition's economic outlook or even to provide a solid base of support should the opposition attain power. As for developing such groupings, the existing opposition leaders had no feel for labor support in the urban strongholds, were by background and disposition unsuited to be real champions of the small farmers, and were too far from the seats of power to be able to command strong business backing. The opposition leaders were consciously and conscientiously "conservative," consistently appealing more to values and to generalized conditions than to specific mass groups.[44]

Finally, the opposition elements faced a really critical difficulty in that the forms of opposition were themselves limited. With a government that had restricted the latitude of political activity as well as of public debate and which had itself preempted many of the issues of the April 1960 revolution, the opposition gathered to it all the sources of dissent, from the covert sympathies for the now outlawed "progressive" parties to the more conservative outlook exemplified by the opposition leadership, though it could only articulate the latter. Therefore, despite the apparent uniformity of its leadership, it was a conglomeration of interests, vulnerable to the blandishments that the government could increasingly hold out to its diverse supporters.

In summary, the opposition to the new government predominantly symbolized, in its outward appearance and mannerisms, the prerevolutionary generation. It was not without influence; it had captured the majority of popular votes in the elections and thus reflected the large measure of distrust that hung over the new government. In 1964 and again in 1965, the opposition would help galvanize popular opinion on the critical issues of democratic rights and the Japanese settlement, in the latter bearing much of the brunt of a nationwide struggle. It was, moreover, the official "opposition," and to a Korean population sensitive to the institutional requisites of a democratic system, this fact entitled it to a general measure of support and to demands for protection against the overwhelming legislative majority of the DRP. But the opposition's parliamentary position had been badly crippled, and its public prestige lowered as well, by the outcome of the 1963 Assembly election. With the DRP in firm control, the politics of the Assembly were to prove again and again an exercise in frustration, exacerbating the negativism and the factionalism that had already existed within opposition ranks. As national interest turned, moreover, from the emotional issues of democracy and Japan to those of economics, and closely related to the latter, to international initiatives and prestige, the opposition, with its makeup and outlook, found it increasingly difficult to compete with the growing professionalism of the executive and the aggressive recruitment of the younger generation by the Democratic Republican party.

3 / The Struggle for Democracy

The issue that hung most heavily over the newly elected government of 1963 was whether, and how, it would achieve one of the main ideals of 1960: the development of democracy. The military coup had cut off the first really free democratic experience Korea had known since independence. With all its turmoil and disappointments, the period of the Interim and Democratic governments, 1960–1961, remained for many Koreans, intellectuals and others, a period of great national experimentation and even political uplift. Even well after the return to civilian government, the coup was seen by these persons as having cut off Korea's chance for political development, defined to mean the development of a fully free and functioning democracy.

This feeling was very deep, extending beyond those especially antagonistic to the military intervention of 1961. For though there was no historic tradition of democracy in Korea, it had, during the struggle for independence, very largely become the accepted norm for the country; after independence democracy had been absorbed with amazing rapidity into the political culture of South Korea. Among the intelligentsia, the press, and increasingly among the students, democratic ideals came to have a very special importance. These groups became the strongest and most vocal defenders of democracy in times when it was most threatened. But other parts of the society—bureaucracy, military, farmers—also developed a stake in, and a degree of ideological attachment to, democratic principles, and this influenced the overall political milieu.

Thus as soon as it permitted resumption of open political activity in 1963, the Military Government was faced with a widespread demand for a quick end to military rule and a restoration of some form of civilian, democratic government. Conflict on these matters continued, moreover, after the reestablishment of a type of civilian government. Throughout 1964 and 1965, when the government and its critics were pitted in a bitter struggle over the normalization of relations with Japan, the degree of allowable political opposition and open dissent was put to a severe test. The struggle over relations with Japan brought to the fore some of the more extreme authoritarian influences within the government on the one hand, and the more reckless and turbulent forms of popular dissent that had done so much to weaken the strength and stability of the democratically elected government of 1960–1961, on the other. As a result, the new government, and the whole constitutional system, were very soon under great stress.

Yet by the end of 1965, a compromise was reached of considerable significance for the future attitude and actions of the regime. The government did not accept a return to the openness and freedom of action that had existed in 1960–1961. Moreover, it proved determined to use strong measures to cut off dissent where it seriously threatened order or its own survival. But a general recognition of limitations on the legitimate use of government power in this area and of protected areas of free speech and dissent was also established. The framework for both order and preservation of democratic institutions was thus more clearly established. The result, moreover, was to encourage Park's administration to adopt a political and economic strategy at home that would in the next two years promote a freer and less regimented society.

SOURCES OF DEMOCRATIC VALUES

It is important to look more closely at the sources of democracy in Korea in order to understand the intensity of the struggles in this period, as well as the nature and significance of the compromise that was achieved. In Korean political culture, democracy has largely been an import from the West.[1] Its early acceptance as the norm for an independent Korea originated in part during Japanese rule, in the close association between nationalist efforts within Korea and the sympathetic operation of Western missionary schools and churches. A large number of the expatriate leaders had also early identified the nationalist cause with the West and with general Western principles of liberalism and democracy. But such doctrines, associated primarily with nationalism, remained in conflict with more traditional values.[2]

The conflict between acquired values and traditional habits of thought continued after independence. Under American influence, the non-Communist nationalists in the South set up democratic forms of government. By then a hospitable environment existed in South Korea for a democratically oriented society, in both economic and political terms. The land reform of 1947–1950 had created a rural sector of predominantly small owner-tillers. Partially as a result of Japanese policy restricting the rise of a Korean industrial or management elite, the business caste in South Korean industry was small. And by 1945 considerable fluidity and laxness were evident in the older class structure as a result of the long decline in the political and economic foundations of traditional class distinctions.[3] Many of these leveling influences, particularly the economic ones, were further reinforced by destruction during the Korean War.

But the practice of democracy in the South was hampered from the beginning by a lack of suitable institutions or experience, by the first president's determined quest for autocratic power, and by the international cricumstances surrounding South Korean independence. As has already been pointed out, the first few years of independence were marked by fierce rivalries, instability among political groupings, and the gradual concentration of power in the hands of President Rhee and his followers. The anticommunist posture of the Rhee government and its feud with the North encouraged and gave cover to government persecution of "Left" or "progressive" political activities, many of which however were reflections of genuine indigenous opposition to the regime. This set the tone for a continued narrow perception of permissible boundaries of political thought in South Korea. Finally, especially following the Korean War, new business interests rose in wealth and influence through the political favoritism, corruption, and the misallocation of resources that occurred in the haste and confusion of postwar reconstruction; thus a new aristocracy was established.

The presence, side by side for over a decade after independence, of democratic ideals and institutions, on the one hand, and the autocratic realities of the Rhee government on the other, bred considerable frustration and even cynicism in South Korea. Yet the democratic ideal gave some sanctity to the democratic institutions themselves and helped develop a measure of genuine popular support for them. Some of this was a response to political realities, and indeed connected with the desire for survival; for example, for the older politicians in opposition to Rhee, these institutions were the only means of defense and of continued legitimate operation against him. The cause of democracy also provided a bond between them and the new forces of opposition that were rising.

However, for the younger generations, coming to maturity or prominence in the postwar period, and under the influence of this hybrid of democracy and dictatorship, the democratic norms were much more internalized. They had been exposed to them in their education and their professional training, as well as through the political system; some were drawn to them even more in search of a new course for their frustrated nationalistic energies. The attachment to democracy among younger Koreans was not uniform but their actions reflected its having become rooted in much of Korean culture by the time of the 1960 revolution.

One reason for this extensive postwar political acculturation was undoubtedly the very important American influence in South Korea after 1945. America's role affected not only the values and norms of Korean politics but some of its specific actions as well. The United States had for some time served as a source of ideological doctrine for the Korean nationalist movement. But from 1945 on—through the American Military Government of 1945–1948, the leading role in the Korean War, and the massive aid programs thereafter—American influence extended directly into nearly every aspect of Korean political and economic development. Thus in the first few years after World War II the United States largely shaped the structure of the independent government, the postwar education system, the country's internal and external economic relationships; and increasingly thereafter, through its training and education programs, it shaped the attitudes and abilities of key groups, especially in the education sector, bureaucracy, military, and business community.[4] Ideologically, moreover, the United States was not only reinforced in its earlier role as the source of liberal-reform doctrine, but after 1945 it became the fulcrum of South Korea's anticommunist ideology and the model on which South Korea's political and economic development was presumably patterned in its struggle with the North. In this regard, as described later, the United States was called upon by some Koreans to intervene directly in Korean political developments, and on occasion did so, giving substance to its role as ideological as well as military protector.

The American influence on the attitudes of several key groups in society deserves perhaps the most attention. In education, a long Western, largely American, missionary tradition had been influential on Korean thinking. But the infusion after 1953 of teacher training programs, aid-financed university contracts, and increased private opportunities for study in the United States extended American influence even further, beyond the formal structure of postwar education, to the attitudes of a significant body of educational leaders whose training and outlook were oriented away from traditional concepts. These leaders posed a challenge to their seniors in the education system, who were largely Japanese-trained, and to the traditional concepts of education that had quickly enough become part of the postwar system. In these persons, and in those students and teachers whom they influenced in Korea, were internalized instead the newer concepts and objectives of education, which included "democratization."[5]

The bureaucracy was another group significantly affected by the American presence. In addition to officials trained in the United States, those in government operations within Korea, in nearly every field of economic development, were exposed to the influence of American advisors. Regulations governing the aid projects also brought not only Korean bureaucrats, but ministers, assemblymen, and private businessmen into contact with Western concepts of management, organization, and legal procedures. The United States in 1959 also helped found the first Graduate School of Public Administration in Korea, located at the country's most prestigious university, whose graduates were to make up a large proportion of the nation's bureaucracy after 1960. Persons exposed to these several sources of American influence were thus infused with new concepts and standards, particularly related to organization and management, public responsibility, merit systems of promotion, and technical specialization. As in education, they presented a contrast and a threat to their seniors, whose basic orientation had been shaped by education and experiences in the Japanese colonial period. They were also, in outlook and orientation, closer than their seniors to the post-liberation Korean college graduates who began to enter the bureaucracy in large numbers after 1960. It was, in fact, these two groups—the younger postliberation university graduates and those exposed to foreign training—who, along with the military, increasingly came to the forefront in the bureaucracy after 1960 and shaped much of that institution's outlook and output in the following years.[6]

Finally, as described in the previous chapter, the military establishment was built almost entirely under American direction and almost exclusively on American principles of organization and function. American influence in this case was largely through American military channels and focused more on techniques and certain behavioral matters than on democratic ideology. Moreover, the intense exposure and contact with the United States did not prevent the military coup of 1961 against an elected government, even though there were strong expressions of disapproval from the United States at the time. On the other hand, it is probably true that the ambivalence of many senior officers about the duration of military rule, and the splits that occurred in the Military Government between 1961 and 1963 over this and related issues, reflected a genuine attachment by many officers to the principle of a nonpolitical role for armed forces. But American influence was even more significant as regards the military in developing overall the skills and strengths of this particular group in Korean society, which was to play such an important role in Korean politics after 1961. The military, like elements of the bureaucracy, thus became as noted earlier one of the more "modernized" institutions in Korea, that is, more responsive to advanced concepts of administration and more likely to share general Western emphasis on program performance. This separated the military from much of the older elite. It was also to create a mutuality of interest with American officials that, after the restoration of civilian government in 1963 and particularly after the focusing of attention on economic issues, was to lead not only to a rapid rapprochement with the United States but to a renewed receptivity to American political and ideological influence as well.

Nevertheless, it is important to distinguish between American influence and the growth of democratic ideology in Korea. The two were not entirely synonymous. The United States was not consistent in its actions in this regard: it condoned the April 1960 revolution and denounced the military coup a year later. But before that the United States had lived with the many autocratic actions of the Rhee regime.[7] The very buildup by the United States of the Korean military to such large proportions, though done for obvious defense reasons, made a military entrée into Korean politics at some point inevitable. Nor was exposure to American education or training a guarantee of a democratic outlook. Of all the Korean governments after 1952, none had as many American-educated persons among its leaders as did the Rhee government.[8] When accused of being a dictator, Rhee would point to his 40 years in the United States and cite as his major ambition to give Korea a government "of similar feature and ideals."[9] Finally, the younger generation of military and bureaucratic leaders, who had benefited most from foreign exposure and technical training, were ambivalent about the democratic content of Western political values. Imbued with respect for concrete program goals, professional expertise, and efficient management, they often became impatient with democratic-style politics in their country, which seemed to slow progress toward their goals and open up the government as a whole to various forms of political pressures and dissipating forms of corruption.

American influence on the growth of democracy was nevertheless great, as important in its indirect effect upon the forces of change as in the setting of an ideological environment. It helped give to the younger generation of bureaucrats, educators, military men, and others the skills and orientation for a changing, economically developing country, and thus aggravated their impatience with and revolt against the politics and administration of the Rhee regime. At the same time, by its presence and its importance to South Korea internationally, the United States reinforced the symbols and values of democracy, encouraged them in education, helped establish them in the constitutional provisions of government, and backed them generally in various phases of its assistance programs, both military and economic. Democracy thus became the accepted norm for the elite as for the population at large, for the modernizing groups as for the traditional nationalist in Korea. In this atmosphere, an internal and quite indigenous attachment to democratic principles was able to develop. For some it was abstract, for some very real and meaningful. But it touched most groups.

INTERNAL PRESSURE GROUPS

By the late 1950s the most ardent and vocal spokesmen for this attachment were the academic intelligentsia, the press, and the students. These three groups in Korea, which have played such an important political role in recent years, are closely related. The relationship between professors and students is obvious. But in Korea there is also a very significant link between the academic intellectuals and the press, through the regular feature and editorial writing for the daily papers in which many professors engage. Yet the commitment and motivation of these three groups in the struggle for democracy have been slightly different.

The academic profession in Korea is in a stage of difficult transition. It is moving from a traditionally prestigious role in the social hierarchy to one of uncertain influence, relatively lower pay than many other professions, and increasing competition for prestige and influence with such new contenders as business and the military. In response, the academic profession appears to have become defensive rather than radical. The same absence of radicalism is true of all three of these groups. One can speculate whether the long outlawing of any Left-wing politics or ideology in South Korea has not simply precluded the open expression of radical sentiments or the growth of any radical movements. But this bent among the academics appears to be a reflection of genuine sentiments as well. The academic profession as a whole is not a radical defender of human rights or of either social or economic equality. The members reflect instead a reaction against the long periods of instability in Korean politics and a growing concern with the solution of Korea's economic problems. They reflect, furthermore, a vestige of class consciousness, seemingly aggravated by the perceived loss of status of their profession and by a somewhat negative outlook generally on Korean character.[10]

Yet the academic profession has at the same time developed and still manifests a strong distrust of government. This was nurtured during the long decline of the Rhee regime into nearly absolute totalitarianism and in the unhappy experience with the Military Government when intellectuals were at the same time both persecuted and sought after for advice but in the end left without influence or respect in the government.[11] The defense of democracy has thus become important to the academic profession, as defense of the freedom of the university, the freedom and status of the intellectual, and the right to criticize the government, from which the profession has been alienated.[12] In these areas particularly, the academics have been a formidable influence.

It would be a mistake, moreover, to judge the attitude and influence of this profession by its general outlook only. Among the profession there is a sizeable group more fervently involved in the struggle for democracy, per se. Their attachment is more closely related to the struggle for human and individual rights, to the idealism of the students, and to the identification of democracy with Korea's national identity.[13] These have often been the most active persons, moreover, in political writing and organizational activity. To these persons, as to the students, the contradictions between the slogans of the Free World and the fact of authoritarian rule in South Korea—between the norm and the practice of democracy—have become a rallying cry against government and, in harder times, one more counsel of despair. Long pessimistic over the country's economic future, seeing in prospect for a divided country either permanent dependence on the United States or resubjugation to Japan, they read into the struggle for democracy the one measure of national identity for South Korea. "Without democracy," observed a brilliant and tense Korean scholar at the height of the struggle with the government over the Japanese settlement in 1965, "there is no distinction between North and South Korea."

The journalists of Korea have been much less exposed than the academics, and perhaps even the students, to the direct influence of the United States. Certainly much less than the academic community have they studied abroad or shared in the benefits of United States assistance programs.[14] They represent, therefore, the very genuine indigenous attachment to principles of democratic government in Korea, which the press indeed has done much to forge. Journalists generally also represent a slightly younger group than their academic colleagues, and as such are much more a product of the postwar Korean education system. Perhaps for this reason, or perhaps because of their own lower economic position, they show greater concern than the academics with the problems of "economic democracy," that is, distribution of wealth and full employment, and with economic questions generally in defining the process of modernization. They appear also more receptive than the academics to considerable disruptions in society for the sake of modernization. But they, too, as a whole tend to stress responsibility well over human rights as most important for democracy in Korea, and pessimistically view the lack of self-governing ability among Koreans as one of the greatest obstacles to democracy in their country.[15] Thus their support of democracy is tinged more with negativism and sometimes even despair at its outcome than with the more positive and optimistic character of nineteenth-century Western liberalism. Perhaps for this reason, the more general restrictions on the freedom of the press in South Korea, for example, on manifestations of a political Left, are sometimes met more with resignation than revolt.[16]

Yet one has the sense of a greater degree of political activism in the Korean press than in the academic community as a whole, perhaps simply the reflection of a more active and continuing participation in the process than the intermittent action of the academics, who can withdraw to the tasks of education and preoccupations of university life whenever the issues of politics are not overriding. The press, moreover, provides an outlet to those academics whose concern with political issues is more continuous and active; there the two strands of activist influence converge.

The modern press as an institution in Korea has its roots in the pronationalist publications of the Japanese period, and some of the leading papers today have a long, proud tradition of having challenged the authority of government—Japanese and Korean—when dissent was a clearly dangerous activity. In addition to the newspapers, several intellectual journals have provided a continuous forum for some of the most outspoken internal criticism of postwar Korean governments and some of South Korea's most progressive political thought. To some extent, the press adopted these principles of a free press from Western democratic societies during the nationalist struggle. But it has taken them over and made them practically the cornerstone of Korean democracy. Because of its wide readership in a highly literate country, its outspoken and almost unrelenting "opposition" character, and its association with the prestigious academic leaders, the press exerts great influence on the nature and intensity and even the tactics of political opposition in South Korea.[17]

The press, despite (or perhaps because of) its long established tradition of dissent, has been constantly in danger of suppression. Under the Rhee and Park governments, the press has had to walk a narrow line to avoid either outright closure or indirect methods of control such as threats of violence or economic pressure. It has been plagued as well by its internal problems. In the 1960–1961 period, when the press was largely unrestricted, papers sprang up everywhere, many using the printed word for mere sensationalism or political blackmail. While this extreme abuse was arrested after 1961, the press has consistently had to worry about excesses of sensational and generally irresponsible reporting in what is a highly competitive, low-paid profession. Successive governments have sought to use these as excuses for curbing the press. Thus the Military Government, in a move designed in part to eradicate the most irresponsible journals of the 1960–1961 period, clamped very severe controls on the press as a whole and reduced to one a day the number of editions of even the most responsible papers.[18] In 1964 and 1966, as discussed below, the press would again find itself faced with the threat of overt government regulation in response to problems of internal press management and control.

In this milieu, like most academics and students, journalists have sought to carve out an area of freedom of movement and expression that would maintain a reasonable and meaningful voice of dissent in the country, but without trying to break down—in what might be but a futile gesture—all those prerogatives of restriction that the government had gathered to itself in the postwar era. Thus, with occasional but still rare exceptions, the press has maintained unremitting anticommunism, and only gingerly questioned the official policy on reunification, which is in many ways the touchstone of orthodoxy in Korean politics. It has, on the other hand, usually been sharp in criticizing corruption and irregularities in electoral or parliamentary procedure, and almost vitriolic on issues of nationalist concern such as Japan. Most important, the press as a whole is generally quick to react to a gross violation or a flagrant disregard of the minimum processes of a democratic system. For it sees in these processes not only the means of preservation of the system in which it operates, but an opportunity for the growth of those characteristics and practices, of both people and institutions in Korea, that would make possible a more complete and genuine democratic state, to which the press is strongly committed.[19]

On the question of the freedom of the press, finally, it has shown an amazing capacity for organization, concerted action, and political effectiveness in defense of its interests. The press, it should be noted, is connected in many cases with large business interests, which has helped its effectiveness. It has also been willing to use its influence on the students in its own defense or in defense of issues on which it feels strongly. The success of the press, however, has clearly been greater in blocking overt forms of press control than covert. Thus financial pressure on business owners, government-influenced bank foreclosures on loans, secret threats, harassment, and even editorial censorship by CIA members, have been used successfully to curb and control the press despite the absence of legal restrictions. Such curbs, common under Rhee, have become intensified again since 1968 with apparently significant effect.[20] Nevertheless, the press clearly remains a very powerful institution in Korea—too cautious or conservative to be branded as dangerously radical, and too strong to be ignored.

If the professors and journalists have thus helped define many of the issues of democracy in Korea, the students have become the *force majeure* for their political activities. As a group, students had been an important locus of nationalist fervor and activity under the Japanese. But it was in the April 1960 revolution that they acquired the prestige and power that, in the postwar era, led them to be looked upon as a major independent political force. Afterward their actions became almost a bellwether of Korean stability. In 1964 and 1965 they were looked upon by government and opposition alike as having one of the most critical roles in determining the outcome of the struggle over the Japanese settlement and the fate of the government as a whole.

Like the students of many developing countries, the Korean students have been at the center of the many currents and conflicts of a changing society and, as a result, often the most sensitive to those changes. Education itself has been one of the most explosive forces of postwar Korea. From 1945 to 1965, the rate of literacy rose from 22 percent to over 80 percent. But perhaps even more significant was the rise in secondary and higher education noted in Chapter 1, which set Korea off from many Asian and Western countries as well: a 13-fold increase in secondary education and an 18-fold increase in college enrollment.[21] The education sector, moreover, was a vivid example of the many crosscurrents of Korean, Japanese, and American influences that operated in Korea after liberation. The students in Korea have also been massed to help both the rate of communication and the relative ease of organization for political activity. In 1965, of Korea's 142,000 college students, 90,000 were in Seoul.

The political role of Korean students, nevertheless, has been distinct from that in some of the other developing countries, where students have been a major element of influence or power. Unlike many other countries, students in Korea are not organized in strong national organizations. They are also, as are professors, prohibited by law from having direct affiliation with political parties. While this situation is largely the result of government preference, it also suits the students' preference. For, influenced greatly by the relatively unplanned rush of events that resulted in the revolution of April 1960, the students have come to prefer their actions to have the appearance—if not always the actuality—of spontaneity, or of ad hoc response to issues of great national importance. The students thus see themselves as the "conscience of the nation," a nonpartisan force that rises in defense of the national interest at critical moments, when more partisan forces have failed to defend them. And it is nationalism, more than democracy or any other issue, that arouses student emotion and forms the core of unified student action.[22]

Democracy, however, has become identified with this nationalist tradition. This flowed almost naturally from the postwar generation's being raised in a world of information—textbooks, newspapers, journals—in which democracy played an important role, in complete contrast to their elders' world. It has happened also, however, because of the frustration of other outlets for nationalist energy. The issue of reunification, a popular one with students, has been frustrated first by the shortage of realistic alternatives for reunification since the Korean War, and second by the fact that the debate on the issue has been largely proscribed under the strictness of anticommunist directives. Anti-Japanese sentiment offered another external outlet, which the Rhee regime long fanned. But with the nearly total exclusion of Japanese involvement in Korea after 1945, it became difficult to make Japan a scapegoat for internal difficulties of which the students along with others were becoming increasingly conscious. Nationalist energy, therefore, became increasingly focused inward on the contradictions in South Korean society and the obstacles they posed to national growth and prestige. The contrast of large inputs of aid and still glaring economic weaknesses was one such contradiction. The gap between the formal adherence to democratic principles and the increasingly corrupt practices of the Rhee regime was another. The events leading up to 1960 strengthened students' identification with the second of these issues. Hopes for change had become increasingly pinned to the strong potential electoral showing of the Democratic party and were bitterly frustrated by the election-rigging of 1960. It was the election, followed by the repression of student protestors, that touched off the April revolution.

The Korean students' attachment to democracy, which emerged so strongly at that point, has been described with some justice as more value- than norm-oriented, more idealistic and concerned with universal causes than related to specific injustices.[23] But the students' outlook on democracy is even less clear-cut than that description would imply, and also more tied to other relatively concrete objectives of equal importance to them. The students' overall attitude toward democracy, particularly Western democratic principles, is filled with the same conflicts noted among academics and journalists.[24] Similarly, however, these views have not led students into adherence to revolutionary new forms of government or economic organization. As noted earlier, the proscription on left-wing or radical political activities in South Korea makes it difficult to gauge the depth of real attachment or potential for attachment to radical activities. But, even in the freer atmosphere of 1960–1961, the students did not exhibit much interest in radical social or economic revolution.[25]

One has the impression, instead, that in their personal insecurities generated by the economic and political conditions of postwar Korea, the students, conscious of a still prevalent elite status accorded them by most of society, are concerned more with finding jobs, prestige, and satisfaction within the present system than in remolding it altogether. Their national outlook, similarly, is geared to removing the apparent and fairly immediate obstacles to Korean economic progress and political justice, though their program for doing so is not sharply defined.[26] Defense of democracy, as an ideal and as a protest to the corruptions and frustrations of the later 1950s and beyond, has become part of that outlook, but part too of something at once both larger in concept and more concrete in its anticipated results for the students themselves.

The April 1960 revolution, however, did add another dimension to the students' attachment to democratic ideals that has an important bearing on their proclivity to political action. In the revolution, the students found themselves at the head of a truly national uprising, assuming for the first time since independence a leading role in Korean political life in the tradition of student forces in the nationalist struggle against the Japanese. Not surprisingly, therefore, the 1960 experience has shaped much of the students' self-perception of their political role in Korea today. In the legacy of that experience, democracy looms large. It was not the only issue but it was the most dramatic, and it gave the revolution its idealistic character. For students since then, the defense of democracy has become part of the student tradition. They have come to look to themselves—and others have looked to them—to rise up in protest against any similar gross violation of the rights of the people and the basic forms of democracy, as occurred in 1960.

Finally, in a related but indirect way, the April revolution contributed in one more manner to the identification of the student movement with the struggle over democracy. It thrust the students into a generally active political role from which they were not soon to draw back. But if they were to act in defiance of constituted authority on any issue, they were of necessity, given their form of action, to be involved in testing the rights and limits of protest. And in fact, in most of the major student demonstrations from 1960 on, the students took to the streets over one issue which, in the face of reprisals, shifted to a defense of students' rights and the rights of protest generally. Thus directly and indirectly, students moved to the forefront after 1960 in testing the basic principles and practices of democracy, including both the right of dissent and the legitimate use of authority and power.

THE TRANSITION TO CIVILIAN RULE

These then have been the several influences—foreign and domestic, passive and active—promoting the demands for democracy in Korea, which played such an important role in the 1960s. From the first gap in the solidity of military rule in 1963, they began actively to influence events. The Military Government had from the beginning indicated that at some reasonably early point it would return the country to civilian rule.[27] That promise, plus the probably widespread if tacit recognition that the 1960–1961 period had been almost dangerously turbulent, and also the rather impressive reformist record of the Military Government in its first few months, made military rule tolerable in Korea for nearly the first two years. But as the country approached the termination of

Military Government, all the seams began to crack. The civilian elements became impatient, the military regime, through the scandals of 1962, lost much of its reformist reputation, and the junta itself began to divide over the issues of party formation and power.

In the early months of 1963, the country went through a series of vacillations and crises over the nature and timing of a return to civilian rule. The Military Government was divided internally between those who wished the country returned to civilian rule without much military involvement afterward, and those who wanted the junta leadership to assume control in the new government.[28] On the other side, the newly freed civilian politicians engaged in a fratricidal scramble for nomination to the presidency, especially at those times when it appeared that General Park Chung-Hee would not be in the running. Parties formed, split, and reformed. By election time, as many as six opponents of Park had received nominations from various party groupings, four of whom remained in the election to the end. Whatever his true intentions throughout all this, the feuding of the civilian parties gave General Park, spurred on by open declarations of support from military elements, the excuse to hint first at a possible extension for four more years of military rule and later as a more acceptable move, to announce his own intention to run for president.

In this turbulent and uncertain period when military rule might have been extended, the major elements of Korean society mitigating against autocracy were in evidence. The military establishment as a whole could not unite in a desire to maintain military autocracy in Korea and, reinforced by the antipathy of some to party leader Kim Chong-pil, could not even agree on the means by which the ex-military should participate as leaders in a civilian government. The crack in military unity opened the way to a host of other influences in Korean politics. The United States played a major direct role at this point. When Park, in the spring of 1963, indicated a possible reversal of the Military Government's earlier position on returning the country to civilian rule, the United States was outspoken in its opposition and exerted a good deal of diplomatic persuasion on the government not to upset its original timetable. Some Korean commentators have pointed to this as the decisive influence.[29] United States intercession was allied, however, with the quite fervent feeling that now existed within Korea. Once the process of transition had begun in early 1963 with the resumption of political activity, the pressure for civilian rule built up so quickly that extension of military rule past that year could have touched off demonstrations and even open acts of rebellion. Civilian politicians—divided on almost everything else—united to oppose the government on this point.[30] And the press, still under intermittent censure, supported the battle. This combination of forces prevailed.

The country thus returned at the close of 1963 to the constitutional forms of a democratic republic. There was of course one great change; the involvement of the military now as a major political force, with Park Chung-Hee elected president and the Democratic Republican party swamping the Assembly elections. There was also the fact that the government, through the use of the Political Purification Act to free or withhold politicians from participation in the elections and through other actions, had helped sow disunity in the opposition ranks.[31] The Military Government had also given the country a constitution that provided for very strong executive powers.[32] With the former military leaders in control of both the executive and the Assembly, the degree of really democratic government remained therefore something of a question mark.

The test of the reality of constitutional government came quickly enough. In 1964, the government pushed ahead with secret negotiations on a settlement with Japan. Although the Japanese issue is discussed at length in Chapter 5, it can be stated in summary fashion here that the issue touched upon and raised nearly all the fundamental issues facing Korea at this point: the political future of the country, the direction of its economic policies, its future foreign relations, the hopes for reunification, and the question of national identity. The circumstances of the negotiations were such, moreover, as to arouse the emotions of the country even more than might otherwise have been the case. In 1964 particularly, they involved tactics and personalities that raised suspicion about the intentions and trustworthiness of the Korean negotiators. Thus there also came to the fore all the suspicion and mistrust that had been generated against the new leaders since 1961—by the coup, the scandals surrounding the formation of the DRP, and the closeness of the 1963 election, which the losers contested sharply. In time, therefore, the issue became a test of the very legitimacy of the government. Not all the persons involved in the struggle over the Japanese settlement saw it in this fashion. But more and more, as it progressed, the struggle took on this character.

Very early in 1964, uneasiness over the government's policy toward Japan started to become the focal point for political criticism of the new government. Soon thereafter the issue struck a responsive note with the students. By March 1964 they had taken to the streets to protest the negotiations with Japan. Their initial action led to countermeasures by the government, some constructive, others not. The latter exacerbated the situation.[33] By May and June the lines of communication between the government and the students had broken down altogether. Demonstrations had become violent, and the government itself was under attack. In May the cabinet resigned. In June the government was forced to declare martial law.

In the aftermath of this series of events, the government moved to silence the major sources of popular opposition that had arisen. Divided internally and outnumbered by DRP votes in the Assembly, the opposition political parties were not considered a major threat. But, to the extent that they could ignite the fires of the press and the students, they were potentially a spearhead endangering the very existence of the government. The government thus saw the press and the students as the major threat. And it believed that the press itself had done much to fan the flames of student emotion and to instigate the demonstrations. As a result, President Park proposed to the National Assembly that the conditions for lifting martial law include the passage of two laws, one aimed at control of the press and the other at control of the students. Known as the Press Ethics and the Campus Protection Laws, they became the first real test of the political dynamism and flexibility of the new regime.

In the first stage of maneuver, the government was able to obtain agreement with elements of the opposition in the Assembly to pass the Press Ethics bill as part of the agreement to lift martial law.[34] Significantly, it was outside the Assembly that the effective opposition took place. The press banded together and refused to accept the conditions of the bill. The government sought to exert pressure but without success. Once again international pressure came to bear on the Korean government, as suppression of the press aroused criticism from other countries.[35] Meanwhile various political and civic leaders in Korea joined the battle on the side of the press, and the opposition Assembly members, embarrassed by their earlier acquiescence, denounced the bill. The issue threatened to become a cause for major confrontation between the government and a conglomerate of popular opposition. The government decided instead to compromise. Extracting a promise from the press of voluntary self-regulation, the president agreed not to enforce the Press Ethics Law. Shortly thereafter, the government withdrew the Campus Protection bill without pressing for a vote.[36]

The compromise on these two bills was significant and far-reaching.

It did not mean that the press had won complete freedom for itself, for the threat of renewed government pressure was implicit in self-regulation. The press would also find itself subject to less overt but not insignificant pressures from government agencies on a number of occasions thereafter. With respect to the students, the events of the following year were to show that lack of formal controls would not prevent the government from curbing political activity on the campuses. But the compromise was still very important. Had the laws been passed and enforced, the distinction between the Park and Rhee governments would have been greatly narrowed. The possibility of real dialogue between the government and some of the most important voices of popular opinion would have been diminished. And without that dialogue, the later evolvement of genuine consensus behind government policies would probably have been impossible.

The effects of the compromise were not seen in this light immediately, however, for the next year was again one of turbulence and one in which the division between government and campus almost came to the breaking point. If 1964 had been something of a victory for opposition forces, 1965 was a year in which government power was firmly exerted. The issue was again Japan. In the winter of 1964–1965, when the government resumed negotiations with Japan, the general atmosphere of the country was calm.[37] But as a final settlement with Japan began to take shape in the spring, things changed rapidly. The opposition parties united in June for what they described as a "do-or-die" struggle. Student demonstrations began even earlier, in April, and continued off and on throughout the summer. This time, however, the government was better prepared in many ways. Its control of the demonstrations was more effective. Whereas in 1964 thousands of students had reached the central parts of Seoul, they were unable to do so in 1965. The government was forced to close the schools for early vacation, and in August to bring in troops. But formal martial law was not declared, and the security of the government was never really in doubt, as it had been in the previous year.

The government was also more confident in 1965: of the waning of the Japanese issue among the population at large, of its ability to put the settlement through the Assembly, and finally of its ability to control the situation throughout the country afterward. Consequently, it moved against its opponents, particularly on the campuses, in a final calculated show of force that seemed to risk revolt but which actually brought an end to the demonstrations. First, the Japanese settlement was finally pushed through the Assembly by means of a highly questionable parliamentary maneuver. Then in response to continuing student demonstrations, the government ordered the universities, including some private ones, to expel a number of student leaders and professors for being involved in the demonstrations. When some of the universities demurred and demonstrations resumed, it sent troops onto two campuses—an almost unprecedented act—and brought the demonstrations to a close.[38]

There was a generally widespread feeling of relief in the country over the end of the demonstrations. But the government's actions to accomplish this had struck deeply at the integrity of the universities and the basis of constitutional government itself. The feeling on the campuses in 1965 was thus probably more bitter than at any time under the Park regime. There was shock elsewhere as well. Political and press leaders variously labeled the government's actions as unconstitutional, cruel, and undemocratic.[39] The DRP-dominated Assembly unanimously passed a resolution calling upon the government to relax its position on the expelled professors and students. Yet, in this case, the administration stood firm. Over a year later, a similar attempt by the Assembly to win a reprieve for those expelled continued to fall on deaf ears.[40] The administration had taken the position in 1965 that it would not allow student demonstrations to dictate the course of political events, particularly to threaten the government itself. It made clear, furthermore, that on an issue on which the government felt it had a reasonable measure of popular support—as the government felt it had at this time on the Japanese settlement—it would not hesitate to stop forcefully any dangerously large or continuous demonstrations or other threatening acts of opposition outside the normal institutions of government. Thus not only the students and professors, but other citizen groups formed that year to oppose the Japanese settlement, experienced government reprisal through arrest or intimidation.[41]

The events of 1965 thus clarified the nature of the compromise that was to exist between the new government and its opponents over permitted forms of political protest and activity. Fragile as it had been in 1964, the constitution had survived and seemed to have won more real commitment from all sides. As pointed out more fully in Chapter 5, the opposition parties' acceptance of the basic legitimacy of the government, or at least of the system under which it ruled, came only in the aftermath of these events. Only then did their attention turn to the electoral process as the only relevant means of turning the government out of office. For their part, the administration and the Democratic Republican party took several steps after the Japanese settlement was completed to ease the return of opposition members boycotting the Assembly and to restore the normal functioning of that body. The regular institutions of government, generally, survived and in some cases were strengthened. The Assembly, though shaken, was intact. The cabinet was able to remain in office throughout the turmoil of 1965. Moreover, in contrast to the negotiations of 1964, cabinet officials had been in charge of the final and largely open negotiations with Japan.

In its relations with nongovernment institutions, the government's role was further clarified. After 1964 the press continued to operate free from overt controls, though the restrictions emanating from the anti-communist and other security laws, plus a variety of pressures both subtle and otherwise, were sources of constant constraint.[42] There would be, moreover, no more attempts to create vehicles of permanent censure of university activity, despite the actions taken in 1965. For the average citizen, as for the press and universities, one of the greatest problems of political liberty was uncertainty. In 1965, many an individual, deeply concerned over the direction of the government's policy toward Japan, had been genuinely unsure of what degree of opposition would risk reprisal or arrest. In some ways that creates a worse tyranny than well-defined limits.[43] After 1965, however, some of these limits became a little bit clearer and, until the election fever began in late 1966, a little broader as the tension diminished. One could criticize the government on its overall domestic policies and its foreign policies (within the general anticommunist framework of the latter), on the means by which it carried out these policies, and even on the degree of honesty in government if not approaching calumny against the most senior officials. One could not call into question the very legitimacy of the government or seek to turn opposition to policies into a force that threatened the fall of the government itself. To summarize, the government recognized in this period that on the issues on which it was most vulnerable—the preservation of democratic forms of government and the basic integrity of government policies—the potential of not only the politicians, but also of the press and the students was great and that these could not be overcome by force alone.

It should be clear that the events of these years were more significant in the atmosphere they created, particularly in the administration's thinking, than in the development of institutional safeguards for democratic politics. The result in the latter case was, in effect, to return the operation of government to the formal institutions which had been established for that purpose in the new constitution. This was not unpopular in itself. There was much sympathy with the students in 1964, but in 1965 it faded somewhat when the intensity and continuation of demonstrations seemed to threaten more harm than possible good.[44] But the problem with the formal institutions of government was that they were limited by the weak state of the political party apparatus and other elements of the political structure, such as the law and courts, which were all largely subject to executive control. The opposition parties in the Assembly were in even more disarray, after the Japanese settlement, than before. On issues of less than vital concern, that is, on which they could hope to stir mass interest, they were therefore left again to debate hopelessly against an overwhelming government majority, or else to obstruct parliamentary procedure or even to use violence to win compromise.

The power of the government in the Assembly, in the final analysis in the streets, and even in some measure over the press thus made the constitutional system only a framework that kept open the dialogue. The limitations on the dialogue and what it produced were very much at the discretion of the government, and the opportunity to set in motion major new trends in thought in either domestic or international policy rested on government initiative or at least sanction. It was to this situation that much of the uneasiness and mistrust of 1964–1965 was directed. But it was in this area of discretion that the events of these years had their most significant effects.

For the government had already by the end of 1964 begun to give ground, to respect more the demands of public opinion, and to encourage a greater degree of open discussion of major policies and programs. This was evident in the handling of the Japanese issue in 1965, as contrasted to 1964. Diplomatic negotiations were switched to normal and relatively open channels. The government made a virtual campaign of publishing, discussing, and defending before the public the terms of the final agreement. The change in administration thinking, however, went deeper. The preservation of the general framework of constitutional government in this period and the acceptance of a generally free press created basically new political requirements for the regime. If the press could not be completely cowed, and the Assembly, political parties, and universities were all to be permanent parts of the system, the administration would have to build more of a genuine popular consensus in its favor, not only to maintain stability but to face the elections of 1967. This had become evident in the struggles of 1964 and by the time of the compromise with the press at the end of that year. It became even more so after the showdown with the universities in 1965. The government was not as unpopular in 1965 as some of its bitterest critics maintained. But even those who welcomed the restoration of order within the framework of constitutionalism still questioned whether this result and this set of leaders would produce any real change in the generally frustrating history of South Korean political and economic development.

To meet this questioning, and to secure itself in a formally democratic system, the Park administration by the end of 1964 began to focus the nation's attention much more successfully on the economic elements of its program. The administration, for other reasons, had already begun to place more emphasis on the concrete objectives of economic development. But it now began to turn to these as the basis also of a new national consensus and of a genuine measure of popular support for the regime. In the process, with a newly developing mutuality of interest and objectives between the government and people, the whole nature of the interaction between government policy and popular participation, as it had existed from 1963 to 1965, began to change.

4 / Growing Economic Emphasis

In justifying the 1961 military coup before the presidential election of 1963, Park Chung-Hee devoted the better part of his argument to the economic state of the country. To start with, he reiterated a familiar-enough lexicon of criticisms of the Rhee regime: the large amount of foreign aid "frittered away," the overemphasis on consumer goods, the depressing effect of aid-financed agricultural imports on domestic agriculture, the heavy dependence of the budget on aid receipts, the inefficient management of state-run enterprises, and the lack of long-range planning.[1] He identified the military revolution with the frustrated hopes of the April 1960 revolution. He also said that, for the leaders of the military coup, economic resurgence was an integral part of a nationalistic vision of a more independent South Korea to come—more independent of United States aid and control, and, as an economically stronger and independent entity, more able to deal with North Korea.

The issue of economic development had thus grown in importance in Korean politics. In the early years after liberation, the issues of independence, partition, and the Korean War had all engaged public concern much more immediately than had economic development. The basic direction of postwar politics, whether to be dominated by the Right or Left, and indeed, the very fact of access to power had also been more critical issues.[2] Economic development was generally desired but it was considered largely a function of these other problems.

In the late 1950s attitudes began to change. As has been pointed out earlier, the large military buildup and the influx of foreign aid after the Korean War changed the basic character of the economy, creating new sources of wealth, new opportunities, and new problems. At the same time, the growth of urban centers, education, and mass communications contributed to an acute and widespread awareness of these changes. For many critics it was the disparity between large scale, well-publicized aid and low living standards that symbolized much of their frustration over economic conditions in this period. Dissatisfaction with the Rhee regime therefore focused more and more on his seemingly fruitless references to early reunification and his preoccupation with the preservation of his own power, while following policies and practices to the detriment of sound development programs and more honest and productive use of aid funds. These were the major themes of the Democratic party in the 1956 campaign when, though lacking a presidential candidate, the party defeated Rhee's vice-presidential candidate.[3] Nevertheless, as Rhee's Liberal party apparatus became stronger, movements for sounder development policies within the bureaucracy were choked off. Such action only further divided the government from growing popular concern on this issue, a division aggravated by the economic stagnation that began in 1958. By 1960, the list of economic grievances had become part and parcel of the intellectuals' and students' view of the Rhee regime and probably of a wide range of other Koreans as well.

A desire for different and more effective development programs was thus one issue common to all the regimes—Interim, Democratic, Military, and Democratic Republican party—after 1960.[4] Moreover, that there had by then been a genuine revolution in outlook and leadership from Rhee's time is made clear by the fact that, in 1962–1963 even in the face of economic setbacks and political diversions, there was no return by the Military Government to the more protective and politically inhibited approach to economic development of that earlier period. Rhee's approach had not been negative; indeed, he had had some major aspirations for Korean development. But they had been distorted by other objectives, while the technical and professional needs for successful policy performance had been ignored.[5] Thus the Rhee government could counsel its ministries to understate Korean harvests regularly in order to try to maximize the inputs of United States agricultural products under the aid program, obtaining a short-range political advantage at the cost of sound domestic agricultural production.[6] It could persist in maintaining overvalued exchange rates and in generally discouraging exports, again strengthening the case for aid at the cost of economic growth. Finally, the regime as a whole remained resistant to the ideas of those within its ranks who had professional economic expertise, blocking their advance in the bureaucracy and otherwise failing to encourage their work.[7]

Many of these barriers fell in the first few years after 1960. For the new regimes, self-sustained development was a more immediate political objective. Their stronger identification with younger professional people was reflected in changes within the bureaucracy. Furthermore, after 1961, the military leadership had an agressive nationalism and a strong desire for achievement—at times a headlong optimism—that distinguished it from the hesitant and sometimes self-defeating earlier economic approaches. But the most significant *political* development in the economic policy of the Park administration as it developed after 1963, was that economic policy became the central thrust of the regime's entire political effort at home and, to a large extent, abroad. The political role of economic performance developed gradually in a period of considerable turmoil and frequent confrontation between the administration and its critics over other issues. As the government faced press and student opposition from 1963 onward and realized the need to compromise in the use of its power, and also as it began to gain confidence in its ability to achieve a new burst of economic growth in Korea, it began to turn increasingly to economic development as the means by which it could accept, shape, and live within, a civilian and largely democratic political structure. By the end of 1964, this became its fundamental political strategy and the cornerstone of its drive for consensus and, finally, reelection in 1967. Instead of being a piece of a larger nationalistic program of somewhat vague dimensions, as had been the case with the Military Government, concrete economic performance became the touchstone of political performance and national progress.

In retrospect, the growing emphasis on economic development as a source of final legitimization and popular consensus for the new regime seems natural. The growth of economic awareness during the previous decade had made economic performance almost a "must" for any regime that hoped to succeed after 1960. Economic success was important also to most of the nationalist objectives animating the new post-1961 leaders, particularly since they eschewed the more unrealistic hopes for early reunification on which Rhee had relied. But with all this manifestation of awareness and concern, there were also great doubts and serious conflicts in Korea about actually undertaking a long-range development program, which reflected political and psychological attitudes that were part of the heritage of the new as well as of the old leadership. As a result, for three years after the return to civilian rule, really until the latter part of 1966, the full commitment of the Park administration to a vigorous development program, particularly as the core of its political strategy, encountered reservations within the administration and doubts among the population at large.

The reservations and conflicts that have surrounded economic development in Korean thinking help explain not only some of the issues that faced the country in the period under discussion, but also the striking political reaction which after 1965 followed the successful development effort. Self-doubt was at the heart of this ambivalence. It was a self-doubt connected with prospects for South Korea as a separate economic entity and for the future of Korean nationalism in the South. It extended also to uncertainty about the qualities of character and leadership available in Korea for the implementation of a just and effective economic development effort.

The division of Korea had long provided what seemed to many a case against separate development in the South and for emphasis instead on reunification as a prior or at least concurrent objective. North Korea had the better deposits of coal and iron, the only economical and well-developed hydropower sites, and almost all the heavy industry developed during the Japanese colonial period. Complementing these resources, the South had the better agricultural base, the bulk of textile and other consumer industry, and twice the population. The last was seen as a mixed blessing: with virtually no natural power sites and little mineral base for heavy industry, the possibility that the South could, alone, absorb its underemployed and unemployed in industrial development seemed slight. Furthermore, comparisons between economic growth in the North and South in the decade following the Korean War seemed to confirm the disadvantages of a separate development program in the South.[8] Finally, the South's difficulties were compounded by its large military establishment, which was seen as a major obstacle to growth, particularly in the mobilization of domestic resources for investment.

The results of this thinking were largely negative. The stalemate over reunification and the continuing state of hostility between North and South ruled out both a unified development effort and a reduction in military expenses to ease the cost of development in the South. There was also the effect of inefficient and unpromising use of economic resources and aid in the late 1950s. Together these factors contributed to a general sense of despair and pessimism about the prospects for economic growth in the South, even among advocates of improved policies and practices. Such an attitude was, for example, reflected in much of the academic writing on economic matters, both in the late 1950s and beyond. Even as late as 1965, when exports, agriculture, and overall GNP were showing considerable progress, a Korean professor, not atypically, saw the period of the First Five-Year Development Plan as having produced the following main results: (1) inflation worsened, (2) "medium and small industries were ruined," (3) "the privation in farm economy went from bad to worse," (4) income distribution widened, (5) unemployment increased, and, (6) as the only positive point, there was significant inducement of foreign capital. The author then recommended that, to avoid such problems in the future, the goals of the Second Five-Year Plan being formulated be restricted and the development pace "slowed down."[9]

Furthermore, even if separate development were possible for the South, to embark upon a long-range program for this purpose encountered nationalist objections. It seemed to be a tacit, or even open, acceptance of permanent division between North and South and an abandonment of any real unification policy. Moreover, some felt development would make reunification more difficult because the economic structures of North and South would become less complementary. Korean sensitivity on this point was great enough to affect Korea's investment decisions, as well as the aims of the American aid program.[10] There was also another question that troubled nationalist Koreans when they thought of development. Separate development of the South seemed to demand great, and perhaps nearly permanent, dependence on either the United States or Japan. If the former was resented, the latter was feared. The seriousness of this issue became evident in the struggle over the Japanese settlement, which some Koreans saw as a struggle over national identity: Was South Korea to sacrifice its independence to Japan, and its hopes for reunification with the North, for the benefits of economic gain?[11]

The pessimism and skepticism about economic development reflected more, however, than these issues, which seemed rather to have intensified and magnified more fundamental doubts about Korea and Koreans. Among all classes in Korea there was an inclination to identify factionalism, selfishness, and other shortcomings in the Korean character and sometimes to feel that they were major obstacles to economic or political progress.[12] Doubts also showed in the skepticism expressed at the early signs of economic upswing from 1963 to 1965, and particularly, in the questioning—not altogether unjustified in terms of past practices—of the honesty of the government's data showing that such improvement was real.[13] Such doubts were also quite sharply reflected in the character of some of the opposition to the Japanese settlement, namely, in the suggestion that the leaders of Korean government and business could not be trusted not to "sell out" to the Japanese. This seemed in its intensity to extend beyond overt accusations about the incumbent government and business leaders to an indictment of the Korean national character as a whole. As one editorial plaintively remarked, "We are not yet ready to receive Japan, politically, economically, culturally."[14]

These feelings, especially among the intellectual articulators of political thought, were undoubtedly magnified by the problems of social change and adjustment created by economic modernization. Since, traditionally, businessmen did not occupy a respected place in Korean society, their rise during the 1950s created a resentment and suspicion that were compounded by the existing level of corruption. The suspect nature of business relationships with government was, moreover, accepted by the businessmen themselves, as they dealt largely covertly in defense of their interests and privileges, thus often reconfirming the prejudice. Attitudes toward businessmen were changing, as one oft-cited survey of college women in Korea seemed to highlight.[15] But strong indignation registered in late 1964 at suspected favoritism in the distribution of bank loans appeared to reflect more than a righteous anger over corruption—it seemed to harbor a distrust of large business and banking circles in general.[16] The problem of social adjustment was further aggravated by the rise of the military after 1961. Military leadership in development efforts and the benefits it would receive from successful development made acceptance of the changes after 1961 all the harder for older political elite groups and for the intellectual community. It was a bitter pill to swallow, even for objectives they all outwardly supported.

Doubts about the Korean character and about South Korean prospects, plus fear of neighboring powers (Japan on the one side and North Korea and China on the other), contributed to one final element in the conflict toward economic development: the attitude toward the United States. The demand for a more independent, self-sustaining economy in Korea carried with it a demand for changes in the relationship with the United States. This included not only changes in the use of American aid to support more investment, especially in heavy industry, but a reversal of what appeared to be a deepening dependence on the United States. Yet at the same time the level of such aid had become a touchstone of the strength of American commitment to Korea, a measure of the arms and political support that South Korea could expect from the United States.

There were, of course, other measures of this commitment—the level and type of military assistance, the continued assignment of United States troops to Korea, the exact wording of United States defense commitments—all equally sensitive. But economic aid formed an important part of this complex. Politicians in the 1950s and early 1960s had prided themselves on the level of aid they could obtain from the United States. Students who questioned American officials forcefully on the "colonial-type" effects of aid questioned them equally so on any rumors or plans to reduce that aid. Newspapers speculated anxiously each year on the levels of aid for the coming year.[17] And when the United States supported the early conclusion of a settlement between Korea and Japan, opponents immediately suspected that the United States was trying to shift to Japan the burden of its Korean aid, and beginning an even more general unburdening of United States responsibilities in Asia, to the detriment of Korean security.[18] Thus, while nationalist fervor and the very definition of economic independence demanded a reduction of dependence on United States aid, confrontation with that reality immediately raised doubts and questions, at least as to how far and how fast Korea should allow itself to be moved in that direction.

All these doubts and conflicts were thus part of a tradition that had grown side by side with the new awareness of economic issues and the impatience with the older manner of dealing with them that emerged so clearly by 1960. The persistence of this uncertainty and conflict, even among the leaders and direct heirs of the April 1960 revolution, was one of the reasons the military coup leaders of 1961 gave for taking over and seeking to direct, with authoritarian firmness, the objectives of the earlier revolution. But even the post-1961 military leadership was not free of them.

The leaders of the 1961 coup had viewed economics largely as a poorly directed part of the national structure which could, as much else in Korean life, be set quickly and dramatically on the right path. Moreover, economics was seen as one means of several toward the end of an overall political-economic entity sketched vaguely in terms of "purer politics," greater national independence and vigor, and improved international stature. The economic policies of the Military Government reflected these attitudes. They were often bold and designed to produce sweeping results. Some of the longer-term trends set in motion—in trade, industrial incentives, foreign capital inducement, and agricultural extension and distribution services—were of great significance. But, during military rule, the measures did not succeed in producing all the economic and political results desired by the new leaders. As a result, despite the importance at first laid upon economic problems by the Military Government, the overall economic decline that had begun in 1958, on the whole continued through 1962, aggravated by both political instability and some of the economic measures taken by the new leaders.[19]

These early setbacks dissipated much of the military leaders' earlier confidence and diminished the importance accorded by at least some of them to economic development in relation to other, political, objectives of the regime. Some of the junta leaders, for example, came to feel that economic development was less an immediate key to power in the approaching transition to civilian government than were political organization and political funds. Several major and economically damaging financial scandals that broke into the open in 1962 were believed to have been engineered by these elements through the CIA and connected with the funding of the then incipient Democratic Republican party.[20] Even after Park's victory in 1963, elements within both the executive and the DRP's Assembly membership continued to feel that, while development should be pursued, it was not a necessary vehicle for consensus and political stability. These, it was felt, could be obtained by centralized party organization, limitations on freedom of speech and press, and strong military backing to the government's programs. As pointed out in Chapter 2, this point of view still had its representatives in the executive structure after 1963.

Finally, strong resistance developed within the new Park administration, as it had in its predecessors, to some of the specific consequences of an economic development program, especially where they encroached upon traditional means of support. The Ministry of National Defense was, for example, strongly opposed to acquiescence in the decline of American grant aid because the proceeds of that aid had long supported the bulk of the Korean defense budget. Others in the government and outside were equally concerned about the domestic tax burden for defense that would result. The Ministry of Foreign Affairs and some of the other ministries were still inclined, much as in the Rhee period, to look upon further concessions of such American aid as political assets and measures of diplomatic success. A long internal debate on these issues preceded President Park's visit to the United States in May 1965, where new agreements on aid were to be announced in advance of the settlement with Japan.[21] They continued under active debate until well into 1966, when the Second Five-Year Plan was issued.

The movement under the Park administration toward a political strategy emphasizing economic performance, that is, one in which internal political strategy and foreign policy would be shaped and redefined almost entirely around the economic emphasis of the administration, was thus not entirely natural or altogether inevitable. It developed gradually, beginning with the president's commitment, and later, that of his cabinet members, to a more professional and executive-controlled management of economic affairs. It grew during the interaction between the confrontations over political liberties and dissent raised by the Japanese issue, on the one hand, and the momentum of economic achievements that was becoming apparent, on the other.

GROWTH OF ECONOMIC EMPHASIS

The specific economic policies and programs that led to the economic upsurge after 1962 are described in detail in Chapter 8. At this point it is only relevant to sketch the growth of political commitment to these policies and their political ramifications. The difficulties of the 1962–1963 period, as described in Chapter 2, caused Park Chung-Hee to turn more to professional civilian experts in the cabinet and the bureaucracy for the management of economic affairs. With the departure of some of the more revolutionary elements of the Military Government into the organization of the DRP in early 1963, there was also greater opportunity to reassess some of the earlier economic approaches that had followed the coup. One of the first steps agreed upon by the cabinet in 1963, therefore, was a stabilization program involving reductions of budget and credit outlays, which forced a general cutback in the Military Government's earlier economic goals. The targets of the First Five-Year Plan, issued with such fanfare and hope by the Military Government in 1962, were thus officially lowered in 1963.[22] The new emphasis on stabilization, plus the onset of a food crisis, also led to a rapprochement with the United States in connection with the formulation of economic policy, signaled by the reestablishment, for the first time since 1961, of a Joint United States-Korean Economic Cooperation Committee.[23] These two changes laid the basis for better economic management and planning in the years to come, including better coordination of United States aid resources for development.

In 1964 the government proceeded to make more fundamental changes. Economic and fiscal policies came under the very firm direction of the deputy prime minister, concurrently chairman of the Economic Planning Board (EPB) in May 1964 cabinet, Chang Key-young. The EPB had both budget and planning functions, as well as responsibilities for foreign aid; under Chang it used these in concert to become the central directing point and clearing house for all economic policy. Under Chang also, the stabilization program, which had been developed primarily as an anti-inflation device, began to broaden out to cover interrelating monetary and fiscal measures, institutional changes, and policy emphases that were needed not only to make stabilization efforts more effective, but also to support a more aggressive growth policy. Chang's assertiveness, ability, and self-confidence won the support of the president if not the love of the DRP leaders in the Assembly, nor that of other cabinet ministers. As pointed out later, Chang was in succeeding years to become a focal point of political debate over economic policy.

The organization and coordination of economic programs under one cabinet minister enjoying strong presidential support in itself represented an important institutional change. It made possible better and more concentrated analyses of economic problems and furnished a central point for introducing economic changes. There were other important achievements in 1964 as well. In May 1964, as one of its final acts, the first cabinet under the new civilian government had put through a 90 percent devaluation and established a unitary exchange rate. In the coming months, the administration succeeded in controlling inflation which had, despite the earlier stabilization program, continued into the spring of 1964. A bumper crop in the fall, though caused as much by good weather as by good programming in agriculture, raised confidence generally and offset the memory of the 1963 food crisis. There was still uncertainty in this period, however. For example, while carrying out the devaluation, the government throughout 1964 delayed allowing the exchange rate to float freely, a step the government had indicated it would take at the time of devaluation as part of a larger program to free the trade sector generally of controls. Critics had maintained that a floating rate would mean a steady and continuing devaluation. The government was as yet not confident enough in its stabilization, export, and other economic policies to risk their being right.

However, by the end of 1964, confidence was building up in several areas. Exports had more than doubled between 1961 and 1963 and they rose another 50 percent in 1964; government emphasis on exports began to play a dominant role in economic, including investment, policy. Expectations—and targets—in this area began to rise. In the field of stabilization, not only had the inflation been brought under control but the government found itself able to ward off the pressures of special interest groups particularly sensitive to that program: farmers who had had to accept higher fertilizer prices occasioned by devaluation without relief through budget subsidy, and businessmen both large and small who, by year's end, found the credit squeeze occasioned by monetary controls increasingly uncomfortable. Contrary to dire predictions, with the bumper crop of that year, farmers went on, at the end of 1964, to buy fertilizer in greater amounts than before. The stabilization measures, however, did have a very restrictive effect on the growth of industrial and other non-agricultural output in 1964, even if the rumors of widespread business failures proved exaggerated.[24] The boost in agricultural output, nevertheless, plus the rise in exports of manufactured goods contributed to evidence of a substantial recovery from the recession of 1958–1962. The Gross National Product rose 9.1 percent in 1963, the highest annual rise since the Korean War, and 8.3 percent in 1964. Furthermore, in a resumption of financial diplomacy outside the United States, President Park paid a state visit to the Federal Republic of Germany in the closing months of 1964, receiving a warm welcome and paving the way for new German capital assistance that would make Germany the second, later the third, largest aid and capital donor to Korea (after the United States and Japan).[25]

Thus, by the end of 1964, the government in many ways—in organization, politics, and economics—felt itself in a better position to press ahead with an aggressive and comprehensive development effort. At the same time, as described in the last chapter, the government had come to accept a compromise in its efforts to control the press and universities, as well as limitations on its ability generally to use military power and political pressure to achieve consensus. The economic recovery of 1963–1964 therefore encouraged the government to shift its political strategy to an emphasis on economic achievement. President Park had designated 1964 as the "Great Year of Reform." However, politically it was not a happy year, what with student demonstrations, the rupture of negotiations with Japan, the declaration of martial law, and the near disintegration of the constitutional system. In his New Year's message of 1965, the president set a new tone that was to be a consistent theme of future years. He declared 1965 the "Year of Work" and made clear the administration's three major targets: production, export, and construction.[26] It was almost entirely an economic emphasis.

The seriousness of this emphasis was registered in the scope of economic programs undertaken during the new year. The work on the Second Five-Year Plan began to acquire degrees of priority, technical competence, and broad participation that would enable it when completed to surpass all previous Korean planning efforts in both professional soundness and popular acceptance.[27] Concurrent with the emphasis on better planning came several major policy decisions. In the spring, the government went ahead with the floating exchange rate system. It also began a liberalization of import restrictions. Both steps were fundamental. Economically, they signified confidence in the country's ability to maintain the export momentum, to absorb and afford the imports required for export and domestic production as the market demanded, and to control tendencies toward inflation through improved management of the stabilization program. Politically, they signaled the government's willingness to provide incentives and opportunities for the private sector as a whole and to dismantle the complex set of controls and licensing system that had played such an important part in the corruption of government and business under the Rhee regime.

The freeing of the trade sector was closely followed by another major reform of both economic and political significance. In September, the government put through an interest rate reform that revitalized the banking sector through the attraction of private savings. From a political point of view, the interest rate reform had two notable effects. It brought the public into the development process in dramatic fashion. The flow of private savings into the banks, which more than tripled in the first year of the reform, indicated the degree to which Korean citizens were ready to respond to economic incentives, in this case, the opportunity to earn high but safe rates of interest in the commercial banks instead of accepting the risks of the informal or "curb" market, to which most small savers had in the past turned. Second, by enlarging the bank's loan resources, the government took a step toward eliminating one major cause of favoritism and corruption in bank lending. Formerly, the banks had had to lend their limited resources at rates fixed by the government well below the market rates. As a result, not only was the competition for bank loans great, but borrowers could relend the money at great profits. These conditions, like those under a closely controlled import licensing system, invited corruption and had led to the concentration of bank loans in the hands of large, politically influential companies. With the reform, the resources were enlarged, the disparity between official and market rates greatly reduced, and the controls on bank lending relaxed. Not surprisingly, big businessmen had opposed and small businessmen had favored the interest rate reform.[28]

The export emphasis, which grew in importance in this period, also had political and psychological repercussions. South Korea's export performance, long dormant, was a symbol of its capacity or lack of capacity for economic independence. Along with its international character, it was also one set of statistics that could not readily be faked. It thus became not only a measure of growth but a means of overcoming doubt and cynicism. The administration did not hesitate to make exporting into a national campaign, almost a patriotic duty. Export producers were given priority in investment decisions, credit allocations, and other benefits. Each province set its own export target. And each year the administration's year-end targets became an object of watchful waiting and, when made, the subject of widespread public discussion.

During 1965 there was another important political-economic milestone that captured public attention. In May, President Park visited Washington and obtained a multi-year commitment of $150 million in loans. In the same visit, it was mutually agreed that there would be no change in the United States policy of steadily reducing levels of grant aid for general commodities, which in the past had formed the main portion of United States aid. This agreement marked a turning point, for it gained, from Korea, adherence to what had for some years been the trend of American aid policy and, from the United States, a formal recognition of recent Korean development efforts. The worldwide United States aid program had begun shifting its emphasis after 1961 from grants to loans, with the latter aimed more at longer range development plans and projects. Korea had only slowly come under this umbrella: The level of grant aid to Korea had been declining since 1957 with the intention on the American side of "pressuring" the Korean government into greater self-sufficiency and better long-term planning. But the level of economic planning and administration in Korea had not reached the point at which it could get very much United States loan support. Only 5 percent of United States aid receipts from 1961–1964 had been in the form of capital project loans. The American loan commitment of 1965 thus marked a recognition by the United States of the successful economic momentum created in Korea since 1962, and Korea's place in the "development" category of countries. Within Korea, in the context of the long political and emotional debate over past use of aid for "consumer" rather than "capital" goods, and of the uneasiness over recent reductions in grant aid, the loan commitment had a positive psychological effect. It eased concern over the continuation of United States support and encouraged the Koreans to believe in their own development potential.

In style, the government's economic efforts throughout 1965 were a combination of "push and pull," of coercion and incentives. Key export industries were given targets to fulfill and put under considerable political pressure to turn their production and sales efforts to foreign markets. Compulsory savings programs were initiated for civil servants. To obtain a passport one had to show a new deposit of 10,000 *won* ($37) in a commercial savings account. On the other side, credit incentives, import privileges, and tax benefits served as important inducements to voluntary production for export. High interest rates soon proved effective in drawing private savings into banks without much further pressure. As a result, the extent and intensity of direct government controls lessened gradually, while more weight was given to incentives.

The process of decontrol was slower in the rural areas, where the government in this period relied much more heavily on a centrally directed, highly bureaucratized approach to achieving major developments in agriculture.[29] Two elements of the administration's rural program, however, undoubtedly had immediately positive political effect. One of the rural priorities given added weight in 1965 was land development, which aimed at adding 15 percent more agricultural land to Korea by the reclamation of hillsides and tideland areas and by making irrigation and other improvements on existing farmlands. This was a labor-intensive program. Supported by over 100,000 metric tons of United States agricultural products per year in a food-for-work program, it employed hundreds of thousands of rural workers. Also, the newly developed public land was divided up and made available to the people who had developed it or to others whose holdings were below one *chongbo*.[30] A second, well-received development was the over sixfold increase in the number of agricultural extension workers between 1961 and 1967, which resulted in lowering the number of farms served per worker from 1,365 to 375. These extension workers had little coercive authority but were well trained and well liked. They soon became one of the more popular elements of government representation in the rural areas.[31]

Summarizing, increased attention to economic development after 1962 had led to government pressures, internal reforms, and other steps that were not only of economic importance, but also of considerable political significance, particularly in widening the level of participation in development and in removing some of the traditional forms of corruption that had been among the most visible "political" obstacles to Korean development. They demonstrated, too, that the new administration had a serious commitment to economic development and, even more, that it was capable of engineering policies and programs for this end far more effectively than the Military Government or other earlier regimes. All these steps were gradual in their political effect, however. In 1965 the administration was still operating largely from a position of exceptional parliamentary and military strength, with the goal of widespread popular support still elusive. This situation was dictated largely by the continuing dispute over Japan. The strife that once again erupted over this issue in 1965 clouded over, though not entirely, as the government's success in that endeavor showed, much of the political change being generated by economic progress.

The government's political-economic strategy was thus fairly clearly developed by 1965. But its concept of timing and of detailed execution of the transition from force to consensus was less sharply delineated. Its hope for popular political support increased with the success in economic development, encouraged further by the political and psychological side effects of the particular economic policies chosen. But until that popular support came, the government was prepared to use its political advantage and, where necessary, its military backing, to maintain the basic direction of its policies in the face of opposition. Even its policies were largely geared to their economic effect, first, and their popular political effect, second. For example, in the liberalization of trade and the change of interest rates, the administration was clearly motivated more by their economic rationale and their contribution to economic objectives than by any effect they might have on the "democratization" of the development process. Yet the government, beleaguered by political storms in this period, was quick to recognize and seize upon the political opportunities that did develop from economic reform: in pushing economic development to the forefront of national priorities in both 1965 and 1966, in pointing to the tasks of development as justification for strong measures to quell demonstrations and political strife, and in publicity campaigns— including banners, speeches, increasingly open discussions of economic issues being considered by the government, and so forth—which appealed to both patriotism and private gain in supporting the government's development efforts.[32] These efforts were to bear remarkable political fruit in 1966 and 1967.

POLITICAL POWER AND POLITICAL COMMITMENT

In terms of economic policy and development, the period from 1963 to 1965 was thus one of growing confidence, innovation, reform, and success. But it was at the same time a stormy period. The reform and redirection of economic policy were carried out amidst strife and opposition, over the often loud cries of special interest groups, and in the face of continuing and widespread pessimism and mistrust. Almost every major economic reform of this period encountered doubt and skepticism at the outset.[33] The ability of the government to pursue its economic policies with such success, and of the country to make the transition in economic outlook and performance that it did by 1966, point therefore to the importance at that stage of Korea's development of the government's political-military strength, on the one hand, and its particular convictions, on the other.

In regard to the former, there is no doubt that the administration had a certain indisputable strength against its opponents and critics. It had the votes in the Assembly to push through every major bill and to vote down every contrary motion. It had the backing of the military, which enabled it to take on the most controversial of issues, that is, the Japanese settlement, knowing that if the constitutional system of control broke down, the administration had the force of martial law to replace it. And finally, it had a unity of organization and relative unity of purpose that the opposition lacked. All of these contributed not only to the administration's power, but to its will and confidence.

On the other hand, this degree of power could have been the death knell for political democratization. But in the use of power, the administration was fortunately guided by certain convictions that enabled and encouraged it to move in more constructive directions. As pointed out in Chapter 2, the Park administration was a product of the revolutionary period of 1960–1961, and reflected its desire for change and national economic development. With origins in the military, moreover, the administration was socially and politically removed from the traditional elite groups that had previously ruled the country, some elements of which were indeed now actively opposed to it. As a result, it operated with different priorities than had the Rhee regime, and felt greater freedom and incentive to break down older governmental patterns. This shift was evident in the economic policies that were pursued after 1963. The restrictive system of import quotas and the manipulation and control of scarce banking resources had together formed the backbone of a mutually corrupting and mutually profiting system of cooperation between a limited number of businessmen and government officials under the Liberal party regime.[34] In the reforms of 1964 and 1965, both of these systems collapsed, to the vain cries and behind-the-scenes maneuvering of those who had long lived by them. It was not the end of cor-

ruption, not even the end for most of the biggest business interests of
the previous era. But it was an end to that system of corruption to which
the Park administration had not been a party and which it found economically debilitating. Other forms of corruption, some of quite major
proportion, grew quickly enough in its place.[35] But they at least fitted
into a different set of priorities over the next few years in which, in
contrast to the Rhee regime, the independent economic growth of Korea
was rated as a major objective to which older forms of corruption, as
well as many previously favored interests, were sacrificed. The growth
in turn provided a basis for a political accommodation between the new
government and the populace, and a growing consensus in favor of the
government's overall program and priorities.

By its makeup the new administration was also inclined toward some
restraint in the use of the power at its disposal. That restraint was not
always exercised. But there were many members of the new government—in the cabinet, the presidential secretariat and in DRP ranks in
the Assembly—who had come to power in the post-1963 civilian government and who had a stake in preventing a return to narrower military-
dominated rule. Also, among those in the cabinet and bureaucracy who
were concerned with concrete program objectives, there was a growing
desire to find a compromise settlement on the political issues that seemed
to be threatening both stability and economic progress, and to "get on"
with the tasks at hand. There was finally the pressure on the government
of such articulate groups as the students and press.

The rapprochement with the United States was also very influential
in this regard. For the Park government, the close relationship that
developed with the United States after 1963 became an integral part of
its overall political-economic strategy. The United States was not only a
source of considerable technical and capital help, but of political encouragement and assistance in such difficult areas as the settlement with
Japan. For its part, the United States saw in the development of a
reasonably moderate, stable, civilian form of government that could
produce economic results, an answer to many of its political and ideological objectives in Korea, which had been so confused and complicated
by the aftermath of events since 1960. A growing mutuality of interests
between the two governments therefore became apparent after 1963, as
well as an interest in reconciling their political and economic views. This
undoubtedly helped both economic development and political democracy
in Korea. United States representatives could not dictate Korean moves
in these areas, but they could and did encourage and support members of

the government who were inclined in this direction, counseled the wisdom of restraint and judiciousness in the use of power for their own sake—furthermore pointing out the international repercussions for Korea's image if this were not done—and increasingly shaped the aid program to give maximum support to the development emphasis. Much of the above was achieved through informal contacts on a wide range of issues. Some was done by more specific and open means; one example was the clear statement of United States sympathy with the press during the dispute of 1964.[36] The aid agreements of May 1965 were another.

Of particular importance, finally, was the personal conviction of President Park. It is clear from his actions, his speeches, and his decisions that he was interested in building up Korean strength and national confidence and was not, especially in these first years, overly concerned with personal glorification. He shared with Rhee a strong sense of nationalism. But, unlike Rhee, he became convinced that the future of Korean nationalism in South Korea lay primarily in building up the independent economic strength of the South and in greater political stability.[37] To these ends, he was not reluctant to use the power at his disposal. But the ends did not get lost in the means. The strength of his convictions was crucial, for on numerous occasions the president personally made the decision on critical economic issues which determined the margin of priority given to economic development over other political objectives. In so doing, he sometimes went against not only established favored interests but elements of his own supporters. One example was in agricultural policy. At a critical point in 1964, the president, despite heavy political pressure, refused to weaken the effect of devaluation by continuing indefinitely the subsidies on fertilizer. In this decision, and in the general movement of the administration toward more emphasis on new land development, technological improvements, and greater market efficiency—as substitutes for the more traditional agricultural subsidies and the Military Government's liberal credit policies in the rural areas—the president exposed the administration to charges of having betrayed one of its 1963 election slogans, "Agriculture First." These policies and the heavy growth of industry would indeed cost the administration some of its original rural support in the next elections.[38]

On the other hand, the president was equally, if not more, prepared to risk the opprobrium of urban-centered opposition, for example, in his policy toward Japan, the pressure of big business against the interest rate reform, and the dissension that some of the administration's economic policies created within the Democratic Republican party. On this last point, the president frequently faced serious party challenges to the basic organization and direction of the economic program, centered usually on the controversial cabinet member in charge of economic planning and programming, Chang Key-young. Yet the president twice intervened personally, in 1965 and 1966, to choke off an attempt from within the DRP to obtain a vote of nonconfidence in Chang.[39] This was not an issue of virtue versus vice, for these could be distributed on both sides of the struggle for economic power. But the president was prepared to defend the highly centralized and aggressive direction of economic policy that had since 1964 developed under Chang and to keep that power in the hands of those primarily loyal to himself and his policies, rather than to the more diverse interests of the party. Similarly, the president was determined to maintain the cabinet largely intact as a whole against repeated appeals from the DRP for a major shake-up—in 1965 after the Japanese settlement, again in early 1966 after the DRP convention.[40] In addition to wanting to maintain his control over the cabinet, President Park seemed particularly guided by advice that the rapid turnover of cabinet ministers, common in earlier regimes, was largely incompatible with any sustained attack on the country's economic ills.

For the economic development of the country, and perhaps for its political development as well, this combination of concentrated power and constructively oriented political conviction seems in retrospect to have been necessary to achieve so much redirection of economic policy and programs in so short a period of time. The various steps to spur economic growth in 1964 and 1965 were taken against a drumfire of criticism, some of it from political opponents who, still refusing to recognize the legitimacy of the regime, were primarily trying to bring it down, and amidst the turmoil of the struggle over relations with Japan. Under other circumstances of power and leadership, therefore, their achievement might at best have been stretched out over many more years. In the light of the deep-seated pessimism of many Koreans about their economic future, it is questionable whether such gradual changes could have had the same dramatic political effects that the accelerated and concentrated economic emphasis of this period would produce in 1966 and 1967. In referring to the earlier attempt at economic reform made by the ill-fated Chang Myon government of 1960–1961, Henderson's comment seems pertinent: "Pushed slowly through cantankerous debate or heated charges in the Assembly's two houses, these reforms somehow failed to impart publicly the same confidence which the swift acts of a determined executive might have conveyed."[41]

The change in emphasis in the period from 1963 to 1966 thus represented something much more fundamental than an economic development program or even an astute political strategy using economic development. It represented a concrete step toward a radical change in Korean outlook and actions: a step away from an unhappy dependence on the United States and a generally pessimistic attitude regarding a South Korean state, and a step toward an aggressive policy of economic growth, more international diplomacy, and clear expressions of national self-confidence. Some of the positive aspects of this movement were becoming apparent by 1965. But all the forms of resistance to this movement—political, psychological, and emotional—were still active. They became fused with other more immediate frustrations in the last act of the complex and long fight over relations with Japan.

5 / The Climax of Dissent: The Japanese Settlement

As is evident from the previous discussion, the negotiations with Japan ran like a thread through all political and economic events from 1961 to 1965. This was so because, caught up in the dispute over the restoration of Korean relations with Japan, were nearly all the political, social, psychological, and economic issues raised in Korea's transition from a traditional society to a modernized state. The Japanese issue not only touched on these issues directly, it served as a vehicle for bringing them to an emotional climax of tremendous intensity.

The issue of Japanese relations was fraught with emotional problems and technical complexities. Japan had for centuries been one of Korea's most dreaded foes: Korea's national hero, Admiral Yi Sun Shin, is celebrated for his remarkable defeat of the Japanese navy in the sixteenth century. But the primary determinant of contemporary relations was Japan's annexation of Korea in 1910, followed by 35 years of colonial rule. In the beginning, Japanese rule was harsh, reflecting manifestation of the growing militaristic element of Japanese politics at the time. The nationalist Korean uprising of 1919, followed by criticism of Tokyo's colonial policy from within Japan itself, led to some moderation. Modern Korean newspapers date from this later period; some degree of Korean cultural freedom was also allowed. However, in the 1930s, and increasingly as World War II intensified, the colonial policy again became both harsh and degrading. The Korean language was outlawed in the schools, emperor worship became mandatory, and a deliberate policy of "Japanizing" Korea—though hardly on terms of equality—was enforced. Koreans were drafted to fight in the Japanese armies in Manchuria and elsewhere, and to work in war industries. The production of rice and other goods was increasingly diverted to the war effort. The privations and cultural indignities of this last period added a final bitterness to that which had been generated by continuous discrimination in opportunity, education and wealth, and by military and police brutality.[1]

Anti-Japanese feelings were deliberately sustained after liberation by Syngman Rhee. This practice did not involve prosecution of Korean "collaborators" in the bureaucracy or police, which was a source of conflict between Rhee and some of his opponents.[2] It did, however, involve a continuing anti-Japanese national sentiment, fostered through textbooks, constant reminders of Japanese colonial rule in speeches and declarations, and in extraordinary demands upon Japan as the price for restoring normal diplomatic relations.[3] Bitterness against Japan was further generated by the Korean War: Many Koreans believed that Japan had profited greatly from the conflict economically, to such a point that it was the key to Japan's postwar recovery, but without contributing any direct support, or sacrifice, to the fighting.[4] Consequently, throughout Syngman Rhee's presidency, although trade was reestablished, there was very little diplomatic contact. Intermittent attempts at restoring full diplomatic relations were made but without great enthusiasm on either side; they were pursued largely at the insistence of the United States, with the first talks being held under the auspices of the Supreme Command for Allied Powers in 1951, before the end of Allied occupation of Japan. Over the next eight years, talks were held off and on, but were broken off for various issues or insults.[5] The Chang Myon government resumed the talks on a somewhat more promising note in 1960, but they were cut short by the coup.

During this time the issues between the two countries grew terribly complex.[6] They fell into four major categories. The first was "basic relations," which included the very sensitive matter of South Korea's desire for Japanese recognition of the Republic of Korea as the only legitimate and sovereign government of all Korea, to the exclusion of the North Korean government.[7] It also included the disposition of previous treaties between the countries. The Koreans demanded a repudiation by Japan of its colonial rule, either by formal apology or through abrogation of the Annexation Treaty of 1910 at its origins. Though expressing regret over the "unfortunate period" in Korean-Japanese relations, the Japanese shied away from a formal apology and preferred to have the treaties abrogated on the basis of Korean independence in 1948.[8]

The second category was that of property claims. This included indemnification of Korea, both for direct losses of property taken by the

Japanese and for indirect losses to the country incurred by colonial rule. This was somewhat the equivalent of reparations agreements between Japan and other Asian countries after World War II.[9] After 1961, basic agreement actually turned out to be possible most quickly in this area, though it was no less controversial within Korea for that. In fact the very speed invited suspicion of "secret deals" and treason, by the government's opponents.[10]

The third category was fisheries. Probably no more complicated problem existed between the two countries. In 1952, President Rhee had proclaimed a zone from 18 to 60 miles wide around Korea, for exclusive fishing and defense rights—known as the "Rhee Line" until 1960, and the "Peace Line" thereafter. The line was maintained in light of the great superiority of Japanese fishing equipment and in the hope of defending the rich fishing resources near Korea for Korean exploitation. Aside from questions of international law, the problem with the Peace Line was that it could not be defended. It thus became a sore point of national pride: a defense line of Korea's "basic rights and livelihood" on the one hand, but, in the face of flagrant violation by Japanese fishermen who neither recognized it nor worried very much about Korean reprisal, a source of anger and humiliation on the other. Very difficult technicalities were also involved in the fisheries question, such as determining the rights of Korean fishermen in the areas between the mainland and the Korean island of Cheju, over 100 miles off the southern Korean coast; equipment and tonnage limitations in jointly fished zones; and patrolling arrangements. But they all boiled down to the problem of preserving meaningful opportunities for Korea's crowded, low-income fishing population, and for Korea's access to the rich resources off its coast for its own development, in the face of Japanese technical superiority, the laws of the sea, and the practical problems of policing so large an area.

The fourth category concerned the legal status of Koreans resident in Japan. Totaling over a half million, these residents did not enjoy full rights of citizenship in Japan, although many had lived in Japan for generations. They were victims as well of discrimination in education, employment, and wealth. The objective of the Korean government was to win for them full rights of citizenship and to facilitate business and other transactions between them and Korea. The issue was complicated by the fact that the Korean residents in Japan were split between those loyal to the North and those loyal to the South. There was also the agreement Japan had in 1959 allowed to be arranged through the Red Cross, for voluntary repatriation of Koreans to North Korea, to which

South Korea strongly objected. On the other side, there was considerable resistance in Japan to giving full and equal citizenship rights to the Korean minority and also some hesitation about allowing Koreans full freedom to transfer their personal assets from Japan to Korea.

Each of these categories of issues was capable of arousing emotion in Korea. When, in April 1965, the Park government reached final agreement with Japan on a treaty covering all these points, nearly every aspect of the settlement came under attack. Most at issue was the abandonment of the Peace Line in return for a 12-mile limit on exclusive fishing rights, and jointly agreed limitations on the size of catch and the nature of equipment in the areas beyond. Also sharply criticized, however, was the "basic relations" treaty, which recognized the Republic of Korea as "the only lawful government in Korea" but did not mention the extent of its territorial jurisdiction. The property claims settlement, amounting to $300 million in grants, $200 million in loans, and $300 million in commercial credits, followed closely the understanding reached in earlier talks between Kim Chong-pil and the Japanese during the period of the Military Government. For that reason it was open to suspicion, as well as feared for the entrée it gave to Japanese economic interests. Other aspects of the agreement were similarly criticized as representing one-sided concessions.[11]

But the issues between Japan and Korea were not really at the heart of the confrontation between the government and its critics. In all the unrest during 1964 and 1965 surrounding the treaty, there was not one significant demonstration against Japan, per se, or against Japanese in Korea. What was really at issue was what the Japanese settlement had come to symbolize to both sides in the dispute within Korea itself. By the end of the first major confrontation on the settlement in 1964, the issue had acquired the significance of something fundamental and momentous. In its denouement, a year later, a decision was taken affecting the whole future direction of Korean society.

THE STAKE OF THE GOVERNMENT

For the Military Government, and later for President Park's administration, the Japanese settlement began as a kind of unfinished business left behind by the traditional elite, which stood as one of several obstacles from the past to Korea's modernization. For the new leaders, the settlement also had special significance as it promised major new economic resources that could help broaden Korean economic, as well as international, relations. Consequently, after the coup, the Military Government had moved relatively quickly to resume talks with Japan. Kim Chong-pil, director of the Central Intelligence Agency and one of the key figures in the Military Government, met with Japanese Foreign Minister Ohira in the fall of 1962 and reached basic agreement on the sums for the property-claims settlement. After the formation of the civilian government under President Park, steps were taken to resolve the other issues. The respective ministers of agriculture met in March 1964 to discuss the fisheries question. In the same month, Kim Chong-pil, now an assemblyman and chairman of the Democratic Republican party, went to Japan, apparently to arrange for a final settlement.

At this point the serious dispute erupted. It is not entirely insignificant that this was the first spring in three years that military rule had been lifted and that student political expression was possible. It also seems apparent that the negotiations with Japan, particularly Kim Chong-pil's semisecret agreement with the Japanese in 1962, served to stimulate the suspicions that the students, the press, and others already had about the new leaders—especially after the financial scandals of 1962 and the controversies over the organization and funding of the DRP.[12] The Japanese issue provided a nationalist focus for such suspicion, which drew on the long history of anti-Japanese feeling, as well as on more immediate fears that Japanese economic power would become allied with internal corruption. In March 1964, therefore, a report that Kim Chong-pil had worked out a timetable for completion of the negotiations and that a treaty would be signed by May, electrified opponents, who felt that the matter was being rushed through in unusual haste. The students took to the streets in the first really spontaneous demonstrations since before the coup, and vented their criticism on the leadership as a whole. Government leaders were impugned as traitors and Kim Chong-pil was particularly criticized for his eagerness to reach agreement with Japan. By May the situation had become so critical that the cabinet resigned.[13]

By this time, it had become clear that the Japanese settlement was to be a major and unavoidable point of conflict between the government and a rapidly forming coalition of politicians, students, intellectuals, and journalists. The new cabinet, appointed on May 9, 1964, announced immediately that the Japanese settlement was to be among its highest priorities and that it was to be achieved within a year. With an almost instinctively hostile reaction to the announcement, the students once again took to the streets. The new wave of demonstrations led to a declaration of martial law in early June. Politically, the next few months were taken up with the disposition of martial law and the issues it had raised. But by December the administration had resumed negotiations with Japan and the country waited apprehensively for the next spring.

The government's determination to push ahead with the Japanese settlement in 1965, in the face of all this opposition, was based on several motives. One was that the original reasons for the settlement had become all the more imperative. In the continuing reassessment and reorganization of economic policies, the development of major new sources of investment capital was seen as more necessary than ever. And it was obvious, despite overtures to Europe, that Japan was the largest and most accessible source. (Events would show that once re-lations were reestablished, capital availability from Japan would exceed the formal agreements.)[14] Second, in its rapprochement with the United States, the government had come to appreciate and accept the American emphasis on restoring relations with Japan, which flowed from strategic and economic considerations.[15] President Park and the new cabinet, headed by a former ambassador to the United States, were not inclined to try to reverse the American position, even if they were prepared to fight some rearguard actions, for example, to slow the pace of American aid reductions. Instead, they saw the American outlook as one more in-centive for Korea to develop more independent sources of international support and capital investment. Related to this, finally, was the admin-istration's general interest in expanding its diplomatic efforts, which would be weakened considerably by inability to gain recognition and support from Korea's largest and closest neighbor. In terms of Asian policy alone, the lack of contact with Japan inhibited any serious leader-ship role Korea might play and, as events in 1966 were to show, Korea did covet such a role.[16]

But in addition to these motives, the administration acquired new and compelling reasons for pursuing its policy toward Japan from the very nature of the controversy. In the resistance that burst forth in 1964, the administration saw a brand of politics to which it was instinctively opposed and which it was determined to overcome. The military coup had in 1961 taken place in the midst of considerable student unrest; it had been justified by its leaders in large part in terms of the chaos that such demonstrations, as well as political party disputes, were creat-ing. In the course of 1964 and 1965, President Park was to make clear that he considered the continuation of such instability destructive and one of the major obstacles to Korea's going beyond the revolution of

April 1960 to concrete achievements in political and economic development. The student movement, in his opinion, had gone beyond its rightful boundaries and needed to be curbed. It had become a force that disrupted both education and national policy.

In his statement to the nation of August 25, 1965, justifying the government's controversial order to the universities to expel some student and faculty activists, President Park expressed this view pointedly. He paid tribute to the reasonableness of early demonstrations on so troubling an issue as Japan and even credited them with strengthening the government's hand in the negotiations. But, he continued:

> A new disease spread in this country after the April 19 student uprising. It is the notion that demonstrations can do everything . . . Students! Have you seen any country prosper in which the students habitually take to the streets, disturb society, and try to interfere in problems? . . . How much of our national power, which should have been directed to construction and production, was wasted and how great were the damages to public properties from the student demonstrations? . . . But what I am worried about most is not the personnel and material losses we have suffered so far but the loss we shall suffer 10 or 20 years hence.[17]

The second element of domestic opposition to the settlement that the government particularly resented was the attitude of its political opponents. In the eyes of the administration, they opposed the settlement primarily for partisan reasons, at the expense of national interests.[18] Moreover, the more adamant among them were seen as acting out of revenge for their defeat in 1963 and out of a quite specific desire to bring down the government. Thus, for them, the Japanese issue was merely a vehicle. As will be described later, the opposition parties were not entirely innocent of these charges. As a result, the administration saw little possibility of a successful domestic effort at compromise, short of abandoning the settlement altogether. But more important, the government saw in this attitude, and in the increasing belligerency of the students as well, a major challenge to its legitimacy. Not only in the demands of the more easily dismissed adamant opposition but in those of other critics, the government's honesty, integrity, and competence in this matter, indeed, its right to carry out a task of such importance to the nation, were being questioned. Not infrequently, for example, critics argued that a settlement with Japan was desirable in principle, but not *this* settlement by *this* government.[19] As agreement with Japan came closer, the government felt it all the more important to respond strongly to this criticism and in clear defense of its own authority. With the importance that the Japanese settlement held for all of the government's other major programs, the issue thus grew into a challenge to its right to reshape the course of the nation's development, not only in this area but in others.

There was also one other factor in the administration's coming to feel, by the end of 1964, that the Japanese settlement was a cornerstone of all it hoped to achieve. The administration sensed in the opposition to the settlement the nation's insecurity about its ability to compete as a sovereign state, that is, its capacity for economic growth, and for wielding independent national power generally in the shadow of its larger neighbors or protectors. It sensed this insecurity in what it felt to be the purely negative and destructive politics of the opposition parties, and in the emotional fears that the prospects for settlement had aroused in the students and other segments of the population. This lack of confidence was anathema to the positive nationalism of the coup leaders and was in basic conflict with the type of stable and secure political order and economic growth the Park administration was trying to foster. On the occasion of the signing of the final treaty in June 1965, President Park spoke directly about this problem:

> I know that some use such extreme words as "humiliating," "low posture," and even "sellout" with respect to the results of the Korea-Japan negotiations . . .But if their assertions come out of a genuine fear that we might again be invaded by Japan or be economically subjugated to Japan, I wish to ask them: Why are they so lacking in confidence, so unreasoningly afraid of Japan, and so enslaved by a persecution mania and inferiority complex?
>
> Such timid mentality is in itself humiliating! We should first of all discard the inferiority complex, the defeatist feeling that we are bound to be defeated by the Japanese whenever we confront them. The biggest factors obstructing our modernization are defeatism, inferiority complex, and retrogressive inactivism which occupy one corner of our hearts.[20]

In a joint communique a few weeks later, defending the settlement as well as asserting the government's determination to keep order, the cabinet addressed itself to the same issue:

> We should get rid of the unfounded worries, persecution mania,

passive attitude, and defeatism, and [should instead] strive to cope with other nations and achieve a superior position in the community of nations . . . What is most essential is to embrace a concrete sense of sovereignty, sense of independence, national pride, and self-encouragement.[21]

THE SOURCES OF OPPOSITION

The above description of the government's motives suggests some of the main sources of opposition to the settlement. But it does not reveal the depth of bitterness, emotional fervor, dismay, and fear that moved the opponents of the government's policy in these years. The opponents labeled the treaty being negotiated with Japan "country-ruinous," treasonous, a crime perpetrated by an antinational regime. They called upon the people to "oppose to the death the humiliating and treasonable negotiations with Japan."[22] Caught up in the struggle, the opposition parties raced headlong toward destruction. And the students struggled to the point of endangering their lives and the political sanctity of the universities that had been so narrowly preserved in 1964.

One of the sources of the emotion and violence of opposition was a genuine fear of Japan. This was an ambivalent feeling, composed of admiration and emulation of Japanese character and methods, on the one hand, and jealousy and fear of Japanese strength and ability, on the other.[23] In the aftermath of 1945, the Koreans had seen Japan rise to be one of the richest and potentially most powerful nations in Asia, while Korea had suffered war, instability, and comparatively poor economic achievement. The Koreans had not even had the psychological lift of having defeated Japan in a colonial revolution; liberation had come as a product of Japan's defeat in World War II by the United States and its allies. The United States had indeed emerged in this light as an important protector of Korea against Japan. Therefore, not a little of the opposition portrayed United States policy as shortsighted in betraying Korea by pushing it into the arms of Japan.

Fear of Japan made acceptance of almost any terms with the Japanese difficult. In the area of property claims, for example, there was a desire for just repayment. But the larger the figures, the greater the fears of Japanese neocolonialism. The Koreans feared the Japanese would export outdated machinery to Korea, exploit Korean cheap labor, and gradually assume management control over Korean industries that received Japanese loan capital.[24] That these fears were not confined to the opposition groups was demonstrated by an editorial in the semigovernmental *Seoul Sinmun*, shortly after the treaty was signed:

> The way for Japanese economic infiltration is opened widely . . . With this huge financial power and advanced experience as a backdrop, the Japanese are clandestinely but concretely and correctly surveying our situation to find our weak points. When the time comes for them, they will jump on them to exploit maximum profits.
>
> As ink permeates blotting paper, so does Japan soak into Korea . . . At this juncture, it is a big problem whether Korea can expect much from the so-called "'friendly economic cooperation" with Japan without losing her economic independence.[25]

The editorial went on to note government plans to protect the country from these dangers. But if this editorial appeared in a progovernment paper, how much deeper were the fears of those who lacked confidence in the government's ability or willingness to safeguard the nation from such domination.

Attacks on American policy in this regard were often sharp. The United States' position on the Japanese issue was well known. The United States had initiated the first serious talks in 1951 and had used its good offices in both countries during subsequent years to facilitate a settlement. To opponents of normalization, this policy represented a near "sell-out" of Korean independence, a "second Taft-Katsura agreement"—a reference to the United States acknowledgment in 1905 of Japan's predominant interest in Korea, which Koreans feel was the prelude if not the signal for Japanese annexation a few years later.[26] The American policy was also seen as based on a false premise. Critics charged that United States policy in the Far East was anchored on Japan. But, they argued, as the fulcrum of anticommunist policy, Japan was a bad risk. Japan was not as strongly anticommunist as Korea. In a rather striking appraisal of the domestic attitudes of the two countries, one professor stated that Korean anticommunism had been "more or less similar to McCarthyism," while in Japan it was only a matter of "political party policy."[27] Further, critics charged, for Japan, normalization of relations with South Korea was no more than a prelude, in deference to American wishes, to more active trade and other relations with the Communist countries of Asia. After agreement, Japan would thus step up its relations with North Korea, to the humiliation of South Korea, and with Communist China, to the embarrassment of the United States.[28] The bitterness toward the United States was thus compounded of a feeling of betrayal and blame, as well as a warning. "I think that the U.S. will not wake up," exclaimed opposition leader Yun Po-son, "before it suffers another Pearl Harbor several more times."[29]

Fears about Japan and uneasiness over the loss of United States protection against that country, were reflections as well of insecurity over the strength and reliability of Korean national and moral character, as touched upon in Chapter 4. It was to this aspect of the opposition that the government reacted strongly, as mentioned earlier. But the depth of this concern was not overcome by government preachments. It ran deep in Korean culture, from a tradition of factional politics, and a long history of dependence on outside protection, to the reinforcing disappointments of postliberation history.[30] Some of this mistrust was directed specifically at this government.[31] But the most frequent accusation was that of a "humiliating diplomacy." The government was castigated for nearly every concession: for not exacting a specific apology from the Japanese for its colonial rule, for compromising on the Peace Line, and for accepting the recognition of the Republic of Korea as "the only lawful Government in Korea" but without specification of its jurisdiction over territory north of the 38th parallel.[32] One can disagree over specific points, but the general argument of the critics suggested that any concession reflected defeat and humiliation before Japan. And that attitude seemed to reflect a deep sense of inferiority that no Korean government could have satisfied in a practical negotiation with Japan.[33]

Much of this questioning, moreover, went beyond the government to the society at large.[34] There was fear of a cultural invasion, with Japanese ways overwhelming the Korean. There was fear of "comprador capitalists," that is, businessmen who would become mere figureheads for Japanese control. There was fear that politicians would be unable to resist the blandishments of Japanese financial support and that Korean democracy in general would bend to the "Oriental style" of Japan rather than hold to the Western influence of the present. One editor, in very personal terms, stated the individual fear of many about the future of Korean independence and moral integrity in the face of Japanese wealth, power, and influence:

> My opinion . . . is that I am fundamentally against the normalization should the present state of our nation seem to remain as it is. For I personally believe that under such a situation, normalization would simply mean subjugation of our nation to Japan.
>
> I do not know what the real hidden intention is of those people

who daringly swear to work for prompt modernization of our nation, or those [who would commit] "hara-kiri" should normalization become a fact . . . At the moment, I do not place much trust either in what the government says about the issue or what the opposition shouts forth these days . . . My most immediate and probably most ultimate concern . . . is, should the wave of Japanese influence and economy sweep over our land, would I be able to maintain and carry out in action my attitude of opposition, and if I could do so, how long.

Suppose a Japanese comes to me offering a great reward to do work for them which will be against our national interest. Would I then be able to reject such an offer or be able to resist the temptation or inclination of my mind to compromise? . . . If a Japanese article of a little better quality is offered about the same price as our domestic made article, will I be able to choose the domestic made item without hesitation so as to protect our frail national economy? . . .

When the majority of people pursue their own interests forgetting what they had shouted so confidently before, then I am not sure what course I would follow, because I believe that a human being is a very minor thing in such a society where majority rules, and [I do not know] how far the efforts of an individual can go against the tide.[35]

Very close to this type of fear, but more clearly rooted in nationalist feeling, was concern over national identity. For many intellectuals, particularly as the struggle between the government and the universities reached a climax in 1965, the Japanese settlement posed a basic question of direction. Some opponents, for example, felt that the settlement would lead to the South Korean economy being absorbed into that of Japan as the North Korean was becoming absorbed into the Communist bloc, thus making reunification a more distant prospect.[36] But the issue ran even deeper. The Japanese settlement marked a major new departure in modern Korean history, perhaps opening Korea as much to Japanese economic and political influence as the early postliberation period had opened it to American.[37] It marked also an endorsement of the government's priority and basic program for national development. To many, these steps were being taken before some fundamental internal questions had been answered: One was whether the move toward Japan did not place Korean hopes for reunification at the mercy of Japanese international policies, as it had previously been tied to American policy. Were there no possibilities yet to be explored, asked these opponents, for a more truly independent course vis-à-vis the North? What would happen, they argued further, to Korean nationalism—particularly that of the students—if no such prospects were opened up to them? One professor argued very emotionally that many would in time turn to communism as the only satisfying alternative. Similarly, there was the unresolved question of democracy. For those pitted in opposition to the government in 1965, this issue seemed very far from settled. If overlooked or overwhelmed by "realistic" arguments for the Japanese settlement related to economic benefits and international politics, a vital element of postwar political culture in South Korea would be destroyed. The meaningful distinction between North and South Korea would be lost for the younger generation, and the alternative for nationalist-minded students would become compromise with the North in opposition to subordination to Japan.[38]

Finally, partly in response to these feelings, and partly promoting them, were the internal dynamics and motivations of the opposition political parties. Their internal struggles for leadership in this period were bound up with their tactics of opposition to the treaty with Japan. In turn, their tactics and overall strategy very largely shaped the nature and duration of the national debate.

The failure of opposition politicians to unite in the elections of 1963 had carried over into the subsequent period which saw two large and two small parties, all in opposition to the DRP, represented in the Assembly. During 1964 and 1965, these parties gradually began to merge, but in July 1965, two main opposition parties still remained distinct, one led by defeated presidential candidate, Yun Po-son. In ideology, there was not a great deal of difference between the two.[39] But there was considerable difference in temperament and in approach to national politics. Yun Po-son's opposition to the Park government was unremitting. He believed that the Park regime was illegitimate, from its origins in the coup through the 1963 elections which, he believed, had been either rigged or falsified. His tactics of opposition were similarly unremitting. He denounced compromise with the government on almost any issue. His interpretation of opposition was to bring the government down, without reference necessarily to constitutional means, rather than to try to modify its policies or to achieve some sort of working relationship with it. In his keynote speech of 1965, he went so far as to call for a new "coup d'état" to topple the regime.[40] Yun also dominated his party as an individual. He not only insisted on maintaining ultimate control of strategy and tactics; he was determined to remain the party's standard bearer in any presidential election.[41] By contrast, the other opposition group, the Democratic party, was somewhat more conciliatory. It was apparently prepared in early 1965 to accept the Japanese settlement with modifications if it could obtain a share of influence and credit for such modifications. In her keynote speech of 1965, party leader, Mme. Pak Sun-chon demonstrated a clear interest in a "loyal opposition" role.[42]

Without doubt, this competition for leadership of the opposition influenced the steps taken to oppose the Japanese settlement. The two opposition parties began to take steps toward a merger in early 1965 as they sensed the impending climax of the Japan issue and the need for concerted action.[43] In preliminary steps, Yun appeared to have the upper hand and was setting a fairly strident tone.[44] However, when the merger actually took place in June, Yun was defeated by Mme. Pak as Supreme Commissioner of the new People's party, and was not even included among the party's top three officials. There was a feeling at the time that this marked a trend toward moderation.[45] But events proved that the issue of party leadership and strategy was less easily resolved. Yun offered to step into the background. But, in fact, he and his supporters used the Japanese issue as a means of forcing a difficult and indeed impossible strategy upon the new party, in the end nearly bringing about its dissolution. It was in the months following the merger that the struggle for leadership in the new party became most intense and moved the opposition into a nearly tragic role.

Not all of the adamancy on the Japan issue that pressed upon Mme. Pak in the next few months, however, came from Yun's supporters. There were people in opposition ranks who were not comfortable with Yun as a leader but who shared from personal conviction his determined opposition to the Japanese settlement. Thus Mme. Pak had among her principal lieutenants in the new party men who were also opposed to any compromise that betrayed basic opposition to the treaty or the emotions of the students, intellectuals, and others actively against the settlement.[46]

In her first statement after election, therefore, Mme. Pak set forth a position designed to retain party unity and avoid any charge of weakness. The ratifications of the agreements, she stated, would be "blocked at all costs." She pledged stronger efforts both within and outside the Assembly to do so. In a prediction of near cataclysm, moreover, she said, "The Korea-Japan normalization pacts shall never be ratified at the Assembly unless and until some Assemblymen get killed." If the pacts should be ratified, she added, "the political arena would see its end." At the same time she took a step away from advocating overthrow of the government. She spoke of parliamentary strategy for issues to be taken up after the Japanese issue. And she made it explicit that the People's party was making its plans for "taking over the Government in the next election."[47]

But the moderates in the opposition were placed in an impossible position. Their only hope rested upon the possibility of forcing the government into a compromise—either another cessation of the negotiations as in 1964 or some very major concessions on either the content of the agreements or the makeup of the negotiating delegation. But the government was not so inclined and was convinced that the settlement it had negotiated by early 1965 was the best obtainable. It was also convinced that further delay on the matter would only prolong the political crisis in the country. In June, therefore, the government proceeded to sign the newly negotiated treaty with Japan and, in July, showed its determination to obtain ratification. In the course of a fist-swinging melee in the Assembly, the DRP formally introduced the newly signed treaty to the Assembly for consideration, using its overwhelming majority to roll over the vehement protests of the opponents.[48] The handwriting was on the wall. There might be further attempts at delay and at compromise but the government would ratify the treaty in 1965, come what may. And the opposition—which had promised to fight the treaty "to the death" and block it "at any cost"—could not stop it, not at least within any reasonable bounds of constitutional protest, and probably not at all. The question then arose as to what the opposition should do.

Into this situation the "adamants" stepped, urging a strategy that was ostensibly aimed at forcing the government to the wall but was at least equally aimed by Yun's forces at taking revenge upon the new party. Essentially, it called for the opposition members to resign from the Assembly through mass resignation from both the Assembly and their party.[49] The government, they argued, "would not dare" to pass the treaty in a one-party Assembly, therefore forcing a postponement of the treaty and perhaps even a new general election.[50] The tactic, also, of course, would mean the dissolution of the new opposition party.

The weeks of July and August 1965 were filled with great tension, debate and—for the opposition parties—frustration, dispute, and ultimate defeat. The tension was everywhere in July. The student demonstrations had finally been halted but only by calling an early vacation, which was to end in mid-August. Both sides were girding for a showdown before then, particularly as the government was anxious to complete ratification while the students were away, and the opposition just as anxious to postpone an Assembly vote until they were back.[51] In a vain attempt to avoid a crisis, Mme. Pak met with the president on July 20, and the two agreed on steps to maintain constitutional procedures and order.[52] But the meeting produced sharp attacks on Mme. Pak from the "adamants" and the opposition split worsened. At the end of July, Yun announced his intention to resign from the new party and called upon others to follow suit.[53] The moderates argued that should the party be dissolved, the government would indeed ratify the treaty in a one-party Assembly, the people would revolt and the government would reply with worse repression—thus the desperate need to preserve the constitutional order. The adamants argued in rebuttal that ratification could be blocked only by dissolution of the party and new general elections, and any government action to the contrary, such as ratifying the treaty in a one-party Assembly, would be met by overwhelming popular resistance. Each side charged the other with a strategy of "aiding the enemy."[54]

In August the slim "working agreement" between Mme. Pak and President Park dissolved. In an unannounced move, later known in Korea as "the snatch," the DRP suddenly voted the consent bill out of committee while physically barring opposition members from the rostrum.[55] The opposition members of the Assembly, realizing that final ratification was at hand, submitted their resignations en masse from the Assembly. But the government, proving the moderates only too right in their prediction, proceeded to ratify the treaty in a one-party Assembly.[56] The students, returning to school at this time, stormed into the streets in protest over this action. The government then replied, as described in Chapter 3, by bringing in troops, expelling academic and student activists, and closing two major universities.[57] By September the crisis over Japan was over. The universities were in shocked silence. The government had won. There had been no revolution.

THE UNWINDING OF TENSION

The events of spring and summer 1965 had a tragic character to them throughout—a sense of individuals and associations struggling inexorably and helplessly against an outcome that was almost from the beginning inevitable. The sense of gloom and at times alarm ran through the press commentary throughout the summer. The period, however, had provided for an outpouring of emotion; in the process a transition in national outlook took place. In June, on the eve of the treaty-signing with Japan, the *Tonga Ilbo*, the country's largest newspaper, wrote despairingly of the national state of affairs at such an historic moment. But it focused on the settlement as the cause of such a state:

> A great and grave turning point, which will tragically affect us and our offspring is about to be effectuated. It is indeed a national tragedy that the normalization agreements, the contents of which are unsatisfactory to almost every citizen, are to be formally signed while the opposition wages extreme struggle, the doors of schools are closed down, and hunger strikes and demonstrations [occur] among the students.[58]

Though maintaining a kind of negative neutrality on the partisan aspects of the dispute,[59] the press had in fact during the summer kept up pressure on the issue: on the opposition party, reminding it of its pledge to block the agreements, and on the government, pointing out the disunity over the agreements.[60]

But in the aftermath of the summer's events, the tone changed. It was the state of the nation, in a different sense, that now occupied the concern of most writers: the loss of normal Assembly operations, the plight of the universities, and the general "absence of politics," that is, the absence of a normal procedural means for carrying on the nation's business. The *Tonga Ilbo* on August 14 now denounced the opposition for choosing political crisis rather than ratification of the treaty.[61] Its editorial of September 3 summed up the feeling of the opposition press at this point and presented an interesting contrast to that of June:

> Brazen graft and corruption evolving around the [seats of] power; dirty factional strife within the opposition, which boasts of its "turn" to assume the forthcoming regime; deeds destroying order perpetrated by some elements of military personnel; some students swarming through the streets, stoning in the name of demonstrations; and the general public who do not know what to do except sighing— these are our images at the moment . . .
>
> Most lamentable is the absence of politics. Leaving their forum to military personnel and students, the politicians have stepped down to the position of by-players and on-lookers.
>
> Politics must return to the hands of the politicians first of all. This is the first task to be achieved at this moment. After that, they should discuss momentous problems.[62]

In September the press was in fact almost unanimous in calling upon the opposition assemblymen to return to the Assembly, not being very kind to the opposition in the process. The major concern became a restoration of the normal processes of government.[63] The Japanese issue faded in this context. At the end of September, Mme. Pak led her followers back into the Assembly, apologizing formally for the party's "wrong policy line."[64] Yun and his followers broke away and formed a new "clear-cut opposition" party. But early in 1966, even Yun announced his readiness to accept the Japanese treaty as a fait accompli.[65]

As an issue of political importance, therefore, the Japanese treaty disappeared with amazing rapidity. Concern in political circles, as in the rest of the country, turned elsewhere. Disputes continued over the disposition of Japanese funds and other matters under the treaty.[66] But these were issues within the normal range of political dispute. A year after the settlement, when a major smuggling incident was uncovered involving Japanese goods, with alleged compliance of government officials, the reaction was substantial within the Assembly; student demonstrations occurred on a small scale. But at no time was there a revival of the emotion or the crisis atmosphere of 1965.[67] The quick acceptance of the Japanese agreement, once completed, was one of the striking characteristics of the period after 1965.

The Japanese settlement, nevertheless, represented a major turning point. Many changes had been in process in the years prior to 1965. The outline of post-Rhee politics was becoming clear: not a return to the chaotic freedom of 1960–1961 or a maintenance of the military autocracy of 1961–1963, but a relatively unromantic, imperfect, but workable, compromise between the two. The economic uncertainties of the postwar period were giving way to a more certain path of success in export and internal development. The shibboleths of the past—anti-Japanese feeling, early reunification hopes, semipermanent protection (political and economic) by the United States—were also disappearing. But the acceptance of these changes and of the attitudes required by them was not complete. The Japanese issue symbolized the resistance to these facts of change and indeed to the requisites of Korea's postliberation position: Japan had been a reality which, with Rhee's encouragement, the Koreans had put out of their minds for nearly 20 years. As the *Tonga Ilbo* put it, more poetically,

One may wake up in the morning and say to himself, "Oh, Japan is right beside me as ever" . . . But during the past 20 years since

Liberation, we had no time to stop to remind ourselves of this, and thought it the safest way to pretend to be unaware of this.[68]

To avoid Japan, a large neighbor and even before normalization a major economic factor in trade, was to avoid other realities as well. One was that Korea was indeed divided and not likely to be reunified soon in a shattering resumption of hostilities between the United States and the Communist countries to the north, as Rhee had continued to hope since 1953, and from which hope the population had never really freed itself.[69] And if Korea were divided, what were the real prospects for South Korea? A greater sense of nationhood required broadening international ties, relinquishing some of its dependence on the United States, and above all taking its chances in a commitment to self-reliant development. It meant a government not only interested in development but strong and stable enough to carry out programs of long duration and major transformation. That meant a new kind of politics, with surer and more professional administration in the executive and greater unity and organization of its supporters in the Assembly. This in turn placed new requirements upon an opposition: the development of a cohesive body of support less dependent upon factional defections from government supporters and capable of putting forth an alternative comparable to the professional and program-oriented image of the administration. It meant, finally, that it was South Korea as it existed—its quality of leadership, its political strengths and weaknesses, and its share of economic resources—that would have to undertake these tasks.

By 1965 much of this change was already being accepted throughout Korea. Those in opposition to the Japanese settlement probably greatly overrated the dissatisfaction of the population at large. For one thing the government had done quite a job in publicizing its position and justifying the settlement. But for another, the advantages were not small. There was, for example, little hard evidence of deep fear or overt dissatisfaction about the settlement among the fishing population, despite the national debate over the compromise on the Peace Line by which they were the most affected.[70] In all likelihood, the large amount of Japanese capital earmarked in the settlement for fishing equipment as an offset for that compromise appeared more promising for improving their livelihood than maintenance of a theoretical preserve which had not been effective as a real barrier to Japanese competition. Businessmen and laborers, already feeling the effects of the upswing of 1964–1965, must also have felt the pull of advantages that the opening of Japanese capital sources would mean.[71] There was no doubt that the student demonstrations of 1965 lacked the widespread support of 1964.[72] Nor did they attract other participants. The government's action against the universities drew nothing like the reaction it might have in the previous year, and nothing like the resentment that antistudent action had produced in 1960. It is also worth noting that the military's attitude in support of the government was unwavering.[73]

But for those groups, that is, the intellectuals, the press, and the students, who had for so long been the articulators outside the government of national sentiments on politics and nationalism, these changes were more difficult to accept. It was harder in part because these same groups had been in almost constant struggle with the incumbent government over political issues. They found it difficult therefore to acknowledge this government, this leadership, as the actual heirs of 1960. But more important, they now articulated and represented what were really all the nation's fears and uncertainties about the course that the government was determining. They thus laid the basis for a major confrontation between the sentiments and emotions that had guided and protected the past and the challenges and requirements of the future. It is possible that some concessions on the part of the government to the demand for a pan-national negotiating team in 1964, or perhaps to a longer period of debate in the Assembly in 1965, would have lessened the intensity of confrontation, though probably stretching it out for a much longer period of time. But it is hard to imagine that any of these measures would have avoided the need at some point for a painful confrontation between these opposing forces. In the emotional intensity of the summer of 1965—with the fistfights between assemblymen, the frenzy of the students, the despair of the columnists—all the frustrations of the past several years and the fears of the commitment to what so clearly lay ahead came to a climax. It was, as one sad and wistful observer commented at the time, "the going to the couch of a whole nation."

The very intensity of the Japanese experience seemed to release much of the tension that had existed up to that point. In the next two years, the nation would be caught up in the economic upsurge that would in 1966 produce the highest growth rate in South Korea's postliberation history, and in the dramatic new, and not entirely unrelated, involvement of South Korea in the politics of Asia and very directly in the war in

Vietnam. The main opposition party would also turn its attention to economics in 1966. By the time of the national elections in 1967, Japan was no longer even an issue, while the future of Korean economic development was one of the most important. Building up from the long period of postwar reconstruction, the growing forces of economic change thus came once again to the forefront of Korean politics.

Part II

6 / The Dimensions of Economic Growth and Structural Change

In recent years the Korean economy has to an extreme degree exemplified the dual process of growth and rapid structural change. All aspects of structure, from the composition and uses of output to the allocation of inputs, have been in a state of flux. Such a rapid and positive transformation is not likely to result solely from natural economic forces; special external factors, and more often government policy actions, must also be present. In the Korean case both were important. The initial recovery from severe war damage was distorted and unbalanced. Economic policies contributed to this unbalanced recovery and to a structure of relationships between imports and exports and savings and investment that was not only unsupportable without massive external assistance over the longer run, but increasingly harmful to growth. A drastic change in policy in the first half of the 1960s caused a rebound from past distortions and a positive response to government policies and actions which accelerated and guided the transformation. In many instances, as suggested in Chapter 4, the ramifications of these policies were not fully perceived by the policy-makers. But their tendencies were anticipated and, once they proved relatively effective, the policies were often pushed very forcefully in order to speed up the process of structural transformation.

While many peoples might shy away from the conscious pursuit of such rapid change, the Koreans have, by and large, been willing to undergo the inconveniences and uncertainties involved. The pressures of poverty exacerbated by war, the political need to try to keep up with North Korea, and eagerness to achieve even a part of the affluence seen in Japan and the West all contributed to a desire for rapid growth and development. As pointed out in Chapter 4, this desire had, by the late

121

1950s, translated itself into strong political pressures for economic change. Also, the Japanese occupation, land reform, wartime destruction, and finally revolution had eliminated many of the strong vested interests that might have resisted such change. Consequently, it was possible to implement aggressive measures and to achieve dramatic results.

In addition to this capacity and will for transformation, Korea possessed certain special characteristics in the development of its human resources and in the makeup of its industrial structure. It was in fact the convergence of these factors—a comparatively well-educated and highly motivated population; an industrial structure based largely on light and relatively labor-intensive industry; and policy changes which maximized the advantages of these and other factors in the Korean scene, and which in so doing departed in several instances from some of the more common approaches to economic development—that made possible the scope and pace of change experienced in the mid-1960s.

This chapter will deal with the dimensions of Korea's economic growth and structural change and briefly compare Korean patterns with those of other countries at comparable levels of development. In the succeeding chapters we shall try to explain the causes of the recent transformation of Korea's economy: first in terms of changes in supply, demand and technological conditions, especially in industry and agriculture (Chapter 7); and then in terms of changes in the structure of economic policies (Chapter 8) and the approach to policy-making as embodied in the planning process (Chapter 9).

PRE-KOREAN WAR DEVELOPMENT

Modernization of the Korean economy began during the years of Japanese occupation, when the first factories and such infrastructure as power, railways, and some communications facilities were built. During the 1930s industrialization was greatly accelerated to support the buildup of Japanese military strength. By the end of the decade the value of industrial production for all of Korea was equal to that of agriculture.[1] Most of the industry and the better farmland were owned and managed by the Japanese, with Koreans serving as laborers and lower-level supervisors.

The withdrawal of the Japanese in 1945 and the division of the country at the 38th parallel left South Korea with an economy of very limited capabilities. The loss of Japanese management, the rupture of trade with Japan and North Korea, and the subsequent shutting-off of power supplies from the North eliminated most of South Korea's normal patterns of exchange and adversely affected the productivity of its economy as a whole.

By 1950 a number of these problems had been at least partially alleviated and, with the help of substantial foreign aid from the United States, the economy was beginning to recover. In the spring of that year, trade missions began to explore new export markets for textiles and other light manufactured goods in Southeast Asia. The land reform program was implemented; a new central bank was created; and other institutional reforms were laying the foundation for future growth.

All this was lost in the summer of 1950, with the North Korean invasion and occupation of all of South Korea except for the extreme southeast corner—the so-called Pusan Perimeter. Industrial facilities outside the perimeter not destroyed in the fighting were heavily bombed, thus eliminating most of South Korea's limited industrial capacity. The new institutions, such as the central bank, which had been created to bring order and growth to the economy, were used instead to finance and fight the war, an experience from which they were slow to recover. While the agricultural and rural areas were not much affected, the main urban area around Seoul was heavily damaged. It has been estimated that the overall physical destruction attributable to the war was the equivalent of $2 billion, that is, roughly equal to the value of one year's Gross National Product at that time. After one year of intense fighting over the whole country, the front stabilized near the present truce line, and it was possible to start the process of rehabilitation and reconstruction.

POSTWAR RECOVERY AND DEVELOPMENT

Since the end of the Korean War, Korean economic development has gone through three relatively distinct periods. The first, from 1953 through 1958, was a period of reconstruction, when much that had been destroyed during the war was rebuilt, and when production grew at a satisfactory rate. It was also a period of imbalance and instability. Large scale foreign aid supplied the imports needed for investment and consumption, but inflation was continuous and domestic resource mobilization of limited effectiveness. The second period, from 1959 to 1962, was one of stagnation and political unrest. The growth of output declined— to nearly zero in per capita terms. Restraints on aggregate demand resulted in idle capacity in many industries. The easy investment guides of reconstruction had not yet been replaced by new indicators and stimuli for investment. Declining aid and import levels acted as a brake on production and investment. Also, adverse weather conditions affected agricultural production in 1960 and 1962.

The third period, beginning in 1963, has been characterized by high growth of output and employment and structural change in the form of rising ratios of investment, saving, and exports and imports. In practically all respects the economy has pushed ahead at such rapid rates that the people have been able to perceive the improvements and to have a clear sense of sharing in the benefits.

Variations in the growth record are indicated most sharply by the changes in per capita production (see Figure 1). This rose from the equivalent of roughly $80 at the end of the Korean War to about $90 at the end of the reconstruction period in 1958. Through 1962 it remained nearly constant at that level, but, since that time, it has risen at an average annual rate of 7 percent, reaching nearly $140 by 1968. In the six years from 1962 through 1968, per capita real output grew by 50 percent. The overall growth rate of GNP averaged 6.8 percent a year

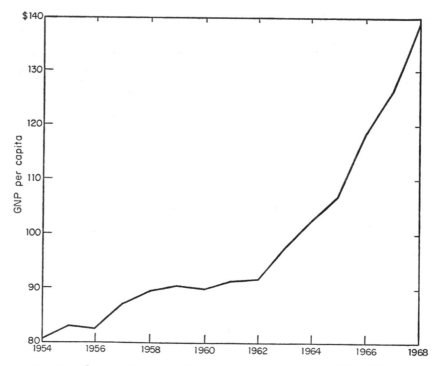

Fig. 1.   Gross national product per capita in constant 1965 dollars.

from 1954 through 1968 but ranged from 5.5 percent during reconstruction to 3.6 percent during the stagnation period and up to 10.1 percent from 1963 through 1968.

The growth rates of the main producing sectors have varied with the rate of overall growth. The average rates for all sectors during the stagnation period were below those of the postwar recovery, and well below those of the subsequent high growth period (see Table 6.1).

Table 6.1   Rates of Growth of GNP by Industrial Group[a]

Industrial group	Average rates of growth			
	1954–1958	*1959–1962*	*1963–1968*	*1954–1968*
Agriculture, forestry, and fisheries	4.0	0.8	4.8	3.5
Mining and manufacturing	15.1	9.4	17.8	14.7
Social overhead[b]	12.4	10.0	18.9	14.4
Other services[c]	4.1	3.8	9.3	6.1
Total	5.5	3.6	10.1	6.8

Source: See Appendix Table 3.

 [a] Based on GNP series in 1965 constant market prices.

 [b] Includes construction, transportation, storage, communication, electricity, water, and sanitary services.

 [c] Includes trade, banking, insurance, real estate, ownership of dwellings, public administration, defense, rest of world, and other services.

Agriculture, forestry and fisheries, and mining and manufacturing declined most markedly between 1954–1958 and 1959–1962, but then all sectors raised their growth rates substantially thereafter.

For the 15-year period 1954–1968, mining and manufacturing, and social overhead (which includes construction, transportation, storage, communication, electricity, water and sanitary services) have had average growth rates of nearly 15 percent. Other services have averaged 6 percent and agriculture, forestry, and fisheries only 3.5 percent. Inevitably this has meant significant shifts in the relative shares of the main sectors in total GNP. Agriculture, forestry, and fisheries have dropped from nearly half of GNP in 1954 to less than one-third by 1967–1968. During the same period, mining and manufacturing rose from less than 10 percent to nearly one-fourth and social overhead from below 5 percent to over 10 percent (see Appendix Table 2).

These changes in the structure of production are in the direction that is expected for developing countries, but the rate of change in Korea has been more rapid than normal. This can be demonstrated by comparing the Korean shares at various levels of per capita GNP with those predicted by Chenery and Taylor from their cross section studies of many developing countries.[2] As shown in Table 6.2, the share of what

Table 6.2 Comparison of Korean and Normal Industrial Shares of GNP at Various Levels of Per Capita GNP

Per capita GNP in US dollars	80	90	100	120	140
Relevant time period for Korea	1954	1958– 1962	1963– 1964	1966– 1967	1968
Shares of GNP in Korea:[a]					
Primary production[b]	49.7	43.7	42.2	39.6	30.9
Manufacturing and construction	11.1	16.1	18.8	21.9	28.0
Normal shares of GNP:					
Primary production[b]	46.2	44.2	42.6	39.3	37.0
Manufacturing and construction	13.0	14.5	15.6	17.5	19.1
Ratio Korean shares to normal shares of GNP:					
Primary production[b]	1.08	0.99	0.99	1.01	0.84
Manufacturing and construction	0.85	1.11	1.21	1.25	1.47

Source: From estimates of normal shares for "large" countries in H. B. Chenery and Lance Taylor, "Development Patterns: Among Countries and Over Time," *Review of Economic Statistics,* Nov. 1968.
[a] Shares of GNP in Korea are the averages for the years shown as derived from Appendix Table 4.
[b] Primary production here includes agriculture, forestry, fisheries, and mining, to make it consistent with the Chenery-Taylor classification.

Chenery and Taylor classify as primary production—agriculture, forestry, fisheries and mining—was slightly above the norm in the immediate postwar period, about at the norm for the decade 1958 to 1967 as per capita GNP rose from $90 to $120, and then fell well below the norm in 1968, partly as a result of poor crops. Manufacturing and construction, on the other hand, started below the norm in 1954, but were above the norm thereafter and had reached nearly 50 percent above normal for a country with per capita income of $140 by 1968. These departures from the norm are symptomatic of South Korea's relatively poor natural resource base, which tends to limit the share of primary production.

International comparisons of the social overhead sectors are less meaningful than those for agriculture and manufacturing because the value of production is biased by the degree of government ownership or regulation. It appears, however, that the output of the social overhead or infrastructure sectors in Korea has been relatively low and has acted as a brake on the overall growth rate. These were the sectors that were most adversely affected by partition and the Korean War, so that heavy investment was required to build them up to satisfactory levels. Much of this investment has been implemented in the 1963–1968 period, which has made possible the high rate of increase of nearly 19 percent per year in social overhead output.

GROWTH AND STRUCTURE OF DEMAND

Since the end of World War II, aggregate demand has consistently exceeded domestic output in Korea. The country has therefore in this period had not only a large import surplus, but also continuing inflationary pressures. These pressures have varied in intensity, from relatively severe during the Korean War and most of the reconstruction period to more constrained in the stagnant period from 1959 to 1962 (see Table 6.3). Inflation became serious again in 1963 and 1964, the first two years of the high growth period, but was thereafter held near a rate of 10 percent per year. Because of this long inflationary experience, with

Table 6.3   Index of Inflation: Annual Change in Prices as Reflected by the Implicit GNP Deflator

Year	Percent Change
1954	32.8
1955	67.4
1956	30.1
1957	20.9
1958	−0.7
Average 1954–1958	30.1
1959	2.3
1960	9.3
1961	16.1
1962	13.9
Average 1959–1962	10.4
1963	30.9
1964	34.5
1965	8.3
1966	12.9
1967	10.5
1968	12.0
Average 1963–1968	18.2
Overall average	20.3

Source: Bank of Korea, *Economic Statistics Yearbook*, 1969.

annual price increases averaging 20 percent, most Koreans have come to expect some continuing inflation. Annual rates of price increase of 10 percent or less are judged to represent relative stability and have become the guideline of recent stabilization policy.[3] By these standards there have been only four years from 1954 to 1967 that have been noninflationary.

It is difficult to measure the size of Korea's import surplus relative to GNP, because one has to translate foreign currency values into domestic currency during a period when the official or the effective exchange rate was held at unrealistic levels. The magnitude of the disparity is indicated in Table 6.4, where the import surpluses in current prices and in 1965

Table 6.4   Imports, Exports, and Import Surplus as Percent of GNP

| Year | In constant 1965 prices | | | Import surplus in current prices |
	Imports	Exports	Import surplus	
1953	22.1	5.6	16.5	6.6
1954	14.9	3.7	16.3	5.2
1955	18.9	4.0	14.9	6.9
1956	21.8	3.5	18.3	10.8
1957	23.7	4.0	19.7	9.7
1958	19.4	4.4	15.0	7.9
1959	15.2	4.8	10.4	6.8
1960	17.0	5.2	11.8	8.5
1961	14.8	6.2	8.6	8.5
1962	18.9	6.8	12.1	10.8
1963	22.1	6.7	15.4	10.7
1964	15.2	7.4	7.8	7.1
1965	16.0	9.5	6.5	6.5
1966	22.2	12.8	9.4	8.5
1967	27.5	16.4	11.1	9.1
1968	35.5	19.8	15.7	11.7
Average 1953–1968			13.1	8.5

Source: Bank of Korea, *Economic Statistics Yearbook*, 1969.

prices are shown as a percentage of GNP. The discrepancy is particularly great in the years 1953–1957 but it exceeded one-third in 1958–1959 and again in 1963. During the other years devaluation or special exchange taxes and subsidies narrowed the gap. Neither series is a good indicator of the "real" size of the surplus. The best approximation may be an average of the two percentages, which for the whole period would be about 11 percent of GNP. Thus, during the 15 years from the end of the Korean War, domestic output has been augmented by an import surplus equal, on the average, to 11 percent of that output. But aggregate demand has still been excessive, resulting in an average annual price increase of about 20 percent.

Despite the large import surplus and the resulting availability of goods in excess of domestic production, Korea was unable to bring about a significant shift in demand from consumption to investment until the high growth period beginning in 1963 (see Table 6.5). Throughout the

Table 6.5 Consumption and Investment Expenditures as Percent of Total Available Resources

	Consumption				
Years	Private[a]	Govern-ment	Total	Invest-ment	Total
1953–1958	78.9	9.2	88.1	11.9	100.0
1959–1962	76.1	12.9	89.0	11.0	100.0
1963–1968	72.6	9.4	82.0	18.0	100.0

Source: Derived from Appendix Table 6.

[a] The statistical discrepancy in the National Income accounts has been deducted from private consumption in arriving at the share of private consumption in total available resources.

decade after the Korean War, consumption averaged nearly 90 percent of total available resources and investment only 11 percent.[4] In the six years from 1963 through 1968, the average investment share climbed to 18 percent and consumption accordingly dropped to 82 percent.

As with estimates of the real size of the import surplus, there are also statistical and valuation problems in connection with investment estimates. Because the exchange rate was considerably overvalued in the 1950s, especially for investment goods, and because a large share of the investment expenditures was for imported capital goods, the real cost of investment during that period is understated. It is difficult to estimate a suitable correction factor for this bias, but at least we can caution that the apparent upsurge in investment demand is somewhat overstated.

The changing patterns of consumption are also significant. While the total consumption share did not change much from 1954 through 1962, there was a shift from private to public consumption during the low growth period, 1959–1962. This was reversed thereafter as the government share declined in 1964–1965, to be followed by the drop in private consumption's share in 1966–1968. Movements in the share of government consumption have been strongly but negatively influenced by the rate of inflation. During periods of high inflation, government revenues and wage payments lagged behind the price change; the reverse occurred when inflation was limited.

In terms of comparison with normal shares of total expenditures for countries of comparable per capita income levels, Korea's private consumption share was above the norm of 74 percent prior to 1963. The average share for government consumption has been near the norm of 11 percent but has swung below the norm in the high growth and inflation periods and above the norm in the stagnation period.[5] Investment was consistently below the normal level of 15 percent until 1963. In general these comparisons show that only in very recent years has a shift in private consumption and investment shares moved Korea to a high growth pattern of demand.

THE PATTERN OF FOREIGN TRADE

Shifts in the structure and financing of foreign trade have been among the most notable changes in the Korean economy and have had a major influence on the whole development pattern. Total imports have tended to move with changes in the level of domestic production. There were high ratios of imports to GNP in the reconstruction years, a decline in the stagnant period and a resurgence in the high growth period (see Table 6.4). Regular commodity exports, on the other hand, were negligible prior to the high growth period, when they started to expand very rapidly. They have since been a major stimulant to the whole economy, particularly manufacturing, which has supplied most of the new exports. Along with these changes in the levels of foreign trade have come major changes in the patterns of financing and in the main countries of origin and destination.

The most notable change in import composition has been the steady rise in the capital-goods category, machinery, and transportation equipment, which by 1966–1968 accounted for 32 percent of total imports, compared to 14 percent in 1959–1962.[6] Manufactured goods also increased, but less rapidly than capital goods (see Table 6.6). Many of these manufactured products were intermediate or semifinished goods destined for Korean industry. The types of imports that have declined in relative importance include fuels and lubricants and chemicals, an area in which there has been substantial import substitution.

Between 1958 and 1967–1968 the principal origin of Korea's imports shifted, largely from the United States to Japan (see Table 6.7). This

Table 6.6 Commodity Imports by SITC Classification, 1957–1968
(in millions of dollars)

		1957–1958		1959–1962		1963–1965		1966–1968	
		Avg.	%	Avg.	%	Avg.	%	Avg.	%
Food, beverages, tobacco	0,1	92.3	22.4	36.9	10.7	84.2	17.9	112.1	10.6
Crude materials	2,4	66.2	16.1	74.2	21.4	108.8	23.1	217.8	20.5
Fuels, lubricants	3	40.4	9.8	29.8	8.6	31.4	6.7	59.8	5.6
Chemicals	5	72.9	17.7	75.2	21.7	89.1	18.9	125.9	11.1
Manufactured goods	6	55.7	13.6	49.4	14.3	68.3	14.5	183.7	17.3
Machinery, transport	7	39.6	9.6	48.5	14.0	81.6	17.3	338.4	31.9
Miscellaneous	8,9	43.1	10.6	32.2	9.3	7.6	1.6	22.4	2.1
Total		410.2	100.0	346.4	100.0	471.0	100.0	1,060.3	100.0

Source: Ministry of Finance, *Foreign Trade of Korea, 1968* (Seoul, 1969).

Table 6.7   Commodity Imports by Region and Major Country of Origin
(in millions of dollars)

Region and country	1958		Annual average for 1967–1968	
	Amount	%	Amount	%
Asia	79.2	20.9	699.1	56.7
Japan	49.9	13.1	533.6	43.3
America	216.3	57.1	395.3	32.1
United States	209.0	55.2	374.7	30.4
Europe	72.8	19.3	118.8	9.6
Other	9.9	2.6	19.1	1.5
Total	378.2	100.0	1,232.2	100.0

Source: Economic Planning Board, *Major Economic Indicators,* 1969.

was explained in part by an even more sizable change in the sources of financing for imports. In 1957–1958, grant aid, mainly from the United States, paid for roughly five-sixths of total imports, with Korean foreign exchange being used for only 12 percent (see Table 6.8). By 1967–1968, commercial imports with Korea's own exchange covered two-thirds of the total and foreign loans accounted for 17.6 percent. A significant proportion of the loans and some of the grant aid came from Japan and could be used only for purchases from that country. But, more important, Korea was able to use its own foreign exchange to buy from the lowest-cost source, and for many commodities this source was Japan.

Until as recently as 1962, Korean exports consisted predominantly of sales of goods and services to foreign military forces stationed in Korea. Although regular merchandise exports have grown steadily and dramatically since 1960, it is only since 1963 that they have amounted to 50 percent or more of total exports. Since 1964 both military transactions and other service exports expanded along with general merchandise exports so that total current-account earnings more than quadrupled from 1964 to 1968. (See Table 6.9.)

Merchandise exports have exhibited two distinct (but related) shifts since 1960. One is the greatly increased share of manufactured goods in total exports (see Table 6.10), and the other is the diversification of markets (see Table 6.11). In 1960 manufactured goods accounted for only 18 percent of total exports. In 1965 the comparable share was 62 percent; by 1968 it was 77 percent. The shift of markets has been away from Japan toward more balanced sales, especially in the developed countries. While the traditional exports to Japan of sea products and minerals have grown somewhat, most of the new manufactured-goods

Table 6.8 Commodity Imports by Source of Financing
(in millions of dollars)

	1957–1958		1959–1962		Annual averages for 1963–1965		1966–1968	
	Amount	*%*	*Amount*	*%*	*Amount*	*%*	*Amount*	*%*
Own foreign exchange	47.8	11.7	115.1	33.2	221.9	46.6	680.0	64.0
Grant aid	342.5	83.5	214.5	61.9	170.2	35.8	139.7	13.2
Foreign loans	0	0	1.1	0.4	39.4	8.3	186.2	17.6
Relief and others	19.9	4.9	15.6	4.5	44.5	9.3	54.3	5.1
Total	410.2	100.0	346.3	100.0	476.0	100.0	1,060.3	100.0

Source: Economic Planning Board, *Major Economic Indicators,* 1969.

Table 6.9   Exports of Goods and Services
(in millions of dollars)

Year	Merchandise	Military transactions	Other services	Total
1960	32.8	62.6	21.5	116.9
1961	40.9	79.7	25.0	145.6
1962	54.8	84.7	23.7	163.2
1963	86.8	58.3	30.4	175.5
1964	119.1	63.7	28.2	211.0
1965	175.1	74.0	40.7	289.8
1966	250.3	100.9	103.5	454.7
1967	334.7	162.6	145.6	642.9
1968	486.4	216.6	172.2	875.2

Source: Economic Planning Board, *Major Economic Indicators*, 1969.

Table 6.10   Composition of Exports by Type of Commodity

Commodity	1960	1965	1968
Agricultural products	21.9	8.7	4.3
Marine products	17.7	13.7	10.2
Mining products	42.2	15.3	8.2
Manufactured products	18.2	62.3	77.3

Source: Economic Planning Board, *Major Economic Indicators*, 1969.

exports have gone to North America and Western Europe. To some extent Korean exports have replaced those of Japan in these markets, but so far Korean manufactured goods have not penetrated the Japanese home market to any significant degree. A new and perhaps transitory

Table 6.11   Composition of Exports by Region and Major Country
of Destination (percent)

Region and Country	1960	1965	1968
ASIA	73	49	33.4
Japan	62	25	21.9
Hong Kong	8	6	3.2
Vietnam[a]	0	8	1.2
AMERICA	11	37	55.1
United States	11	35	51.7
EUROPE	13	12	8.0
OTHER	3	2	3.5
Total	100	100	100.0

Source: Economic Planning Board, *Major Economic Indicators*, 1969.
   [a] The exports to Vietnam do not include those financed with United States economic and military assistance funds.

market has arisen in Vietnam for certain types of manufactured goods, financed mainly by United States aid. But this market has accounted for only a limited share of Korea's regular exports in recent years.

Total foreign exchange earnings associated with the war in Vietnam became significant only from 1966, when a large Korean military force went to Vietnam, as did numerous civilian workers. The remittances from Koreans stationed in Vietnam accounted for a large share of Vietnam earnings; the total earnings from Vietnam reached nearly 20 percent of current account earnings and private transfer receipts in 1967. This compares with 10.6 percent in 1966. (See Table 6.12.) Although

Table 6.12   Korean Earnings from Vietnam, 1966–1968
(in millions of dollars)

Type of earnings	1966	1967	1968
Commercial exports	$ 13.8	$ 7.3	$ 5.6
Military goods sales	9.9	14.5	30.8
Construction and service contracts	12.3	43.5	58.4
Remittances:			
Civilian	9.7	40.6	38.4
Military	13.2	30.0	34.4
Others	0	8.8	4.6
Total	$ 58.9	$144.7	$172.2
Total receipts from exports of goods and services plus private transfers	$558.0	$744.8	$993.0
Vietnam earnings as % of total	10.6	19.4	17.3

Source: United States Operations Mission to Korea, 1969.

the earnings continued to rise in absolute terms in 1968, they declined as a share of current account receipts plus private transfers. Thus the Vietnam War has been responsible for some of the recent spurt in foreign exchange earnings, but it has not been a major element in the expansion of commodity exports.

SUMMARY

To sum up briefly the growth and structural change in Korea since the Korean War, there have been cyclical movements, or parallel swings for many of the major variables over the 15 years here reviewed. Reconstruction (1953–1958) was a time of moderately rapid growth in primary and secondary industry, moderate investment, high imports, low exports, and necessarily sizable inflows of foreign aid. The stagnation period (1959–1962) showed declines in many areas, with only government consumption going up relative to GNP. Finally, in the period since 1963, all productive sectors have experienced increased growth rates, and the demands from investment and exports have mounted rapidly, leading to a similar increase in imports. Only government and private consumption have declined as shares of GNP, thereby expanding domestic savings and releasing resources for investment and exports.

7 / The Causes of Economic Growth

Having described the general dimensions of growth and structural change in Korea, we turn now to their causes. In this chapter we shall be concerned with the more proximate causal factors of growth: the availability of natural and human resources, as well as the changes in supply and demand conditions that had direct effects on the level and composition of output. In the following chapters we shall take up the main policies and institutional changes that provided the framework for, and influence on, the direct causal factors.

NATURAL AND HUMAN RESOURCES

South Korea has an unbalanced pattern of productive resources: a very limited endowment of natural resources and an abundant and relatively highly trained stock of human resources. Despite recent efforts to reclaim new land, less than one-fourth of the total land area is cultivated and there is roughly one-fifth of an acre or one-tenth of a hectare of cultivated land per capita. The extremely mountainous nature of the country seriously limits opportunities for increasing the cultivated area. Mineral resources are also in short supply. Anthracite coal is found in various parts of the country and is mined intensively. Other major minerals include tungsten, copper, lead, zinc, and iron ore, but these and several lesser minerals, even after considerable efforts at development, still account for less than 2 percent of GNP. There is no petroleum in the country and, despite considerable exploration, there have been no discoveries of major new mineral deposits in the past decade. Thus natural resources have made a limited contribution to recent growth and offer little ground for optimism in the future.

Table 7.1 Labor Force and Employment[a]

Year	Population 14 years and over	Labor force	Employed	Labor participation rate, %	Employment rate, %
1963	15.7	8.7	7.9	55.2	91.9
1964	16.3	8.9	8.2	54.4	92.3
1965	16.6	9.2	8.5	55.4	92.6
1966	16.8	9.3	8.7	55.4	92.9
1967	17.2	9.5	8.9	55.4	93.8
1968	17.4	9.8	9.3	56.0	94.9

Source: Economic Planning Board: *Major Economic Indicators,* Mar. 1969.
[a] In millions of persons.

Human resources, on the other hand, have for some time been recognized as relatively highly developed for a country of Korea's per capita income. According to one study, based on conditions in the late 1950s using formal education as a measure, South Korea was the most extreme deviant, on the high side, in a correlation of an index of human resource development with per capita GNP.[1] According to this index, Korea's human resource development was comparable to that of countries with median per capita GNP equal to three times the Korean level. Since that time Korea's educational effort has increased and become even more advanced or "overdeveloped," in relation to the country's level of real output.[2]

In addition to the underlying strength deriving from the educational system, the Korean labor force has other atributes that have enhanced its contribution to economic growth. Korean workers have been described by one manpower specialist as "adaptable, trainable, manually dexterous, and accustomed to arduous work for long hours."[3] The country's climate undoubtedly contributes to the industriousness of the people.

The labor force has been increasingly absorbed in production and shifted from the less to the more productive sectors, so that output per worker has risen rapidly. Unfortunately, the labor force statistics are only available for the years since 1963, but these serve to illuminate the changes during the high growth period. Between 1963 and 1968 the labor force increased by 12.5 percent, while the number fully or partially employed rose by 18 percent; the employment rate went up from 92 to 95 percent of the labor force. At the same time the average number of hours worked per week rose and the share of all workers who were working less than 18 hours per week dropped from 9 percent to 5 percent.[4] Thus underemployment declined. During this same period, as shown in Table 7.2, employment in agriculture, forestry, and fisheries was constant, while that in mining and manufacturing went up by 86 percent, and in social overhead and services by 41 percent. If these employment changes are related to the changes in value added for these same broad sectors between 1963 and 1968, it can be seen that the value added per worker, measured in constant prices, increased by slightly less than one-fourth in each of the sectors, but that because of the shift of workers away from agriculture into the more productive sectors, the value added per worker for the whole economy went up by 37 percent (see Table 7.2). Looked at somewhat differently, of the roughly 60 percent increase in value added, one-third can be attributed to increased employment and about two-thirds to rising production per worker. Clearly, this is not simply the result of an improved labor force but reflects the expansion of capital facilities and generally improved efficiency of economic organization.

One of the critical questions for both economic welfare and the political stability of the country is the extent to which the labor force has shared in the benefits derived from this growth of productivity. Some insight into this can be gained from the information on earnings of production workers in Table 7.3. This shows that real wages have been significantly influenced by changing rates of inflation, but that in 1967 and 1968 real wages seem to have responded to the growth in productivity and scarcity in the labor market. Real wages in mining and manufacturing, which had risen in the late 1950s when prices were stable, dropped sharply in 1963–1964 when inflation was high. They recovered slowly in 1965–1966 but then went up rapidly in agriculture, mining, and manufacturing during the next two years. A comparison between 1963 and 1968 shows roughly a 30 percent increase in real wages, which is nearly the same rate as the increase in real value added per worker during the same period.

Thus the Korean labor force offered a favorable resource for achieving rapid growth. It was characterized by almost total literacy, relatively high levels of education, industriousness, and relatively low wage rates in terms of either domestic or international prices. Also, there was a large number of unemployed and underemployed workers who could be drawn into new or more productive employment as the opportunities and demands arose. Labor or manpower was clearly not a constraining factor on growth. However, it could not be counted on to generate much

Table 7.2 Change in Number of Workers and Value Added per Worker between 1963 and 1968

	Number of workers[a]			Value added[b]			Value added per worker[c]		
	1963	1968	% Change	1963	1968	% Change	1963	1968	% Change
Agriculture, forestry, and fisheries	5.0	4.9	− 2	271	331	+ 22	54	67	+24
Mining and manufacturing	0.7	1.3	+86	124	280	+126	177	216	+22
Social overhead and services	2.2	3.1	+41	693	1,127	+ 63	88	121	+37

[a] Millions of workers.
[b] Billions of *won* in 1965 prices.
[c] Thousands of *won* in 1965 prices.

Table 7.3   Index of Monthly Earnings of Production Workers
(1965 = 100)

Year	Index in current prices			Seoul consumer price index	Index in real terms		
	Agriculture	Mining	Manufacturing		Agriculture	Mining	Manufacturing
1957		36.6	43.5	45.5		80.4	95.6
1958		38.0	47.8	43.8		86.5	109.1
1959	42.6	45.1	52.0	45.3	94.0	99.6	114.8
1960	43.1	46.5	50.0	49.8	86.5	93.4	100.4
1961	47.6	53.5	56.5	53.9	88.3	99.3	104.8
1962	51.5	59.2	60.9	57.5	89.6	103.0	105.9
1963	65.2	66.2	70.3	68.8	94.8	96.2	102.2
1964	88.5	78.9	84.3	88.0	100.6	89.7	95.8
1965	100.0	100.0	100.0	100.0	100.0	100.0	100.0
1966	116.9	118.3	117.4	112.1	104.3	105.5	104.7
1967	142.7	154.9	143.5	124.2	114.9	124.7	115.5
1968	178.3	171.8	182.6	138.0	129.2	124.5	132.3

Source: Economic Planning Board: Major Economic Indicators, Mar. 1969.

growth unless combined with additional amounts of complementary factors.

Recent writings on the growth of agriculture have generally agreed that a number of factors are required to bring about rapid increases in productivity. These include appropriate incentives to reward the farmer who expands output; research on the most productive techniques and plant varieties, availability of water and of the new physical inputs such as fertilizer, pesticides, and improved seed; marketing, credit, and similar institutions to service agriculture; and finally extension and information systems that make the farmers aware of the possibilities open to them.[5] There is further agreement that these factors need not be combined in fixed proportions but may vary from country to country, and even among regions within countries. The problem is to identify, in any given setting, the most critical factors that are either holding back growth or may act as a sort of catalytic agent to activate the process of technological change and increased application of the whole range of growth-promoting factors.

While this conception of a relatively complex production function for agriculture is undoubtedly realistic, it also means that there is real difficulty in trying to quantify the influence of individual factors on the growth of output. In reviewing the experience of a particular country, one is likely to find the combination of inputs growing in rough proportion, so that one or two main inputs may serve as a surrogate for the whole complex. Only if there are basic changes in the mix of inputs or extreme variations over time is it possible to sort out the differential effects of the individual inputs in a statistically meaningful way. This problem is clearly prevalent in Korea's recent experience. There have been parallel movements over time in agricultural output, in cultivated area, and in the various other agricultural inputs, but they have not grown at a constant rate. Agricultural output has experienced alternating periods of rapid and slow growth. These changes in the growth rate of output have been approximately matched by changes in the input complex. But periodic bouts of adverse weather conditions as in 1962–1963, 1967, and 1968; the short period for which statistics are available; and the limited reliability of those statistics make it hazardous to push the analysis very far in the direction of sorting out the influence of individual inputs.

Consequently, the main objective of the discussion that follows will be to show the changes in the complex of inputs and other influential factors over time, which will suggest the varying capability of the government and the economic system to marshal the resources needed for agricultural development. The analysis is not carried beyond 1966 for two reasons: complete data were not available for the subsequent years, and severe droughts in different parts of the country in 1967 and 1968 had sizable affects on production quite unrelated to the longer run factors affecting agricultural productivity.

A picture of changing growth rates and the relative growth of the different field crops can be obtained by using average production for several years at the beginning and end of the period, expressing output values in constant prices and deriving growth rates. This is done in Table 7.4 for the main categories of farm crops. The compound annual growth rate for crop production thus increased from 3.7 percent in the late 1950s to 6.2 percent in the early 1960s. Along with the rising rate of growth, there has been considerable diversification. Where rice and barley accounted for 75 percent of output and 87 percent of the increase in output between 1956–1957 and 1960–1961, these had dropped to 68.5 and 47 percent, respectively, for the more recent period. Potatoes, fruits, tobacco, and vegetables have achieved high rates of growth since 1960–1961 and have accounted for half the increase in total real output.

The changing composition of output is undoubtedly in response to changes in consumer demand as rising incomes become manifested in greater consumption of vegetables, fruits, and other crops. This change has induced farmers to increase their production of the higher profit crops and to adopt new cultivation techniques, such as hothouse vegetable production, which has sprung up around all the major cities. Increased supplies resulted in a moderate decline of fruits and vegetable prices relative to grain prices from 1961 through 1964, but this did not seriously affect the growth of output (Table 7.5).

Aside from the diversification of production that has raised farm output and income by raising the relative share of new high value crops, the other major source of agricultural growth can be attributed to increased inputs of land and yield-increasing ingredients of modern agricultural technology.

The expansion of the land input can be achieved by cultivating more land, or making more intensive use of a given area through double cropping. Also the productivity of land or the extent of double cropping can be influenced by the availability of irrigation systems. Over the

Table 7.4 Shares, Growth Rates, and Contributions to Growth of Main Farm Crops

Crop	1956–1957		1960–1961		1965–1966		1956–57 to 1960–61		1960–61 to 1965–66	
	Average value	% of total	Average value	% of total	Average value	% of total	Growth rate	% of total growth of output	Growth rate	% of total growth of output
Rice	78,785	58.6	94,105	58.4	108,523	50.0	3.7	57.6	2.9	25.8
Barley	20,530	15.3	28,356	17.6	40,100	18.5	6.7	29.4	7.2	21.0
Cereals	1,640	1.2	1,771	1.1	2,172	1.0	1.6	0.5	4.2	0.7
Pulses	4,587	3.4	4,493	2.8	5,281	2.4	−0.4	−0.3	3.3	1.4
Potatoes	5,375	4.0	6,416	4.0	17,386	8.0	3.6	3.9	22.0	19.6
Fruits	2,234	1.7	3,016	1.9	6,264	2.9	6.2	2.9	15.7	5.8
Tobacco	4,322	3.2	4,928	3.0	10,495	4.8	2.7	2.3	16.3	9.9
Vegetables	14,056	10.4	15,763	9.8	24,648	11.4	2.3	6.4	9.4	15.9
Special crops[a]	2,981	2.2	2,239	1.4	2,209	1.0	−5.9	−2.8	−0.3	−0.1
Total:	134,510	100.0	161,087	100.0	217,078	100.0	3.7	100.0	6.2	100.0

[a] Special crops include ginseng, hemp, herbs, and tobacco.

Table 7.5   Indexes of Prices Received by Farmers for Various Crops

Year	A Grains	B Fruits and vegetables	Ratio B/A
1959	82.7	87.3	1.05
1960	100.0	100.0	1.00
1961	124.2	86.9	0.70
1962	132.8	116.4	0.87
1963	214.6	210.4	0.98
1964	271.5	232.1	0.85
1965	247.8	276.5	1.07
1966	259.1	259.3	1.00

Source: Bank of Korea, *Economic Statistics Yearbook*, 1967.

decade from 1956 to 1966, as indicated in Tables 7.6 and 7.7, there has been an expansion of the cultivated area, the cropped area and the fully irrigated area. The cultivated area grew very slowly prior to 1963, but in the two succeeding years it expanded by nearly 10 percent. Planted area, which is a summation of the total area on which crops are planted and therefore allows for double cropping, increased steadily from 1961 to 1965. The extent of double cropping went up from 49 to 57 percent of the total cultivated area. Much of this expansion of cultivated area was the result of bench-terracing on the lower slopes of Korea's many hillsides. This was a labor-intensive activity that provided 45 million

Table 7.6   Cultivated and Planted Area[a]

Year	Cultivated area	Planted area	Ratio of planted to cultivated area
1956	2.01	3.02	1.50
1957	2.02	3.07	1.52
1958	2.03	3.07	1.52
1959	2.03	3.00	1.48
1960	2.04	3.02	1.48
1961	2.05	3.05	1.49
1962	2.08	3.15	1.51
1963	2.10	3.20	1.53
1964	2.19	3.40	1.55
1965	2.28	3.59	1.57
1966	2.31	3.48	1.51

Source: Bank of Korea, *Economic Statistics Yearbook*, 1967, and NACF, *Agricultural Yearbook*, 1966.

[a] Area is given in millions of *chongbo* (1 *chongbo* = 2.45 acres).

Table 7.7 Comparisons of the Extent of Irrigation

	1956	1960	1965
Fully irrigated rice paddies (1,000 hectare)	544	669	744
Partially irrigated rice paddies (1,000 hectare)	615	547	553
Total paddy area (1,000 hectare)	1,159	1,216	1,297
Ratio of fully irrigated to total	0.47	0.55	0.57

Source: United States Operations Mission to Korea, *Rural Development Program Evaluation Report* (Seoul, 1967).

man-days of employment at the peak in 1965. These efforts were organized by the Korean government and supported by United States surplus agricultural commodities, which were used to pay part of the workers' wages. Not only have the cultivated and planted areas been increased, but the area of effectively irrigated rice paddies has also been expanded. Major expansion of the fully irrigated area took place between 1956 and 1960. Somewhat slower growth has followed.

In addition to land and water, other critical direct inputs for raising agricultural productivity include fertilizer, pesticides and improved seed. There are no good quantitative indicators of the seed variable in Korea, but fertilizer and pesticide usage is indicated in Table 7.8. The application of fertilizer tripled from 1956 to 1966 but most of the increase oc-

Table 7.8 Use of Fertilizer and Pesticide

Year	Fertilizer[a]		Pesticide	
	1,000 MT	Index	1,000 MT	Index
1956	184	82	4.9	83
1957	221	98	6.8	115
1958	219	97	5.1	86
1959	243	108	5.6	95
1960	225	100	5.9	100
1961	262	116	5.6	95
1962	308	137	7.4	125
1963	347	154	18.8	319
1964	372	165	23.4	397
1965	480	213	22.0	383
1966	534	237	26.5	450

Source: Bank of Korea, *Economic Statistic Yearbook*, 1967.

[a] Fertilizer is measured in metric tons of plant nutrients. The figures from 1956 through 1962 are those shown for the previous years in the published statistics, but they actually related to a period from Aug. 1 of the previous year to July 31 of the year here indicated. From 1963 on, they are based on the calendar year.

curred after 1960. Also during this later period, there was greater use of mixed fertilizers, rather than only urea or nitrogenous fertilizer. This kind of qualitative change had been proven effective on a test basis, but its consequences for total output are difficult to estimate. The use of pesticides also rose sharply in 1963 and has continued at high levels.

Another direct agricultural input that is important in Korea because of the acidity of the soil is the application of lime or crushed limestone. Statistics on the amount of lime applied are inadequate, but it has been indicated that, after a relatively large increase in lime use from 1963 to 1965, the level dropped from a target of 750,000 metric tons to a realized figure of only 144,000 tons in 1966 because of shortages of rail transport to move the lime from the deposits to the countryside.[6] The same source indicates that annual lime needs are 1 million metric tons, but how closely the use of lime in past years has approximated this target is not clear.

Factors that have an indirect effect on agricultural output include credit, extension and marketing services, and the incentive effects of relative prices received and paid by farmers. The agricultural credit picture is not easily perceived because of the changing balance between loans from organized financial institutions and from private moneylenders, concerning which information is limited. Also, the nominal amount of credit outsanding over time must be adjusted for changes in the price level. A shift in the balance of loan sources from private lenders to the banks or cooperatives is presumably advantageous to the farmers because bank credit is generally provided at lower interest rates and on other more favorable terms. In 1961 and 1962, with strong political motivation as described in Chapter 2, the Korean government made a major effort to substitute loans from the government-organized National Agricultural Cooperatives Federation (NACF) for those of private moneylenders. This resulted in a significant increase in the nominal and real magnitude of bank credit to farmers, as shown in Table 7.9. But inflation in 1963 and 1964 drove the real value of bank loans down sharply.

These changes were apparently matched by changes in the ratio of bank loans to total debt of the farm households. According to the estimates presented in Table 7.10, which should be regarded as only very approximate, the share of private debt to total farm household debt declined fairly steadily from 82 percent in 1956 to 58 percent in 1960. We do not have any estimates for 1962, when private debt probably reached its lowest proportion; but by 1964 the estimated share had risen to 70 percent. Considering that there had been little increase in the real value

Table 7.9 Agricultural Loans by Banks and Credit Sales of Fertilizer
(in billions of *won*)

Year	Loans by banks[a]	Credit on fertilizer	Total	Total converted[b] to 1965 prices
1956	3.6	1.0[d]	4.6	13.5
1957	7.3	1.4	8.7	23.4
1958	7.9	1.4	9.3	24.8
1959	8.2	1.2	9.4	24.5
1960	11.5	1.4	12.9	30.9
1961	16.5	2.0	18.5	38.3
1962	17.3	4.9	22.2	40.4
1963	19.7	5.3	25.0	35.5
1964	24.3	5.4	29.7	32.0
1965	23.7[c]	10.3[c]	34.0	34.0
1966	27.8[c]	12.9[c]	40.7	35.4
1967	34.0[c]	12.0[c]	46.0	35.7

Source: 1956–1964 from National Agricultural Cooperatives Federation, *Problems and Means of Improvement of Agricultural Credit System in Korea* (Seoul, 1965); 1965–1967 from Bank of Korea, *Economic Statistics Yearbook,* 1967 and *Tables on Stabilization,* prepared monthly by the Bank of Korea.
[a] As of the end of August of the respective years.
[b] Conversion to 1965 prices is based on the implicit GNP deflator.
[c] As of the end of September.
[d] Estimated.

Table 7.10 Ratio of Private Debt to Total Farm Household Debt (in *won*)

Period	Total debts per farm household	Private debts	Private as % of total debts
End of			
Oct. 1956	3,997	3,273	82
Oct. 1957	4,623	3,592	78
June 1958	5,625	4,433	79
Sept. 1959	6,779	4,743	69
Sept. 1960	6,693	3,885	58
Aug. 1964	19,808	13,936	70

Source: 1956–1964 from National Agricultural Cooperatives Federation, *Problems and Means of Improvement of Agricultural Credit System in Korea* (Seoul, 1965), p. 32; for 1964, from National Agricultural Cooperatives Federation, *Rural Credit Survey in Korea* (Seoul, 1965), p. 162.

of bank loans and fertilizer credit between 1960 and 1964 (see Table 7.9), any real increase that did occur during this period came mainly from the private moneylenders. Thus we appear to have the somewhat surprising situation that both the real value and the relative share of organized credit for farmers increased during the period when agricultural production was growing most slowly (1958 to 1962), and that both declined in subsequent years, when production increased substantially. This is clearly not sufficient evidence to suggest that organized credit to farmers has had a negative effect on farm output, but it does indicate that such credit has not been an important positive factor for increasing agricultural production.

Despite the apparent diminution in the role of organized credit to farmers after 1962, a continuous expansion of other services provided to the farmers by the NACF and by the Office of Rural Development (ORD) took place. The former organization was involved in supplying fertilizer and pesticides, as well as credit, to the farmers; it also bought up or assisted in the marketing of farm crops. The ORD is mainly concerned with extension activities including distribution of improved seed, and information on new crops and cultivation techniques. Prior to 1962, the distribution of fertilizer had been carried out by both NACF and private business, but in that year NACF took over full responsibility. This step led not only to increased supplies of fertilizer but also to increased sales of fertilizer on credit; a relatively low, subsidized price for fertilizer through 1964; better timing and wider distribution of the supplies; and some pressure to encourage the use of mixed, rather than plain, nitrogenous fertilizer.

Between 1960 and 1966, the number of rural guidance or extension workers under the Office of Rural Development increased sixfold, so that the average number of farm households served by each worker dropped from 2,100 to 375. Of the new workers, over half had at least a junior college degree and more than a third were graduates of a four-year agricultural college. This increased the flow of information on new farming technology to the farmers and contributed to the rapid adoption of better seeds, crop diversification, mixed fertilizer, spraying, and other measures to increase productivity. These workers were also involved in the programs for expanding arable land.

The total number of employees of the Ministry of Agriculture and Forestry and affiliated agencies such as the NACF and Fisheries Cooperatives tripled between 1956 and 1966 (Table 7.11). While the number of civil servants engaged in a particular activity is not necessarily a meaningful measure of their contribution to the output of that activity, one expert group reviewing the Korean experience has concluded:

It is clearly evident that the ROKG [Republic of Korea Govern-

Table 7.11   Employees of the Ministry of Agriculture and Forestry

Year	Number of Employees	Index 1960 = 100
1956	9,110	67
1960	13,497	100
1961	14,281	106
1962	17,406	129
1963	18,597	138
1964	21,415	158
1965	24,481	181
1966	28,116	208

Source: United States Operations Mission to Korea, *Rural Development Program Evaluation Report*, p. 272.

ment] bureaucracy over the past ten years had made a major impact upon many facets of the agricultural sector. Increases in both manpower and budgetary allocations are measurable manifestations of the ROKG will to force this change and development to take place. While some part of the top-down bureaucratic drive and accompanying financial resources have been politically motivated and the latter wastefully used, on balance the benefits side of the performance ledger far outweighs the negative component of the total effort.[7]

Another potential influence on the growth of agricultural production is the relative prices of goods sold and purchased by farm households—the farmers' terms of trade. Changes in these terms of trade can, of course, have both positive and negative incentive effects. Recent studies have generally shown that Asian farmers respond positively to improvements in their terms of trade.[8] A rise in price of farm products in relation to other prices usually means that output is likely to increase; furthermore, farmers are more likely to adopt new production technologies if the price relationships yield substantial gains from increased output.

In Korea an index of prices received and paid by farmers has been compiled since 1959, and the ratio of grain to nongrain prices in the wholesale price index can be used as a rough but apparently exaggerated indicator of the terms of trade index for earlier years. In Table 7.12 these series show that from 1956 to 1959 the price relationships moved strongly against the farm sector, improved continuously through 1963, and declined thereafter. The peaks and troughs were accentuated by above normal harvests in 1958 and 1959, and poor harvests in 1962 and the summer of 1963. But the underlying cycles in the terms of trade seem

Table 7.12 Measures of the Terms of Trade for Farmers

Year	Wholesale price index			Index of prices received and paid by farmers[a]
	Grain	Nongrain	Ratio of grain to nongrain	
1956	101	75	137	
1957	116	87	133	
1958	95	86	111	
1959	84	100	83	93
1960	100	100	100	100
1961	124	111	111	104
1962	131	123	108	106
1963	208	139	149	124
1964	263	190	139	115
1965	247	217	114	109
1966	260	234	116	104

Source: Bank of Korea, *Economic Statistics Yearbook,* 1967.
[a] Prices received are for main farm products, whereas prices paid are for farm supplies, farm labor, and household consumption goods.

to precede cyclical movements in agricultural output by several years. The decline in farmers' terms of trade from 1956 to 1959 precedes the leveling off of output growth from 1958 to 1962. Then the improvement in relative prices from 1960 to 1963 is followed by rising output. It is difficult to be sure what has been cause and effect in this experience. There may in fact be a cobweb type of movement with several years' lag in which improved terms of trade lead to higher output which depresses prices and eventually output, etc. Even if the experience is too short to test such an hypothesis, it does seem safe to conclude that the shift in terms of trade in favor of the farmers from 1959 to 1963 gave some stimulus to the growth of output that occurred from 1963 onward.

We can now draw together the various causal factors relating to agricultural production and trace their influence over time. The pattern can be seen most readily by presenting the several output and input series as indexes based on 1960 values (Table 7.13). In broad terms the increase in the real output of agricultural crops from an index of 100 in 1960 to 155 in 1966 is a composite of three types of change: diversification and rapid increase of the nongrain crops, increase in planted area, and increase in yields. The planted area expanded by about 15 percent, while higher average yields in grains had by 1966 added another 20–25 percent.

Table 7.13   Indices of Agricultural Output, Inputs, and Relative Prices
(1960 = 100)

	1956	1957	1958	1959	1960	1961	1962	1963	1964	1965	1966
Output											
Value of all farm crops	85	95	103	103	100	115	106	117	136	135	155
Value of rice and barley	81	91	100	104	100	114	101	115	128	125	140
Value of all other crops	97	101	106	100	100	117	122	117	160	175	211
Inputs											
Cultivated area	99	99	99	100	100	100	102	103	107	112	113
Planted area	100	102	102	99	100	101	104	106	113	119	114
Fertilizer supply	82	98	97	108	100	116	137	154	165	213	237
Pesticide supply	83	115	86	95	100	95	125	319	397	383	450
Organized farm credit		76	80	79	100	124	131	115	107	110	115
Government workers in agriculture	67				100	106	129	138	158	181	208
Relative prices											
Ratio of grain to nongrain prices	137	133	111	83	100	111	108	149	139	114	111
Prices received and paid by farmers				93	100	104	106	124	115	109	104

The remaining expansion of the overall index by roughly 15 percent can be attributed to the secondary crops: potatoes, fruits, and vegetables.

Of the inputs that contributed to raising yields, fertilizer, which more than doubled between 1960 and 1966, was probably the main factor. Limestone and pesticides were also significant. The role of organized credit for farmers was negligible. However, the organization of distribution, marketing, and extension services to assist the farmers improved and expanded rapidly in this period and appears to have made a significant contribution. Finally, the swing in relative prices in favor of the farmers from 1959 to 1963 probably gave an added stimulus to the adoption of new technological inputs, expansion of cultivated area, and willingness to experiment with new crops.

In addition to quantitative changes in inputs, there was also a qualitative change: efforts to help were better organized and technical competence improved to identify the farmers' specific needs.

CAUSES OF MANUFACTURING GROWTH

The main factors influencing the rate of growth and the structure of manufacturing since the Korean War have been: changing conditions of demand for manufactured goods, the supply of intermediate inputs and the stock of productive industrial capital, which factors have in turn been intimately tied to the patterns of foreign trade and the policies affecting foreign trade. Although these are to be explored more fully in the following chapter, some aspects of the trade picture should be discussed here. As already indicated, manpower has not been a significant limiting factor on the growth of manufacturing, but it has influenced the structure in the direction of labor- and skill-intensive industries.

An overview of the growth of manufacturing and some of the main influences on that growth since the Korean War can be obtained from Table 7.14, which shows the value added in manufacturing, the estimated stock of fixed capital in manufacturing, the imports of all kinds of intermediate goods, and the exports of manufactured goods. When capital stock, intermediate imports, and manufactured exports are employed as explanatory variables in a least squares regression, they seem to explain much of the growth of manufacturing. Capital stock and intermediate imports are primarily supply or input variables, although they do have implications for demand in that capital formation uses some output from manufacturing, whereas intermediate imports may be a substitute for domestic manufactures. Exports of manufactures are, on the other hand,

Table 7.14 Manufacturing Production and Some Major Related Variables[a]
(Amounts in billions of *won* at 1965 prices)

Year	Value added in manufacturing at producers' prices		Estimated net fixed capital stock in manufacturing[b]		Imports of intermediate goods[c]		Exports of manufactured goods	
	Amt.	Index	Amt.	Index	Amt.	Index	Amt.	Index
1953	29.8	23.1	25.0	18.9	71.4[e]	80.5	0.3[e]	0.9
1954	36.0	27.9	27.5	20.7	50.3[e]	56.7	0.3[e]	0.9
1955	44.1	34.2	30.2	22.8	73.3	82.6	0.4	1.4
1956	52.0	40.3	34.5	26.0	82.8	93.3	0.7	2.3
1957	57.8	44.8	44.8	33.8	83.7	94.4	1.1	3.8
1958	62.3	48.3	58.4	44.1	77.0	86.8	0.7	2.3
1959	67.7	52.5	72.6	54.8	64.7	72.9	0.6	2.1
1960	72.8	56.4	84.1	63.8	75.0	84.5	1.1	3.9
1961	74.8	58.0	91.0	68.7	64.2	72.4	1.5	5.4
1962	85.9	66.6	99.4	75.0	82.6	93.1	2.5	9.0
1963	100.8	78.1	106.2	80.2	87.4	98.5	10.2	36.3
1964	105.5	81.8	116.6	88.0	72.3	81.5	15.3	54.2
1965	129.0	100.0	132.5	100.0	88.7	100.0	28.2	100.0
1966	149.7	116.0	145.6	109.9	127.2	143.4	40.5	143.8
1967	185.5	141.8	165.9	125.2	162.2	182.8	56.4	200.0
1968	238.0	185.0	216.0	163.0	213.0	240.0	89.0	315.0

Sources: Value added in manufacturing is from the Bank of Korea, *National Accounts.* Estimated net fixed capital stock in manufacturing consists of an estimate of initial capital stock plus the annual fixed investment in manufacturing from the *National Accounts* minus annual depreciation, which is assumed to be 7 percent.

[a] The results for the years 1953 through 1967 of the least squares regression of manufacturing value added (V^m), against net fixed capital stock in manufacturing (K^m), imports of intermediate goods (M^i), and exports of manufactured goods (E^m) are as follows:

$$V^m = 6.49 + 0.601\,K^m_{t-1} + 0.241\,M^i + 0.68\,E^m$$
$$(0.043)\phantom{\,K^m_{t-1}}(0.09)(0.182)$$
$$R^2 = 0.994$$

The standard error of estimate adjusted for degrees of freedom = 3.85.

[b] Capital stock is lagged by one year. The estimate of initial capital stock was derived from the incremented capital output ratio for the period 1953–1967 times the value added in 1953.

[c] The imports of intermediate goods are the United States dollar CIF values for all SITC codes, except 04 and 7, converted to *won* at the average 1965 exchange rate of 265 *won* per dollar.

[d] Exports of manufactured goods are United States dollar FOB values of SITC codes 6, 7, and 8 converted at the 265 *won* per dollar exchange rate. The estimated intermediate import and manufactured export figures for 1953 and 1954 are based on the ratio of such imports and exports to total imports and exports in 1955 applied to the total import and export levels in 1953 and 1954.

[e] Estimated.

a demand for industrial output; this has become a significant factor only in very recent years.

Both output and capital stock have grown by roughly the same percent, and the implicit ratio of net fixed capital to value added (one form of the capital output ratio) is slightly less than one for the whole period. By international comparison this is a relatively low ratio. It is probably due both to concentration of investment in noncapital-intensive industries and to some underestimation of past investment. Intermediate imports have grown much more slowly than has manufacturing production, suggesting a considerable amount of import substitution. Still, the ratio of imported intermediate goods was 90 percent of the value added in manufacturing in 1967 and 1968. While these imports include a number of items that are not direct inputs to manufacturing, such as fertilizer, they still do suggest a fairly high degree of import dependence and indicate why the growth of manufacturing has been influenced by the availability of such imports. We turn now to a more detailed examination of these and other influences on manufacturing production.

During the reconstruction period from 1953 to 1958 the principal constraint on manufacturing output was the shortage of productive capacity. The many factories that had been damaged or destroyed during the war had to be repaired or rebuilt and gotten back into production. Demand for industrial commodities was generally in excess of domestic supply plus imports. Inflation persisted throughout these years, and rising prices generally assured that manufactured goods could be sold at a profit. While imports of competitive goods were supplied through foreign assistance, such imports were cut back as domestic productive capability was restored. Assistance was shifted to financing imports of the intermediate goods required by industry. This assured an abundant supply of such inputs at a favorable, consistently overvalued, exchange rate. Thus manufacturers had adequate markets and raw materials and mainly needed capital goods to expand production.[9]

The rehabilitation of facilities started even during the war and was supported by foreign assistance. Initially, it was concentrated on the consumer-goods industries that could supply the basic needs of the population. By 1953, production of a number of commodities such as cotton textiles, rubber shoes, and soap had equaled or exceeded prewar levels. Textiles and other consumer-goods industries were further expanded in the following years; a few industries, such as rubber products and soap, appear, however, even by 1953 to have attained a condition of excess capacity which persisted throughout the next five years.[10]

Also during this period a number of new industries were started in South Korea in an effort to provide substitutes for imports. A few of these, such as cement and sheet glass, were based mainly on domestic raw materials. Others, however, such as wool and synthetic spinning, plywood, and newsprint, were heavily dependent on imported materials. In the latter case the amount of import substitution resulting from the new investment was relatively limited, but so long as the supply of intermediate inputs (through aid) was abundant and the domestic market was both protected and growing, production could increase rapidly.

This pattern of forces, which contributed to high growth in manufacturing, began to fall apart in the late 1950s. Both private consumption and investment demand were curtailed by a tightening of fiscal and monetary policies. At the same time the supply of foreign assistance was reduced, which resulted in a decline in imports and shortages of raw materials for the import-dependent industries. The government imposed strict import controls and end-user allocation systems, which spread the reduced supply of intermediate imports among existing producers. Despite the existence of considerable excess capacity in many areas of manufacturing, investment continued, although at a slower rate than during the previous rehabilitation period because the system of import controls and investment subsidies encouraged the buildup of idle capacity.

The constraints on aggregate demand in this period are indicated in a number of ways. The rate of growth of private consumption declined from an annual average of 6 percent from 1953 through 1958 to 3 percent from 1958 to 1961. The marginal propensity to consume in relation to changes in GNP dropped from 95 to 70 percent. The share of private consumption in gross expenditure declined from 80 to 76.5 percent. The share of gross fixed investment also fell slightly. Evidence of the actual fiscal and monetary constraints is found in the rise in the ratio of taxes to GNP, from 7.7 percent in 1957 to almost 10 percent in 1960–1961, and in the slower growth of bank credit and money supply during the same period. As a result of these measures, for the first time since Korea's independence the annual rate of price increase dropped below 10 percent.

The cutback in foreign assistance, which occurred after 1957, was due to a phasing-out of the UN Korean Reconstruction Agency Program and a reduction in direct United States aid. The Korean response to the decline in external resources was mainly in the direction of tighter controls, rather than changes in the exchange rates or tariffs. Thus the reduced supply of intermediate imports had to be divided among a growing number of domestic producers, who were generally able to raise the prices of their products and increase profits per unit of output even though the volume of output was diminished.

Some indication of the depressed state of raw materials imports for manufacturing from 1958 through 1961 can be gained from Table 7.15,

Table 7.15 Imports of Raw Materials for Manufacturing
(in millions of United States dollars)

Raw material	1958	1959	1960	1961	1962
Raw rubber	4.5	6.7	7.6	5.8	5.9
Lumber	11.1	6.5	8.1	7.4	18.4
Pulp	1.7	2.7	3.4	5.0	8.3
Oil	2.7	2.5	2.5	3.9	3.9
Others	1.5	1.1	1.4	1.7	3.2
Chemicals	22.6	20.7	20.7	21.4	32.0
Papers	15.7	7.1	7.7	4.5	3.6
Textile yarns	12.7	15.8	18.1	18.8	28.8
Fabrics	48.8	43.9	46.4	42.1	50.2
Base metals	18.5	12.1	14.7	11.1	29.4
Total	139.8	118.9	130.6	121.8	184.8
Percent change from previous year		−15.0	9.8	−7.0	51.7
Growth rate of manufacturing		8.7	7.5	2.7	15.0

Source: Economic Planning Board, *Economic Survey 1963* (Seoul, 1963), p. 52, for all statistics except the growth rate of manufacturing, which is derived from the GNP accounts in constant 1965 producers' prices.

which shows that such imports were actually below the 1958 level for the three succeeding years and that the growth of manufacturing output declined steadily.

The dependence of manufacturing production on imports is given in Table 7.18, which shows the total import requirements per unit of output from the interindustry tables of 1960. The average import coefficient for all manufacturing was 26.9 percent, and 20 of the 27 manufacturing sectors have coefficients above .2. This degree of import-dependence, spread out across most types of manufacturing, made it inevitable that changes in manufacturing output would be reflected in changes in imports of intermediate goods, or vice versa.

During the stagnation phase, investment in manufacturing declined from the high levels of the mid-1950s, but was still apparently adding to capacity more rapidly than output was growing (see Table 7.14). Evidence on these developments is not fully reliable because there are no statistics on investment by type of manufacturing industry. But by 1961 estimates of unused capacity show that it was very substantial, especially in heavily import-dependent consumer-goods industries such as food processing.[11] These estimates of available capacity may be exaggerated because quotas for the import of raw materials were generally allocated on the basis of existing capacity. Not only was there an inducement for industrial producers' associations to overstate the industry's capacity in order to justify a claim for more imports of that industry's main raw materials, but individual producers within the industry also tried to increase their share of the market by claiming that absolute or uneconomic capacity was in fact operable or even by building new capacity despite the fact that their existing facilities were not being fully utilized.

From 1958 through 1961 these problems of the manufacturing industries provoked considerable debate within Korea over the country's basic industrial structure and policies.[12] Most observers suggested that the structure was seriously unbalanced because consumer goods rather than intermediate and capital goods were being emphasized, because of overdependence on imports, and finally in terms of producing only for the domestic market rather than for both domestic and international markets. While there was fairly general agreement on the existence and nature of the imbalances that were contributing to stagnation, there was disagreement about causes and proper corrective actions. One dilemma was that a shift of emphasis to intermediate and capital goods industries would mean more capital-intensive, less labor-absorbing industries, which was undesirable and probably uneconomic given the large number of unemployed and the generally skilled nature of the labor force. This was reinforced by investment project analyses, which frequently showed that production costs for relatively small scale plants to meet the intermediate and capital goods needs of the domestic market would be well above prevailing world market prices.

This led, however, to a second dilemma. Because such cost comparisons were frequently made with the prices of Japanese suppliers, they raised the issue of whether Korea should continue and even increase its dependence on Japan for the more capital-intensive intermediate and capital goods, or whether it should produce its own even if at higher prices. Strong nationalistic sentiments, personified by President Syngman Rhee, argued against tying Korea's economy to that of Japan. The foreign aid agencies which were being asked to finance new investment in the capital-intensive industries were more influenced by the international cost-comparisons and a desire to strengthen relations between Japan and

Korea. They were therefore slow to take on new projects.[13] But the slow-down in industrial growth and the growing excess capacity in the lighter industries kept up the pressure to move in some direction to escape from these dilemmas.

The means of escape devised by the Military Government in 1961 and 1962 involved movement in several directions. As short-run measures, they relaxed the restraints on aggregate demand by shifting to more expansionary monetary and fiscal policies. After a devaluation in early 1961, they also eased up on import quotas, and the inflow of imported raw materials jumped sharply in 1962 (see Table 7.15), with industrial production going up by 15 percent.

The longer-run measures, as spelled out in Korea's First Five-Year Economic Plan, involved expansion of investment in power and energy sources for industry; further import substitution in basic or key industries such as cement, fertilizer, iron, and steel; and, finally, policies and incentives to increase exports.[14] While the last of these measures—the efforts to raise exports—was the object of considerable uncertainty and skepticism, in fact the response of exports proved to be more rapid and more pervasive in its effects on the whole economy than even the most optimistic proponents had anticipated.

This response was strongest in manufacturing, despite the fact that South Korea had never before been a significant exporter of manufactured goods. The absolute growth of commodity exports and the relative increase of the manufacturing share are indicated in Table 7.16. Total exports in 1968 were 14 times the 1960 level, giving a compound growth rate of nearly 40 percent for the period. The share of manufactured goods rose from a range of 10 to 20 percent of total exports prior to 1960 to nearly three-fourths by 1968. It is clear that 1963 was a turning point, in that exports of manufactures increased fourfold or by $29 million and accounted for practically the total increase in exports over the 1962 level. The expansion of manufactured exports was only $20 million in 1964, but in the three succeeding years it averaged over $50 million increase per year.

The impact of these changes in exports on total and sectoral production can be approximated by using the input-output tables for 1963 and 1966 to estimate the total direct and indirect demands generated by exports. The results of such an analysis are shown in Table 7.17. The dependence of total production on export demand more than doubled between 1963 and 1966. Agriculture, forestry and fisheries, and manufacturing had larger relative increases, whereas mining, which is the

Table 7.16 Exports of Manufactured and Nonmanufactured Commodities, 1955–1967 (in millions of U.S. dollars)

Year	Manufactures[a] Amount	%	Nonmanufactures Amount	%	Total Amount	% Change
1955	1.5	8.3	16.5	91.7	18.0	
1956	2.5	10.2	22.1	89.8	24.6	+36.7
1957	4.0	18.0	18.2	82.0	22.2	− 9.8
1958	2.5	15.1	14.0	84.9	16.5	−25.7
1959	2.2	11.1	17.6	88.9	19.8	+20.0
1960	4.1	12.5	28.7	87.5	32.8	+65.6
1961	5.7	13.9	35.2	86.1	40.9	+24.7
1962	9.6	17.5	45.2	82.5	54.8	+34.0
1963	38.6	44.5	48.2	55.5	86.8	+58.4
1964	57.7	48.4	61.4	51.6	119.1	+37.2
1965	106.4	60.8	68.7	39.2	175.1	+47.0
1966	153.0	61.1	97.3	38.9	250.3	+42.9
1967	212.8	66.4	107.4	33.6	320.2	+27.9
1968	335.1	73.5	120.3	26.5	455.4	+42.2

Source: Economic Planning Board, Korea Statistical Yearbook, 1964 and 1967.
[a] Manufactures are SITC codes 6, 7, and 8.

sector most dependent on exports, showed a lower rate of increase. By 1966 both mining and textiles derived roughly one-fourth of their total demand from exports, light manufacturing and metal products were near 15 percent, and the rest of manufacturing was around 10 percent. As exports continue to rise as a proportion of GNP and as manufactured

Table 7.17 Dependence of Sectoral Production on the Direct and Derived Demand for Exports in 1963 and 1966 (in percent)

	1963	1966
Agriculture, forestry, and fisheries	1.8	4.7
Mining	17.8	26.0
Manufacturing	6.6	14.8
Food, beverages, and tobacco	3.2	7.6
Textiles	8.3	24.0
Other light manufacturing	6.1	15.5
Chemicals and ceramics	3.5	9.7
Metal products	13.5	17.1
Overhead and services	6.3	10.3
Total	4.7	10.6

Source: Derived from the 1963 and 1966 Input–Output Tables in the Bank of Korea Economic Statistics Yearbook, 1966 and 1969.

goods increase as a proportion of total exports, the dependence of manufacturing production on export demand can be expected to increase further.

Exports not only substantially stimulated demand for manufactures but also earned the foreign exchange to buy more imports. Furthermore, the government removed all taxes and restrictions on imports of intermediate goods that were to be used to produce exports. Thus the import constraint was effectively removed for those industries that were supplying the export markets, and they were able to expand production up to the limits of export plus domestic demand or of their available productive capacity.

As has already been indicated, there was much unused capacity in manufacturing at the beginning of the rapid growth period, especially in the light manufacturing industries that also depended heavily on imported raw materials. Beginning about 1963, many of these industries found that they could effectively compete in world markets. They had idle capacity and were given unrestricted access to imports. These conditions were the basis for the rapid growth that followed.

One further condition contributed to the competitiveness of Korean exports and the capability to expand exports quickly. This was the so-called unbalanced structure of manufacturing, resulting from the slower development or even absence of the more capital-intensive intermediate-goods industries. If Korea had invested more heavily in such industries during the 1950s and early 1960s, then it would have been reasonable to expect that the export industries would depend on domestic sources for their intermediate goods; if these domestic sources had production costs in excess of world prices, the export industries would have been at a disadvantage in trying to compete in world markets. As it was, the export producers were permitted to import intermediate goods even if comparable goods were available domestically, thereby assuring them access to such inputs, from either domestic or foreign sources at world prices. Therefore, the unintegrated structure of Korean manufacturing and the heavy dependence on imported inputs, which had been harshly criticized in the past and cited as a harmful effect of foreign aid, resulted in a lower domestic value-added from export production than might otherwise have occurred, but it also enhanced the competitive position of Korean products in world markets.

The effects of this can be seen by comparing the import coefficients of the manufacturing sectors in 1960 and 1966, shown in Table 7.18. These show that the import dependence of most light industries

Table 7.18 Import Coefficients for Manufacturing

Manufacturing sector	Direct plus indirect imports	
	1960	1966
Processed foods	.225	.159
Beverages and tobacco	.109	.066
Fiber spinning	.595	.532
Textile fabrics	.426	.387
Finished textile products	.358	.273
Sawmills and plywood	.241	.561
Wood products and furniture	.163	.278
Paper	.280	.302
Paper products, printing, and publishing	.288	.190
Leather and leather products	.181	.177
Rubber products	.537	.451
Basic chemicals	.259	.331
Intermediate chemicals	.360	
Chemical fertilizer	.235	.181
Finished chemical products	.365	.323
Coal products	.096	.094
Cement	.149	
Other ceramic, clay, and stone products	.201	.152
Iron and steel	.261	.508
Steel products	.261	.457
Nonferrous metals and primary products	.178	.241
Finished metal products	.275	.387
Machinery, except electrical	.209	.284
Electrical machinery	.261	.278
Transport equipment	.232	.315
Miscellaneous manufacturing	.260	.307

Source: Bank of Korea, *Economic Statistics Yearbook,* 1966, 1969.

decreased between these two years but that the import dependence of all the heavier industries went up. Thus there was growing integration in the lighter industries, which were the major export producers. The exceptions were plywood and wood products, for which import coefficients went up sharply because of the need for imported logs. In the heavier industries, on the other hand, integration and import substitution were not forced. These industries were permitted to import much of their raw materials and intermediate goods, which helped to hold down production costs.

The resultant growth of Korea's manufacturing industries became to a degree self-reinforcing for a number of reasons. Improved foreign exchange earnings from exports and receipts from other sources eventually permitted a broad relaxation of restrictions on imported raw materials, a step that stimulated most sectors of manufacturing, whether they were producing for the export or the domestic markets. As idle capacity was used up and the demand for new manufacturing investment increased, the external resources were available for the accelerated investment that came in 1966 and 1967.

For the postwar period as a whole, the growth and structure of manufacturing appear to have been guided by a shifting pattern of supply constraints and demand pressures. Initially, limitation of productive facilities was most acute and the abundant supplies of imported intermediate goods plus a strong demand for basic consumer goods caused a rapid buildup of capacity in the import-dependent, consumer-goods industries. This investment was financed mainly by foreign assistance. After 1957, restraints were applied to both consumer demand and intermediate imports, and these became the limiting factors on industrial output. Continued investment resulted in substantial excess capacity throughout most industrial sectors. Then, from 1963 on, a restructuring of foreign trade policies gave a strong stimulus to exports, especially of manufactured goods. This absorbed the redundant capacity and directly or indirectly generated the foreign exchange resources for additional intermediate imports and new investment. Thus, the export-led industrial growth removed the immediate or proximate demand-and-supply constraints. This resulted in rapid expansion that eventually pushed up against the barriers of infrastructure and organizational capacity. Export growth also took some pressure off the demands that were frequently expressed in earlier years for more rapid expansion of heavy industry.

8 / The Patterns of Economic Policy

The critical role economic policies played in transforming the structure of the Korean economy, as well as in moving it in to a high growth path, has been noted at various points in the preceding discussion. Before undertaking a systematic appraisal of these policies and their effects, it will be helpful to indicate the general economic objectives that were being sought by the Korean government. Inevitably, there is some difficulty in identifying objectives with precision. There is even more difficulty in assessing the relative importance attached to them by the policymakers, as well as the changes in their importance that occurred over time.

OBJECTIVES OF KOREAN ECONOMIC POLICIES

As indicated in Chapter 4, the Military Government in 1961 brought with it a relatively strong emphasis on economic development and eventual achievement of national self-sufficiency. Earlier, economic goals had been less clearly defined. There had also been much more of a mixture of competing political and economic objectives before 1961, with a resulting conflict regarding certain aspects of development.

In the immediate postwar period, the main economic objectives of the Rhee government were: (1) rebuild the infrastructure and industrial capacity that had been destroyed by the war; (2) maintain strong military forces to forestall any new attacks from the North; and (3) improve the private consumption levels within the limits of domestic production and available foreign assistance.

These objectives called for high levels of investment and of government and private consumption, and they competed with each other for the available supply of resources. In the short run the major means by which resources could be augmented was foreign assistance. Therefore, the Korean government sought to mobilize additional resources by maximizing such assistance. This approach to the three primary objectives of the reconstruction period inevitably encountered some resistance from the main aid supplier, the United States, but there was nevertheless a steady increase in aid until 1957. The average inflow from 1953 through 1958 was $270 million per year, or roughly $12 per capita per year; this was nearly 15 percent of the average annual GNP per capita at that time.

As the productivity of the Korean economy increased, the conflict of objectives between aid donor and recipient sharpened. The basic issue was over domestic resource mobilization, that is, over the share of the increasing output that should be saved or taxed to provide resources for investment, for the maintenance of military forces, and for other essential government services. This conflict had a major impact on the entire range of economic policies in Korea throughout the postwar period. Taking many forms, it at times had harmful effects on the political and economic development of the country.

Unfortunately, quite often this issue was posed, by both Korean and American officials, in terms of a direct conflict between domestic resource mobilization and foreign assistance. Conceptually, a target rate of growth and "required" military expenditures were assumed, so that any additional resources that could be diverted from domestic consumption were expected to be matched by a reduction in external aid. Eventually this concept was changed so that the rate of growth and the level of investment were transformed from fixed targets into variables. This change meant that domestic resources and foreign assistance or foreign capital inflow became complementary, rather than being considered as pure substitutes for each other.

From the inception of the Military Government, there was a growing and finally predominant emphasis on achieving an accelerated growth of output. Within several months after the military coup, the target growth rate of the First Five-Year Plan (1962–1966) was pushed up to 7.1 percent, from a previously contemplated 5.2 percent per annum. The target for the Second Five-Year Plan (1967–1971) was again set at 7 percent, but because realized growth averaged nearly 10 percent from 1963 through 1966, the government in 1967 raised its planning sights to the 10 percent level. Along with, and related to the rise in growth targets, there was a growing willingness to utilize commercial loans from abroad,

Both the military and DRP governments exerted major efforts to induce such capital, as well as to increase domestic savings in order to push up the investment level. The availability of private capital, combined with the politico-economic objective of greater self-sufficiency and independence from foreign influence, had thus by the mid-sixties led the Korean government to accept and even advocate a phased reduction in foreign assistance. This was a major departure from the past, when although the objective of self-sufficiency had been frequently enunciated by Korean officials, it was generally treated as something to be achieved eventually, not as any defined target toward which progress was being made.

Since the Korean War, there have been several other more political objectives or considerations that have influenced economic policies and had significant economic implications. Throughout the Syngman Rhee period the eventual reunification of South and North Korea had been much emphasized. As a consequence, there was an unwillingness to build up the South as an independent and integrated economy. The possibility that unification would again give access to the electric power and heavier industries of the North was given as a reason for holding down the growth of such facilities in the South. After the Rhee period, it was generally recognized that reunification would not occur in the foreseeable future and that investment decisions should not be influenced by its possibility.

Another major objective of the Korean government and people, discussed in Chapter 5, has been to contain Japanese influence in Korea. At times this has taken the extreme form of completely excluding Japanese citizens and of an embargo on trade with Japan; more often it has involved attempts to define the limits of Japanese involvement in matters as varied as the use of coastal fishing areas, foreign trade, forms and terms of capital inflow from Japan to Korea, the residence of Japanese in Korea, and the rights of Koreans resident in Japan. This objective results both from resentment toward a former colonial power and fear that the Japanese would be able to dominate the Korean economy and subvert Korean political processes to serve Japanese interests. Gradually the Koreans have become more confident of their ability to limit Japanese influence; they have also come to see that Japanese activities within Korea could be basically consistent with Korean objectives. Since the restoration of normal diplomatic and commercial relations in 1965, the Koreans have endeavored to increase the inflow of Japanese capital and to make greater use of Japanese resources, though still within a system of constraints.

It is interesting that, throughout the postwar period, the redistribution of income or wealth has not been a major concern of economic policy. This presumably reflects the equalizing effects of a colonial status during which the Japanese had held most positions of economic power and the Korean aristocracy had been largely destroyed; of the land reform carried out in 1949–1950; and of wartime destruction, which eliminated any large elements of extreme wealth in the country. There has been concern about poverty and underemployment, but little evidence of a conviction or expectation that the government should or could do much of a direct nature about these problems in the short run. The experimentation with the National Construction Service in 1960–1962, a labor-intensive reconstruction program, was perhaps an exception but not a successful one.[1] Instead, the tendency has been to look initially to foreign assistance as a source of relief for the extremely impoverished, and subsequently to a high growth rate as the means of providing employment and more equitable income distribution.[2] Thus, to the meager extent that this objective did exist, it could be subsumed under the aid-maximizing and growth-maximizing objectives.

To sum up, in the decade and a half since the end of the war, Korean economic objectives have shifted from the multiple concerns of reconstruction, defense, and maintenance of minimum consumption standards to a more single-minded concentration on growth. Rough surrogates for these two sets of objectives were, in the initial period, the maximization of foreign assistance, and, in the later period, the maximization of investment and production. Defense has continued to be an important objective but, until the attacks from North Korea in early 1968, resource allocations for defense had stabilized. After 1956 there had been no really strong pressure to increase military forces or the share of output going to defense, and the division of responsibility between Korea and the United States for support of the defense effort, once Korean potential for growth was evident, had become a less contentious issue in the mid-1960s. Thus defense needs were in the nature of a minimum constraint that had to be satisfied, rather than one of several objectives to be maximized.

It should also be pointed out that policy objectives, and the changes that took place in them, were intimately related to time horizons. During the years when Korean leaders were concentrating on augmenting the supply of immediately available resources by obtaining additional aid, they were less concerned with the longer-run effects of the uses to which those resources would be put. They were trying to cope with immediate or short-run problems of security, hunger, and survival, rather than with the future growth of output. It was only as the immediate problems became less serious and the prospects for survival improved, as they did in the latter part of the 1950s, that the time perspective became more extended and the people attached increasing importance to the future in relation to the present. Part of the failure of the Rhee government was that it did not adjust to this extension of the time horizon, whereas the military and successor governments, and even the Chang Myon government, which emphasized planning and future growth, responded to, and stimulated, popular expectations as to the future.

With the shift from short-run to longer-run objectives came a parallel movement away from a simplistic notion of mobilizing resources quickly by maximizing aid, regardless of the side effects. Instead, the government and the people became more aware of the importance of resource allocation as the determinant of future growth. Increasingly by the late 1950s, questions were raised about the wisdom of building more factories when many existing facilities were idle, or of importing large amounts of relief grain that depressed domestic farm prices. Consequently, pressure built up to restructure policies that had been instituted to meet the short-run objectives but that stood in the way of growth. Eventually this pressure resulted in a more balanced emphasis on resource mobilization and allocation and a realization that some aspects of resource mobilization through foreign aid could have adverse effects on growth. With this perspective, we can now turn to a more detailed analysis of policies and their effects over the postwar period.

OVERALL RESOURCE MOBILIZATION

The Korean approach to mobilization of economic resources has evolved over time as both the objectives of economic policy and the potential availability of various types of resources have changed. In the reconstruction period the emphasis was on foreign grant aid as the principal source that could be expanded quickly and with the least harm to the country's other objectives. There was also a willingness to rely on inflationary financing, rather than to increase public revenues as a means of gaining control over domestic resources. Only after five years of large aid inflows and considerable inflation did the emphasis shift to the domestic fiscal sector. This was due to a prospective decline in aid and heavy pressure from the aid donors to curtail the inflation. As a result of this shift in emphasis, public sector revenues were increased, aid was reduced, and inflation considerably slowed down, but the economy stagnated, so that within a few years the Military Government, impatient to revive production and investment, reverted to expansionary monetary policies. It also began to draw upon external financing other than aid to augment the resource inflow from abroad.

Once again, however, inflation threatened to get out of hand and to have harmful effects on resource allocation. By the close of 1963, heavy United States pressure induced the Korean government to avoid further deficit financing of the budget. While this resulted initially in a drastic retrenchment of public sector resource use, it eventually led to more serious efforts to expand public revenues. As grant foreign assistance continued to decline, further efforts were made to broaden financing sources by means of an all-out campaign to encourage private saving and through the continued expansion of foreign borrowing.

The effects of these more recent measures are amply illustrated by changes in the level of investment, and the sources of saving by which it was financed between 1962 and 1968 (see Appendix Table 7). During this interval investment went up from 13 to 26.7 percent of GNP, domestic savings went from 1 percent to 15 percent of GNP, and foreign savings first dropped from 11 to 6.5 percent of GNP in 1965 and then rose again to 11.7 percent in 1968. The composition of foreign savings, however, shifted from almost exclusively grant aid (transfers from abroad) to a nearly equal division between grants and loans. Domestic savings continued to be dominated by the private sector, but at least the government sector moved from dissaving to positive saving. Because the policy measures that brought about these changes in the pattern of resource mobilization were in many cases the reverse of earlier policies directed toward inducing and absorbing foreign aid, their role and extreme effectiveness can best be appreciated by tracing their evolution from the narrow focus on aid to the broader, more diversified approach.

Korea received foreign aid in the postwar years for the combined purposes of reconstruction and stabilization. While it was generally agreed that additional real resources were needed to meet both minimum levels of current consumption and investment for reconstruction, there was disagreement over the appropriate kinds of real resources and often confusion between the real resources gap and the financial gap. As indicated by Reeves,[3] the Korean government objected to the undersupply of investment goods and the oversupply of intermediate or consumer goods that the United States government insisted were needed for stability purposes. In the United States view, such goods were required not only to meet normal import demands but also to mop up the domestic currency which, in lieu of tax revenues and private savings, was necessary to finance both government (including defense) and business activity in a noninflationary manner. In large part, the confusion about how the financial gaps might be filled was due either to a lack of comprehension of how flexible prices might help to narrow the gaps or refusal to permit the kinds of price adjustments that might bring this about.

Thus, in Rhee's time, the Korean government followed a set of policies that clearly kept the internal and external financial gaps wide open to facilitate financial and real-resource transfers from abroad and to help justify the need for more aid. These policies consisted of an overvalued exchange rate, relatively low tariffs on imports, no efforts to encourage exports, a deficit budget financed by borrowing from the Central Bank when taxes and aid-generated revenues were insufficient, Central Bank financing of commercial bank credit to the private sector, and low interest rates that assured excess demand for credit. Such policies inevitably produced an internal financial gap between government revenues and expenditures, and between financial savings and lending. They also insured an external financial gap between import demand and foreign exchange availabilities. A higher exchange rate would have curtailed import demand and probably increased export earnings. A higher interest rate would have restrained credit demands and would probably have increased savings. Higher taxes would have restrained consumption and added to savings. But the Rhee government insisted on holding to the low exchange, interest, and tax rates so that the imbalances persisted. Their persistence was in turn cited as evidence of the need for more assistance at existing exchange rates to satisfy the excess demand for imports and the excess demand for internal finance.

The main features of the policies for maximizing the inflow of foreign aid during the 1950s can be seen in a comparison of the actual exchange rates on imports and exports with an approximate parity rate based on recent relations in the semifree exchange market (see Table 8.1). Another manifestation was the low ratio of government revenues to GNP and the sizable government borrowings from the Central Bank, despite the large flow of aid-generated counterpart funds to the government (see Table 8.2).

As a consequence of these policies and the willingness, albeit sometimes grudging, of the United States to try to fill the internal and external financial gaps, the levels of foreign grant aid rose steadily from the end

Table 8.1 Comparison of Average Effective Exchange Rate on Imports with Simple Parity Rate

Year	Wholesale price index (1965 = 100)	Average exchange rates for imports	Parity exchange rate based on 1965–1967 ratio of free exchange rate to wholesale price index	Average import rate as percent of parity rate
1955	27.8	34.1	70.1	48.6
1956	36.6	50.7	92.4	54.9
1957	42.5	51.0	107.2	47.6
1958	39.9	55.2	100.7	54.8
1959	40.8	69.5	103.0	67.5
1960	45.2	82.8	114.1	72.6
1961	51.2	115.2	129.2	89.2
1962	56.0	130.0	141.3	92.0
1963	67.5	136.5	170.3	80.2
1964	90.9	207.2	229.4	90.3
1965	100.0	265	252.3	105.0
1966	108.8	272	271.5	100.2
1967	115.8	273	287.9	94.8
1968	125.2	278	313.0	89.0

Source: Wholesale price index from Bank of Korea, *Monthly Statistical Review,* May 1969 and earlier years. Average exchange rate for imports from Bank of Korea, *National Accounts Estimates.*

of the war to the peak of $383 million in 1957. Thereafter they declined somewhat erratically to the $100 million level by 1966–1967. These figures refer only to grant aid from the United States and the United Nations Korean Reconstruction Agency. Since 1966 there has been some grant aid from Japan to Korea, but such aid will be dealt with subsequently in the discussion of more recent efforts to mobilize external resources.

In time, the effects of the aid-maximizing policies of the mid-1950s became increasingly harmful to the growth of the Korean economy. As recognition of these adverse consequences became more widespread, a growing demand to restructure the policies also developed. This was encouraged by word from the United States that the aid level must be expected to decline in subsequent years and that external and internal resource gaps would have to be narrowed accordingly. The Rhee government resisted these pressures for change, a policy that led to the charge that it was following an old and out-moded strategy which was no longer consistent with the longer-run interests of the country.

There was some progress, nevertheless, in raising public revenues and thus reducing the budget deficit and curbing inflation during the last years of the Rhee regime, as will be discussed below. But none of the other basic policy changes was adopted until after the change of governments. Immediately thereafter, the short-lived Democratic party government carried through a major devaluation and the successor Military Government made a first attempt at stimulating private savings by raising interest rates and at encouraging exports by direct subsidies. Along with the continued growth of public revenues, these measures probably would have brought about a steady reduction of the gaps that the grant aid was expected to fill, had it not been for serious crop failures in 1962 and 1963. The food grain shortages not only necessitated a temporary increase in grant aid levels during those two years but also contributed to a new round of inflation that undercut public revenues. But these temporary departures from the new longer-run trends served only to emphasize that grant aid was of diminishing importance in the general area of resource mobilization and that public and private savings and foreign loan capital were becoming the critical variables. It also became clear that policies directed mainly toward justifying and facilitating the inflow of large amounts of grant aid were no longer appropriate.

PUBLIC SECTOR RESOURCE MOBILIZATION

As measured in the national accounts, average government consumption levels in Korea have been about typical for countries at Korea's level of income. But these measures understate the total resources available to, and utilized by, government in Korea. On the other hand, they suggest a higher level of resource mobilization than has actually been achieved. If corrections are made for these two types of distortion, it becomes clear that the government has been a relatively ineffective mobilizer of resources through the normal channels of taxation and a large user of resources. While the gap between normal resource mobilization and utilization was earlier filled by external assistance, in recent years this assistance has been declining and the decline has put heavy pressure on the government to raise more revenues.

These several relations and patterns are represented in Table 8.2, which shows the components of revenues and expenditures in relation to GNP since 1957. The regular revenues, consisting of all taxes, charges, and net proceeds of government enterprises, rose to relatively high levels from 1959 to 1962, the stagnation period. They then dropped precipitously in the following two years, which were years of substantial inflation, and then improved steadily and rapidly from 1965 through 1968. These revenues are the most meaningful measure of public sector resource mobilization, and they show that performance has been very erratic. This will be analyzed in more detail subsequently.

As for the counterpart revenues, they are derived from the sale of grant-type foreign aid. The level of counterpart proceeds used to finance the budget was at a peak in 1958. It declined in the subsequent two years as grant aid was reduced, then rose in 1961 and 1962 as the result of a devaluation in early 1961, which meant that more *won* were generated by each dollar of aid. Thereafter, the relative importance of counterpart declined quite steadily, paralleling the decline in grant-financed imports. The total revenues available for financing government budgetary expenditures were augmented by borrowings mainly from the banking system in each year until 1964, after which borrowings were discontinued. The deficit financing was highest in 1962 and 1963, when the sharp increase in government expenditures in 1962 triggered the inflation that undermined revenue collections in 1963.

In addition to the regular budgetary revenues and expenditures, Korea has received a large amount of military assistance from the United States that is not recorded in the budget, the balance of payments, or the national income accounts.[4] Although there are problems in valuing these military assistance resources, we have developed estimates in Table 8.3 to give some indication of the relation of such assistance to the other resources over which government disposes. The military assistance, which consists of equipment, weapons, ammunition, and other military supplies, declined sharply from the equivalent of 17 percent of GNP in 1958 to about 10 percent in the next three years and then down to an average of 5 percent for 1964–1968.

Viewed in broad terms, the disposition of resources by government thus declined from the very high levels that prevailed from 1958 through 1962. The resource mobilization capability, however, which was improving during the 1958–1962 period, was severely set back in 1963–1964 but recovered rapidly thereafter. Military assistance and the counterpart funds generated by economic assistance have declined very markedly from about 25 percent of GNP in 1958 to 7 percent in 1967–1968. This

Table 8.2 Total Availability and Disposition of Government Resources as Percent of GNP

	Revenues				Expenditures				
Year	Regular	Counter-part	Borrow-ings	Total	General	Defense	Military assistance	Invest-ment	Total
1957	7.3	11.4	2.8	21.5	4.5	5.7	13.4	7.5	31.1
1958	8.8	11.9	2.3	23.0	6.7	6.1	17.0	7.0	36.8
1959	11.4	8.5	.6	20.5	6.2	6.3	9.7	5.6	27.8
1960	12.0	6.8	.8	19.6	6.8	5.9	9.5	4.2	26.4
1961	11.1	8.1	1.4	20.6	7.2	5.6	10.1	6.4	29.3
1962	12.6	8.3	5.9	26.8	12.3	5.9	7.9	7.1	33.2
1963	9.5	5.4	7.0	15.6	6.5	4.2	7.5	4.1	22.3
1964	7.4	4.0	0	11.4	4.6	3.6	4.9	2.4	15.5
1965	8.6	4.5	0	13.1	5.2	3.7	7.2	2.7	18.8
1966	11.2	3.7	0	14.9	5.7	3.9	4.9	3.9	18.4
1967	12.9	3.1	0	16.0	6.8	4.0	4.1	3.7	18.6
1968	14.9	2.0	0	16.9	7.5	4.1	4.8	5.3	21.7

Source: Derived from the statistics on the General Government Budget in Economic Planning Board, *Major Economic Indicators, 1957–1968*, Mar. 1969, p. 28. Military assistance figures are from Table 8.3.

Table 8.3 Estimates of Military Assistance and Its Relation to Korean Defense Expenditures and GNP

Year	U.S. military assistance[a]		Government consumption expenditure[b] (in billions of won)		U.S. military assistance as percent of	
	In millions of U.S. dollars	Converted to billions of 1965 won[c]	Total	Defense-related[a]	Defense-related consumption	GNP
1956	231.2	61	65.7	31.2	195	12.7
1957	265.5	70	66.3	34.1	205	13.4
1958	353.5	94	70.5	33.3	282	17.0
1959	212.4	56	69.8	31.2	179	9.7
1960	213.1	56	71.1	28.7	195	9.5
1961	232.7	62	69.8	28.2	220	10.1
1962	189.5	50	70.4	29.1	172	7.9
1963	194.8	52	73.8	27.1	192	7.5
1964	137.8	37	71.2	28.2	131	4.9
1965	219.2	58	76.0	29.7	195	7.2
1966	168.7	45	84.8	32.4	139	4.9
1967	153.2	41	92.4	33.7	122	4.1
1968	204.1	54	101.7	37.6	144	4.8

Source: U.S. Military Assistance is the sum of regular military assistance plus grants from excess stocks as reported in *Agency for International Development (AID), US Overseas Loans and Grants and Assistance from International Organizations, July 1, 1945–June 30, 1966.* Special report prepared for the House Foreign Affairs Committee (Washington, D.C., Mar. 1967). General Government consumption and GNP estimates are from the Bank of Korea, *National Accounts.*

[a] Military assistance figures are for U.S. fiscal years and are therefore not exactly comparable with the Korean Government consumption expenditure series.

[b] In constant 1965 market prices.

[c] Converted at an exchange rate of 265 *won* per dollar.

[d] Defense-related consumption in constant 1965 prices is estimated by using the ratio of defense expenditures to total government consumption from the current price series.

decline in the relative role of external resources for government has been offset mainly by reducing the share of government in the economy, but also to a degree by better domestic revenue mobilization.

Declining levels of counterpart aid after the peak year of 1957 seemed initially to stimulate a stronger tax collection effort, so that current government revenues went up from 10 percent of GNP in 1958 to 13.8 percent in 1960. Then the devaluation of early 1961 raised the flow of counterpart from a given amount of assistance, and revenue growth stopped. Subsequent inflation shrank the real value of both revenues and counterpart even more, with a consequent decline in the total budget. Finally, from 1965 on, as the relative importance of counterpart became quite limited, the pressures to raise the real size of the budget and increase the government's command over resources by noninflationary means forced a new attack on revenue problems. This produced quick results.

Two notable features of the Korean governmental revenue system have been the perverse response of real revenues to the rate of inflation and the positive response to more forceful tax administration. It is not possible to isolate these two effects and to measure their relative significance because changes in the rate of inflation and in the efficiency of tax enforcement have occurred at the same time. During the periods of relatively limited inflation, as from 1958 through 1962, and from 1965 to 1967, tax administration was tightened, but in 1963 and 1964, when inflation accelerated, tax collection was lax.

While there has been a lag of nearly a year in the assessment and collection of several taxes, which can account for part of the perverse response to changing rates of inflation, the main feature of the Korean tax system is the degree of administrative discretion allowed in assessing most types of taxes. In general the legislated tax rates have been quite high, so that actual assessments have characteristically been well below the legal limits. Bargaining, compromise, and payoff were common features of the assessment process. These conditions meant that the way to increase tax collections was not to raise tax rates but simply to raise assessments. The main tools used by the government for this purpose were to allocate collection quotas among regions, districts, and individual tax officials, and to maintain a system of rewards and penalties for the collectors who met or failed to meet their quotas.

To further strengthen the administrative apparatus, the government in 1966 set up a new Office of National Taxation, and the president took a strong, personal interest in its effectiveness. He appointed one of his trusted subordinates (a member of the original coup group) to head the office and apparently supported him against the political and economic pressures brought by persons who sought relief from the higher taxes. The president also gave public recognition to the largest taxpayers and tried to stimulate an awareness among the public of the importance of paying taxes. While there have been objections to the excessive pressure of tax collectors who were trying to meet their collection quotas, there also seems to have been a general recognition that additional revenues were needed by the government. During a period of high growth such as the country has experienced since 1963, it has been easier to achieve a high marginal rate of taxation without encountering undue taxpayer resistance.

Because of a growing feeling that the limits of increased revenue through stronger tax enforcement were being reached, some new tax legislation was pushed through the National Assembly in late 1967. The new laws broadened the tax base, raised tax rates, and introduced a number of equity and incentive features into the tax system. Whether these changes were needed for continued improvement in the revenue expansion and resource mobilization efforts of government is not clear, but the legislation at least confirmed the government's intention to continue to expand revenues and government savings to levels consistent with the high rates of investment, growth, and levels of public services that have been set for the country.

Western observers have tended to underestimate the capability of the Korean revenue system to expand revenues mainly by stronger administrative action. They have also expressed concern over the equity of a tax system that gave so much leeway to administrative discretion. On the latter point it is very difficult to test the equity of the system because no reliable information is available on the real tax base against which the tax is theoretically assessed. Also there are no grounds for positive assurance that the discretionary judgment of individual collectors is any less equitable than rigid application of the existing laws.

The flexibility of the Korean system has not been fully demonstrated. It may well be, as Musgrave has suggested, that there are upper limits to administrative improvement and that the tax base needs to be broadened and rates increased to expand revenues in the future. But in the recent past, rate and base changes have not been a significant influence on the actual level of collections.

INCENTIVES FOR PRIVATE SAVING

Failure to mobilize significant private savings had been one of the outstanding characteristics of the Korean economy to be noted and lamented as a nearly hopeless cause by both Korean and foreign analysts. Many reasons were offered for the low savings rates, including the low levels of per capita income, inflation, uncertainty about the future stability and even existence of the country, and lack of a savings habit and of institutions to accumulate and allocate savings efficiently. Each of these, except perhaps the one about the absence of a desire or habit to save, had some substance. Taken together they seemed to offer severe obstacles to the expansion of private saving.

The government had on occasion launched campaigns to stimulate saving, most notably in 1962 when the Military Government blocked all demand deposit accounts in the commercial banks and tried, largely without success, to force their conversion into longer-term deposits. But this was typical of government efforts for most of the postwar period, which were based on coercion and exhortation rather than on creating a structure of incentives and conditions to encourage voluntary savings.

These failures, together with the increasing need for savings to support high growth, in 1964 and 1965 led to renewed interest and analysis in the area of mobilizing savings. Several studies assessed the deficiencies of the past and suggested appropriate directions for future policy.[5] There was general agreement that the combination of inflation and low ceilings on the interest rates paid by banking institutions was a strong disincentive to the accumulation of savings deposits in the banking system. This in turn caused the stagnation and decline of organized financial institutions that were primarily dependent on monetary expansion to keep them alive. But such expansion, if excessive, caused further inflation and perpetuated the basic sickness of the banking system. At the same time it was noted that the unorganized financial institutions, which were traditionally quite widespread in Korea,[6] were flourishing and obviously taking over more of the roles of the organized institutions.[7] They were not subject to the interest rate ceilings and could afford to pay interest rates well above the prevailing rates of inflation. As the demand for finance from the business sector increased, because of the high growth and high returns on investment in 1963 and 1964, and as the expansion of credit through the banking system was curtailed in an effort to halt the inflation, the real interest rates on both deposits and loans in the unorganized money markets advanced. They became the main source of readily available funds and most businesses depended on them to some degree.[8]

Finally the Park administration, after reviewing studies of the monetary institutions by Korean economist Lee Chang-Nyol and American consultants Gurley, Patrick, and Shaw,[9] and after being pressed strongly by the United States government as well as the International Monetary Fund, obtained Assembly approval of higher interest rate ceilings in August 1965 and pushed through an approximate doubling of interest rates at the end of September 1965. The change in rates, as shown in Table 8.4, raised the rate on 18-month time deposits to 2.5 percent per month or

Table 8.4   Change in Interest Rates of Banking Institutions
(as of Sept. 30, 1965)

	Percent per annum	
	Old rate	New rate
Interest rates on bank deposits		
Time deposits		
3 months	9.0	19.6 (1.5)[b]
6 months	12.0	26.8 (2.0)[b]
over 1 year	15.0	30.0 (2.2)[b]
Over 18 months	—	34.5 (2.5)[b]
Notice deposits	3.65	5.0
Savings deposits	3.60	7.2
Installment savings deposits	10.0	30.0
Passbook deposits	1.8	1.8
Extra deposits	1.0	1.0
Interest rate on bank loans		
Discount on bills	14.0	24.0
Loans for export and supply of goods to US forces[a]	6.5	6.5
Loans for purchase of aid goods	14.0	26.0
Loans for military supply goods production	14.0	26.0
Rice lien loans	11.0	11.0
Loans on other bills	16.0	26.0
Overdraft	18.5	28.0
Loans overdue	20.0	36.5
Call loans	12.0	22.0

Source: Bank of Korea, *Economic Statistics Yearbook,* 1967 (tables 33 and 34).

[a] In the case of unperformed export or supplies of U.S. offshore procurement, the rate on other bills is applied.

[b] Indicates the actual rate agreed upon by the Korean Banking Association. The rate given in parentheses is the monthly interest rate, corresponding to the annual rate compounded monthly. The maximum rate decided upon by the Monetary Board is 2.5% per month for all time deposits.

34.5 percent per year compounded, which was higher than any of the loan rates except the 36 percent rates on overdue loans. A number of loans, especially those for exports and for longer-term capital expenditures, were continued at relatively low rates and of necessity subjected to continuing loan ceilings or other rationing devices. On regular bank loans, however, the long-standing and pervasive system of ceilings was withdrawn. This meant a shift to indirect means of credit control, which had not really been applied in Korea since independence.

The extent of the needed increase in bank deposit rates was not arrived at in any very scientific manner, being based upon rough comparisons with prevailing rates in the unorganized market, which at that time ranged from 4 to 7 percent per month. It was expected that bank deposits would be more attractive than deposits in the unorganized markets because the former would be less risky. But the government also wanted to set the bank deposit rate high enough to assure a strong favorable response.

It seems fair to say, however, that no one involved in the so-called interest rate reform anticipated anything like the response that did occur.[10] Total time and saving deposits increased by 25 percent in one month, tripled in one year and doubled again the following year. Of more relevance, the increases in these deposits in the two years following the reform were equal to 5 and 6 percent of GNP in the respective years (1966 and 1967). Or, as Kim Kwang-Suk shows, real time and saving deposits (deflated by the wholesale price index) had not increased at all during the three years before the reform, but rose by 372 percent over the succeeding two years.[11] Other dimensions of the growth of savings can be seen in Appendix Table 7.

In an excellent analysis of the effects of the interest rate changes, Kim Kwang-Suk has found that they were a significant influence not only on time and savings deposits in the banks, but also on household saving and gross domestic saving.[12] He goes on to show how the inflow of savings to the banks made possible an expansion of bank lending activity by 80 percent in 1966 and another 75 percent in 1967.[13] He notes also that the Bank of Korea had to adopt strong measures to mop up banking system reserves, so that a multiple expansion of bank credit would not be possible. In part this growth of the reserve base resulted from rising foreign exchange holdings that were to some extent also attributable to the high interest rates (see below).

A final and most significant aspect of the revival of the banking sector following the interest reform was that, while bank lending to business increased greatly, it still could not meet the full range of needs for loan funds. The commercial banks were neither accustomed nor equipped to enter into longer term financing. Their business was confined mainly to meeting working capital needs, especially financing imports of raw materials. The main longer-term lending institution, the Korean Reconstruction Bank, had not tried to attract time deposits and had not raised its deposit or loan rates to the levels of the commercial banks. It preferred to continue to rely for funds on allocations from the government and repayments of past loans.[14] These have proven to be limited sources.

Private enterprises, confronted with a lack of equity financing facilities, a shortage of longer-term loan finance at home, and high interest rates on shorter-term funds, were very much inclined to look abroad for financing their capital expansion needs. The government and the foreign aid programs took some steps to increase such financing through the two longer-term lending institutions, the Korean Reconstruction Bank and the Medium Industry Bank. But, more important, the government opened the doors to external credits from private sources in order to fill the gap in the domestic financing institutions. The Japanese settlement in 1965, and Korea's rapidly improving economic condition and foreign exchange situation had laid the foundations for tapping such sources. And most important, the Korean government had begun to implement policies that encouraged private lending from abroad.

INDUCING FOREIGN INVESTMENT

The first serious efforts to attract foreign private loan and equity investment into Korea were made in 1962. Faced with the prospect of declining grant aid levels and the high investment requirements of the First Five-Year Plan, the Military Government decided that private foreign lenders were one of the more promising sources of capital. It therefore adopted new laws to encourage foreign investment and to provide guarantees of repayment to foreign lenders. The guaranteeing institutions at that time were the Korean Reconstruction Bank and the Bank of Korea; they received government authorization on a case-by-case basis. As was acknowledged in an official government report, this active pursuit of private capital was "quite in contrast to the previous policy of this country, which depended heavily on gratuitous aid."[15]

The attempt to increase the inflow of both public and private loans was viewed not only as a matter of practical necessity but also as a means of moving toward self-support and diversifying the sources of external capital, thus reducing Korean dependence on the United States. It was also part of an effort to broaden Korea's diplomatic ties with Western Europe and other developed areas.[16] The conditions for attracting private credits were relatively favorable because Korea had practically no foreign debt obligations, and also because it was generally felt that the United States would not for the foreseeable future allow Korea to fall into default on debt repayments. The main obstacles to borrowing abroad were the poor performance of the economy in the early 1960s, but the new system of repayment guarantees eliminated much of the risk to the lender.

The response to these inducements was very favorable. Where there had been practically no private foreign loans to Korea prior to 1962, from 1963 the approvals of private loans exceeded those of government loans in every year except 1966 when the amount of government loans approved was exceptionally high. In 1967 and 1968 the approval of private loans increased rapidly when the government introduced a new system of repayment guarantees by the commercial banks that bypassed the need for review and approval by the National Assembly, a process which had proven very unwieldy, requiring much maneuvering and often payoffs by the borrower, and which was sometimes politically embarrassing to the administration. Under the system of commercial bank guarantees, the main responsibility for approval rested with the Economic Planning Board, and frequently the commercial banks, which are all controlled by the government, did not scrutinize the proposed investment before agreeing to guarantee the borrower's repayments. This was clearly an unsound arrangement that was likely to result in many projects being financed by foreign private loans on unrealistic repayment terms. But it reflected in part the failure of the banking system to transform its own resources into suitable types of credit for financing investment, and also the government's desire to expand investment rapidly.

By the end of 1968 the total value of private foreign loans and private investment that had been approved was nearly double that of the government loans (see Table 8.5). Approximately the same relation held for arrivals of imported goods under these loans and investments. This influx of private capital and several other developments brought about a significant change in the pattern of financing of Korea's balance of payments deficit (see Table 8.6). The deficit was relatively large in 1963, then reduced following devaluation in 1964 and 1965. Then it mounted rapidly in the next three years. Net transfer payments were the

Table 8.5 Foreign Loans and Investments (in millions of dollars)

Year	Approvals				Arrivals			
	Government loans	Private loans	Invest- ments	Total	Government loans	Private loans	Invest- ments	Total
1959– 1962	72.7	1.8	2.1	76.6	7.3			7.3
1963	9.2	54.1	5.4	68.7	42.6	23.6	5.5	71.7
1964	36.2	62.1	0.8	99.1	11.6	11.9	0.6	24.0
1965	76.3	78.1	22.3	176.7	5.7	36.1	6.3	48.1
1966	152.9	104.4	4.6	261.9	72.8	110.0	14.5	197.3
1967	87.9	147.7	24.8	260.5	105.2	123.9	9.7	238.8
1968	82.6	469.5	32.5	584.6	73.2	267.1	16.7	356.9
Total	517.8	917.8	92.5	1,528.1	318.1	572.6	53.1	944.1

Source: Economic Planning Board.

Table 8.6 Summary Balance of Payments

	1962	1963	1964	1965	1966	1967	1968
Current account deficit	292.0	402.8	221.0	198.6	323.0	417.1	673.0
Imports	455.2	578.3	432.0	488.4	777.7	1,060.0	1,548.2
Exports	163.2	175.5	211.0	289.8	454.7	642.9	875.2
Net transfer payments	236.5	259.5	194.9	203.3	219.6	225.2	224.0
Private	36.5	52.0	53.9	68.7	97.6	90.7	95.9
Government	199.8	207.5	141.0	134.6	122.0	134.5	128.1
Net capital and monetary movements	55.5	143.3	26.1	− 4.7	103.4	191.9	449.0
Private, net	4.4	49.3	7.3	16.6	183.6	277.7	416.8
Other, net	51.1	94.0	18.8	−21.3	−80.2	−85.8	33.2

Source: Economic Planning Board, *Major Economic Indicators, 1957–1968* (Mar. 1969).

main source of financing through 1966, but thereafter private capital became the dominant element. Even within the transfer payments, there was a shift from government supplied grant aid to private transfers, with much of the latter coming from Koreans working overseas, especially in Vietnam.

Thus, in the relatively brief period of the five years from 1962 to 1967, Korea had moved from an almost exclusive dependence on governmental grant assistance to a predominance of loan financing, especially from private sources, to meet its current account deficit. The total foreign capital inflow in 1966 and 1967 was, in fact, so much larger than the trade deficit that, in each year, foreign exchange reserves increased by roughly $100 million.

There has been serious concern in some Korean and foreign quarters about this greatly expanded reliance on private foreign loans to finance Korean industrial investment. It was charged that the capital goods and even raw materials obtained with these loans were overpriced, making the effective interest rate much higher than the nominal rate; that corruption was involved in obtaining approval of the loans; that the borrowers were receiving undeserved subsidies in the form of lower interest rates on the foreign loans than on funds borrowed domestically; that foreign lenders, especially Japanese, were gaining control of Korean industry and would eventually take over; and that the borrowing was far greater than required to fill the balance-of-payments gap, as evidenced by the buildup of foreign exchange reserves.

On the question of facilitating foreign takeover, the system of repayment guarantees provided considerable insurance since, in the case of default, the Korean Reconstruction Bank or the commercial banks were likely to refinance the debtor, take on the management of the enterprise, and repay the debt, rather than transfer ownership or control to the foreign lender. In fact in 1966 and 1967 the KRB was forced to take over several enterprises, which was cited as evidence that some of the loans had been unsound.

Against the objections to the use of private foreign loans must be weighed the alternatives. The domestic banks were not well equipped to handle such financing, even though after 1965 the commercial banks had the financial resources. The Korean Reconstruction Bank was so slow-moving and so inclined to exact payoffs at each stage in the processing of loan applications that it would probably not have been able to handle a greatly expanded volume of loans even if it had had the funds.

Thus the main alternative probably would have been much lower levels of investment.

Primarily for this reason the government actively promoted the use of private foreign credits. Undoubtedly there was also some collection of payoffs for individuals and for the government's party in connection with the approval of guarantees for these loans; the DRP needed political funds for the election in 1967 and subsequent campaigns.[17] But, equally important, the foreign loan guarantees gave the government, and particularly the Economic Planning Board, a means for influencing the kinds of investment being undertaken.

RESOURCE ALLOCATION: TRADE, AID, AND CREDIT POLICIES

Many of the policy tools that bear upon resource mobilization have also been used in Korea to influence the allocation of investment and other productive resources. Among the most important in the latter connection has been the trade policy complex, including exchange rates, tariffs, subsidies, direct controls, and financing terms. A second major set of tools has involved the allocation of foreign aid and foreign and domestic credits. A third area has involved the use of government investment funds and ownership in selected types of production in order to assure their development. Primarily, the use of these policy tools has been the responsibility of the government, but foreign aid donors have also played a role in the allocation of aid funds for both investment projects and intermediate goods. The aid agencies have even had a significant voice in decisions about longer-term domestic credits derived from aid-generated counterpart funds.

Over much of the postwar period, guidelines for allocation policies have not been well articulated or fully accepted. As a consequence, policies have been changed frequently and forcefully. To a significant extent the erratic nature of policy guidance has been due to the previously described evolution of economic objectives. The transition from aid or short-run, welfare-maximizing objectives to growth-maximizing objectives was not a smooth or clear-cut shift. Consequently the evolution of policies was uneven or sequential, occurring first in one area and then in another.

A second reason for the uneven progression of allocation policies was the ineffectiveness of planning or economic policy coordination (as discussed in the next chapter). There were also some serious conflicts between the Korean government and aid donors as to the objectives of policy and appropriate policy measures. These conflicts included relative emphasis to be put on import substitution versus export expansion, light versus heavy industry, and discretionary versus market-oriented controls as a means of influencing resource allocation. The Korean government, especially during the Rhee regime, favored import substitution, heavy industry, and direct controls. But under the Military Government, and even more so under the successor, elected civilian government, there was a fairly rapid change to an export-based, light industry pattern of resource allocation and greater reliance on market forces, albeit with strong built-in incentives for influencing investment and resource use. Not only did this change contribute to accelerated growth, it also eliminated much of the conflict between aid donors and the Korean government, and also among Koreans. The favorable effects of the shift in policies, while bringing about rapid increase in output and industrialization, offered the promise of expanding demands and thereby justification for the much-desired heavy industry.

Trade policies have clearly been one of the most important tools for resource allocation. In the 1950s Korea employed what Kindleberger has called a disequilibrium system to influence resource allocation.[18] This consisted of a highly overvalued exchange rate that kept down the basic cost of imports; low tariffs or tariff exemption on favored imports such as capital and intermediate goods, accompanied by an extensive set of controls for allocating these goods to producers and other users; and finally high tariffs and/or prohibition on practically all imports that competed with domestic production, especially of manufactures. This system gave the government some very powerful tools for controlling the expansion of industrial capacity and the levels of operation and profitability of existing capacity. It also put the government officials administering the controls in a position to share in profits arising from them; consequently it bred corruption. Finally, the system gave the greatest rewards to those who were most competent at obtaining favorable government actions with the least sharing of the resulting profits.

Because most of the imports in the 1950s were financed by foreign aid, the aid agencies were also involved in initial allocation decisions on capital-goods imports and in subsequent adjustments of import controls to provide protection for new or expanding industries. Here, too, Korean entrepreneurial talents were tested in terms of the ability to obtain agreement from the aid donors on project proposals or import allocation schemes.

The critical issues of trade policy during this period revolved around the magnitude of incentives for favored industries, the kinds of industries that should be favored, and the relative emphasis to be placed on investment goods or intermediate and consumer goods. To summarize briefly, the aid donors generally argued in principle for reduced incentives, although they frequently agreed to high protection for investment that they had supported. They urged a "realistic" or at least a higher, exchange rate to discourage imports, remove some of the excess profits of the import-using industries, and give some encouragement to exports. The aid donors also favored investment in the lighter, final processing industries or the industries using domestic raw materials, rather than in the more capital-intensive intermediate goods industries. And, finally, they insisted upon a mix of imports involving less capital goods than the Korean government wished. Faced with a financial-availability constraint and a desire to forestall inflation, the aid donors wanted to put a large share of their limited resources into intermediate goods that would keep existing productive facilities running, satisfy consumer demand, and avoid the credit expansion and increased domestic spending likely to accompany new investment activity.

The Korean government, which wanted to raise the level of foreign aid, argued repeatedly not only for more investment goods but also for more intermediate goods or food imports if necessary to restrain inflation. It was not willing to raise the exchange rate because low cost capital goods and basic raw materials were particularly important for the new intermediate and capital-goods industries that they hoped to establish. They also wanted low cost food imports to hold down living costs in the cities and to prevent pressure for wage increases.

The disequilibrium system worked effectively during reconstruction, together with the policy of aid donors, to guide investment into the established areas of light industry, but it contributed to the stagnation of the post-reconstruction period. As the level of aid started to decline after 1957–1958, and foreign exchange earnings remained small, the reduced supplies of imports forced cutbacks in both production and new investment. Competition for import quotas for intermediate goods became more intense, and much of the industrial investment was guided by the desire to qualify for larger quotas, even though existing capacity was not fully utilized.[19]

A first step toward disbanding the disequilibrium system was taken by the Democratic party government when it devalued the *won* from an official rate of 65 to a new rate of 100 on January 1, 1961, and then to 130 *won* per dollar on February 2, 1961. The devaluation removed much of the excess demand for imports and resulted in an 8 percent decline in total imports in 1961 as compared with 1960, even though import controls were greatly relaxed for a brief period. It also contributed to the growth of commodity exports by 25 percent and foreign exchange receipts by 50 percent. These trends might have continued had it not been for the renewal of domestic inflationary forces under the Military Government in 1962 and 1963. This caused a rapid expansion of imports and drawdown of foreign exchange reserves in those years and rising internal prices in 1963 and 1964 which pushed the fixed exchange rate back into an overvalued position.

In order to gain more direct control over national resources, the Military Government also restored import controls and made them increasingly detailed and arbitrary. The one major difference between this and the earlier disequilibrium situation was the new emphasis on exports. In 1961 the Military Government had instituted direct export subsidies and in 1962 had added the export-import link system, which continued through early 1964, when there was another major devaluation. Export subsidies in the latter half of 1964 were granted on 71 items and ranged from 5 to 25 *won* per dollar of exports. Han Kee-Chun estimated that the average subsidy on all exports was as follows.[20]

Year	Average *won* subsidy per dollar of export
1961	7.4
1962	10.3
1963	4.1
1964	3.5

The linking rights in addition gave exporters special access to import licenses for the most restricted, and therefore the highest profit, imported goods. These two types of subsidies made possible continued rapid growth of exports in 1963 and 1964, despite the increasing overevaluation of the exchange rate and the high levels of domestic demand associated with the inflation.

Between May 1964 and March 1965 the pattern of trade policies was again largely reversed, with a reduction of direct controls and direct subsidies. The exchange rate was devalued from 130 *won* to 255 *won* per dollar on May 3, 1964. The new foreign exchange regulations adopted at that time provided for a floating exchange rate, but it was not actually allowed to float until after March 22, 1965. Along with the initial devaluation, the linking rights for exports were discontinued, and in the following year, direct export subsidies were terminated. The main source of incentives for exports thereafter shifted to more indirect means, that is, to the exchange rate, favored access to credit and imported raw materials, and almost complete tax exemption on export production. Although the cost of imported capital and intermediate goods went up as a result of devaluation, the expanded and easy availability of such imports for the export producers and the credit to buy them were more than offsetting compensations.[21]

Thus along with the easy access to external private loans, which will be described below, the export industries were given low interest rates and full financing of current production costs. On obtaining an export letter of credit from a foreign buyer, the export producer was able to buy all his imported inputs on a three-to-four-month deferred payment basis and to obtain loans from the domestic commercial banks for the full domestic production costs. Both types of financing were at 6 to 7 percent per annum interest rates, which were negative rates in real terms, that is, corrected for the average rate of inflation, and were about 20 percent per annum less than the general bank short-term rates after the interest rate reform.[22]

On the other hand, the import-substitute industries that were producing mainly for the domestic market found their profits somewhat curtailed. Not only did the costs of imported raw materials go up, but their markets were also diminished to the extent that export producers bought imported rather than domestically produced intermediate goods. Another pressure in the same direction was the continuing if gradual reduction of quantitative restrictions on imports for 1965 through 1967, which increased competition among domestic industries.

While the weight of incentives, both direct and indirect, shifted increasingly away from import substitutes and toward exports in 1965 and 1966, a second major factor was also working in the same direction. This was the political and administrative backing for an all-out government campaign to expand exports, typified by the constant setting of seemingly unattainable export targets, their attainment, and then the setting of even higher targets. The president took a strong personal interest in export expansion and was primarily responsible for continuously elevating the targets. He held monthly meetings to review the progress of the export drive and to ensure that no administrative obstacles impeded export growth. Procedures were simplified; special consideration was given to exporters who were having difficulty filling their orders; and embassy staffs abroad, up to and including the ambassadors, were pressed into service as export-promoters. Briefly, all parts of the Korean government apparatus that could be of any help were recruited for the export drive. The political leadership made it clear that performance would be judged on what an individual or an agency had contributed to the growth of exports. In a relatively authoritarian, achievement-centered bureaucracy such as Korea's, these can be powerful stimuli.

It is difficult to estimate the real value of the various export incentives and even more so the significance of direct government efforts to promote exports. The combination of low interest rates, easily obtained loans, no restriction in imported inputs, tax exemptions and reduced public utility rates, which are available to the export producer, would all have to be compared with the actual or imputed costs incurred by nonexporters. These are not accurately measurable. Any result would most likely be misleading and less useful than a simple suggestion that the incentives and encouragement given to exports were sizable and effective.

It has been argued that these recent government efforts to promote exports have been excessive—that they were inefficient because they provided unnecessarily large rewards to the exporters, that they encouraged exports of commodities in which Korea did not have a comparative advantage, and that many of the exports involved very little real domestic value added when compared to the very large imported inputs. It would be unreasonable, of course, to suggest that such strong incentives should be carried on indefinitely. There has, however, been ample justification for such measures in the past because Korean exports had previously been so low in relation to import levels or normal export levels for a country of Korea's level of development. In other words, the extensive disincentives for exports of the 1950s needed to be counterbalanced by the incentives of the 1960s. These policies should probably be continued until exports reach what seems to be a normal share of GNP.

It would also appear that concern about comparative advantage or low domestic value added has been largely unfounded. It is unlikely that the existing incentives would lead to exports of commodities with a serious disadvantage, because the selling prices are generally set by world market competition, and there are limits to the profits that can be gained by cutting costs on the basis of the incentives. The dangers of misallocation of investment or excessive profits are also much greater for import-substitute industries, where domestic markets are protected and domestic prices can be pushed up to several times the world market prices. This cannot be done with exports. Consequently those exports that are marginally more profitable because of the export incentives are unlikely to be seriously inefficient suppliers of the domestic market should the export incentives be removed.

Finally, in a country such as Korea, with limited raw materials, an unintegrated industrial structure and a skilled labor force that receives low real wages, it is inevitable that exports should consist mainly of labor-intensive processing of imported raw materials and intermediate goods. In time, as a more integrated and capital-intensive industrial structure is developed, the domestic value added in exports will undoubtedly rise, but there is no reason to push for this too rapidly or to move away from export patterns that make maximum use of Korea's most abundant resource. This appears to be precisely what Korea's trade policies of the past few years have managed to achieve, and they are becoming a model for other countries with seriously unbalanced foreign trade and declining traditional export sectors.

In addition to trade policies, allocation of aid funds for projects was, during the 1950s and early 1960s, one of the principal means of influencing investment patterns. Until very recent years, most of the major investments either for reconstruction or for new projects were financed mainly with foreign aid. Therefore the decisions on these aid projects by both the Korean government and the principal aid donors, UNKRA and the United States, were a major factor in setting the investment pattern. Admittedly, the incentive structure from trade and other policies was important in stimulating project proposals from the private sector, but the approval of aid projects served as the screening device on the bulk of the new projects, at least until 1962–1963. To some extent willingness to allocate aid funds to certain kinds of projects undoubtedly led to investment by private or government enterprises in some cases in which the incentives for investment would otherwise have been weak.

Influence on investment, moreover, was not only exerted by the government and aid donors through control of the sources of external capital. Because of the need to finance domestic investment costs, as well as imported capital goods of Korean industry, and especially because domestic savings were not forthcoming in sufficient magnitude prior to the interest rate reform, the Korean Reconstruction Bank was formed in 1954 to provide longer-term loans to Korean enterprises. Also the Agricultural Bank, which later became the National Agricultural Cooperatives Federation (NACF), was used to channel funds to agriculture and fisheries. Both the KRB and NACF depended mainly on aid-generated counterpart funds for their financing. In this way aid inflows were made to support both the foreign and the domestic costs of most projects. By controlling both sources of financing, and also by manipulating import restrictions or domestic price ceilings to affect the profitability of different productive activities, the government and the aid donors had a powerful set of tools for channeling investment activity.

The allocation of grant aid financing from the United States for various projects is given in Table 8.7. The distribution of KRB loans is

Table 8.7   AID Grant Project Assistance by Sector, 1958–1966

Sector	Amount (in millions of dollars)	Percent
Agriculture	20.4	8.6
Mining	11.9	5.0
Manufacturing	39.3	16.5
Power	27.4	11.5
Construction	5.9	2.5
Transportation	61.9	26.1
Health, sanitation	25.0	10.5
Education	15.1	6.3
Miscellaneous	30.9	13.0
Total	237.8	100.0

Source: Bank of Korea, *Economic Statistics Yearbook,* 1965, 1967.

shown in Table 8.8. United States project aid was distributed quite broadly across the productive sectors, with the largest share in transportation (26 percent), the next in manufacturing (16 percent), and the remainder divided about evenly among electric power, agriculture, and social services. The allocation of KRB loans was more heavily concen-

Table 8.8   Outstanding Loans of the Korean Reconstruction Bank by Sector, 1958–1966 (in billions of *won*)

Sector	1958	1959	1960	1961	1962	1963	1964	1965	1966
Agriculture	0.1	0.2	0.2	0.3	0.3	0.3	0.3	0	0.5
Manufacturing	6.5	8.6	9.7	10.5	11.5	12.2	14.2	18.6	23.7
Mining	0.9	1.2	1.4	1.5	1.4	1.8	1.7	1.8	2.0
Electricity	1.6	1.6	1.6	5.2	7.6	9.4	11.1	11.1	13.3
Transportation	0.3	0.6	0.6	0.4	0.6	0.7	0.9	1.3	3.0
Construction	0.8	1.7	1.9	2.1	2.1	2.2	2.3	2.4	3.7
Services	0.3	0.3	0.3	0.4	0.8	1.1	1.2	1.5	0.5
Total	10.5	14.1	15.9	20.3	24.3	27.6	31.7	36.8	46.6

Source: Bank of Korea, *Economic Statistics Yearbook,* 1965, 1967.

trated in manufacturing, which accounted for about two-thirds of loans outstanding from 1958 through 1960 and roughly one-half thereafter. The share for the category of electricity, water, and sanitation (which was mainly electricity) increased sharply in 1961 and remained near one-third thereafter. The combination of financing from these two sources was thus concentrated largely on manufacturing and infrastructure, with a shift toward infrastructure after 1960.

This system of tightly controlled investment activity, based on the allocation of foreign project aid and of long-term domestic credits from the KRB and other government banks, changed when the Military Government and subsequently the Park administration, faced with declining levels of grant aid for projects and limited supplies of foreign government project loans, opened the doors to foreign private credits. At about the same time, the KRB also began to feel a reduction in available funds due to declining aid levels. As a result the focus of control over at least larger private investments shifted to the granting of approval for repayment guarantees for foreign credits. Such credits were generally first agreed to between private Korean borrowers and foreign lenders, who then sought approval from the Korean government for the issuance of a guarantee. While the Korean Reconstruction Bank actually guaranteed the repayment in *won,* and the Bank of Korea assured convertibility of the *won* into foreign exchange (with the KRB bearing the exchange risk), the Economic Planning Board had the dominant voice within the administration on which projects should be approved. Finally, all such guarantees had to be authorized by the National Assembly, which often complained loudly about specific projects but was generally brought around by various inducements to granting approval.

The system for approving loan repayment guarantees obviously involved a certain amount of bribery. The payoffs were probably larger than was characteristic in the typical aid-financed projects, but whether they led to worse or better allocation of investment is difficult to say. Most of the private loan projects were at higher interest rates and shorter maturities than the aid-financed projects, and they had to meet more severe, commercial profitability tests. Also, they were more dependent on private initiative and more responsive to generalized incentive measures such as the export drive than were the public loans or the earlier grant aid projects. On the assumption that the incentive structure in the mid 1960s, with the new trade and financial policies, was more rational and more conducive to growth than it had been in previous years, the greater reliance on private initiative was justified. The more apparent bribery should be viewed as primarily a cost of operating the loan guarantee system rather than as a strong influence for misallocation of investment.

The allocation of foreign financing among sectors has been very different for the recent loans and direct investments than it had been for the earlier grant aid projects (see Table 8.9). Of the total $1,528 million in foreign loans and investments approved by the Economic Planning Board through the end of 1968, nearly half has gone into manufacturing, with the largest amounts in textiles, and fertilizer. Electric power and transportation together account for 35 percent. The government loans were heavily concentrated on infrastructure projects, while the private commercial loans were mainly in manufacturing. The smaller-scale loans and direct investments were predominantly in the export industries.

Thus, over the longer run the allocations of investment through aid and credits and the means for influencing these allocations have changed along with the changes in the composition of savings. In the earlier period when foreign grant aid was the main source of savings, the government and the aid donors controlled the allocation of aid and domestic credit throughout the economy and thereby exerted a strong direct influence over both the public and private sectors. But as private domestic savings and private foreign capital inflows have grown over the past few years, they have assumed a dominant role in the financing of investment and production in the private sector, especially in manufacturing. Foreign government loans and World Bank loans have gone increasingly to public investment in the infrastructure sectors and to government-owned manufacturing enterprises in such industries as fertilizers and oil refining. The government retained control over the approval of foreign private credits, but the approval process was more flexible and expeditious than that previously associated with grant aid projects. Especially favorable consideration has been given in this process to export-oriented projects. On domestic commercial bank credit, the government has given up its direct allocative controls but it has devised special subsidy schemes through the banking system, again designed to favor the export sectors. These trends corresponded to the movement toward decontrol in the trade sector, also favorable to exports. The total picture in the mid-1960s was thus one of a relaxation of what had been a pervasive system of allocative controls and a greater reliance on market-oriented, but still powerful, incentives for guiding the private sector's resource allocation decisions.

Table 8.9 Foreign Investment Projects Approved through 1968, by Industrial Category[a]

	Number of projects	Amounts of foreign loan or investment (millions of dollars)	Percent of total
Agriculture	12	2.9	0.2
Fisheries	26	73.1	4.8
Mining and manufacturing	236	706.4	46.3
Mining	3	15.9	1.0
Food, beverages, and tobacco	8	8.6	0.6
Textiles	64	167.7	11.0
Wood, paper, and leather products	12	16.9	1.1
Chemicals	24	35.9	2.6
Fertilizer	11	121.3	7.9
Petroleum	5	72.2	5.0
Cement and ceramics	20	104.2	6.8
Metals and metal products	23	47.3	3.1
Machinery and transport equipment	44	52.4	3.4
Misc. manufacturing	22	59.1	3.9
Construction	24	82.9	5.4
Electricity	29	290.1	19.0
Water and sanitation	7	17.9	1.2
Communication	13	42.0	2.7
Transportation	35	240.2	15.7
Other	11	72.8	4.8
Total	393	1528.3	100.0

Source: Economic Planning Board.

[a] Includes all government loans, private or commercial loans with repayments extending beyond three years, and direct private investments that had been approved by the Economic Planning Board. The amounts in each category are:

	Mining and manufacturing	Other sectors	Total
Government loans	150.4	367.4	517.8
Commercial loans	483.4	434.4	917.8
Direct investment	72.5	20.0	92.5

GOVERNMENT OWNERSHIP AND INVESTMENT

The last major means by which the government has influenced resource allocation is through direct government investment and through government-owned enterprises. Although the government inherited the former Japanese enterprises at the time of independence, it divested itself of most of the manufacturing facilities, retaining mainly public utilities such as power, railroads, and communications. It has, however, created new government-owned corporations to pioneer in some of the basic import-substitute industries such as fertilizer and oil refining. Government corporations are also planned for petrochemicals and steel. These are all industries in which there are economies of scale, so that in the early stages of development one producer is likely to dominate the market and establish a monopoly position. The government has preferred to control such industries directly, bearing the risk of innovative investment and assuring that production expands to meet domestic needs, rather than trying to regulate private producers and threatening them with competition from imports. As these industries have become better established and there has been room for several enterprises, the government has opened the way to private investors.

One example of this sequence is found in fertilizer, where the government-owned Chungju Fertilizer Company made the initial investment. This very costly facility took over five years to construct and to be put into effective operation. After a second government-owned plant was built, the government drew upon the experienced staffs of these two enterprises to establish two new joint ventures involving government-owned domestic companies and foreign private companies. Finally, a wholly private, domestic, and foreign joint venture was allowed to build the fifth fertilizer plant, but the Korean government subsequently took over the shares of the private Korean investor when his company was found guilty of smuggling prohibited imports, together with construction materials for the plant. Despite this reversion to government ownership, the trend toward private investment in established industries is still manifested. It was repeated in petroleum refining, where the first refinery was a government-owned enterprise in joint venture with a foreign enterprise, but the second and third refineries are to be purely private enterprises.

Attempts to move the coal-mining industry along the same path have been less successful because the strong popular demands to hold down prices of coal—a mass urban consumption item—have squeezed the profit margins of the newer privately owned companies. The government-owned coal corporation has sustained continuous losses but has nonetheless expanded its operations on the basis of direct government investments or loans from the KRB.

Government investment and enterprises have been important in agriculture, where they have contributed to the expansion of agricultural infrastructure, have expanded the supply of inputs, and have influenced the productive patterns of the farming population. Most of the investment in irrigation, land reclamation, flood control, and agricultural research has been carried out directly by the government with the help of foreign aid and technical assistance.

The government-organized National Agricultural Cooperatives Federation (NACF) has also supplied most of the productive inputs to the farmers and handled an important share of the marketing of farm crops. By controlling the prices of inputs and affecting the prices of outputs through various price support or stabilizing schemes, the NACF together with the Ministry of Agriculture not only has a strong influence on farm income but also can induce changes in cropping patterns and production techniques.

Some notable examples of these efforts are the very rapid increase after 1960 in sweet potato production as a consequence of high price supports (see Chapter 7); the expansion of silk production in response to both export demand and government supplies of improved silk worms and production credits; and the increased use of fertilizer and lime, which followed NACF and Ministry of Agriculture assurances of supplies at reasonable prices. As indicated in Chapter 7, it is not possible to explain definitively the factors causing growth of agricultural output, but increased supplies of improved inputs have been important, and these increased supplies have been provided by government agencies such as the NACF.

CONCLUSION: DEVIATIONS FROM CONVENTIONAL POLICIES

The structural changes that have occurred in the Korean economy in this decade are widely recognized as essential elements in the process of moving a country from impoverishment and stagnation toward self-sustaining growth. They have struck at three main barriers to growth: the investment, saving, and foreign exchange constraints. The remarkable aspect of Korean experience has been the speed with which these changes have been brought about. Although it is still too early to conclude that the transformation is irreversible, there is no evidence of backsliding and no apparent grounds for anticipating a reversion. If the current patterns do continue, then in one of the briefest periods of recent record, Korea will have moved from an economy of low investment, low saving, and low export to one of high investment, substantial saving, and high foreign exchange earnings.

The reasons for these rapid changes are several. In part the very un-favorable structural relations of the past—the minimal savings and export levels and the heavy dependence on foreign aid to sustain only moderate levels of investment—meant that even modest improvements looked good by comparison. Furthermore, the poor performance of the past was in large part the result of various negative policies and institutional arrangements which, when removed or changed, contributed to the recovery.

There were also certain underlying strengths in the Korean economy that were supportive conditions for the rapid growth and structural change. The vigorous, relatively well-educated, reasonably frugal population provided an abundant and productive labor force. Sizable unemployment and the weakness of unions or other labor organizations have kept real wages low in relation to the average productivity of labor, in comparison with many developing countries. But the main forces that activated the processes of growth and structural transformation were the series of positive policy measures specifically directed toward expanding exports, savings, and investment, and the weaving together of economic and political strategies in a mutually supporting manner.

The Park government has moved quickly and forcefully to seize opportunities. Its tendency has been to try to overshoot the mark rather than be caught short in providing incentives for such items as exports or savings. Some inefficiency probably resulted, in that policy measures may have been stronger than would have been necessary had there been more knowledge or analysis of the particular situation toward which the policy was directed. On the other hand, the extreme approach did produce results that have undoubtedly far exceeded their costs. More cautious measures might well have failed. The Korean approach to removing the investment, saving, and import constraints, moreover, deviated from the conventional policy lines that had been followed by most developing countries in recent years. This obviously raises some questions about the appropriateness of the conventional measures or the validity of the assumptions on the basis of which such measures have been recommended.

Conventional policies to increase investment have emphasized holding down the costs of capital goods through favorable exchange rates, tax exemption, direct subsidies, and low interest rates. These measures tend to result in the greater involvement of governments, both foreign and domestic, in the process of investment decision-making and execution. This involvement may be justified on the grounds that market forces are not a good guide for investment, but that should not obscure the fact that government decision-making is often slow, costly, and liable to corruption. In particular, the foreign assistance agencies are extremely slow moving. The time lag between original proposal and full operation of major capital projects that they finance is typically at least five years.

When rapid growth is occurring, such delays in carrying out investments, especially in critical areas of infrastructure, can stifle the growth process. In such cases, the growth of demand becomes the primary criterion of investment and the time dimensions of decision-making and implementation are critical. To speed up the investment process and to increase the total volume of investment, Korea strove to increase the general availability of domestic and foreign credit, including that from private sources with its inevitably harder terms, and moved part way in the direction of market forces, rather than government decision-makers as the final arbiters of investment choice. The investment level has thus jumped sharply, and the normal development period on investment projects has been appreciably shortened.

The conventional approach to increasing domestic saving in poor countries has generally been based upon the propositions that the amount of voluntary private saving will be very limited and that whatever saving will occur will be mainly from the higher income groups out of expanding profits. Consequently, the main emphasis has been on the expansion of government revenues but with some tax incentives for the most likely sources of private saving. The development of specialized institutions such as insurance companies, savings associations, and securities markets, which facilitate private saving by the higher income groups, is also commonly encouraged. On the other hand, it has generally been assumed that in poor countries private savings are not very responsive to changes in the interest rate. Nevertheless, after having first tried to expand public revenues and saving and then resorted to credit expansion and inflation, the Korean government finally raised interest rates on bank deposits and instituted a campaign to promote private savings in the banking system. This resulted in a fourfold increase of such deposits in two years and was a significant factor in raising the domestic saving ratio from 7.6 percent to 11.7 percent in one year (from 1965 to 1966). The banking system was resuscitated and replaced the unorganized money market as the primary source of loanable funds.

The most common approach to solving the import constraint has been to accelerate the import substitution process so as to reduce, or at least avoid, increases in the ratio of imports to GNP. Although there has been growing concern among students of economic development over the efficiency of rapid import substitution, there has also been widespread skepticism about the expandability of exports by the developing countries. Confronted with this dilemma, most countries have been advised to follow a selective approach of import substitution and export expansion guided by comparative advantage.

Korea followed a purely import substitution strategy in the 1950s and rapidly reached the barriers of inefficiency that contributed to the declining growth rates at the end of the decade. In the 1960s, the dominant strategy has been export expansion, especially for manufactured goods destined for developed countries. This resulted in a sevenfold increase in commodity exports from 1960 to 1966 and a rise in the ratio of goods and services exports to GNP from 4 percent to 11.4 percent during the same period.

In essence, Korea has relied upon the efficiency and speed of private investment decisions and private capital inflow, the expansion possibilities of manufactured exports, and the interest elasticity of private savings as the three main devices for overcoming barriers to growth. It would be incorrect to imply that these were the only elements of the growth strategy or that they were responsible for all the growth and structural change that has occurred, but they have probably made the difference between good and exceptional performance.

Korean development strategy, emphasizing inducements for private foreign capital, high interest rates for private savings, and incentives for exports, also had important political implications that were quite different from those associated with the more customary strategies. Whereas the traditional emphasis involves government allocation of underpriced foreign assistance funds and import licenses (with all the possibilities for corruption this entails), as well as strong tax enforcement and high tariffs on imports, the Korean program in the 1960s generated large amounts of realistically priced foreign exchange, which reduced the need for government allocation. It also relied on a system of rewards for savers and exporters. This to some extent transformed the role of government from that of policeman to that of partner. The government helped to secure additional commitments of foreign financing; it raised the incomes of those who saved and those who produced for export; it was active in trying to remove the barriers to obtaining raw materials, finding export markets, and generally improving the efficiency of operations of export producers. There were still many areas in which the government seemed to be more of an adversary than an associate, but the balance shifted to a degree, and the effects on the attitudes of the general population toward the administration and the bureaucracy were favorable.

It was obviously difficult for political leaders and for the bureaucracy to give up many of the sources of income deriving from direct controls over import licensing and bank lending, especially at a time when government salaries had not recovered from the recent inflation. The government's ability to cut back on such controls and to develop a more positive relationship with the private sector was thus due, as pointed out in Chapter 4, to strong government leadership, a nationalistic or public-spirited response of the bureaucracy when they saw that the changes were actually accomplishing something in terms of growth, and undoubtedly some ingenuity in discovering new sources of private income and political funds to replace that previously derived from administering the controls.

9 / The Significance of Economic Planning

Economic planning is a politico-economic process that draws together the techniques of economic analysis and the forces of consensus-building, decision-making, and action-taking that are the heart of the political process.[1] Recent Korean experience attests to the interdependence of the political and economic facets of planning. A series of planning attempts between 1953 and 1961 were sidetracked because the political conditions were inimical to serious consideration, much less adoption and implementation of the plans. Eventually, in 1962, a plan was formally accepted by the government but was subjected to serious criticism as being mainly a political device, rather than a technically sound economic program. Finally, in 1966, when an analytically competent plan was supported by an appropriate political environment, not only were the economic decisions of the government and the private sectors influenced significantly but also the legitimacy of the government was strengthened and the antagonism of some alienated groups toward the government was mitigated.

The first efforts at planning in Korea were begun during the Korean War by the foreign assistance agencies that were trying to assess the patterns and the potential costs of rehabilitating the Korean economy. The main result of this work was a program prepared by Robert R. Nathan and Associates for the United Nations Korean Reconstruction Agency.[2] In 1958, a second planning effort was initiated by the newly established Economic Development Council of the Korean government. This was to be a seven-year plan divided into a three-year and a four-year phase. The plan for the first phase, covering the years 1960–1963, was formulated in 1959 and approved by the cabinet in January, 1960.[3] Three months later the Rhee government was overthrown and the plan was set aside.

In the following year, a new five-year plan was presented by the Economic Development Council, but it suffered the same fate as the three-year plan.[4] The draft was completed just prior to the military coup of May 1961 and was not acceptable to the new government that assumed power after the coup. It did, however, provide the basis for a third planning attempt that was finally carried through to completion and approved in late 1961 as the First Five-Year Economic Plan, 1962–1966.

As a result of criticism leveled against this plan and the poor performance of the economy in 1962, the government decided in 1963 to revise the growth targets and investment program downward. This revision was completed in 1964 but was never given much consideration, because the government was concerned with the more immediate problems of financial stabilization. In time the revised version of the First Five-Year Plan was forgotten altogether, since the overall performance of the economy from 1963 onward was approaching or exceeding the so-called over-ambitious patterns of the original plan.

The Second Five-Year Economic Development Plan was prepared in 1965 and 1966 and approved by the president in August 1966. This basic program has since been supplemented and modified by annual plans, called Overall Resource Budgets (ORBs), prepared each year since 1967.

In the following discussion we shall review Korea's experience with planning in terms of who did the planning, what were the main lines of development strategy in the several plans, and, finally, what was the impact of the planning in both economic and political terms?

The early planning work in Korea was done mainly by foreigners— the Nathan team and others associated with the United Nations and United States assistance programs—because there were very few Koreans with any experience in this area. In the second round of planning activity, from 1959 through 1961, Koreans played the major role, with only limited help from foreign technicians or advisors. A number of Koreans who had recently completed training programs abroad, especially in the United States, were drawn into the staff of the Economic Development Council and the Ministry of Reconstruction where the planning work was concentrated; they were given the main responsibility for preparing the Three-Year Plan and the first version of the Five-Year Plan. An advisory team from the University of Oregon was attached to the Economic Development Council at this time, but, according to its own summary report, the team played a very limited role.[5]

After the military coup, the Supreme Council for National Reconstruction, which had assumed all legislative, executive, and judicial powers, also took an active interest in the planning work. It transformed the Economic Development Council into the Economic Planning Board, combined planning, budgeting, and foreign assistance administration, and charged the planning group with revising the draft Five-Year Plan to conform to some new guidelines laid down by the Supreme Council.[6] The revised plan was drafted mainly by the Korean staff of the Economic Planning Board. It was then reviewed by various Korean advisory groups during the last quarter of 1961 and finally approved by the Supreme Council.

As a result of criticisms of the Five-Year Plan and the continuing irrelevance of planning to current policy decisions, many of the leading planners left the government or shifted to other positions; a new, younger group assumed responsibility for planning. When it was time to begin work on the Second Plan, a number of foreign advisory groups were drawn into the planning work to help the still relatively inexperienced Korean planners. In 1964 the United States Agency for International Development contracted with Robert Nathan Associates to provide a second team of planning experts. In contrast with the earlier Nathan group, this one was to work with and for the Korean government—specifically the Economic Planning Board (EPB)—and was to help prepare the Second Plan. In addition to the Nathan Group, an economic and technical advisory team of the German government attached to the EPB assisted with the planning work. The United States AID mission also took a very active and direct interest in the Korean government's planning beginning in 1965 and, in contrast to the normal pattern of relationships, functioned as a planning advisory group. The AID mission and the Nathan team brought a number of experts in various aspects of planning to Korea in 1965 and 1966; they further contributed to the formulation of the Second Plan.[7] Finally, several teams were brought in to develop programs for particular sectors. These included an AID-supported study of the power industry and a World Bank-supported study of transportation.[8] Thus there was much more participation by foreigners in the preparation of materials for, and the formulation of, the Second Five-Year Plan than there had been in any of Korea's previous planning efforts, except the original Nathan Plan which was a purely foreign product.

This broadening of involvement in the planning process for the Second Plan also took place among Koreans. The various ministries of the government were not only asked to propose projects for inclusion in the investment program, but their representatives also participated in the deliberations on development strategy and planning methodology. Staff from the ministries and government-owned development banks made up the group of ten industry committees that were responsible for assessing the existing structure of production, estimating the future patterns of development, and reviewing the projects proposed for their industries.[9] A number of academic and research groups made studies of topics that were relevant to planning.[10] Finally, some special interest groups and representatives of the public were consulted periodically, over the roughly 18 months during which the Second Plan was being prepared, to obtain their views on national priorities and the approaches being contemplated by the government.

PLAN STRATEGIES AND TARGETS

As W. Arthur Lewis has suggested, there is no single unifying theme to a discussion of development strategies, but instead a judgment as to which issues are important in a particular setting.[11] The issues of strategy that have been of most concern in Korean planning since the end of the Korean War appear to have been: (1) the overall rate of growth, (2) the structure of industrial production and foreign trade, and (3) the division between domestic and foreign savings and between various forms of domestic saving.

Although there are in any given setting practical upper limits on the potential rate of growth, there is also a range over which the rate can be expected to vary, depending upon the commitment of the populace to achieving high growth; the effectiveness of the economic policies of government; and the uncontrollable influences of weather, international politics, and similar factors. In selecting the target growth rates for planning purposes, the planners or policy-makers are likely to be most influenced by what they think is a reasonable upper limit and by the degree of commitment to growth that they either perceive or can hope to instill in the people. Conceptions of a reasonable limit to growth are influenced in turn by recent performance, at least during what are considered to be favorable periods.

In the Korean plans there has been an alternating pattern of projecting continuation of past growth rates when those have been relatively high or of projecting sharp increases in the growth rate when the immediately previous record has been unfavorable. The Nathan Plan, coming right after the Korean War in which so much of the industrial capacity and infrastructure had been destroyed, proposed a very rapid but de-celerating recovery with an implicit compound growth rate of 8.6 percent per annum. In view of the limited information on the previous per-formance of the economy and the fact that this was a reconstruction program concerned with rebuilding along established lines, which was believed to be easier than charting new paths of development, the high growth target did not at that time seem unreasonable. In fact it proved to be far above actual achievement. In the subsequent Three-Year Plan the target growth rate was set at 5.2 percent, which was about equal to the average growth rate of the preceding five years. Then, the First Five-Year Plan, prepared in the midst of the stagnation period, contained a target rate of 6 percent in its first version and 7.1 percent in the final version issued by the Military Government in January 1962. This was roughly double the growth rate of the preceding three years and was much above the levels that the Korean economy had previously been able to sustain for more than one or two years. Thus it had to imply either major changes in policies, commitment, and performance or it simply represented wishful thinking. The government clearly intended the former, but was accused by its critics of the latter. Poor performance during the first year of the plan supported the critics and caused the scaling down of the plan to a 5 percent growth target, but, as previously noted, this was subsequently set aside when the realized growth rate from 1963 on pushed up above the original 7 percent target.

After experiencing several years of very high growth, the 7 percent growth target of the Second Five-Year Plan seemed relatively modest. In subsequent, annual planning exercises the target has been raised to 10 percent,[12] which is only slightly above the average growth rate for the four years 1963–1966. This move to a very high planning target was prompted in large part by experiencing the severe constraints of bottle-necks in key infrastructure areas, such as power and transportation, where it is not possible to fill the shortages with imports. The planners concluded it was necessary to assume the highest possible growth rates in planning for these sectors to avoid constraining the growth of the whole economy.

As the various plans have been drafted and revised over the past 15 years, and the growth targets have been moved about in the range from 5 to 10 percent, there has been little disagreement over the desirability of striving for the highest practicable rates of growth. The arguments have been mainly over what was realistic, with the implied concern that too high targets would result in over-investment in some areas and the release of inflationary forces. The planners have generally tended to advocate the higher growth targets, while those concerned with financial policy have urged more caution.

The other direction in which growth targets have had relevance is in terms of Korea's relations with the suppliers of foreign assistance. The Nathan Plan was explicitly intended to contribute to agreement among aid donors on overall reconstruction objectives and related assistance needs. It failed to serve this purpose because the Korean government never accepted the plan or agreed to its general directions. The high 7.1 percent growth target of the First Five-Year Plan and the related level of investment were judged by one foreign group to exceed by far the potential of the economy, and to need scaling down.[13] Another group, doing an evaluation on behalf of the United States government, while acknowledging that the growth target seemed very high, went on to say that there was not sufficient information on the Korean economy to estimate a practicable rate of growth. As a result of these reports and other assessments, neither the United States nor the World Bank accepted the plan as a basis for determining appropriate levels of their assistance.

More recently, the World Bank formed an international consultative group on assistance to Korea and has been evaluating Korea's growth record and targets as a basis for determining assistance needs. In its initial assessments during the preparation of the Second Five-Year Plan, the World Bank experts concluded that the growth targets were too ambitious and recommended that consideration be given to adjustments necessary to scale down from a 7 percent to a 6 percent growth target.

In time, as Korea's actual growth continued to average near 10 percent in 1966 and 1967, the World Bank raised its sights and accepted 7 percent as near the lower rather than the upper end of the feasible growth range, with the upper limit reaching 10 to 11 percent. The Bank also was increasingly inclined to accept the Korean estimates of the investment and external resource requirements to attain these higher rates of growth.

The main choices confronting Korean planners in the area of industrial structure have involved the division between agriculture and manufacturing, and within manufacturing, the relative emphasis on light and heavy industry. The latter choice also has been related to the split between labor-intensive and capital-intensive production, the degree of integration of the industrial structure versus international specialization, and thus the questions of international trade patterns. As pointed out in the previous chapter, there have been a number of shifts in the thinking of Korean policy-makers since the Korean War, which have been reflected in the plan targets and strategies relating to industrial structure.

The Nathan Plan emphasized the expansion of primary production—agriculture, fisheries, and mining—to satisfy domestic demand and to meet minimum necessary export levels. It also projected extensive import-substitution to meet consumption and investment demands and to bring the import level down to roughly 10 percent of GNP by the end of the plan period. This move toward a more closed economy was deemed necessary because of the apparently limited prospects for boosting the export ratio above 10 percent, and also because of the objective set by the Nathan Plan, that the economy be self-supporting by the terminal year, 1958. Thus the program involved a turn toward self-sufficiency as the only apparent means of achieving trade balance. These trade and production projections proved very wrong, in part because they were not accepted by the Korean government, which therefore did not implement the policies that might have contributed toward their realization, but also because the projections were unrealistic from the very beginning.

One of the critical assumptions of the Nathan Plan was that rice production could be raised quickly and that, by substituting other grains for rice, a large surplus of rice would be available for export. This increase in rice production and exports did not occur. Instead, Korea continued to be a sizable importer of grains into the 1960s and has been able to export limited amounts of rice only in years following exceptionally good harvests.

The other major hope for exports was minerals, which it was assumed would amount to nearly $70 million by 1958, or one-fourth of total exports. Minerals did prove to be the main export, but they were valued only at about $10 million in 1958, which was nearly two-thirds of the total exports of $16.5 million. Even in 1968 when exports were approaching $500 million, mineral exports were only $34 million, or half the level originally suggested for 1958. While the failure of total exports to expand during the 1950s along the lines suggested in the Nathan Plan should be attributed mainly to the unwillingness of the Korean government to implement the exchange rate and other policies that would have encouraged exports, it also seems clear, on the basis of the subsequent experience with exports during the 1960s, that Korea's comparative advantage is mainly in the area of light manufactured goods, not in the agricultural and mining areas suggested by the Nathan Plan.

The proposals for broad import-substitution in manufacturing also failed to materialize, which was probably fortunate for the long-run growth of the economy as discussed in Chapter 7. The availability of substantial foreign aid, beyond the period originally contemplated in the Nathan Plan, made it possible to continue imports of intermediate as well as capital goods (imports of finished consumer goods dropped practically to zero) and reduced premature investment in capital-intensive intermediate goods industries.

The Three-Year Plan followed many of the same lines as the Nathan Plan in the areas of industrial and trade structure, but it called for "progress toward" rather than "achievement of" a balance between exports and imports. The export targets were less ambitious, and recognition of the need for a continuing import surplus, including imports of grains to meet the food deficit, was very different from the earlier program. But, like the Nathan Plan, the new plan called for major import-substitution in key industries, such as chemicals, metals, machinery, and nitrogenous fertilizer, and projected an absolute decline in the import level of 8 percent between 1958 and 1962, despite a planned 22.6 percent increase in real GNP. This proposed pattern of investment reflected the Korean objections to excessive growth of consumption goods industries and the desire to build an integrated or balanced industrial structure, which was generally conceived of as an increasing share of capital goods in total manufacturing production. The Three-Year Plan stated: "It is hoped we can change the ratio between the production of capital goods and consumer goods from 25–75 in the base year (1958) to 35–65 in the target year (1962)."

With the First Five-Year Plan the emphasis began to shift away from a self-sufficient industrial structure. Although there was still concern about raising the relative output of capital goods, there was also a growing acceptance of the need for relatively high levels of imports and of the idea that the trade gap would have to be closed mainly by raising the export ratio. As stated in the plan:

> The ultimate course of the Korean economy lies in industrialization. During the plan period, the period of preparation for industrialization, emphasis will be placed on development of power, coal, and other energy sources, increase in the earnings of farm households

by raising agricultural productivity, expansion of key industrial facilities and adequate provision of social overhead capital, utilization of idle resources, some improvement in the balance of international payments, primarily through increased exports, and technological advancement.[14]

The investment programs in electric power and related expansion of coal mining were effectively implemented, so that by 1964 the country had sufficient supplies of electricity and coal for the first time since the end of World War II. Also the plans for expansion of agricultural production were effective. The targets for increased cultivated and irrigated areas, and the application of fertilizer and pesticides were approximately met; the effects on agricultural output were of the magnitude that had been predicted.

While there was provision in the First Five-Year Plan for a number of import-substitute industrial investments, these were less important than in the previous plans. As a consequence, the ratio of imports to GNP was projected as being about 20 percent in the terminal year, or approximately the level as in the base year. A rise in the import ratio was also called for during the plan period to cover needed investment goods. Clearly, this implied moving toward a more open, trade-oriented economy. Even so, the import projections proved conservative. Actual imports over the whole plan period were about 7 percent above the plan levels, and in the final year they were 45 percent higher than the plan.

The export projections seemed unrealistically high at the time the First Plan was issued, and it is doubtful that the planners had much of an idea as to how the targets might be achieved. But the implementation of a series of export incentive measures, beginning in 1961 and continuing over the next several years, resulted in such spectacular growth of exports that by 1966 the realized export level of $250 million was nearly double the target level of $137.5 million. The composition of exports predicted in the plan followed the traditional assumption that agricultural and mineral products would predominate. This, too, proved very inaccurate as manufactures accounted for over 60 percent of the total by 1966. Thus, while the First Five-Year Plan had anticipated at least the direction of some of the changes in industrial and trade structure, it clearly underestimated the extent of those changes and it did not contemplate many of the policies that were subsequently used to bring about these changes.

As the preparation of the Second Five-Year Plan was getting under-way, the favorable results of these new policies were becoming apparent; as a consequence the questions that had to be answered in connection with industrial structure for the Second Plan were more in terms of how far the existing trends would or should be pursued and what marginal adjustments seemed appropriate, rather than what major shifts in direction or policy were needed. One set of proposals argued for con-tinued expansion of exports and of agricultural production, but with increasing reliance on a rural-oriented industrial sector to supply the export commodities. This was intended to provide stronger linkages between the urban and rural populations and to improve the incomes of the rural inhabitants so that they could buy more of the rapidly growing industrial production.[15] The basic strategy of export-led in-dustrial development was generally accepted, but the rural industry emphasis was not, in part out of concern that decentralized, small scale producing facilities might be less efficient and therefore impair the competitiveness of Korean exports in world markets. Although there was a willingness to give at least equal, if not some preferential, treatment to smaller scale industry, there was a reluctance to try to push such industry out into the rural areas. Furthermore, there was a disposition to continue the agricultural programs of the First Plan, which seemed to be successful. While recognizing that the output of the agricultural sector would grow less rapidly than that of manufacturing, it was expected that farm income would continue to rise at a satisfactory rate, that the shift of population from rural to urban areas was inevitable, and that rapid expansion of employment opportunities must occur in the cities.

The main questions concerning industrial structure for the Second Plan were (1) how rapidly exports could be increased, (2) whether the growth of demand for certain intermediate goods would be sufficient to justify building efficient-sized plants within Korea, and (3) whether to permit the large scale importation of machinery and equipment to sup-port a rapid expansion of investment or to try to divert some of this demand to the domestic machinery and capital goods industries.

The export alternatives were posed as a choice between target levels for commodity exports in 1971 of $500 million or $700 million. These implied compound annual growth rates of 19 and 26 percent from the 1965 level of $175 million. The Ministry of Commerce and Industry and others advocating high growth and rapid industrialization supported the high target. Those who were more concerned about financial stability and a balanced industrial structure argued for the lower target.[16] The target finally chosen for the plan was $550 million, or a growth rate of 21 percent. But this figure had hardly been agreed upon when current developments indicated that it was conservative. Current account earnings have continued to run well above planned levels, and consequently there has been a continuing process of raising export targets and increasing the support for export activities as the current export results have exceeded earlier expectations. The strategy decisions involved in the formulation of the Second Plan were just one stage in this process.

At the time the Second Plan was being prepared, two major investment projects were under consideration for which it was recognized that economies of scale were important and, therefore, that the prospective rates of growth of demand were very significant. These were an integrated steel mill and a petrochemical complex.

The decisions incorporated in the Second Plan on these two big industrial projects were reached after an analysis of the overall growth of industrial demand and of the investments required in the lighter industry sectors to sustain that growth. It was then concluded that the petrochemical complex should be undertaken in the early part of the plan period, both because it required less total investment and because sufficient demand for its output seemed likely. The steel mill would be built in the latter part of the Second Plan and would come into production only in the Third Plan period. This kind of confrontation of demand prospects, overall investment availabilities, and the investment needs of other sectors was an essential feature of the decision-making on industrial structure in the Second Plan and was made possible by the multisectoral framework within which the plan was formulated. The framework both required and provided a basis for the reconciliation of conflicting demands in order to arrive at a feasible overall program.

The third critical decision, on whether to protect the machinery industries, was dominated by the desire to maintain high rates of growth and investment and to take advantage of the potential foreign capital that would be available for financing the importation of machinery and equipment. Therefore, despite statements at various points in the Second Plan about the importance of building up the machinery sectors, which were designed to appease nationalistic sentiments, the investment tentatively earmarked for them was not very large and much of it was expected to go into electric and mechanical appliances for the export and consumer markets, rather than into the heavier machine-tool industries.

In summary, the Second Plan decisions on industrial structure were dominated by the desire for high rates of growth and increased efficiency. By capitalizing on the rapid growth of exports, which emanated mainly from the less capital-intensive manufacturing industries, by delaying some of the more capital-intensive projects until adequate demand for their output was assured, and by relying heavily on imported machinery, the plan was intended to keep the economy moving ahead strongly. Growth was so rapid in 1966 and 1967 that what had previously seemed to be ample capacity in the infrastructure areas of power and transportation proved to be seriously deficient. Early revisions of the Second Plan involved major acceleration and expansion of investment in these two sectors, so that they would "not become more serious bottlenecks to growth."[17]

The prospects for increasing domestic savings and reducing dependence on foreign assistance have been among the most controversial issues of Korean planning. Throughout the postwar period the level of domestic savings in relation to GNP has been low by comparison either with other countries or with Korea's investment needs and targets. As a corollary, the level of foreign assistance has been high. While most Koreans have expressed a desire to redress this balance and the foreign assistance providers have supported this idea, there has been continuing disagreement on the speed with which the shift should be effected. There have also been differences as to whether the shift would be achieved mainly by pushing for higher domestic savings rates or accepting lower rates of growth. The conflict is illustrated by a comparison of the macro economic projections of the Nathan Plan and the First and Second Five-Year Plans (see Table 9.1).

All three of these plans postulated a very sudden increase in investment at the beginning of the plan. The Nathan Plan was most extreme in that it provided for an increase in investment equal to 72 percent of the growth of GNP while GNP was assumed to grow at 15 percent. Thus the proposed investment increase exceeded 10 percent of GNP, a very unrealistic target, given the conditions in the country at that time. The investment increase projected in the early years of the First Five-Year Plan was also large, relative to the change in GNP, but because that change was relatively small the investment target was less ambitious. The Second Plan assumed a more modest initial increase in investment and a fairly steady marginal increment thereafter, whereas the earlier plans contained sharply declining marginal increments. Here again the Nathan Plan was extreme in that it assumed investment in the final year would decline absolutely by an amount equal to the rise in GNP.

Table 9.1 Marginal Rates of Investment, Domestic Savings, and Foreign
Capital Inflow, as Projected in Three Korean Plans

Plan	Base year[a] to year 1	Year 1 to year 2	Year 2 to year 3	Year 3 to year 4	Year 4 to year 5
Nathan Plan (1954 to 1958–1959)					
Marginal rate of:					
Investment	0.72	0.12	0.16	−0.23	−1.00
Domestic saving	0.45	0.42	0.46	0.16	0.20
Foreign capital inflow	0.27	−0.29	−0.62	−0.39	−1.20
Per annum growth of GNP	15%	10%	9%	5%	5%
First Five-Year Plan (1962–1966)					
Marginal rate of:					
Investment	1.38	0.66	0.39	0.14	0.16
Domestic saving	0.89	0.64	0.52	0.33	0.25
Foreign capital inflow	0.48	0.04	−0.13	−0.19	−0.09
Per annum growth of GNP	2%	6%	7%	8%	8%
Second Five-Year Plan (1967–1971)					
Marginal rate of:					
Investment	0.54	0.27	0.27	0.28	0.23
Domestic saving	0.27	0.25	0.34	0.35	0.33
Foreign capital inflow	0.26	0.02	−0.07	−0.07	−0.09
Per annum growth of GNP	7%	7%	7%	7%	7%

[a] Base years were for the Nathan Plan, 1953–1954; for the First Five-Year Plan, 1960; for the Second Five-Year Plan, 1965.

The domestic savings projections of the first two plans were similar, in that they assumed very high marginal savings rates during the first half of the plans and then a sharp tapering off in the last two years. In the Second Plan the marginal savings rate was less high on the average and was expected to increase significantly in the later years of the plan. All three plans had similar patterns of foreign capital inflow with a significant increase in the first year and then an absolute decline at least after the second year. The Nathan Plan assumed a precipitous drop in foreign capital receipts in the final year.

A simple comparison of the three plans shows that the earlier expectations of dramatic change have become more cautious and conditioned by reality with the passage of time. The kind of adjustments called for in the Nathan Plan were extreme, and some similar ones were repeated in the First Five-Year Plan. By the Second Plan there was greater awareness of comparative experience in other countries as well as in Korea. The limits of change in marginal savings and investment rates were better appreciated, but also the structural relationships in the Korean economy were less seriously out of balance than at the beginning of the earlier plans. There was also a recognition that Korea should expect to have a sizable net capital inflow for the foreseeable future, but that the sources of financing for the inflow would shift from mainly grant aid to public and private loans and equity investment.[18] For these several reasons the Second Plan projected smoother and more reasonable adjustment in the structure of domestic and foreign savings than had the earlier plans.

The extreme assumptions about the potential increases in savings and foreign capital during the early years of the plans provided the basis for planning comparable expansion of investment. By attempting to carry out these investment programs, despite the failure of domestic savings to grow as expected, the potential for severe inflation was created. It is therefore not surprising that prices rose rapidly during the first years of both the Nathan Plan and the First Five-Year Plan. The clearest example of this is found in the 1962–1963 period when investment was expanded substantially, but still not as rapidly as planned. Foreign capital inflow also rose, but savings did not respond at anything like the contemplated rate. As a consequence inflationary forces were unleashed. Domestic credit was doubled in two years to finance a large budgetary deficit (despite the highest ratio of taxes to GNP in Korea's postwar experience up to that time) and foreign exchange reserves were severely reduced. This experience, as described earlier, led to the imposition of strong stabilization measures and the postponement of planned investment in 1964–1965. Thus the unrealistic projections of domestic savings, noted by Wolf and Nam,[19] contributed to financial instability and disruption of plan implementation.

THE IMPACT OF PLANNING

After nearly a decade and a half of planning activity in Korea, what can be said about its impact on the effectiveness of government operations and on relations between the government and the people? Beyond this, can anything be concluded on the contribution of planning to the overall growth and efficiency of the economy?

The early planning efforts, including the Nathan Plan, the Three-Year Plan of 1959, and the first version of the Five-Year Plan, did little to raise the government's effectiveness. The Nathan Plan's main significance was that it introduced the concept of overall planning to Korea, but the concept remained quite abstract and irrelevant for government operations. If anything, the government leaders during this period (1953–1958) rejected the idea of overall planning and were not interested in trying to define longer run economic objectives or an integrated set of policies. This probably reflected a belief on their part that they could retain more flexibility and achieve better results in negotiations with aid donors by proceeding on an ad hoc basis and avoiding the overall commitments and constraints of a plan. The Nathan Plan called for very forceful policy action by the Korean government and set ambitious targets of self-support that the Koreans were not prepared to accept. To have agreed to the plan would have exposed the government to serious political risks.

Despite the government's rejection of the Nathan Plan, there was still some tendency to judge the country's economic performance against the standards of the plan and to attribute the failures manifested in continuing inflation, rising trade deficits, and declining growth rates to the absence of an overall plan. It was as a result of these views that the Korean government established the Economic Development Council under the Minister of Reconstruction and initiated its own planning efforts in 1958. But this too proved to be mainly an educational experience and was not effective in influencing government operations.

The group responsible for formulating the Three-Year Plan was too isolated from either the operational or policy-making levels of government to draw upon the experience or guidance of either level in trying to articulate a meaningful development program. Also the Korean planners had no experience and practically no outside assistance in their work. The overthrow of the Rhee government shortly after the plan was drafted meant there was no opportunity to test its possible influence on the government. Still, some government officials had at least been exposed to the ideas and problems of planning and had gained some experience in those areas.

Consequently, the formulation of the first and second versions of the First Five-Year Plan under governments that openly espoused planning, showed somewhat more sophistication and the prospects for greater influence on government programs. The main reasons why these prospects were not fully realized was that the Supreme Council for National Reconstruction imposed what seemed to be very unrealistic targets on the planners. The subsequent criticism cut the ground out from under the planners and reduced their influence in the government. The very poor performance of the economy during the first year of the plan, the subsequent inflation, and the time-consuming but fruitless efforts of the planners to scale down the plan to satisfy the critics completely removed the planners from the mainstream of decision-making. The First Plan as such was hardly referred to until work was started on the Second Plan, and also until it became apparent that a number of the seemingly too ambitious First-Plan targets were going to be exceeded.

Some aspects of the investment program of the First Five-Year Plan were influential and contributed to the subsequent growth of the economy. The emphasis on agriculture and infrastructure helped to remove serious bottlenecks and activate lagging sectors of the economy. These were also the areas in which government had primary responsibility (as in power and railroad transport) or was able to carry out more effective programs than the private sector had been able to do (e.g., fertilizer distribution). Other more questionable areas emphasized in the plan were either ignored, as with the steel mill, or postponed until the economy was better prepared to implement them (e.g., the fertilizer plants). Thus the investment program of the plan served only as a rough guide and investment decisions continued to be made on a case-by-case basis, often without the planners having much say in the final decision.

Although the First Five-Year Plan did not present a well-worked-out set of economic policies, it did imply a number of policy directions that were subsequently followed and that provided the real impetus for Korea's rapid growth. These included the encouragement of exports and domestic savings and maintenance of realistic, market-oriented interest and exchange rates. While it is difficult to assess the importance of these policy suggestions in the plan in bringing about the actual implementation of the policies, and it would undoubtedly be misleading to attribute a significant role to them, it can at least be said that the tendencies expressed in the plan were not contrary to the policy directions followed, mainly after 1964.

By the time work began on the Second Plan in 1964, planning as such was definitely not a well-established or influential process in the Korean government. The First Plan had been discredited, its revision ignored, and the planning staff was not significantly involved in the current major economic policy deliberations. It is therefore remarkable that within little more than a year the planning function and the planners became integral parts of the government's decision-making process. This can be attributed to the following factors: the quality of the statistical and analytical work that went into the preparation of planning models and projections; the leadership of the Vice Minister of the Economic Planning Board, Kim Hak-yul, in organizing the planning effort and the active participation of many officials from all parts of the government; the support and involvement of the foreign aid agencies in plan formulation; and finally the realization that the plan was likely to have some continuing influence on the budgetary and policy actions of the government. Because the various agencies of the government began to suspect that the planning might have such an influence, they took it more seriously and thereby contributed to its increased significance.

In the policy areas, the Second Plan largely confirmed the policy directions that were established while the plan was being formulated. These included the measures discussed in the previous chapter for increasing public and private saving, limiting inflation, encouraging exports, and freeing controls on imports. As regards investment, the Second Plan began to face up to the possibilities and needs of high growth rates. But it did not consider or accept the possibility of very high growth (e.g., above 7 percent per year), partly because of the criticism of such high targets in the First Plan, and also because of continuing admonitions from the World Bank to hold the growth target of the Second Plan to 6 percent. As for the composition of investment, the planning process led to some deferring of large, capital-intensive investment projects and some squeezing of the investment recommended for transportation. Such cuts were understandably resisted by the ministries concerned, but because representatives of those ministries had participated extensively in the plan deliberations, they were well aware of the overall resource constraints. Thus the total investment program of the Second Plan was accepted by the various parts of government without serious disagreement and became a general but not an inflexible guide for the government's capital budget and decisions on approval of foreign investments within Korea.

The weakest part of the Second Plan was its program for agriculture, which failed to define a comprehensive set of targets, to relate investments and policies to those targets, or to indicate the other kinds of inputs required to expand agricultural output. Consequently, the agriculture program in the Second Plan was largely ignored and agricultural investment has subsequently been decided without reference to the plan. Perhaps equally weak were those sections on social infrastructure such as education and health, on which relatively less amounts of time were spent in the planning process, but which perhaps reflected accurately lower government priorities in these areas.

Although it became obvious during the first year of the Second Plan period that the overall growth targets of the plan were too low and, in particular, that the investment programmed for the power and transportation sectors was grossly inadequate, this did not result in discrediting the planners and the planning process. If anything, it strengthened the conviction that more and better planning was needed. In part this was because the limitations of predictive accuracy had been clearly acknowledged in the Second Plan and procedures recommended for revising the investment program annually to take advantage of new information and to meet changing conditions. Also the sectors in which shortages became acute were those that would benefit most from good medium-term demand projections. Finally, in Korea it is probably easier to revise estimates of growth and investment upward rather than downward, without "losing face," because it attests to the conservatism of the planners.

It seems fair to conclude that the Second Plan achieved an important influence on the Korean government and that the annual overall resource budgets that have been formulated since 1967 have so far provided a focal point for review and revision of policies, investment programs, and projections of Korean economic growth.

The Second Plan also for the first time had the effect of strengthening the political stature of the government, both at home and abroad. Where the Nathan Plan and First Five-Year Plan had resulted in major disagreements with foreign aid donors and had exposed the government to criticism and embarrassment within Korea, the Second Plan elicited much more favorable reactions and thereby generated greater recognition and cooperation for the government.

When the Second Plan was made public in the summer of 1966, many of its provisions were already well known through advance publicity and press conferences by the officials of the Economic Planning Board. Thus there were no surprises in the plan, but it immediately attracted a great deal of attention and comment in the press and on television. The government organized an effective program to publicize the plan and to answer questions or criticism of it. The president indicated his approval and commitment to carry out the plan that the cabinet had endorsed to him. Thus the government presented the plan to the public with a united front and an air of confidence.

The principal reactions to the plan by the initial reviewers, moreover, both domestic and foreign, were that it was honest and represented a relatively high degree of competence. The admission in the plan document of past errors of policy and statistical misrepresentation, and the projection of growth rates below those of the recent past were all taken as evidence of a new integrity in the government. While there were criticisms of various aspects of the plan, most critics first acknowledged the apparent sincerity and conscientiousness of the planning effort. A sample survey of the opinions of Korean professors and journalists conducted in late 1966 found that 80 percent expected some success from the Second Five-Year Plan.[20] No comparable survey was taken after the earlier plans were completed, but the fact that such a large proportion of traditionally skeptical and antigovernment groups were favorably disposed toward the Second Plan and relatively confident about the benefits to be derived from it was a noteworthy political achievement. The fact that many Korean academicians had had a part in formulating analysis and goals for the plan undoubtedly had some influence. There was even some tendency, in the glow of enthusiasm and confidence at the time the plan was made public in mid-1966, to talk as though the targets of 1971 had already been achieved. This was remarkable for a people who had previously been inclined to live from day to day and to view the future without hope. The obvious improvements in living conditions during the mid-1960s helped to change such attitudes, but the Second Plan marked a turning point in infusing the Korean people with a more optimistic conception of the future. The direct political consequences of this atmosphere are described more fully in Chapter 10.

Part III

10 / Emergence of a
New Consensus

As the country approached the national elections of 1967, the economic emphasis of the mid-1960s and the success achieved under it came to have a profound effect on political attitudes. Within the government this success led to greater confidence and, therefore, to the more energetic pursuit of its economic progress. It also led the government to undertake an unprecedented policy of initiative and leadership abroad that added further to the sense of national achievement. Among the population at large, these developments combined to create a new confidence and a new commitment, both to economic growth and general political stability.

This mood was tested by a number of serious political issues in 1966–1967. Policy on reunification of Korea, probably the most sensitive issue in Korean politics, received its first full airing since the coup. As noted in Chapter 5, one of Korea's most serious political scandals in some time erupted in late 1966 over a smuggling episode, provoking small student demonstrations and some bitter political exchanges. In 1967 a shadow was cast over the whole political system by evidence of corruption in the Assembly elections—an event that carried the seeds of later more serious divisiveness and turmoil, as described in the next chapter. But none of these challenged the stability of government or the direction of events in these years, until 1969. Popular reaction to them instead seemed to show that, while a good deal of mistrust and cynicism about the government persisted, there was no great desire to overturn it or to shake it seriously such as underlay much of the political and popular opposition in 1964 and 1965.

In essence, not only had the basic conditions for rapid economic development been established, but a fundamental problem of Korean political development had been solved: For the first time since the early days of independence there was a really widespread belief in a South Korean state—one that would not only survive but would grow as an independent political and economic entity. A genuine consensus also developed around the emphasis on economic development as a key to other national goals, on the basis of which some of the most sensitive political issues in South Korea could be redefined and accommodated. And in the wake of this new consensus some of the tensions that had gripped the first years of the Park administration began to dissipate.

THE SENSE OF ACCOMPLISHMENT

The changes in the country in this period were manifest in a number of ways. One was the greater popular preoccupation with, and direct participation in, the growth itself. The year 1966 was exceptional in this regard because growth was greater than in any year since independence, and there were upward trends in nearly all key areas—exports, manufacturing, agriculture, private savings, government revenue, and foreign capital inflow. For example, in real terms, private savings doubled in 1966 over 1965 and permitted a corresponding increase in bank lending without serious inflationary consequences. Approved foreign government loans also doubled in 1966 and private foreign loans increased by 50 percent, the latter representing the first effects of the Japanese settlement. In fact the number of private Japanese loans pending approval mounted so rapidly in 1966 that it became apparent that the $300 million for these loans, designated in the Korean-Japanese settlement for over a ten-year period, would actually be committed in from three to five years.[1] Rapid industrial growth was also having a substantial effect on employment.[2] And in 1966 there began the first of a three-stage, 100 percent pay raise for civil servants and military personnel. The raises were made financially possible by the recovery of tax revenues as a percentage of GNP from the low of 1964. They belatedly rewarded groups that had suffered greatly from the earlier inflation and that, in the case of the civil servants especially, had played a large role in the economic upsurge since 1963.

There was an important new visibility to development also in 1966, particularly in the cities. Some of this was obviously politically motivated, the cities having been the major source of opposition votes in 1963 and the location of the strongest dissent during the disputes of 1964 and 1965. But it was nevertheless psychologically effective. In early 1966, the president appointed new mayors for the three largest cities and directed them to initiate new efforts in urban redevelopment. In Seoul, the new mayor immediately embarked upon the most energetic public works program seen in that city since reconstruction after the Korean War. Over 800 new projects—street widening, paving, bridge construction, water and sewer projects, and so forth—were begun in 1966–1967 at a cost of $87 million. In the course of 1966 alone, these projects provided for 2.9 million man-days of work.[3] The overall effect of this activity was indeed spectacular. Some observers, especially foreigners, gasped at the fairly stark concepts of leveling and reconstruction and questioned the selection of priorities. Some newspaper editorials questioned the high costs. But the effect on the average citizen (and on others as well) was quite likely favorable. There was a great sense of change, particularly of "modernization" in the wide streets and sleek new buildings. There were advantages for the average citizen too, in traffic safety and public services.[4] There was, in general, a welcome new image of energy in contrast to the rather lethargic previous administration of Seoul.

Changes were not as rapid or spectacular in the countryside. Despite its original concern with the rural sector, it was not until the droughts and the serious drop in agricultural production of 1967–1968 that the government took cognizance of the lag between urban and rural modernization in this period. Nevertheless, there were clear signs of new growth in the countryside, particularly with the absence by 1965 of the long-traditional food shortages during the off-harvest season. The newly cultivated uplands could be found by then in nearly every part of the country. There was a noticeable increase, too, in the use of consumer goods—cloth, radios, bicycles—and in investment in children's education, though none of these on the scale of the urban areas.[5] Finally, in the rural areas as in the urban, though much more slowly, the government was beginning to allow more play to market forces and to locally inspired and administered development efforts, through more delegation of authority to local officials, plans for relinquishing the government monopoly on fertilizer distribution, and efforts to promote agriculturally related industry.[6]

The changes taking place so vividly on the domestic scene were accompanied by remarkable successes in foreign policy. Earlier, the Military Government had initiated some changes in South Korean foreign policy, designed to reduce Korea's diplomatic reliance on the United States and its Western allies and to overcome the sense of isolation with regard to the growing number of Asian and African nations making up the neutral bloc. These efforts had produced results, particularly in opening up new sources of capital and increasing generally the country's international involvement.[7] But after several years, the efforts to gain diplomatic recognition and support among neutral nations had proved more difficult and less productive than anticipated, with particular disappointment in the United Nations votes on the Korea question.[8] Korean diplomacy was thus still caught between its desire to broaden South Korea's international prestige and the fact that diplomatic entrée and opportunities still remained greatest among nations committed to anticommunism or at least diplomatically close to the United States. However, a way out of this dilemma on both the economic and political-military fronts began to emerge in 1965.

On the economic side, the reestablishment of relations with Japan paved the way for formation of a long talked-about international consultative group on Korea, chaired by the World Bank and made up of the major European countries plus Japan and the United States. Although not a consortium as Koreans had once hoped it might be, the group did provide a prestigious international forum in which Korean developmental progress could be reviewed—and, as it happened, quite favorably—and where capital could be sought for fulfillment of the Second Five-Year Plan. It was thus formal evidence of South Korea's movement away from exclusive reliance on American assistance and into the international framework of aid and finance. Furthermore, the government had independently pursued the introduction of foreign private capital from several sources, particularly seeking to accelerate the introduction of Japanese capital following the settlement. Thus commercial loans from abroad grew tremendously in the mid-1960s and in 1966 exceeded by far the introduction of government loans. The growth of debt associated with these loans occasioned some concern in domestic circles, but on the whole they were evidence of the attractiveness of South Korea's economy to international financial interests and the prospects thereby of achieving rapid growth even while lessening dependence on aid.[9]

Korea's role abroad received another great boost from its decision to provide military support to South Vietnam. In early 1965, Korea agreed to send a 2,000-man noncombat unit to Vietnam and, a few months later, one division of combat troops. In subsequent years, these were augmented to bring total Korean forces in Vietnam to about 50,000 men, second only to the United States and far above any other contributing ally. The Korean involvement in Vietnam had been actively debated within Korea and had been the subject of long and sometimes difficult negotiations with the United States.[10] But once the commitment had been made, domestic support for the Korean role was almost unqualified. Very quickly, in fact, it became a source of unprecedented pride. The Korean performance particularly in the early days was described by the press as "brilliant," "glorious," "amazing," "a wonder to the world."[11] There was particular satisfaction in the stories relating that Koreans were being better received by the Vietnamese than the Americans and that, in both military and civic action roles, it was a case of "teaching the teacher."[12] There was also the satisfaction of having paid back Korea's debt to the Free World for help during the Korean War and of thus having achieved a new sense of dignity and equality.[13]

In addition to pride, however, the Vietnam involvement opened up a specific direction by which Korea could pursue the more active international role it had been seeking. The government now spoke of a diplomatic "advance to Southeast Asia" and began to take an active role in Southeast Asian affairs.[14] It was in this context also that Korea was able, after two years' effort, to bring Japan, Australia, New Zealand, and several Southeast Asian nations into a new regional organization, the Asia and Pacific Conference (ASPAC), which met in Seoul for the first time in March 1966. Unquestionably, the role of South Korea in Vietnam, its growing economic success, and the establishment of normal relations with Japan all contributed to South Korea's being able to draw these nations into an organization bearing the imprint of South Korean leadership and direction, especially in light of the hesitation that Japan and some of the others had had regarding the whole concept. At home, ASPAC was recognized as a triumph for Korean diplomacy.[15]

Other examples of a new and more effective Korean role in international affairs also became apparent in a rapid fashion after 1965.[16] But perhaps none was so gratifying as in the fall of 1966 when, after 13 years of desultory and sometimes acrimonious negotiations, Korea signed a Status of Forces Agreement with the United States, signaling a new recognition of Korean sovereignty and prestige in the United States. The sense of isolation, of the "hermit kingdom," of being a ward exclusively of the United States, began to disappear in this period of incredibly rapid activity. It must have been in another era, remarked one paper, that Korea had been considered an "orphan nation" in Asia.[17]

The new prestige and activity abroad was not lost at home. The signs in Seoul, almost every day of 1966 welcoming some international conference (there were nine in that year), raised the popular consciousness of the new place being assumed by South Korea in international circles. The press commented favorably on the new respect and entrée gained in Washington, seeing it as the result of Korea's role in Vietnam and its successful development efforts at home.[18] Vietnam, moreover, provided some direct opportunities, as well as opened up a new perspective on the world for the average Korean. In addition to the troops, over 12,000 Korean civilians went to Vietnam between 1965 and 1967 to fill jobs with the United States government or private contractors. Most of them were able to send back a large portion of their salary, several times the Korean wage scale, to their families. In 1966, such remittances of both civilians and soldiers reached $23 million; in 1967 the figure more than doubled.[19] As one observer noted, Vietnam became Korea's El Dorado: the first place abroad to which average Koreans could go, or just talk about going, to earn their fortune. Beyond that, Koreans generally were becoming conscious of Asia and their role in it, not just as a defense bastion and outpost of the United States but as a possible force for greater regional cooperation, both economic and political. It was not without significance that Korea formed ASPAC with the United States being specifically excluded.[20]

CHANGES IN POLITICAL OUTLOOK

Thus, in contrast to the turbulence, division, and despair of 1965 when the Japanese settlement was concluded, 1966 was marked by rapid and noted advances in economic growth, visible changes in the Korean environment, and growing pride and confidence in the nation as a whole. These changes gave rise to a notion one found in talking to academics, journalists, and other citizens in the period of 1966–1967, namely, that "political stability," achieved in the aftermath of the Japanese settlement, was a key factor in the accelerated economic performance and other accomplishments. Right or wrong, and there was some truth to it even though the economic growth had begun during the earlier, more turbulent years, the notion was affecting attitudes toward politics. While the culmination of this feeling occurred in the 1967 presidential election, the signs of it were evident much earlier.

On the various major issues that were raised in the course of 1966— unification, the revision of the election laws, the increase of the Korean troop contingent in Vietnam, even the smuggling case—the degree of order, compromise, and successful resolution were in considerable contrast to the previous two years. The opposition party, regrouping after the bitter experience of 1965, struck a constructive note at the outset of 1966, attempting to spell out a new economic philosophy, "mass capitalism," by which the party would seek to play a role in determining the direction of the new economic upsurge. On noneconomic issues, there was a similar attempt to propose constructive alternatives. The opposition leader, Mme. Pak Sun-chon, also made a rather eloquent statement in defense of constitutional order and pledged her party's responsibility to safeguard that order. One editorial commented, "When militant and extreme expressions used in the keynote speeches of the opposition party in the past are recalled it seems as if we were in another world.[21]

For its part, the government appeared to make an effort to maintain the opposition in a viable form and in the framework of democratic politics to avoid the crisis atmosphere of 1965. Though the opposition often walked out of the Assembly, compromises were quickly made thereafter.[22] Some of these incidents were crass political maneuvers or desperate attempts on the part of the opposition to share in the spoils of power. As one Democratic Republican party member reportedly remarked during a dispute over approval of foreign loans, "It would be better for them to expressly ask for political funds." But the attitude of the government undoubtedly contributed to the opposition's being able in this period to exert influence beyond its very limited voting power.

It was the treatment of the unification issue, however, that provided the most important indicator in 1966 of a fundamental, rather than only surface, change taking place in the national outlook. Reunification of Korea was, and remains, one of the most sensitive issues in Korean politics. "Radical" proposals in this area, that is, those that depart significantly from the advocacy of internationally supervised free elections throughout all of Korea as the first step, or which suggest some degree of recognition of North Korea as a preliminary move, have often been the testing point of radical opposition in Korea and in some ways—in the response they generated—a thermometer of popular unrest. In 1961, the student demonstrations calling for direct talks with North Korea sent tremors through Korean society and helped bring on the coup, or at least to justify it. Artists and writers run afoul of security laws in Korea most often when they seem to suggest too close a sympathy with North Korean views on reunification or related issues.[23] On the other hand, an emotional meeting of separated Korean family members at the Tokyo Olympics in 1964 touched off a wave of editorials and political cries for new ways to breach the total wall between the two halves of Korea, in which DRP Assemblymen prominently took part.[24] Unification is thus a largely unpredictable issue, both in the motives of those who raise it and in the reactions it may call forth.

When the opposition opened up the subject of unification in 1966, charging that the Park government had neglected it, this was the first full discussion of the matter since the coup of 1961. Since then, the new leaders had not spelled out their views on the question, save for a fairly frank recognition that the formulas of the past held little real likelihood of success. Under the restrictions on political debate during the Military Government, the subject received little further airing.[25] Even in 1966, President Park tried to cut off a widening debate on the issue, cautioning that "unrealistic discussion of methods of unification" was not helpful to the cause.[26] But the Park government's view was becoming clear through both an emphasis on development and its pointed admiration and emulation of the German experience. President Park had from his earliest days of leadership pointed to the example of West German economic growth as an example for Korea. The fact that West Germany was developing internal economic and political strength far superior to its rival, East Germany, was frequently pointed out as an example for Korea.[27]

Unable to contain the discussion during the summer months of 1966, the government made its position explicit: realistic possibilities for reunification would come only when the internal economic and political strength of South Korea was much greater than at present and clearly superior to that of the North. That time might be a decade off. In the meanwhile, the country should concentrate on that aim rather than divert itself with futile and frustrating hopes of alternatives. This position echoed an earlier, more oblique reference of Kim Chong-pil's that the 1960s would be the decade for gathering internal strength and that the 1970s would be "Korea's decade."[28]

The government's position was not altogether satisfactory to the opposition and the public, especially because it aimed at silencing public debate on the subject. Yet, in the months following, even with a proposal from a new splinter opposition party for direct talks with North Korea, and the attempt of the main opposition to make of the question a major political issue, there was no real challenge to the newly enunciated position of the government from the public, press, or even, in the end, the major opposition party.[29] Unification still remained a very real objective for all Koreans, and it remained an issue of potentially explosive force. But in 1966 the public seemed ready to accept the government's basic redefinition of the whole problem, which in effect made it, as so many other national objectives came to be in this period, conditional on national development. The public could also recognize openly and for the first time without great despair or insecurity, the probable long-range nature of the division of the country.

But the reunification debate in 1966 also pointed out one of the lingering weaknesses of Korean politics. As mentioned earlier, the government's attitude toward reunification was governed in part by its fear of divisive and, in its opinion, futile debate on the question. As one DRP member explained:

> They [President Park and DRP Chairman Kim Chong-pil] want the people to face realities squarely, refrain from frivolous talk and actions—not to wait idly for possible changes in the international situation favorable to our goal but to strive for lasting prosperity of the people and the state. In their theory there is a strong hint that the people should no longer be sacrificed by useless political strife, inefficient administration and journalistic activities without well-defined guiding principles.[30]

Unfortunately, that attitude led to the arrest of an opposition leader, So Min-ho, on charges that remarks he made proposing contacts with North Korea had violated the anti-Communist Law.[31] This has been an all too characteristic response of Korean regimes since 1948. In part it was political repression. In part it also reflected the still deep insecurity that the Korean leadership and even some of the public felt about the ability of Korean society to face, debate, and handle controversial topics openly. We shall return to this problem later. We need only add here, however, that even So's arrest, while deplored on grounds of justice, occasioned no great support for his stand on reunification nor for his candidacy for the presidency the following year. Reunification, like smuggling, had failed to relight the torch of strong popular opposition to the incumbent administration.

Finally, the Second Five-Year Plan, issued in late summer 1966, provided an opportunity to measure the change in attitude on a number of fundamental issues. As pointed out in the last chapter, the plan was designed to serve as a political, as well as an economic, document. It contained conclusions on many of the basic issues that the country had been debating in the previous few years. One was the confident belief in rapid growth for South Korea, accentuated by the government's later decision to accelerate even the plan targets. Second, it laid to rest the equivocation over the decline of United States grant economic assistance. The plan stated, more concretely than any official United States pronouncements, that United States grant aid would decline steadily and end completely in 1971. Finally, the plan represented a clear commitment to long-range development of South Korea as the basis of national strength and the prelude to new efforts for reunification. The opening section of the plan contained a discussion of, and projection for, South Korea per se in 1980, which would have been hardly imaginable in any official document even two or three years earlier. The plan thus summed up the issues of emphasis, outlook, and national orientation that had been raised by the administration's policies since 1963.

The favorable reception given to the plan and the absence of great skepticism over its goals, described in the last chapter, were thus clues to the changing outlook of the nation. By the end of 1966 even the more critical elements of the press were acknowledging the reality of the rapid economic growth and were inclined to accept it as the beginning, though still imperfect, of a new self-confidence. One editorial at the close of the year looked back on 1966 as a watershed of Korean history in which "agony evolved into the amplitude of modernization."[32]

THE 1967 ELECTIONS

The real test of a new consensus, however, on which the administration had had its eye for some time, was the presidential election of 1967. This election provided the climax of this particular period of Korean development. More than a blueprint of the future, it was a confirmation of the changes in politics and economics that had taken place in the last four years. At issue, and quite clearly the critical theme of the campaign, was the emphasis of the administration on rapid economic growth as the key prerequisite to other national objectives, as against the appeals of the opposition, not only to qualitative criticisms of the administration's economic policies, but also to competing social and political values that might demand a readjustment of priorities. The election also pitted against each other the same two opponents as in 1963. It therefore provided a retest of the issue of leadership decided so closely in 1963: between the traditional elite that had been deposed in 1961 and the elite that had emerged in the aftermath of the military coup, which had dominated the country as civilian leaders over the last four years.

The opposition to President Park was plagued by many of the same problems as in 1963: disunity, the inability to relate to the themes of modernization, lack of funds, and uncertain prospects for being able to hold power if it should win. But in the atmosphere of growth and progress in 1967, these problems appeared more inappropriate to the times and were more costly. The opposition was particularly slow to heal the scars of its internal battles related to the Japanese settlement of 1965. These had left the opposition once again split into two feuding parties. The more moderate of these had returned to the Assembly, broadened its appeal, developed a constructive platform, and nominated as its presidential candidate a prominent scholar.[33] With all this, however, it could not overcome, or do without, the adamant group led by former President Yun Po-son. Eventually, only four months before the election, the two parties merged once again. The moderates paid the price of giving Yun the candidacy of the united party. The attempt to present a new image was thus lost. Real unity was also lost, as several leaders of the moderate group found it impossible to give Yun wholehearted support during the campaign.[34]

While Yun seemed to personify the old guard, the party—the New Democratic party (NDP)—did nevertheless represent fairly well the spectrum of organized permissible political opposition to the Park administration. South Korea was an anti-Communist state, and it carried this to the point of precluding genuinely socialist or otherwise left-leaning movements. As the foremost opposition party, the NDP, therefore, was conscientiously and positively conservative. While there had been some mention of concern over income distribution and relative shares of the new economic growth, its economic philosophy—"mass capitalism"— stressed primarily greater control of inflation, public sale of corporate shares in large firms, and greater opportunity for small business. The party made its primary appeal to white collar workers, small and medium businessmen, and middle class farmers. It had an appeal also to intellectuals, primarily, however, on grounds of opposition to the government in power. Intellectuals in Korea also were not champions of the lower classes so much as critics of big business and oppressive government. There was, in fact, no political party of consequence in Korea that made its appeal openly to workers, small farmers, or others who might be separated out as underprivileged. The government considered this as divisive and premature at Korea's stage of development. The New Democratic party was not attuned to doing so.[35]

The absence of any real challenge from the "left" is made plain by a brief description of attempts in 1966–1967 to revive and unify what were called the "progressive" or "reformist" parties in Korea. Most socialist leaders in South Korea, those who had survived the Rhee government and the Korean War, had been arrested after 1961 and kept from political activity. A few very moderate ones were, however, allowed in 1966 to organize a United Socialist Party. Calling for liberation of the masses, socialism, and exchanges between North and South Korea, the USP's platform was radical by South Korean standards.[36] But closely watched, and with labor unions in Korea under government control and proscribed from partisan activity, the United Socialist party was little more than a paper activity. The same year So Min-ho, well known for his opposition to Rhee, an adamant member of the united opposition to the Japan treaty in 1965 and one of the founders of Yun Po-son's splinter party afterward, left Yun to form his own Democratic Socialist party. So hoped to unify the DSP, the USP, and remnants of older student radical groups into a new progressive force in Korea. So's efforts were not very successful. He himself was arrested in 1966 for his remarks on a new reunification policy. But So was having other troubles as well. As a traditional conservative, he was looked at with some suspicion in his latest moves. He also failed to get significant funds for his new party. In the end, his attempts to unify the various groups failed.[37] Later, in the midst of the election campaign, he withdrew as the DSP candidate for President. In so doing, he followed the lead of the other small socialist groups who backed the candidacy of the conservative Yun on the grounds that the struggle against the political restrictions of the incumbent regime was a first priority.[38] In general, the attempts at socialist political activity reflected a largely intellectual, closely controlled, and very narrowly based activity. The groups that did exist, moreover, were beholden to the larger conservative parties like the NDP to win them more freedom of movement.

If the conditions of party competition resembled those of 1963, the themes of the campaign itself contrasted greatly with those of the earlier election. In 1963, much of the opposition campaign was based on antimilitarism, insinuations of Communist sympathy in the Park government, and criticism of the coup.[39] In 1967, the themes on both sides were very much centered on the government's economic policy. President Park ran almost entirely on the development record of his first term and the development potential in the Second Five-Year Plan. In the opening statement of his campaign, he proclaimed that "establishment of a self-supporting Korea is my supreme goal."[40] The chairman of the DRP's election committee stated that "the kernel of the DRP's platform lies in its economic policy."[41] For its part, the New Democratic party countered with criticisms of the emphasis on growth, per se. It appealed for greater distribution of wealth, social security, "balanced growth" (more in favor of agriculture, including more subsidies, and small business), a slowdown in the inducement of foreign capital, and the public sale of shares in large corporations and banks. The party also argued for more emphasis on noneconomic matters, for example, developing a new reunification policy now rather than in the 1970s, the need to establish the precedent of a peaceful transfer of power in Korea in order to realize fully constitutional and democratic government, and charges of corruption.[42] The critical point of difference was that the NDP was prepared to argue for a reduction in the rate of investment and the rate of growth, if necessary, to serve these other needs. The DRP argued that without a rapid rate of growth first, the others had little meaning.[43] Other matters which a year earlier would have been almost certain campaign issues, such as the Korea-Japan treaty and the involvement in Vietnam, attracted scarcely any attention.

The results of the election were revealing. In 1963, Park had beaten Yun by just 160,000 votes and had been indebted to the entry of several opposition candidates for a plurality victory. In 1967, Park won by more than one million votes, with a clear majority over Yun and several very minor splinter candidates. The base of his victory was also revealing: Park gained greatly in the cities. In Seoul, the traditional opposition stronghold, Park had in 1963 lost by more than 2 to 1, whereas in 1967 he drew 47 percent of the votes. He carried the second largest city, Pusan, and carried provincial capitals like Taejon, though he lost the province vote. In the city of Ulsan, the site of the country's major heavy industrial complex, he won by a 9 to 1 margin. Park also gained greatly in areas of the southeast as a whole, where new industrialization was prominent, from where he and many of his cabinet ministers came, and where proximity to Japan had most likely led to greater support for normalized relations with that country. By contrast, Park lost the predominantly agricultural Cholla provinces in the southwest, which he had carried in 1963, and other rural support, presumably in response to feelings of discrimination in government policies against agriculture in favor of industrialization. The overall effect, looking at votes within as well as between provinces, was to even out the administration's previous support from rural and urban areas, and greatly to increase its overall margin of victory.[44]

The results provided a confirmation and ratification of the changes in politics and economics over the previous four years. They were not an enthusiastic endorsement of the administration. As the campaign got under way, one sensed a good measure of intellectual and press sympathy with the opposition's criticisms of the administration, but a lack of confidence in the opposition's ability as a political instrument and a questioning of whether its alternatives were really better suited to solving the problems it raised.[45] A clue to this feeling, explaining probably the feelings of many who changed their support from opposition in 1963 to administration in 1967, came early in the year from the leading newspaper in Korea, which had into 1967 remained the most skeptical and critical of the economic achievements of the Park administration. In an editorial reviewing the keynote speeches in January of the two parties, which had in effect set the tone for the campaign ahead, the *Tonga Ilbo* reviewed sympathetically the opposition's arguments for greater distribution of income and social security but concluded that the government's program, which it said was in reality emphasis on production first and distribution second, had "greater feasibility for harmonizing growth with equitable distribution of income" than the opposition's "populist economy," which would lower economic efficiency.[46]

There was also a new concern in Korea with political stability, particularly as it related to economic development. People speculated whether the opposition, which had limited ties with the military and serious internal divisions, could survive in power or at least maintain a reasonably stable atmosphere, should it win. These same questions had been asked in 1963, but in 1967 stability had acquired more value. In the opinion of one journal, the key to the administration's victory was the belief that economic development could be hurt by political instability.[47] In summary, the election confirmed the new consensus in Korea, based on a priority for economic growth, but based too on support for an overall and less ambivalent trend toward modernization in both the political and economic spheres.[48]

THE NATURE OF THE NEW CONSENSUS

The economic growth of this period and the priority given to it over other concerns created a new basis for confidence and identity and therefore a new commitment to the institutions and development of the state. This was a much needed step in Korean political, as well as economic, development. It cleared up much of the conflict and lack of purpose that had plagued the society since liberation. It made possible actions needed to reestablish economic order in the wake of all the changes after the Korean War, and to begin to develop opportunities for South Korea to become a really viable economic entity. Finally, it provided a means for harmonizing strong leadership with democratic government. In the policies and processes of economic growth, the government had found the means for common interest and interaction between itself and the majority of the population, and a basis for consensus by which authority could be sanctioned through democratic processes, that is, open and free elections.

But with all this, the period represented but a first step in the development of a modernized political system in Korea, one that, while promoting economic improvement and major technological change, is both stable and at the same time responsive to the democratic values of postwar Korean society. While economic programs had reduced political tension within the society, they had not in themselves created political institutions that could embody the new consensus and translate it into a consistently workable political system. This was evident in 1967 in the continuing confusion and fragility of the opposition. Subsequent events, from 1967 on, would reveal equally critical if more subtle weaknesses in the government party. These carried the potential for a much different kind of political-economic interaction, one in which economic development could be distorted for very narrow political purposes.

11 / Lingering Constraints

One of the most notable things about the presidential election of 1967 was that it had generally been acknowledged to have been conducted fairly, openly, and with a minimum involvement of police compared to almost all previous Korean elections. The administration seemed to feel confident in testing its position in the elections and to feel no need to distort the results. The nation was therefore shocked when, in the aftermath of the Assembly elections a month later, charges of fraud, election-rigging, and other distortions grew quickly into a national recognition that the country had been subjected to another gross corruption of the democratic process, one reminiscent of a previous era.

The Assembly elections, and the cumulatively serious political developments in their wake in the next three years, threw into stark relief some of the immediate shortcomings of the political system, which the economic breakthrough and the accompanying new consensus had not solved. These weaknesses lay primarily in the operation of the political party system, especially in the capacity of that system to provide for peaceful changes of power. Behind these, however, were underlying problems: the nearly endemic limitations on political freedom, the role of the military, and the repercussions of the security threat from North Korea. Together these problems constrain the prospects not only for continued political development but economic.

The economic breakthrough of the mid-1960s solved some basic problems of structure and philosophy for South Korea. But it opened the door to new problems, some of them associated with the success of these years. These include effective management of the growing foreign debt, allocating major resources to lagging sectors such as agriculture, preventing increasing inequality of income distribution and consumption, accommodating the growing demand of previously dormant or suppressed socioeconomic groups such as labor, meeting the social and economic costs of rapid urbanization, limiting the extralegal exactions of government upon enterprise, as well as the tendency for government to revert to direct controls and interference to solve emerging economic problems. These are problems that need to be solved mainly within the political arena, and, for South Korea, in some sort of framework for democratic politics. If they cannot be, they will surely grow to distort the economy so as to favor special interests at the expense of economic rationale, threaten future economic growth, and make economics once again a source of contention rather than cohesion.

THE POLITICAL PARTY SYSTEM

In the previous chapter, the weaknesses in the political opposition were indicated by its performance in the presidential election, namely, the inability to organize effectively, to represent newly emerging social and economic groups seeking a vehicle of political expression, and to present a realistic political alternative to the present administration. The Assembly elections of 1967 throw a good deal of light on the weaknesses in the party system as a whole, which extend to the much stronger and well-organized government party.

The Assembly elections contrasted to the presidential contest in many ways.[1] The importance of party organization and label diminished compared to a candidate's personal organization and contacts. Similarly, neither inner party unity nor two-party politics were as evident on the local as on the national level. There had been bitter competition within each party for Assembly seat nominations and, in several cases, those who lost their party's nomination not only would not support their successful rivals, but also seceded from the party to run as candidates on various other party tickets. For other reasons as well, there were numerous candidates in almost every district beside the two main parties' representatives; 702 candidates in all were registered for the 131 electoral contests. While only one of these splinter candidates was elected, the effect was generally divisive for the two main parties.[2] Finally, there was a difference in outlook on the part of the local candidate, who in most cases controlled the local party organization.[3] In the presidential election, he was responsive to national perspective, for the district results were part of a national effort and not so significant by themselves. In the Assembly election, on the other hand, national considerations were far less meaningful to him than his own district, where his personal future was decided. His willingness to use all means at his disposal, even when not directed to do so, rose accordingly.

Consequently, the Assembly elections were marked by sharp competitiveness and factional rivalry. By all accounts, the elections were featured by the heavy use of money, the violation of laws on campaigning, and voting irregularities. It was called "depraved" almost before it was over.[4] When the results were announced, the government's Democratic Republican party had won 103 seats, the principal opposition party 27, and a splinter party 1. Nearly all the opposition seats were from Seoul (where the opposition won every seat, despite Park's good showing a month earlier), Pusan and other cities, while the DRP suspiciously swept all the rural seats. What was alarming to the opposition was that, with the proportional representation accorded to the DRP on the basis of these returns, the latter ended up with 130 of 175 seats in the Assembly, giving it more than the two-thirds majority needed to amend the Constitution.[5] The opposition charged immediately that the elections had been rigged nationwide as part of a plot to be able to amend the constitutional two-term limit on the presidency and thus to pave the way for President Park to run for a third term in 1971.[6]

It seems improbable, however, that the elections were rigged in this manner. To do so would have required a willingness to run tremendous risks of political confrontation at this juncture, which was contrary to the strategy of the administration, for example, in its whole approach to the presidential election and its actions toward the opposition during the year and a half following the Japanese settlement. The possibility of confrontation was accentuated by the general prediction before the elections of DRP losses in the Assembly rather than gains, making a DRP sweep immediately suspect. Furthermore, given the struggles for power and even succession going on within the DRP, it is hard to imagine a fully agreed plot at this time, among all who would have had to be involved, to have Park reelected in 1971.[7]

What seems more logical and more reflective of the state of party politics in Korea is that there occurred a loss of communication between the outlook of the central leadership of the party and the individual members, between national perspective and individual ambition. The DRP was indeed fearful of losing seats in the Assembly election, both as a result of the rural defections from the DRP in the presidential election and in response to an opposition campaign that the DRP administration, flushed with its presidential victory, needed to be restrained by strong opposition representation in the Assembly.[8] To minimize that loss, the DRP leadership gave its candidates ample funds, far more than the opposition could muster, and closed its eyes to the use of the government's local administrative apparatus to aid in tipping the balance. What the central leadership probably did not anticipate, however, was how sweeping and energetic would be the individual candidates' use of those advantages. It was thus faced in the outcome with an embarrassingly large majority. Later, though with considerable difficulty, the president would use this majority for precisely the purpose the opposition feared. But in one fell swoop, much of the prestige, confidence, respect, and consensus gained in the presidential returns was lost. For six months afterward, the administration again faced student demonstrations, an outraged press, and opposition boycott of the Assembly.[9]

Thus the political strategy of the president leading up to his reelection, that is, the change in popular political attitudes through emphasis on conditions favoring economic development, had not affected very much the functioning of the political parties. They remained the repository of factional, rather than national or even identifiable socioeconomic group interest. For the government party especially this was a result of the independent leadership of the executive—of the president, the cabinet ministers dependent upon him, and the bureaucracy—in setting national priorities and developing programs to carry them out. The friction between the administration and the DRP over this independence has been constant. On the executive's part, "bending" to party influence was seen as leading to a diversion of government attention from its priority tasks and a diffusion of both spoils and power over a wide area of individual and narrowly partisan interests. On the DRP's part, the limitations on its influence in key areas, such as the selection of ministers and the direction of policy, left it in the role of a subservient instrument of the administration in the Assembly, without respect and without the responsibility and experience in national development to become a strong national political institution.

Both points of view were probably right to a degree. The Democratic Republican party in 1963 was too diffuse, too opportunistically organized, and too new to develop a clear set of programs that would have captured national attention and support. By 1967, on the other hand, DRP assemblymen came to feel that only the "pork barrel" aspects of national programs were sufficiently identified with the DRP label to be relevant as campaign slogans in their election. As one journal put it, the issues of national policy had been exhausted in the presidential election a month earlier.

Limitations on the role and function of the parties were extended to the Assembly as a whole. Here both the DRP and the opposition might have had the opportunity to gain experience with national program direction, and identification with national issues. The Democratic Republican party played a more significant role in this regard. With its strong organization and general loyalty to the president, it performed a very valuable role between 1963 and 1967 in providing the government with the legal means for carrying its programs through the legislature. The party also served as a valuable point of political contact and compromise with the opposition without "deserting" the administration. But the Assembly's functions in this period remained very much confined to debating and passing in almost every case administration proposals, pretty much on the schedule determined by the president.[10] The DRP influence on such proposals was mostly exerted in advance, behind the scenes, which led often to more personal or partisan than public policy influences being brought to bear, and in any case did little to enhance the function of the Assembly. The weakness of the Assembly vis-à-vis the executive was reflected in the fact that the executive ignored nearly all of the Assembly-originated proposals passed and sent to it for action.[11] In frustration, the Assembly, especially the opposition, retaliated by using liberally its prerogative to question cabinet ministers on political issues. This made it a valuable forum for certain public issues but had little more than nuisance value in affecting executive policy.[12]

It seems clear that in South Korea the executive will have to play a major role in changing the role of the political parties if it is to be done in the near future. At present, organized groups outside the government are not cohesive enough to have a major, sustained impact on the national outlook of the parties. Executive stimulus also seems a more feasible and practical possibility than reform from the grass roots. Local autonomy in South Korea, which was abolished in 1961, is often advocated as a means of strengthening democratic participation in politics, freeing local officials from national party control, and building the sense of group interest needed to buttress party solidity.[13] But given the weakness of party organization and disunity on the local level, and the extent of factionalism, it is hard to imagine that local autonomy alone would not at this juncture produce more instability in the party system and just as much if not more corruption of the electoral process. Given the present imbalance between the Democratic Republican party and opposition strength and funds, moreover, locally elected councils and officials might become now as partisan, and perhaps as diverted from constructive functions, as were such councils in the late Liberal party era under Syngman Rhee. Finally, from a purely practical point of view, the present leadership has sought to promote stability in politics by curbing the extent of political party activity (e.g., forbidding party organization below the county level) and narrowing the system as much as possible to two parties (by curbs on independents in the Assembly and other strictures on the system). It is thus more likely to be willing to respond to pressures to expand this approach gradually, that is, by giving somewhat more scope to the main parties on a national scale, than to abandon it wholesale.

Unfortunately, the trend is presently in the opposite direction. Plot or no plot in 1967, forces close to the president began making plans in 1968 to have the constitution amended by the Assembly to permit a third term. The issue deeply divided the DRP, especially alienating the supporters of DRP founder Kim Chong-pil, who was probably the strongest candidate to succeed Park. Increasingly, pressures were put on such dissenters—expelling recalcitrants, cutting off benefits, and so forth—until by 1969 Kim had found it expedient to retire completely from politics and the remaining dissidents were brought into line.[14] In the summer of 1969, in a highly charged political atmosphere and using tactics very similar to those of the final passage of the Japanese settlement, the DRP in the Assembly sent to the president the necessary bill for a referendum to amend the constitution.[15] There were, as noted below, several consequences of this step. But one of the most significant was that it crippled the DRP, making the party very much an appendage of the president and apparently incapable of organizing itself to select a candidate to run on the party's program independent of the personality of its present leader. The DRP, though having done much more to represent a constructive program of development to the country, thus came perilously close to being as much tied to President Park, as a person, as the Liberal party was to Rhee.[16]

The seriousness of this situation is that it is the political parties which in the long run must carry the burden of translating the new consensus on national goals, achieved in the mid-1960s, into political practices and principles. They must also be the vehicle by which changing goals and demands and new social forces are accommodated. They are finally the indispensable institutions for maintaining the framework of democratic politics in Korea, particularly as long as both local political action is weak and authoritarian influences at the center are strong. The problems of the parties are not only, however, those of organization and function— as featured in the history of the Democratic Republican party, the Liberal party, or indeed the various opposition parties. They extend to the whole thinking in South Korea on the role of politics.

POLITICAL FREEDOM

A second serious constraint in the political system, therefore, which goes beyond the party structure but affects it fundamentally, is the continuing restraint in Korean life on political thought and expression. The authoritarian nature of Korean politics has cultural and historical roots of long standing. Postwar Korean governments have preserved this legacy and given it new forms under modern conditions. The heavy emphasis in South Korea on security and anticommunism, reflecting as it did real fears, also fitted well into the tendency of successive governments to ban exploration of large areas of political thought and to limit the freedom of troublesome political opponents. By 1965 the Park administration had acknowledged the right of a basically free press and agreed to refrain from more overt measures to cut off political activities on campus. But the entire Korean political system remains confined to a narrow range of political freedom. In 1966 and again in 1967 (though after the election, in the latter case), arrests of presidential candidates and campaigners served as reminders that the degree of political latitude was still subject to government interpretation.[17] In 1969, student demonstrations in opposition to the presidential third-term amendment were put down with a fair amount of force.[18] Press coverage of the demonstrations and of the third-term issue itself was subject to greater government control than at any time since 1963—evidence that press control laws are not the only vehicle for censorship.[19] The varying degree of government confidence and/or fear of the results of particular ideas adds to the arbitrariness of such restrictions. Thus, as noted in the last chapter, a prominent politician was arrested in 1966 for suggesting contacts with North Korea, while the innocuous United Socialist Party advocated a similar approach without being disturbed.

The constraint is not, moreover, a matter of simple oppression by the ruling party over its opponents. It reflects a more widespread fear in Korea of the danger of the uninhibited freedom of speech. Thus even the Democratic Party Government of 1960–1961 was in its last few days moving toward passage of a National Security Law.[20] The fear arises from the Communist threat across the border and the danger of hidden infiltration and subversion through intellectual or political circles that might take place if open discussion of certain issues and viewpoints, for example, reunification formulas that approach Communist terms, was not strictly forbidden. It reflects too a fear that Korean society is not stable enough to handle free and open discussion of all issues, especially to resist the divisive effects of opportunist politicians and rabble-rousers. It is hard to gauge the depth of these feelings outside government circles; many intellectuals have denounced them in principle. But one has the sense that they are a product of general South Korean insecurity: born of division, war, poverty, and dependence on an outside power for defense and indeed, for long, basic existence. Thus, with all the attachment to democratic values and procedures that exists in press, intellectual, and student circles, the generally narrow range of free speech in Korea is challenged only weakly.

The restraints on political thought increase the difficulties of the party system. Political parties in Korea, as has often been pointed out, are all "conservative." There is a real resistance to class consciousness, especially if it relates to working classes in the cities. Labor unions are proscribed from overt political activity. The DRP, being less consciously conservative, seeks to be "pan-national." This has not been a serious problem in Korea heretofore. Economic groups, except for the business community, have not been well organized, nor have they perceived a common group interest. In the case of urban-rural competition, which is consciously felt, the Assembly and presidential elections have given the rural interests a fairly effective means of exerting their voice in the capital, while the profits and attractions of urban-centered industrialization have balanced that voice. Labor, as noted earlier, has benefited in both employment and wages from the recent growth, even if at a somewhat lagging pace. Overall, there has been and continues to be more common interest in a sound national development program than a strongly felt competition over existing resources. But the rapid pace of industrialization in Korea will create new problems that should be translated into political activity. Labor has already in 1968 and 1969 become newly active, with increased strikes, wage demands, and some restlessness with government control over union political activity.[21] Small farmers, small businessmen, specialized professions, and so forth, are going to find it more important to protect their position and claim their share in a growing economy. This changing situation provides a valuable opportunity for welding the party system closer to the issues of national development.

The problem is greatest perhaps for the present opposition, which serves as a catch-all of critics but under a conservative cloak, and is thus a frustrating mechanism for many groups. But for both parties, the freedom to take on new issues, new social or economic group interests, and new appeals will be essential to their being able to adjust and re-group as necessary to represent a changing society.

The constraint on political thought has another ramification. While the intellectuals have accepted, as have others in Korea, the need for a developmental emphasis, they cannot but feel frustrated at the arbitrary limits on political freedom. The intellectual community is changing. The older generation, educated under colonial rule in Japan and Korea, is in senior positions giving way to a group trained mainly in the United States and Europe. Beneath the latter group is a growing number of Korean-educated intellectuals, and, with relations restored with Japan, persons likely to be exposed over the next few years more to Japanese intellectual influences than to American. It is not likely therefore that traditional proscriptions on Marxism, socialism, or "progressive" activity will be accepted in the same vein as they were by their elders. While the intellectuals of the past two decades have been concerned with political ideology and generalized political values, the rising generation might be expected to be concerned more with socioeconomic issues and ideology, with new approaches to economic organization and to international relations. Not only their own background but the changing emphasis in Korea as a whole to economic concerns and international prestige will contribute to this outlook. None of this can be contained in the traditional South Korean anticommunist mold alone.[22]

THE MILITARY IN POLITICS

A third constraint, which relates to the restrictions on thought as well as to the weakness of political party activity, is the military. It is a large and powerful institution whose place in Korean politics must be recognized as permanent. The changes in the economic situation since the 1961 coup, and in political attitudes about development, have probably made a return to a purely military experiment such as that of 1961–1963 unlikely. Economic development has not only become a tangible reality in the intervening period, but the policies and administration it requires have grown complex and specialized to the point that experienced civilian administrators and the professional bureaucracy are almost sure to play key roles in any future government.[23] Nevertheless, having entered politics once, and having thereby established a channel for continuing influence, the military is unlikely in the future to remain indifferent to either the election of a hostile regime or to any major crisis in national stability. There are several forces impelling the military toward a continuing role in politics, direct or indirect.

The very size of the military poses a delicate political problem. Until recently, the costs of the 600,000-man force were borne largely by United States aid. But reductions in aid in recent years have pushed this cost increasingly onto the Korean economy. The possibility of a reduction of forces has always been a touchy and dangerous issue for Korean governments and will remain so for any future regime.[24] There is also the fact that the military, to maintain its own internal stability, retires some of its best senior officers in their forties. These are vigorous, ambitious, and highly trained individuals, many of whom will seek a place in Korean political life. Finally, the military officers who have recently served in Vietnam are likely to return home with decided attitudes on the strength and confidence of the Korean military, new views on the appropriate symbols of Korean nationalism, and perhaps a view toward their own role in politics—in other words, a new military clique.[25]

The present Democratic Republican party administration has so far provided political outlets for the military through both executive and party channels, and a direct means of communication through former military officers now leading the government. The government has thus protected its rear as it moved gradually since 1963 toward acceptance of the restraints and intricacies of civilian government. But to the degree that the DRP remains a special outlet for military influences, the party weakens its ability to establish itself as a predominantly popular-based institution, responsive to popular control and direction. On the other hand, the more the DRP might break away from the military to represent a more clearly civilian set of interests, the more the party would lose one of its greatest assets, namely, the ability to assure the country a fairly large and stable measure of civilian rule without the threat of direct military intervention. The opposition has a similar problem. By challenging the present government on the latter's close military ties, it appeals to elements who favor more civilian and democratic politics.

But at the same time it raises the question in many minds as to whether the opposition could survive in power should it win. As noted earlier, this was probably a significant factor in its loss in the last two elections.

THE SECURITY SPECTER

One final constraint continues to prevent any easy evolution toward further political democratization and liberalization in Korea. That is the security situation, especially with the uses made of it by antidemocratic forces. The border with North Korea after 25 years of division remains tense, unbroken by any measure of peaceful exchanges, and guarded by large armies on either side, poised for action. The reduction in Cold War tensions in the late 1950s and early 1960s probably contributed significantly to the ability in recent years of South Korea to concentrate on, and reshape, its internal priorities and to achieve a greater relaxation of political tensions within its own society. But the events of early 1968—the assassination attempt on President Park and the *Pueblo* incident—climaxing a long, slow buildup of North Korean attempts at infiltration and reflecting in part the new tensions generated by Vietnam, demonstrated how quickly dramatization of the security issue could change the mood and the priorities of the nation. New defense considerations quickly assumed a priority along with economic growth. Even though criticized by many as laying the basis for a "political army" and providing a step backward toward totalitarianism, a plan for arming reservists to counter the new threat was rushed through the Assembly.[26]

Whatever the validity of such charges in this most recent case, it is unquestionably true that the security threat hanging over South Korea strengthens the influence of the military in Korea and perhaps even more the position of such antidemocratic civilian organs as the CIA, while it militates generally against movements toward the liberalization of political thought. The greater the tension at any particular time, the more the authoritarian forces come to the fore and the more the moderate voices are weakened. Security crackdowns and dramatic spy cases have also served as both diversions from, and justification for, possible harsh internal political methods being employed at the time. Like the presence of the military, therefore, security is a near-permanent consideration in Korea, made all the more serious by the fact that it has been used since liberation as the vehicle of influence for those most fearful of, and opposed to, democracy. Those, either abroad or within South Korea, who would see democracy flourish there must find ways to define and better respond to realistic security requirements, without as in the past igniting unnecessary crusades nor feeding the fires of those who, perhaps unwittingly, would destroy Korean society from within.

ECONOMIC POLICY

The decision to amend the constitution to permit a third term had an effect on the management of the economy, as it did on politics. The administration had won reelection in 1967 on an economic platform and sought justification for extending its rule past 1971 on the same basis. For awhile in 1969, therefore, there was such pressure on economic "performance"—exports, investment, growth rates, and so forth—that the supporting economic incentives were pushed to undesirable limits. The exchange rate became increasingly out of line, some interest rates were kept at unreasonably high levels, exports were pushed higher by government-set quotas more than by market incentives and were subsidized by special loans and the allocation of special import privileges, and very high growth targets for the Third Five-Year Plan were suggested, largely in terms of their political effect. The financing of the DRP campaign in the referendum also inspired political manipulation of bank lending by government-controlled institutions on a conspicuous scale.

In the aftermath of the referendum, some of these distortions were adjusted, for example, by a devaluation and a lowering of plan targets.[27] But they pointed up the continuing potential of the government to manipulate the economy for fairly narrow political purposes. For all the movement toward decontrol and greater play to market forces in the mid-1960s, the Korean economy remains very much a managed economy with varying degrees and forms of government control over trade, banks, approval of foreign loans, agricultural price supports, and a large amount of direct investment. With a highly trained bureaucracy and a development-minded leadership, and, on the other hand, a fairly traditional-minded business community, this can be, as it was in the mid-1960s, the means to get rapid results. But its negative potential is also apparent.

Corruption is the symbol of this negative potential. It is important to recognize that corruption can take many forms. At one extreme on the spectrum of sources, there is the extraction of payoffs from monopolistic or highly protected and favored activities that have low or even negative real productivity. At the other extreme the payoffs can be similar to a profits tax or service charge that is collected quite uniformly and equitably from a broad range of productive activities. The spectrum of uses of the payoffs has several dimensions. The beneficiaries may be a single potentate or small oligarchy who exist in regal splendor (the Saudi pattern), or the benefits may be spread very broadly throughout the bureaucracy as a supplement to recognizedly inadequate salaries. A third possibility is to use the proceeds for extrabudgetary activities, including political, religious, or even military undertakings that for various reasons cannot be financed through normal budgetary processes.

Hard data on the extent of corruption in South Korea does not exist, and estimates—a favorite pastime of foreign and domestic observers— are based on only the tip of the iceberg of public scandals or the revelations of friends in business or government. Nevertheless, whether more or less than under previous regimes, corruption has obviously been a part of the 1960s. The founding of the DRP, the financing of two elections and a referendum, the passage of key legislation, and the allocation of investment funds are all closely linked to various forms of corruption. The contrast to the 1950s is in the source and the effects of corruption.

In the 1950s, as described in Chapter 4, the main source of the payoffs was in the allocation of foreign aid funds and of bank loans. Inflation, an overvalued exchange rate, low interest rates, and elaborate government controls formed an environment in which such corruption operated profitably for those involved but to the detriment of sound investments or national economic development. In the 1960s, the source shifted to the foreign private loans that became so important a part of investment financing by 1966 and, more recently, the allocation of bank loans to refinance the repayments by firms who received the original foreign loans. The foreign private capital, however, was introduced in an environment of growth-oriented economic policies, considerable decontrol of the trade sector, and an improved interest rate structure and thus— despite payoffs and the like—fed an investment boom that followed reasonably accurate market indicators of real benefits and costs for the country. Many of the principal investments approved by the government in the mid-1960s from which payoffs were obtained had also been tested and approved on the basis of feasibility studies and general consistency with the interindustry and sectoral planning models developed in connection with the Second Five-Year Plan.

The uses of payoffs in the 1960s has been largely for partisan political activities and, second, to supplement rather broadly the salaries of the bureaucracy. Few countries have found a satisfactory way to finance competitive politics, and Korea is no exception. In a country in which the organized private sector is weak and the government strong, it is inevitable that the main sources of such financing would be through government control over the economy rather than from voluntary contributions of large special interest groups in the private sector. The dangers in the Korean "solution" are obvious: the line between public and partisan decisions becomes extremely fuzzy; the possibility of distorting national interest for partisan ones is great; the opposition parties become beholden to the government for their own support and a participant thereby in the same corruption; the main elements of the private sector, for example, business, also become dependent on government and perforce involved in the system of corruption to the point that it can be held over their heads. All these factors are true in Korea today.

Still, the present system of corruption in South Korea has not yet destroyed either the emphasis on growth or the impact of the more sophisticated economic planners in the cabinet and the bureaucracy evident since 1963. This is perhaps the principal change in the 1960s. It is a situation subject, of course, to considerable and more than likely continuing pressure, particularly when the government, as in 1969, seeks political ends that are controversial and expensive. The effects on the private sector have also had a positive as well as negative side. On the negative side, the business community and others have become practitioners par excellence of the "art of survival"; it is notable that the principal business firms have been largely constant in South Korea since the 1950s, despite changes of government, economic reform, and periodic attacks on the more conspicuous ones. This inhibits the development of a fully free, market-oriented business community, and it will similarly continue to inhibit, as in the past, the development of independent labor and professional groups. On the positive side, the siphoning off of percentages from business transactions, occasional government-inspired crusades against certain business enterprises (for various reasons), and the threat of further government action have had an inhibiting effect on the growth of political power and of massive concentrations of wealth or indulgence in conspicuous consumption on the part of the major business leaders. In contrast to Japan, the business giants of South Korea do not wield independent political power. They are subject to the pressures of politics as the government sees them, and these can be pressures reflecting from time to time, as in the past, the demands of small and medium industries, labor, or public outrage over scandal.

CONCLUSION

Institutional protection for political democracy in South Korea is fragile. For that reason the future of at least peaceful growth of political democracy lies very much in the hands of the leaders, and is shaped by their outlook and predilections. The third-term issue that came into the open in 1969 was thus more significant than the questions alone of continued growth and stability and of the leadership ability of President Park. These questions are still of great importance to Koreans today: with all the special advantages at the government's disposal, it is still impressive that when the third-term issue was put to a popular vote, Park won handily.[28] But the opposition to the government was also significant, concentrated solidly in the cities and among the more articulate elements of the population. To them, the basic issue at stake was once again the future of democratic politics, made all the more symbolic by the memory of Rhee's use of the popular referendum to extend his tenure, and a similar rural-urban dichotomy in the outcome. Beyond symbols was the reality in 1968–1969 of the rise in influence of the CIA and other forces of coercion to mute press criticism, confront student protests, overwhelm opposition in the Assembly, and raise funds for the referendum.

The consensus of the previous few years was thus considerably weakened, based as it was on both economic growth and minimum guarantees of political democracy, and including of necessity the support of the intelligentsia. It will remain weak and fluctuating until there are stronger institutional and ideological bases for a steadily widening range of political activity and a greater measure of political freedom.

Economic policy is in turn subject to two forces in South Korea today. One is the new national consensus behind rapid growth, with its effect on political attitudes, and backed by the growing economic sophistication of government leaders, bureaucrats, and ministers. Second is the functioning of the political system that—with weak parties, limited support and activity from independent private groups, and the continuing battle between authoritarian and democratically oriented forces—will subject the economy to distortion, corruption, and the threat of major mismanagement. The shifting balance between these two forces over time is still very difficult to predict.

Appendix Tables

Notes

Selected Bibliography

Index

Appendix Tables

Appendix Table 1   Gross National Product by Industrial Origin
(in billions of *won* at constant 1965 market prices)

Year	GNP	Agriculture, forestry, and fisheries	Mining and manufacturing	Social overhead[a]	Other services[b]
1953	421.9	203.4	37.0	17.1	164.5
1954	447.4	219.1	23.0	20.7	164.5
1955	474.5	224.1	52.5	22.4	175.6
1956	480.5	212.2	61.5	24.8	182.0
1957	522.7	230.6	69.1	28.3	194.7
1958	551.7	246.3	74.4	30.6	200.4
1959	575.8	243.7	81.3	35.5	215.4
1960	589.1	244.0	88.8	37.3	219.0
1961	613.6	268.5	91.6	39.1	214.3
1962	635.0	252.4	106.0	44.5	232.1
1963	693.0	270.6	123.5	51.3	247.7
1964	750.3	314.3	130.1	57.5	248.4
1965	805.9	311.6	157.5	70.0	266.6
1966	913.8	345.9	181.4	84.8	301.7
1967	995.4	326.9	222.2	99.8	346.3
1968	1,127.3	330.8	279.6	130.0	386.8

Source: Bank of Korea, *Economic Statistics Yearbook,* 1969.

[a] Social overhead includes construction, transportation, storage, communication, electricity, water, and sanitary services.

[b] Other services include wholesale and retail trade, banking, insurance and real estate, ownership of dwellings, public administration and defense, services, and the rest of the world.

Appendix Table 2   Composition of GNP by Industrial Origin
(percent, based on constant 1965 market prices)

Year	Agriculture, forestry, and fisheries	Mining and manufacturing	Social overhead	Other services	GNP
1953	48.2	8.8	4.0	39.0	100.0
1954	49.0	9.6	4.6	36.8	100.0
1955	47.2	11.1	4.7	37.0	100.0
1956	44.2	12.8	5.1	37.9	100.0
1957	44.1	13.2	5.4	37.3	100.0
1958	44.6	13.5	5.6	36.3	100.0
1959	42.3	14.1	6.2	37.4	100.0
1960	41.4	15.1	6.3	37.2	100.0
1961	43.8	14.9	6.4	34.9	100.0
1962	39.7	16.7	7.0	36.6	100.0
1963	39.1	17.8	7.4	35.7	100.0
1964	41.9	17.3	7.7	33.1	100.0
1965	38.7	19.5	8.7	33.1	100.0
1966	37.9	19.8	9.3	33.0	100.0
1967	32.7	22.3	10.0	35.0	100.0
1968	29.4	24.8	11.5	34.3	100.0

Source: Bank of Korea, Economic Statistics Yearbook, 1969. Notes: See Appendix Table 1.

Appendix Table 3   Annual Rates of Growth of GNP by Industrial Origin
(percent, based on constant 1965 market prices)

Year	Agriculture, forestry, and fisheries	Mining and manufacturing	Social overhead	Other services	GNP
1954	7.7	16.4	21.1	0.0	6.0
1955	2.3	22.0	8.0	6.7	6.1
1956	−5.3	17.0	10.7	3.7	1.2
1957	8.6	12.5	14.3	7.0	8.8
1958	6.8	7.7	8.0	2.9	5.5
1959	−1.1	9.3	16.1	7.4	4.4
1960	0.1	9.2	5.0	1.7	2.3
1961	10.1	3.2	5.0	−2.2	4.2
1962	−6.0	15.7	13.8	8.3	3.5
1963	7.2	16.5	15.1	6.7	9.1
1964	16.2	5.4	12.1	0.3	8.3
1965	−0.9	21.1	21.9	7.3	7.4
1966	11.0	15.2	21.0	13.2	13.4
1967	−6.0	22.5	17.8	14.8	8.9
1968	1.2	25.9	30.2	11.7	13.3

Source: Bank of Korea, Economic Statistics Yearbook, 1969. Notes: See Appendix Table 1.

Appendix Table 4 Detailed Composition of GNP by Industrial Origin
(percent, based on constant 1965 market prices)

Year	Agriculture and forestry	Fisheries	Mining and Quarrying	Manufacturing	Construction	Electricity, water, and sanitation	Transportation, storage, and communication	Wholesale and retail trade	Banking, insurance, and real estate	Ownership of dwelling	Public administration and defense	Other services	Rest of world
1953	46.8	1.4	0.9	7.8	2.1	0.5	1.5	12.1	1.4	5.1	11.0	7.2	1.2
1954	47.8	1.2	0.7	8.9	2.2	0.6	1.9	12.0	1.0	4.9	9.7	7.4	1.7
1955	46.1	1.1	0.8	10.3	2.2	0.5	2.0	13.1	1.3	4.7	9.1	7.2	1.6
1956	42.6	1.6	0.8	12.0	2.0	0.6	2.5	13.5	1.3	4.8	8.7	8.1	1.5
1957	42.3	1.8	1.0	12.2	2.4	0.7	2.4	14.4	1.3	4.5	7.6	7.9	1.5
1958	43.0	1.6	1.0	12.5	2.3	0.8	2.5	14.2	1.5	4.4	6.7	8.1	1.4
1959	40.8	1.5	1.1	13.0	2.5	0.9	2.8	15.5	1.6	4.2	6.3	8.4	1.4
1960	40.1	1.3	1.4	13.7	2.4	0.9	3.0	16.1	1.7	4.2	6.1	7.8	1.3
1961	42.3	1.5	1.4	13.5	2.6	0.9	2.9	15.2	1.6	4.1	5.8	7.3	0.9
1962	37.6	1.5	1.7	15.0	2.9	1.0	3.2	16.3	1.7	4.1	5.8	7.6	1.0
1963	37.5	1.6	1.7	16.1	3.0	1.0	3.4	16.3	1.6	3.8	5.5	7.5	1.0
1964	40.2	1.7	1.8	15.6	2.9	1.1	3.6	14.6	1.6	3.6	5.2	7.2	0.9
1965	37.0	1.7	1.8	17.7	3.4	1.3	4.0	14.8	1.6	3.5	5.0	7.3	0.9
1966	36.3	1.6	1.7	18.1	3.8	1.3	4.1	15.3	1.5	3.2	4.7	7.0	1.4
1967	31.0	1.8	1.7	20.6	3.9	1.6	4.6	16.4	1.5	3.0	4.6	7.0	2.2
1968	27.8	1.8	1.5	23.4	4.8	1.7	5.0	16.9	1.6	2.8	4.3	6.8	2.0

Source: Bank of Korea, *Economic Statistics Yearbook*, 1969.

Appendix Table 5   Total Available Resources and Their Disposition
(in billions of *won* at current market prices)

Year	Total available resources	GNP	Imports of goods and services	Exports of goods and services[a]	Net capital inflow	Consumption		Gross investment		Statistical Discrepancy
						Private	Government	Private	Government	
1953	51.3	48.2	4.7	1.5	3.2	39.9	3.8	7.3	0.4	
1954	70.4	66.9	4.9	1.4	3.5	55.8	6.8	6.6	1.1	
1955	124.2	116.1	11.4	3.3	8.1	100.3	10.1	11.5	2.3	
1956	168.9	152.4	20.0	3.5	16.5	140.6	13.9	11.2	3.2	
1957	217.1	197.8	23.7	4.4	19.3	165.5	21.4	22.2	8.1	
1958	223.7	207.2	22.1	5.7	16.4	170.8	26.2	19.5	7.3	
1959	226.1	221.0	22.4	7.3	15.1	181.5	30.9	15.6	8.2	
1960	267.7	246.7	31.0	10.0	21.0	207.3	35.5	18.6	8.2	1.9
1961	322.1	296.8	43.8	18.5	25.3	245.4	40.1	25.8	13.0	− 2.2
1962	386.3	348.6	58.9	21.2	37.7	293.8	49.6	26.3	19.2	− 2.6
1963	540.4	488.0	79.5	27.1	52.4	399.6	54.7	72.1	17.6	− 3.6
1964	746.0	696.8	96.5	47.3	49.2	586.0	62.0	74.6	26.7	− 3.1
1965	858.5	805.9	128.9	76.3	52.6	669.1	76.0	87.2	31.3	− 5.1
1966	1,119.7	1,032.0	207.8	120.2	87.6	805.9	104.8	173.8	49.3	− 14.2
1967	1,358.0	1,242.4	279.4	166.6	112.8	973.5	132.2	210.3	61.9	− 19.9
1968	1,760.0	1,575.7	416.8	232.5	184.3	1,191.8	175.3	331.0[b]	90.3[b]	− 28.4

Source: Bank of Korea, *Economic Statistics Yearbook,* 1969.
[a] Includes net factor income from the rest of the world.
[b] Estimated.

Appendix Table 6   Composition of Total Available Resources and Their Disposition[a]

Year	Total available resources	GNP	Imports of goods and services	Exports of goods and services[b]	Net capital inflow	Consumption		Investment		
						Private	Government	Private	Government	Total
1953	100	93.9	9.2	3.1	6.1	77.6	7.4	14.3	.7	15.0
1954	100	95.0	7.0	2.0	5.0	79.3	9.6	9.5	1.6	11.1
1955	100	93.5	9.2	2.7	6.5	80.8	8.1	9.3	1.8	11.1
1956	100	90.3	11.8	2.1	9.7	83.3	8.2	6.6	1.9	8.5
1957	100	91.1	10.9	2.0	8.9	76.2	9.9	10.2	3.7	13.9
1958	100	92.7	9.9	2.6	7.3	76.3	11.7	8.7	3.3	12.0
1959	100	93.6	9.5	3.1	6.4	76.9	13.1	6.6	3.4	10.0
1960	100	92.2	11.6	3.8	7.8	77.4	13.3	6.9	3.1	10.0
1961	100	92.1	13.6	5.7	7.9	76.2	12.4	8.0	4.1	12.1
1962	100	90.2	15.2	5.4	9.8	76.1	12.8	6.8	5.0	11.8
1963	100	90.3	14.7	5.0	9.7	74.0	10.1	13.3	3.3	16.6
1964	100	93.4	12.9	6.3	6.6	78.5	8.3	10.0	3.6	13.6
1965	100	93.9	15.0	9.9	6.1	77.9	8.9	10.2	3.6	13.8
1966	100	92.2	18.6	10.8	7.8	72.0	9.3	15.5	4.4	19.9
1967	100	91.7	20.6	12.3	8.3	71.8	9.8	15.5	4.6	20.1
1968	100	89.5	23.7	13.2	10.5	67.7	10.0	18.8	5.1	23.9

Source: Bank of Korea, Economic Statistics Yearbook, 1969.
a Omits statistical discrepancy shown in Appendix Table 5.
b Includes net factor income from the rest of the world.

Appendix Table 7 Domestic and Foreign Saving, Amount and Percent of GNP

| | Amount in billions of won | | | | | Percent of GNP | | | | |
| | | Domestic | | | | | Domestic | | | |
Year	Total[a]	Private[a]	Govern-ment	Total[a]	Foreign	Total[a]	Private[a]	Govern-ment	Total[a]	Foreign
1953	7.7	5.7	−1.2	4.5	3.2	15.9	11.8	−2.4	9.4	6.6
1954	7.8	6.1	−1.8	4.3	3.5	11.6	9.1	−2.6	6.5	5.2
1955	13.8	8.4	−2.7	5.7	8.1	11.8	7.2	−2.3	4.9	6.9
1956	14.4	2.4	−4.4	−2.1	16.5	9.5	1.5	−2.8	−1.3	10.8
1957	30.3	16.9	−6.1	10.9	19.3	15.3	8.1	−3.0	5.1	9.7
1958	26.7	16.7	−6.4	10.3	16.5	12.8	8.0	−3.0	5.0	7.9
1959	23.7	14.6	−5.9	8.7	15.1	10.7	6.6	−2.6	4.0	6.8
1960	26.8	10.8	−5.0	5.8	21.0	10.8	4.4	−2.0	2.4	8.5
1961	38.8	18.8	−5.3	13.5	25.3	13.0	6.2	−1.7	4.5	8.5
1962	45.5	12.6	−4.9	7.8	37.7	13.0	2.7	−1.4	1.3	10.8
1963	89.7	38.6	−1.3	37.3	52.4	18.4	7.8	−.2	7.6	10.7
1964	101.2	48.4	3.6	52.0	49.2	14.5	6.9	.5	7.4	7.1
1965	118.5	51.8	14.0	65.9	52.7	14.7	6.4	1.7	8.1	6.5
1966	223.1	106.4	29.1	135.5	97.6	21.6	10.3	2.8	13.1	8.5
1967	272.2	110.3	51.9	162.1	112.9	21.9	8.9	4.2	13.1	9.1
1968	421.3			237.0	184.3	26.7			15.0	11.7

Source: Bank of Korea, Economic Statistics Yearbook, 1969.
[a] Includes the statistical discrepancy.

Appendix Table 8   Gross Domestic Capital Formation by Industrial Use
(in billions of *won* at constant 1965 market prices)

Year	Total fixed capital formation	Agriculture, forestry, and fisheries	Mining and manufacturing	Social overhead	Other services	Change in stocks
1953	35.3	4.0	7.1	7.1	17.1	34.3
1954	41.7	3.5	6.7	10.5	21.0	16.2
1955	49.0	4.5	13.6	10.5	20.4	12.4
1956	52.8	5.1	18.5	10.9	18.3	4.5
1957	61.3	6.5	20.6	16.7	17.5	26.6
1958	57.8	5.4	18.2	16.3	17.9	19.9
1959	59.3	6.0	13.6	17.2	32.5	−1.5
1960	61.7	7.0	16.2	13.8	24.7	0.8
1961	65.3	8.4	14.2	21.2	21.5	7.7
1962	84.1	6.7	18.5	32.2	26.7	−6.1
1963	106.0	10.3	25.5	41.0	29.2	31.3
1964	93.3	10.7	23.3	28.2	31.1	21.1
1965	117.6	13.7	32.0	32.6	39.3	0.8
1966	190.6	23.2	63.7	58.5	45.2	16.8
1967	232.1	19.2	61.8	93.5	57.6	9.6
1968	325.6	24.4	80.8	129.7	90.7	18.5

Source: Bank of Korea, *Economic Statistics Yearbook,* 1969.
Note: For breakdown of sectors in social overhead and other services, see Appendix Table 1.

Appendix Table 9 Tax Burden to GNP

| Year | Amount in billions of won | | | Percent of GNP | | | | |
| | GNP | Gross tax burden[a] | Marginal tax rate, percent | Gross tax burden | Central government taxes | | | Local government taxes |
					Total	Direct	Indirect and monopoly profits[a]	
1957	197.8	14.7		7.5	6.7	2.9	3.8	0.8
1958	207.2	16.8	21.8	8.1	7.3	2.8	4.5	0.8
1959	221.0	21.3	32.9	9.7	8.7	3.5	5.2	1.0
1960	246.7	24.4	12.1	9.9	9.0	3.0	6.0	0.9
1961	296.8	28.2	7.5	9.5	8.6	3.1	5.5	0.9
1962	348.6	38.2	19.3	11.0	9.5	2.8	6.7	1.5
1963	488.0	44.0	4.2	9.0	7.5	2.5	5.0	1.5
1964	696.8	52.1	3.9	7.5	6.2	2.5	3.7	1.3
1965	805.9	70.3	16.7	8.7	7.3	2.9	4.4	1.4
1966	1,032.0	111.9	18.4	10.8	9.3	4.1	5.2	1.5
1967	1,245.1	154.7	20.1	12.4	11.3	5.0	6.3	1.1
1968	1,575.7	221.4	20.5	14.1	13.1	5.7	7.4	1.1

Source: Economic Planning Board, Major Economic Indicators, Mar. 1969.
[a] Excludes temporary foreign exchange tax in 1958–1962.

Appendix Table 10 Interest Rates on Deposits and Loans of the Commercial Banks

End of year	Deposits			Loans				
	Time deposits of one year	Installment deposits	Notice deposits	Discount on bills	Export trade	Overdrafts	Overdue loans	Call loans
1960	10.0	4.0	3.7	13.8	13.9	18.3	20.0	13.9
1961	15.0	4.0	3.7	13.8	12.8	18.3	20.0	13.9
1962	15.0	10.0	3.7	13.9	9.1	18.3	20.0	13.9
1963	15.0	10.0	3.7	13.9	8.0	18.3	20.0	13.9
1964	15.0	10.0	3.7	14.0	8.0	18.3	20.0	12.0
1965	30.0	30.0	5.0	24.0	6.5	26.0	36.5	22.0
1966	30.0	30.0	5.0	24.0	6.5	28.0	36.5	22.0
1967	30.0	30.0	5.0	24.0	6.0	28.0	36.5	22.0
1968	25.2	25.0	5.0	26.0	6.0	28.0	36.5	22.0

Source: Economic Planning Board, *Major Economic Indicators*, Mar. 1969.

Appendix Table 11   Money Supply and Liquid Assets
(billions of *won*)

Year	Currency	Demand deposits	Money supply	Other bank deposits	Total liquid assets
1957	8.6	5.9	14.5	2.2	16.7
1958	11.1	8.2	19.3	3.3	22.6
1959	12.4	10.9	23.3	2.6	25.9
1960	13.9	10.6	24.5	6.5	31.0
1961	16.7	17.8	34.4	6.9	41.3
1962	18.0	22.8	40.8	15.9	56.7
1963	18.3	23.1	41.4	15.6	57.0
1964	24.9	23.7	48.6	19.3	67.9
1965	31.6	33.1	64.7	45.4	110.1
1966	42.9	41.3	84.2	79.6	163.8
1967	57.6	62.4	120.0	141.3	261.3
1968	81.9	68.0	149.8	305.1	454.9

Source: Bank of Korea, *Economic Statistics Yearbook,* 1969.

Appendix Table 12   Grant Foreign Economic Aid Received by Korea
(in thousands of U.S. Dollars)

Year	Total value	Year	Total value
1951	106,542	1960	245,393
1952	161,327	1961	199,245
1953	194,170	1962	232,310
1954	153,925	1963	216,446
1955	236,707	1964	149,331
1956	326,705	1965	131,441
1957	382,892	1966	103,261
1958	321,272	1967	97,018
1959	222,204	1968	105,856

Source: Bank of Korea, *Economic Statistics Yearbook,* 1969.

Notes

INTRODUCTION

1. "Modernization" might in some ways be a better term here than development, encompassing more clearly both the transition to modern economic structure and the development of political institutions appropriate to a relatively industrialized, mass-participation society. See Cyril Black, *The Dynamics of Modernization* (New York: Harper & Row, 1966), and David Apter, *The Politics of Modernization* (Chicago: University of Chicago Press, 1965). It is also useful in making a clear distinction between the categories for analysis of nonmodernized and modern countries. See Marion Levy, *Modernization and the Structure of Societies* (Princeton, N.J.: Princeton University Press, 1966), 1, 9–32.

In fact we use "modernization" and "development" nearly interchangeably in this book to refer to the economic side of the process. However, aside from being common usage, "development" has somewhat more appropriate value connotations for our view of the political side. When referring to today's developing countries, which still face both the task of economic modernization and some measure of choice in the pattern of political modernization accompanying it, "development" connotes to us more an evolvement toward one type of modernization—that which provides for a relatively large measure of political liberty. "Modernized" political systems, by contrast, can well encompass totalitarian as well as democratic in terms of meeting certain functional requisites of a modern state. See Samuel Huntington, *Political Order in Changing Societies* (New Haven, Conn.: Yale University Press, 1968), pp. 1–8.

2. It should be noted that, with this definition, the concept of "development" ceases to apply when the task of economic modernization is no longer a major national priority. That obviously does not mean that economically modern—i.e., developed—nations do not face major political and economic issues, some analogous to those in the Third World. But it does suggest that the basic circumstances, and particularly the ability to mobilize national resources to meet mass needs, are of such a different nature in modern societies as to call for a different conceptual framework for analysis.

3. A number of studies of this type have been made in recent years by Simon Kuznets. See his series on quantitative aspects of development carried in *Economic Development and Cultural Change*, vols. 5–8 (1956–1964); Hollis Chenery, "Patterns of Industrial Growth," *American Economic Review*, 50 (Sept. 1960), 624–654; Hollis Chenery and Alan Strout, "Foreign Assistance and Economic Development," *American Economic Review*, 56 (Sept. 1966), 679–733; and Lance J. Taylor, *Aggregate Structural Change: Recent Time Series and Cross-Section Evidence* (Cambridge, Mass.: Project for Quantitative Research on Economic Development, Harvard University, 1967).

4. There have been no cross-section studies of policies comparable to the work of Kuznets and Chenery on structure of output and demand. The recent book by Richard A. Musgrave, *Fiscal Systems* (New Haven, Conn.: Yale University Press, 1968) and several others in the series on comparative economic systems have begun to probe the areas of comparative policy. Albert Waterston's *Development Planning, Lessons from Experience* (Baltimore, Md.: Johns Hopkins University Press, 1963) tries to do the same thing for planning.

5. In addition to the Cyril Black work cited earlier, see A. F. K. Organski, *The Stages of Political Development* (New York: Alfred Knopf, 1965). Related to these are the studies of modernization emphasizing major social transformations, often related to major economic changes, e.g., Edward Shils, *Political Development in the New States* (The Hague: Mouton and Company, 1962), and Marion Levy, *Modernization and the Structure of Societies*. By contrast, S. N. Eisenstadt, *The Political System of Empires* (Glenco, Ill.: Free Press, 1963), analyzes comparative political systems of several preindustrial empires in terms of many of the same characteristics associated in recent writings with political and economic modernization.

6. Lucien Pye, "Concept of Political Development," *Annals of the American Academy of Political and Social Science*, 358 (Mar. 1965), 1–14; Gabriel Almond and G. Bingham Powell, Jr., *Comparative Politics, A Developmental Approach* (Boston: Little, Brown, 1966), pp. 16–43; Eisenstadt, *Political System of Empires*, pp. 13–22.

7. W. Arthur Lewis, *Development Planning* (New York: Harper, 1966), p. 93.

8. Lucien Pye and Sidney Verba, *Political Culture and Political Development* (Princeton, N.J.: Princeton University Press, 1965), p. 13. The concept of equality is stressed in numerous recent works on political development; see Fred Riggs, "The Theory of Political Development," in James C. Charlesworth, ed., *Contemporary Political Analysis* (Glencoe, Ill.: Free Press, 1967).

9. On political parties, see Fred Riggs, "Bureaucratic and Political Development: A Paradoxical View," in Joseph La Palombara, ed., *Bureaucracy and Political Development* (Princeton, N.J.: Princeton University Press, 1963), pp. 127–131. On the conflict of political and economic objectives in general, see La Palombara, "Notes, Queries and Dilemmas," ibid., p. 60.

10. Huntington, *Political Order in Changing Societies*, pp. 49–59. See also Huntington's testimony before the House Foreign Affairs Subcommittee on Asian and Pacific Affairs, *Rural Development in Asia* (Washington, D.C.: U.S. Government Printing Office, 1967), 1, 115–121. By contrast, Robert

Packenham recommends closer attention by political development theorists to the interacting factors of political and economic development. *Foreign Aid and Political Development* (Stanford, Calif.: Stanford University Press, 1971), Chap. 11.

11. Apter, *Politics of Modernization*, pp. 357–390.

12. Ibid., p. 372.

CHAPTER 1. THE ANTECEDENTS OF RECENT DEVELOPMENT

1. Gregory Henderson, *Korea: The Politics of the Vortex* (Cambridge, Mass.: Harvard University Press, 1968). Henderson was attached to the American Embassy in Seoul for seven years. In that time and subsequently, he has acquired a knowledge of Korean culture and history rivaled by few Westerners.

2. Hahn-Been Lee, *Time, Change and Administration: Korea's Search for Modernization* (Honolulu, Hawaii: East-West Center, 1968). Professor Lee, "biographer of the Korean bureaucracy," served as Director of the Budget Bureau and later Vice-Minister of Finance in the Korean government. In these posts he pioneered in new administrative methods and in the introduction of young postliberation Korean college graduates into responsible positions within the bureaucracy. Presently he is Dean of the Graduate School of Public Administration, Seoul National University.

3. Henderson, *Korea*, pp. 21–30, 34–35. See also John K. Fairbanks, Edwin O. Reischauer, and Albert M. Craig, *East Asia, the Modern Transformation* (Boston: Houghton Mifflin, 1965), pp. 419–431, 448–449.

4. Henderson, *Korea*, pp. 16–18. For a discussion of differences between the military rulers of 1170–1258 and the Japanese feudal shogunate, see Fairbanks, *East Asia*, p. 423.

5. Henderson, *Korea*, pp. 33–55, 195–198.

6. Ibid., p. 49.

7. One exception should be cited: the Independence Club, which in the late nineteenth century looked to the United States for both ideological inspiration in promoting reform and political influence as an international counterweight to Korea's often predatory neighbors. The group enjoyed considerable popular support for a time. But, though it worked to maintain and modernize, rather than overthrow the monarchy, it was crushed by the conservative forces in the government. See Chong-Sik Lee, *The Politics of Korean Nationalism* (Berkeley: University of California Press, 1963), pp. 58–67.

8. By 1938, Christians were reported to be 500,000. Later estimates vary. Kyu-Taik Kim and Hanh-Bae Ho, using government census figures from 1960, place the figure at 3.5 percent of the population, "Korean Political Leaders (1953–1962): Their Social Origins and Skills," *Asian Survey*, 3, no. 7 (July 1963), 316. Kyung-Cho Chung, *Korea Tomorrow: Land of the Morning Calm* (New York: MacMillan, 1956), p. 60, puts the figure at one million, which would mean approximately 5 percent. The Korea Information Service,

Facts about Korea 1963 (Seoul, 1963), p. 80, suggests "close to two million" believers, equaling perhaps as much as 7–8 percent.

9. Christian schools were reduced by Japanese pressure from 230 in 1917 to 34 schools and 3 colleges by 1937. Henderson, *Korea*, p. 89.

10. Kim and Ho, "Korean Political Leaders," p. 316.

11. Chong-Sik Lee, *Politics of Korean Nationalism,* pp. 129–233.

12. Ibid. Lee concludes that the probability of Korean nationalists being able to work together after 1945, even if the country had not been divided, was not very great.

13. Ibid. See also Dae-Sook Suh, *The Korean Communist Movement 1918–48* (Princeton, N.J.: Princeton University Press, 1967), p. 335. Henderson, *Korea,* pp. 113–147, gives a good account of the struggle among indigenous and exiled nationalist leaders in the period immediately after liberation.

14. This is the central thesis of Henderson's book. For a summary statement, see ibid., pp. 193–194.

15. Felix Moos, *Social Characteristics and Rural Development in Korea* (Seoul: United States Operations Mission to Korea, 1966).

16. Kyung-Dong Kim, "Entrepreneurs and Politics," draft chapter for Chong-Sik Lee and Sung-Chick Hong, *Politics and Society in Korea* (expected date of publication, 1971), pp. 7–8.

17. Another advantage was the absence of strong religious or cultural resistance to family planning. It was not until the 1960s that this became a governmental priority. But when it did, the obstacles were more organizational and financial than cultural—a rather significant factor in the country's recent success in this field. See *New York Times,* Nov. 11, 1967, p. 13.

18. Refugees plus the returning exiles accounted for much of Korea's increase in population which, in the three years after liberation, rose from 16 to 20 million. Henderson, *Korea,* p. 137.

19. Richard Allen, *Korea's Syngman Rhee: An Unauthorized Portrait* (Rutland, Vt.: Charles Tuttle, 1960), p. 104.

20. For accounts of American background preparation and occupation policies, see Won-Sul Lee, "Impact of U.S. Occupation Policy on the Socio-Political Structure of South Korea, 1945–48" (unpublished Ph.D. thesis, Western Reserve University, 1961); E. Grant Meade, *American Military Government in Korea* (New York: King's Crown Press, 1951), which reviews the overall policy of the period and provides a detailed description of administration in one province; and Henderson, *Korea,* pp. 113–162. American policy, in terms of its international framework, is treated in Leland Goodrich, *Korea: A Study of U.S. Policy in the United Nations* (New York: Council on Foreign Relations, 1956), pp. 17–25, and Carl Berger, *The Korea Knot: A Military-Political History* (Philadelphia: University of Pennsylvania Press, 1957), pp. 62–73.

21. For a detailed description of Rhee's rise to power, see Allen, *Korea's Syngman Rhee.*

22. Henderson, *Korea,* pp. 157–161.

23. In 1953 the South Korean government had three times as many officials as Japan had used for the whole country. Ibid., p. 161. An analysis of

the background, training, and outlook of the bureaucracy from 1948 to 1960 is presented in Hahn-Been Lee, *Time, Change and Administration,* pp. 101–108.

24. Henderson, *Korea,* pp. 139–147, 163. Arrests reached nearly 90,000 in the year following the Yosu uprising of 1948. Two years later, about 30,000–40,000 political prisoners were still in prison.

25. Robert Nathan Associates, *An Economic Program for Korean Reconstruction* (prepared for the United States Korean Reconstruction Agency, 1954), p. 38.

26. One of the stimulants to reform was the heavy rise in landholding under the Japanese, which gave rise to popular feelings of the lack of legitimacy in such holdings. Second was the egalitarianism present in Korean thinking, which had originated in the demand for upward mobility and the concomitant decline of class rigidity already evident in traditional society, but now reinforced by the concepts of equality that were part of both Western and Communist-influenced nationalist ideology sweeping Korea. Such thinking affected the landlord class as well, in its drive for status, as its members entered postliberation elections in great numbers, anxious to move from local positions to the center of power.

A third influence was North Korea's land reform program begun as early as 1946. The American Military Government had in turn begun reform in the South in 1947, redistributing some of the Japanese-owned land over which it had assumed control. Finally, in the new government after independence, land reform became a major issue in the almost immediate struggle for power between the Assembly and the president. Assembly members, for this reason, were seemingly willing to eschew class and economic ties to press reform upon a reluctant president.

The land reform legislation was finally adopted in 1950 after a protracted struggle. But even before this, landlords had been selling their holdings in anticipation of it. Henderson, *Korea,* pp. 49, 289–290.

27. There were two types of land distributed: purchased land of Korean landowners of which 918,548 family households were beneficiaries, and confiscated Japanese land of which 727,632 households were beneficiaries—with some overlap between these two groups of beneficiaries. Ki-Hyuk Pak, et al., *A Study of Land Tenure in Korea* (Seoul: Korea Land Economics Research Center, 1966), pp. 94–95.

28. Ibid., p. 99.

29. Hahn-Been Lee, *Time, Change and Administration,* pp. 55–57. See also figures on damage and relief requirements in Message of the President of the United States Requesting Legislation for the Rehabilitation and Economic Support of the Republic of Korea, 1953, reprinted in Gene Lyons, *Military Policy and Economic Aid, The Korean Case 1950–1953* (Columbus: Ohio State University Press, 1961), p. 259.

30. United States Operations Mission to Korea, *Summary of United States Aid to Korea,* 1953–1966 (Seoul, 1967).

31. Bank of Korea, *Monthly Statistical Review,* 9, no. 3 (Mar. 1965), 21, 77, 88. The level of budget assistance from foreign aid grew from a third of

the total budget in 1954 to 58.4 percent in 1956; it was still at 38 percent in 1960.

32. For a description of the variety of United States aid inputs at the peak of the American program, see United Nations Command, Office of Economic Coordinator for Korea, *Program Accomplishments, Fiscal Year 1957* (Seoul, 1957).

33. Serious disagreements over assistance policies and economic matters existed between the Rhee government and the UN Command during the war. These are described in Lyons, *Military Policy and Economic Aid.*

34. See also Chap. 4.

35. Hahn-Been Lee, *Time, Change and Administration*, p. 55.

36. In 1910, only 11 Korean cities had had a population of over 14,000, representing together but 4 percent of the population. In 1940 there were, according to one estimate, at least 50 cities over 15,000, and, by another, close to 75 cities. Population in these cities was estimated at between 14 and 19 percent of the total Korean population. Henderson, *Korea*, p. 100, cites the lower figures; Hahn-Been Lee, *Time, Change and Administration*, p. 61, using figures of the *Korean Statistical Yearbook 1965*, cites the higher ones. Estimates and comparisons of pre-1945 to post-1945 figures are made more difficult by the division of the country.

37. Henderson, *Korea*, p. 100.

38. Ibid., p. 89.

39. Republic of Korea, Ministry of Education, *Education in Korea 1965–1966* (Seoul, n.d.), p. 1.

40. See below, Chap. 7.

41. Hahn-Been Lee, *Time, Change and Administration*, p. 63.

42. Henderson, *Korea*, p. 172.

43. See below, Chap. 3.

44. Hahn-Been Lee, *Time, Change and Administration*, p. 68.

45. Ibid., p. 127.

46. Mun-ak Park, *Kaebal Haengjong-ron* "(On Developmental Administration)" (Seoul: Pak Yong Sa, 1967), pp. 238–239, cites a survey of newspaper editorials written between 1945 and 1947 that showed 66 percent to be political in subject content, and only 11.5 percent economic. An American official could comment in 1947 that "If ever the behavior of a people were conditioned, not to say determined, by noneconomic forces, those people are South Koreans today." United States Military Government in Korea, "South Korea Interim Government Activities" (USAMGIK Rep. no. 25, 1947), p. 1, quoted in Henderson, *Korea*, introductory notes, p. 379.

47. Hahn-Been Lee, *Time, Change and Administration*, p. 59.

48. Figures, official and unofficial, on this subject are consistently weak, both in the categories used and the sources of data. For example, the Ministry of Education, Republic of Korea, *Annual Survey of Education 1965*, showed 58 percent of the previous year's college graduates employed three months after graduation, 14 percent unemployed, the rest unknown. A check on the figures behind the *Annual Survey* revealed that they were based entirely on school records; a check on the latter found such records to be

largely nonexistent wth figures "manufactured" for the survey. See June-Il Rhee, "Student Unemployment," *Reports of the Student Intern Program* (Seoul: United States Operations Mission to Korea, 1965). Newspapers, on the other hand, prefer to refer to graduates "satisfactory employed" and one such survey put that figure at 10 percent (*Korea Times*, Nov. 26, 1964).

49. Henderson, *Korea*, p. 198. See also below, Chap. 4.

50. See below, Chap. 8.

51. During the last two years of the Korean War, Rhee engaged in a fierce debate with United States military officials, demanding the use of UN and other funds for rapid new investment when United States officials were calling for concentration on stabilization and relief measures. Lyons, *Military Policy and Economic Aid.* For a somewhat different, but much more general treatment of the issues involved, see W. D. Reeve, *The Republic of Korea: A Political and Economic Study* (London: Oxford University Press, 1961), pp. 108–116.

52. Allen, *Korea's Syngman Rhee*, p. 213.

53. Hahn-Been Lee, *Time, Change and Administration*, p. 80.

54. Allen, *Korea's Syngman Rhee*, pp. 139–151.

55. Henderson, *Korea*, p. 274.

56. Hahn-Been Lee, *Time, Change and Administration*, p. 66.

57. Ibid., pp. 87–91. This was the forerunner of the First Five-Year Economic Development Plan, finally issued in 1962. See below, Chap. 9.

58. For an analysis of the changes, see ibid., pp. 91–101.

59. Henderson, *Korea*, p. 173.

60. Hahn-Been Lee, *Time, Change and Administration*, pp. 103–108.

61. The details of the events in early 1960 are drawn from Henderson, *Korea*, pp. 174–175, and *Korea Annual 1964* (Seoul: Hapdong News Agency, 1964), pp. 89–91.

62. Henderson, *Korea*, p. 175.

63. Hahn-Been Lee, *Time, Change and Administration*, pp. 113–132, passim.

64. The Democratic party leadership was descended in about the same proportion from landlord families (41 percent for the Democratic, 37 percent for the Liberal). The mean age of the Democratic leadership was 51.8 compared to 53.4 for the Liberals. Almost all the leaders, in both cases, had had their last schooling under the Japanese. Kim and Ho, "Korean Political Leaders," pp. 309, 314.

65. For two analyses of the origins of the factions in the Democratic party, see Henderson, *Korea*, pp. 275–278, 299–300, giving regional, cultural, and political background; and Hahn-Been Lce, *Time, Change and Administration*, pp. 135–138, giving professional experience and outlook.

66. Describing secret student meetings prior to the Mar. 1960 elections, Henderson wrote: "Attending such meetings one had a strong sensation of the call to action and responsibility which such cells felt, sensing no other groups in the society to whom they could turn." Henderson, *Korea*, pp. 174–175.

67. Ibid., pp. 178–179.

68. Hahn-Been Lee, *Time, Change and Administration*, p. 117.
69. Ibid., p. 180.
70. Ibid., p. 179.
71. Ibid., p. 141.

CHAPTER 2. THE CHANGE IN LEADERSHIP: TRANSITION FROM MILITARY TO CIVILIAN GOVERNMENT 1961–1964

1. See Roy Appleman, *U.S. Army in the Korean War: South to the Naktong, North to the Yalu* (Washington, D.C.: Office of the Chief of Military History, 1961), p. 35.

2. A study of the father's occupation of officers graduated from the Military Academy between 1955 and 1962 thus showed 60 percent of the graduates from farmer or small business families, another 20 percent from white collar worker families; only 6 percent had fathers with professional occupations. Jae-souck Sohn, "The Role of the Military in the Republic of Korea," prepared for the International Sociological Association Meetings, Evian, France, Sept. 1966.

3. Of those who participated in the 1961 coup and the subsequent Military Government, only 18 percent had had such previous military experience. This was less than the percentage among those active military officers who did not participate. C. I. Eugene Kim, "The South Korean Military Coup of May 1961: Its Causes and the Social Characteristics of Its Leaders," prepared for the International Sociological Association Meetings, Evian, France, Sept. 1966.

4. Hahn-Been Lee, *Time, Change and Administration*, pp. 149–150. Robert Scalapino, by contrast, has referred to the military leaders as the "least Westernized" elite to govern postwar Korea. "Korea: The Politics of Change," *Asian Survey*, 3, no. 1 (Jan. 1963), 31. This is true by comparison to the Western educational background of the Rhee regime leadership. Whether the latter was really more attuned to Western concepts of modernization or even politics is not certain. This is discussed below in Chapter 4.

5. Of the approximately 100 men graduating in 1946 from the Military English Class—a makeshift preacademy begun by the American Military Government, which provided six weeks of training—42 had reached brigadier general rank or higher five years after graduation; 69 had done so in eight years. Almost all who reached colonel at all had done so in four years. By contrast, the 8th Class consisted of 1801 men who had received from four to six months' training in 1948–1949 from the new Military Academy. Of these, only 7 had reached the rank of colonel by 1957. By 1961, 140 graduates of this class had reached colonel but nearly 80 percent of this number had reached that rank only in that year, or 12 years after graduation; some of these had obviously done so only in the months following the coup. Sohn, "The Role of the Military." On the content of early officer training at the several schools in this period, see Robert K. Sawyer, *Military Advisors in Korea: KMAG in Peace and War* (Washington, D.C.: Office of the Chief of

Military History, Department of the Army, 1962), pp. 11–81. See also, Hahn-Been Lee, *Time, Change and Administration,* pp. 146–151.

Sohn also cites, as a divisive factor in postwar years, factional competition between those who had and those who had not had Japanese training background.

6. Hahn-Been Lee, *Time, Change and Administration,* p. 150.

7. Eugene Kim, "The South Korean Military Coup," p. 24. This compares with only 37 percent of the sample Kim made of 75 prominent military leaders who did not participate.

8. For an overall statement of the justifications for the coup by its leader, see Park Chung-Hee, *The Country, Revolution and I* (Seoul, 1963).

9. A concise review of the major thrusts and accomplishments of the Military Government can be found in the *Korea Annual 1964.*

10. Byung-Hun Oh, "University Students and Politics in Korea," paper prepared for a conference on Students and Politics, sponsored by Harvard University and the University of Puerto Rico, Puerto Rico, Mar.–Apr., 1967, p. 25.

11. Chang Myon, for example, was not released from this restriction.

12. There were other important economic measures in this period, most notably in industrial development and the issuance of the First Five-Year Economic Development Plan. The Plan and the thinking on longer range problems that it reflected are discussed fully in Chap. 9.

13. *Yongnam Ilbo,* Dec. 19, 1964. All references to Korean language press in this book are taken from the *Press Translations: Korea* (Seoul: *North Asia Press,* daily).

14. See Hahn-Been Lee, *Time, Change and Administration,* pp. 152–154, for a very good account of this "inverted" relationship of juniors and seniors in the Military Government and of the different perspectives and concepts they brought to their jobs. See also below n22.

15. One hundred four prominent persons in the Military Government of 1961–1963 were selected by the authors for analysis, including the Supreme Council of National Reconstruction (highest official organ of the Military Government), almost all cabinet members (excluding those of extremely short tenure and no other position) and 14 additional persons who did not hold identifiable formal positions of prominence but could be considered as important figures in the coup. Of the total examined, 45 were of the younger group of colonels, lieutenant colonels, and majors; 47 were brigadier generals or higher; and 12 were civilians.

Of the 65 of these persons who did not become active in government afterward, 17 of the senior military group returned to active duty. A total of 11—6 of the senior and 5 of the junior group—were involved in charges of countercoups and arrested, and another 3 became members of opposition parties. Twenty-five went into private life, a few with positions in government-owned corporations. Twelve, all of the younger group, could not be traced in later years. Presumably some of these 12 returned to active duty; others took jobs in private life or lower levels of the party.

Sources for selection and biography of the 104 persons were Hahn-Been

Lee, *Time, Change and Administration,* pp. 164–168; *The Korea Annual* (Seoul: Hapdong News Agency), editions for 1964–1969, and "Where are May 16 Men Today?", two-part editorial in *Taehan Ilbo,* May 4 and 8, 1965.

16. The 3 members of the original 11 members who became prominent DRP leaders along with Kim Chong-pil, were Kim Tong-hwan, Kil Chae-ho, and Sin Yun-chang. In the executive, Kim Hyong-uk became Director of the CIA. Yi Sok-che, a major at the time of the coup, became Minister of Government Administration, a largely legalistic and administrative post. Hong Chong-chul, a colonel at the time of the coup, became Minister of Public Information. These latter two are the only representatives of the younger officers out of 42 cabinet ministers between 1963 and 1967.

The other four executive posts occupied in these years by members of the Colonels' group were Director of the Office of Fisheries, Director of the Office of Taxation, Director of the Central Officials Training Institute, and Chief of the President's Security Guard.

17. Chong-Sik Lee, "Political Parties," draft chapter for *Politics and Society in Korea,* pp. 52–55.

18. Ibid., p. 54; *Korea Annual 1964,* pp. 139–140.

19. *Korea Annual 1964,* p. 143.

20. *Chosun Ilbo,* Mar. 25, 1965.

21. See also Chap. 3.

22. One example was the currency reform of 1962, which was planned wthout either relevant members of the purportedly dominant Supreme Council for National Reconstruction or the cabinet fully informed. See *Korea Annual 1964,* pp. 123–124.

23. Kim and Ho, "Korean Political Leaders," p. 320. Henderson, *Korea,* p. 216, notes that Rhee used 129 ministers and prime ministers from 1945 to 1960.

24. See particularly discussion of the dispute over this issue following ratification of the Korea-Japan Treaty, in *Chosun Ilbo,* Aug. 17, 1965. *Tonga Ilbo,* Aug. 17, 1965, and *Korea Herald,* Aug. 18, 1965.

25. See "Another Rebellion within DRP," in *Tonga Ilbo,* 1965; also *Chosun Ilbo,* Dec. 23, 1964; Aug. 28, 30, 1966 (series cited in n.36).

26. The analysis of 31 persons excludes 2 persons who held office only briefly in the summer of 1964, when the cabinet was still adjusting, and who did not figure in its work in the coming years.

The number of changes from the original 17 to 31 persons reflects instability in a few areas, rather than general changes. Five persons served in the chronically unstable position of Minister of Finance, a result more of the unshakable stability and domination of the deputy prime minister in economic affairs in this period than instability in economic policy. (See for example *Tonga Ilbo* editorial, Dec. 27, 1966). Five persons also were involved in the appointments to minister without portfolio, a fluctuating category with sometimes one, sometimes two incumbents. The other serious changes began only in 1966, due to a variety of political and public pressures. Still, 7 of the original 17 were in office after the 1967 elections, including the prime minister and the deputy prime minister, and including significantly, five of the seven original ex-military appointees. All appointees during this period are listed in the *Korea Annual 1969*, pp. 449–453. See also "Profiles of Newly-named Cabinet Ministers," *Chosun Ilbo*, Dec. 27, 1966, which discusses the major changes preceding the elections. Biographies are drawn from these sources, discussions with government officials, and various press reports over this period.

27. Ages for previous regimes are from Kim and Ho, "Korean Political Leaders," p. 314. The sample includes cabinet, Assembly, higher civil servants, and some ambassadors. The figure for the equivalent sample for the Military Government of 1961–1962 is 41.7.

28. The key posts held by ex-military were Prime Minister, Defense and Home Affairs (in addition to CIA). The Defense position was filled by a marine general, Kim Song-un, who combined vigorous defense of military interests with proven loyalty to the president. When Park had announced in 1963 that he might not run for president, it was Kim who organized a well-publicized demonstration by military officers, calling upon him to run. Kim proved to be one of the most stable ministers in the government, assuming this position under the Military Government in 1963 and holding it without a break until 1968.

The Ministry of Home Affairs, which controls the police as well as all local officials, was headed from 1964–1966 by Yang Chan-u, formerly a close military supporter of the president. The police, not surprisingly, were thoroughly reorganized and restaffed in this period.

The cabinet positions held by ex-military from 1964–1967 were Prime Minister, Defense, Home Affairs, Communications, Health and Social Affairs (by a former military physician), Government Administration, Public Information, and Commerce and Industry.

29. See below, Chap. 4.

30. See below, Chap. 5.

31. Hahn-Been Lee, *Time, Change and Administration*, pp. 171–173, identifies a small, highly motivated, change-oriented group in the bureaucracy already emerging by 1963.

32. *Korea Annual 1965*, p. 60.

33. *Tonga Ilbo*, Nov. 11, 1965.

34. Chong-Sik Lee, "Political Parties," pp. 63, 67.

35. Eugene Kim, "Significance of Korean Elections," *Asian Survey*, 4, no. 3 (Mar. 1964), p. 770. Kim believes the DRP plurality was a rather strong showing, given the large number of candidates contesting for seats.

36. Aspects of the factional alignments and realignments of the DRP, and the friction with the executive, are discussed in the series "Inside Story of Political Parties," *Tonga Ilbo*, Aug. 23, 24, 1966, and the first two installments of the series "Political Dynamics of Korea Today," *Chosun Ilbo*, Aug. 28, 30, 1966. See also editorials in the *Chosun Ilbo*, Dec. 26, 1964 and Aug. 17, 1965; the *Tonga Ilbo*, Mar. 24, 1965, and May 29, 1966.

37. For a short account of preelection activity among the several parties, see *Korea Annual 1964*, pp. 138–145, 155–159. For election results, see

C. S. Lee, "Korea: In Search of Stability," *Asian Survey*, 4, no. 1 (Jan. 1964), 659–660.

38. Yun was also one of the very few postindependence leaders of noble birth, which enhanced even more his link with traditional society, Henderson, *Korea*, p. 405, n.24.

39. See editorials on this point in *Tonga Ilbo*, May 4, 1965; *Maeil Sinmun*, June 20, 1965; *Seoul Sinmun*, June 15, 1965.

40. Chong-Sik Lee, "Political Parties," p. 69.

41. By the middle of 1964, against a president, 47; a party chairman, 38; a prime minister, 47; several cabinet ministers in their early forties; and hardly a single prominent party leader over 55 on the government side; the opposition presented party leaders Yun Po-son, 66; Pak Sun-chon, 65; Huh Chung, 68; So Min-ho, 60; and for "younger" men Kim Yong-sam, 52, and Yu Chin-san, 58. When the several opposition parties united in 1965 into the People's party, the new party's 15 man leadership council had an average age of 57; only one of the council members was below 50. Council is listed in *Tonga Ilbo*, July 16, 1965.

42. See below, Chap. 3, for further discussion of the press and students and Chap. 10 for discussion of opposition support in relation to the 1967 elections. A critical analysis of opposition support can be found in the series "Diagnosis of Korean Politics by Professors," *Chosun Ilbo*, Jan. 1, 5, 6, 10, 1967. See also the series "Korea's Opposition Parties," *Chosun Ilbo*, Oct. 19, 20, 22, 23, 1965.

43. Chong-Sik Lee, "Korea in Search of Stability," p. 660, Eugene Kim, "Significance of Korean Elections," p. 769.

44. The conservative label was often championed as the function of the opposition. See, for example, statement of People's party leaders in *Tonga Ilbo*, Aug. 23, 1965.

CHAPTER 3. THE STRUGGLE FOR DEMOCRACY

1. For a rather forceful rejection of the idea that democracy, akin to Western concepts and practices, had a foundation in traditional Korean life or culture, see Pyong-Choon Hahm, *Korean Political Tradition and Law* (Seoul: Royal Asiatic Society, 1967), pp. 14–84. Cf. Henderson, *Korea*, pp. 226, 246–252.

2. Chong-Sik Lee, *Politics of Korean Nationalism*, p. 278. Lee points out, nevertheless, that because Korea was colonized by a non-Western power, Korean nationalists, more than other Asian or African nationalists, generally looked to the West as the source of political support and of new doctrines of freedom, self-determination, and democracy. Through Woodrow Wilson, the United States became a particularly important source of such influence.

3. See above, Chap. 1.

4. See Won-Sul Lee, "Impact of US Occupation Policy," particularly the concluding chapter, for a discussion of the effects of the occupation period.

The American role in the development of the first constitution of the new Republic is usefully discussed in John Kie-Chiang Oh, "Korean Democratization and the United States" (Paper delivered at the 20th annual meeting of the Association for Asian Studies, Mar. 1969), pp. 2–5.

5. For an excellent discussion of the philosophy and organization of the postwar education system, see Bom-Mo Chung, *An Image of Education in Korea: A Critique* (Seoul: Seoul National University, 1966). Professor Chung, a foremost educational innovator in Korea, and at the same time an acute student of cultural conflicts in Korea, cites sovereignization, modernization, and democratization as the three national goals of postwar Korea to which education should contribute. However, although Korea had ostensibly adopted these goals in 1948, they were in fact locked in conflict with older traditions and vested interests in the education system. Ibid., pp. 9, 16–17.

6. There was a correlation as well between youth and foreign training. In April 1965, 30 percent of higher level bureaucrats, between the ages of 31 and 40, had had foreign training compared to only 5 percent of those aged 51 and over. Hahn-Been Lee, "Bureaucracy and Politics," draft chapter prepared for Chong-Sik Lee and Sung-Chick Hong, eds., *Politics and Society in Korea.*

In all, nearly 3,000 persons in education, the bureaucracy, and the business community were sent to the United States for training under the aid program following the Korean War (figure from the United States AID Mission to Korea).

7. United States reaction was stronger in the early days of the Rhee regime (1948–1950) than during the Korean War and afterward. See John Kie-Chiang Oh, "Korean Democratization and the United States," pp. 7–9, for a description of actions taken in 1950 when Rhee considered postponing elections. In 1952 and later, the United States was approached for help by opponents of Rhee but did not respond, drawing sharp criticisms for its inaction. See Henderson, *Korea,* pp. 294, 299.

8. Kim and Ho, "Korean Political Leaders," p. 318.

9. Joung-Sik Lee, "Some Characteristics of Korean Political Culture: A Study of Korean Political Leaders' Statements (1948–1960)," *Korean Quarterly,* 8, no. 3 (Autumn 1960) 68.

10. These conclusions are drawn in part from the results of a pioneering study by Professor Sung-Chick Hong of Korea University. Professor Hong surveyed 1,500 professors and journalists on their attitudes toward modernization, disruption of tradition, economic and political development, and the role of intellectuals. In the survey, both academics and journalists were found to emphasize responsibility and order more than freedom and human rights as most relevant for democracy in Korea. Both also indicated a need for Korea to sacrifice a degree of individual freedom for economic development and rated economic development high among the tasks of modernization. Much less than the journalists, however, did academics accept the need for disruption of the existing social order in order to achieve modernization. Somewhat less than journalists, moreover, did academics ascribe importance to economic equality along with political equality. Sung-Chick Hong, *The In-*

tellectual and Modernization—A Study of Korean Attitudes (Seoul: Daehan Textbook Co., Ltd., 1967), pp. 179–242.

In an earlier, smaller survey, professors revealed a striking attachment to the preservation of class differences, in contrast to a sample of farmers and businessmen. Sung-Chick Hong, "Values of Korean Farmers, Businessmen and Professors," in *Report on the Conference on Modernization* (Seoul: Korea University Press, 1966), pp. 796–797. In this survey and in other contexts, the negative opinion toward Korean character was also revealed. See Chap. 5 below.

Some of the lack of a very radical outlook in the profession is, of course, due to the fact that many left-leaning professors as well as politicians were kidnapped or voluntarily went North, during the Korean War.

11. Scalapino, "Korea: The Politics of Change," p. 32.

12. One of the most striking responses in Professor Hong's survey, and perhaps an indication of the sense of alienation and loss of function that academics feel, was to a question on how actively intellectuals in Korea participate in creating and expressing new social values and ideologies. Among the professors, 88 percent replied that such participation was passive or practically nonexistent. Hong, *The Intellectual and Modernization*, pp. 172–174.

13. Professor Hong found a fairly consistent level of from 20 to 30 percent of his academic respondents who departed from the majority tendency on such questions as democracy (where these persons emphasized "human rights"), the need for curtailment of individual rights for economic development ("disagreed greatly"), and the need for disruption of the existing social order for modernization ("considerably necessary"). Ibid., pp. 186, 193, 194.

14. In Professor Hong's survey, 68 percent of the journalists interviewed reported no experience abroad compared to only 39 percent of the professors; only 1 percent reported having studied in the United States, compared to 20 percent of the professors. Ibid., p. 208.

An important form of United States assistance and moral support, however, was in the occasional supply of newsprint to papers during the 1950s when the Rhee government used the cutoff of the supply of imported newsprint as a means of curtailing opposition newspapers. USIA also sent some Korean newspapermen each year to the United States on observation tours during the 1950s and, to a lesser extent, in the 1960s.

15. Ibid., pp. 57, 68–69, 194, 195, 206, 207.

16. For an illuminating example of the attitude of the press on freedom of speech, giving careful weight to the arguments for control of "reckless," "radical" and other statements dangerous to national interest and security, see the editorial, "Controversial Remarks by Yun and So," *Tonga Ilbo*, May 28, 1966. See also "Freedom of Expression and Political Statements," *Sina Ilbo*, May 30, 1966.

17. Reported circulation for Korean papers was just over one million in 1965, of which 320,000 was for Seoul. *Korea Annual 1967*, p. 260.

18. *Korea Annual 1964*, pp. 136, 375.

19. The press is, of course, not monolithic in its viewpoint or inclinations. Even among those consistently at odds with constituted authority, there is a

wide range of orientation and outlook. The *Tonga Ilbo*, for example, is the largest and oldest paper in Korea, and the leading "opposition" journal. It is also connected with one of the oldest and largest business combines in Korea, the one involved in the founding of the Korea Democratic party during the early postliberation days. It is by nature skeptical of almost every government move. But one does not find it advocating any basic economic or social reordering of society, or fundamental changes in international outlook for Korea, and one would not expect it to be much more radical in these terms, were security wraps removed, than it is today. By contrast, there is the smaller, Catholic-owned *Maeil Sinmun*, in Taegu, which expresses a more radical, rural-oriented economic outlook, in the American populist tradition, and which is somewhat more iconoclastic, e.g., in its skepticism about Korean policy on Vietnam, to which almost all other papers eventually lent full support.

20. See n. 42, and discussion of post-1967 events in Part III.

21. Republic of Korea, Ministry of Education, *Education in Korea, 1965–1966* (Seoul: n.d.), p. 1. Korean expenditure on, and spread of higher education were found to be among the highest in Asia and to exceed the European average, "Long-Term Projections for Education in the Republic of Korea," *Report of the UNESCO Regional Advisory Team for Educational Planning in Asia* (Bangkok: UNESCO Regional Office for Education in Asia, 1965), p. 13.

22. For a fuller discussion of the role of nationalism in Korean student politics, see Princeton Lyman, "Students and Politics in Indonesia and Korea," *Pacific Affairs*, 38 (Fall and Winter, 1965–1966) 56.

While national-level student action remains formally unorganized, it should be noted that campus-level politics customarily involves a large amount of cash expenditures, organizational pressures, and the use of regional and other factional ties as important springboards for support—all reminiscent of the national political system. Byung-Hun Oh, "University Students and Politics," p. 44. Some suggest that these characteristics, particularly the liberal use of funds in student elections, are recent products of CIA involvement in the elections. Others point to the rewards in being able to control the student-body treasury. In any case, the costs are becoming quite high; one student estimated the cost of elections to student-body chairman at 500,000 *won* ($1,860). *Kyonghyang Sinmun*, Dec. 18, 1964.

23. Byung-Hun Oh, "University Students and Politics," pp. 52–53.

24. There have been several small, varied studies of student attitudes in Korea, but much of the opinion expressed here, like some of that expressed in the survey results, is impressionistic. These studies, nevertheless, tend to agree on the not surprising fact that Korean students have mixed views about adopting wholly in Korea the principles and practices associated with democratic politics in the West. In one student survey, for example, 40 percent of the respondents felt that Western democracy was not suitable to Korea at all, and 30 percent more felt it to be only partly suitable. Sung-Chick Hong, "Values of Korean College Students," *The Journal of Asiatic Studies* (Korea University, May 1963), pp. 99–100.

Like the academics, moreover, student attitudes reflect a consciousness of elite status and a certain distrust of formalistic institutions for political equality.

For example, one study found students to be less inclined to accept some of the specific requisites of modern democratic society—for example, the role of law, the participation of many in policy decisions, confidence in the political competence of the individual and the nation—than either middle or lower class Korean adults interviewed in the same survey. Bom-Mo Chung, *Development Attitudes and Value-Orientation in Korea* (unpublished, Seoul National University, College of Education, 1967).

25. They were even somewhat surprised at the resignation of Syngman Rhee in 1960, which had only belatedly become one of the demonstrators' demands. Byung-Hun Oh, "University Students and Politics," pp. 19–20. See also his comments on pp. 22–23, 37, 53–54.

26. These are the authors' own impressions. But the student concern with financial difficulties and vocational insecurity in Korea has been demonstrated by at least one survey, Bom-Mo Chung, "Individual Problems of College Students" (SNU College of Education, 1960), and corroborated by others close to the scene. Byung-Hun Oh, "University Students and Politics," pp. 31–37. A positive reaction to better economic prospects also is apparent in the decline of student activism after 1965. See below, Chap. 5.

27. One of the first such statements came in a note to the United States just two days after the coup. John Kie-Chiang Oh, "Korean Democratization and the United States," pp. 24–25.

28. For a description of events leading up to the election, see *Korea Annual 1964*, pp. 137–146. See also Chong-Sik Lee, "Political Parties," p. 54, on the split within the military at this time.

29. *Korea Annual 1964*, p. 189.

30. Ibid., pp. 141–142.

31. The presence of some of the several opposition candidates in the Presidential election was believed by some to be the result of covert government encouragement, aimed at splitting the opposition. See *Korea Annual 1964*, p. 140. The same suspicion was mentioned in connection with difficulties in opposition unity moves for the 1967 election.

32. For an analysis of the Constitution's main features, see John Kie-Chiang Oh, *Korea, Democracy on Trial* (Ithaca, N.Y.: Cornell University Press, 1968), pp. 157–164.

33. Thus, in the spring of 1964, student groups were infiltrated by government agents who sought to influence the direction of the demonstrations. Some student leaders were also implicated, through questionable "evidence," of being in touch with Communist agents. As a result of these tactics, the situation quickly worsened. *Korea Annual 1965*, pp. 17–18. A more extended role of government agents in the student demonstration, as provocateurs as well as compromisers, was alleged by one of the student participants. Rhee June-Il, "Student Demonstrations in 1964 and Government Measures," *The Political Science Review*, Seoul National University, 5 (1967), pp. 153–169.

34. This later became the source, or excuse (for other issues were involved) for a split within the ranks of Yun Po-son's followers in the Assembly and one of the major sources of new factionalism in opposition politics. See *Kyonghyang Sinmun*, Sept. 23, 1964.

35. See statement of the International Press Institute, *Tonga Ilbo*, Sept. 23, 1964. The United States position in sympathy with the press was also made known.

36. *Korea Annual 1965*, pp. 23–25, 44.

37. The press talked during this time of the need for an eventual settlement with Japan; its concern seemed only over the terms and tactics of such a settlement. Much of its criticism, moreover, was aimed at Japan rather than at the Korean government. See editorials in *Taehan Ilbo*, Dec. 19, 1965; *Kyonghyang Sinmun*, Dec. 19, 1965; *Hankuk Ilbo*, Dec. 10, 1964; and *Kyonghyang Sinmun*, Feb. 16, 1965.

38. Later it ordered two major private universities closed until they finally agreed to dismissal of those designated by the government as "politicking" professors and students. *Korea Annual 1966*, pp. 9–19. See also Byung-Hun Oh, "University Students and Politics," p. 27. For the full text of President Park's speech defending the actions of the government, see the *Hankuk Ilbo*, Aug. 26, 1965.

39. See, for example, editorials in the *Kyonghyang Sinmun*, Sept. 9, 1965, and the *Tonga Ilbo*, Oct. 19, 1965. There was a general torrent of editorials at this time calling for reopening of the campuses and reinstatement of the expelled students and professors.

40. Many of the professors involved, however, had been allowed by this time to teach as lecturers, or in other special capacities, at universities other than the ones from which they were dismissed. Others became editorial writers for newspapers. Of the students, 48 remained excluded from college. "A Year since Dismissal of 'Political' Professors and Students," *Tonga Ilbo*, Dec. 17, 1966.

41. In the most prominent example, members of a group called "National Council for the Defense of the Fatherland," many of them ex-military men who had broken with the junta during the Military Government, were arrested on charges of defaming the government. *Kyonghyang Sinmun*, Aug. 30, 1965.

42. In the midst of the political strife in 1965, for example, terrorists bombed the homes and offices of some journalists and broadcasters. The perpetrators were never caught, and some persons voiced suspicion that they had been agents of the government, or of the military acting independently, who felt that opposition to government policies deserved repressive measures. See the editorial, "Tactics of Terror Without Intention to Kill," *Tonga Ilbo*, Sept. 11, 1965.

In 1966, the *Kyonghyang Sinmun*, which had in 1956 been the object of government censure under Syngman Rhee, was forced into bankruptcy and sale with the apparent compliance of government officials. The incident followed by a few months the arrest of the publisher and some of the staff in relation to the exposure of Communist affiliations on the part of the paper's sports editor. The banks, which are partly government-owned, moved shortly after to collect all the loans outstanding, forcing the paper to be sold. *Korea Annual 1966*, p. 254.

On the other hand, when the country became upset in late 1966 at a rather crass case of a business combine using the paper it owned to defend itself against investigation for smuggling, the administration drafted a law aimed at controlling the types of business interest in and control of the press, and withdrew it just as quickly when the press made clear its opposition to such a bill as a wedge of general government control. *Korea Annual 1967*, pp. 253–254; see editorial of the *Tonga Ilbo*, Nov. 22, 1966.

In summary, the situation was one of uneasy truce, a delicate balance between granting necessary respect for the press's basic rights, on the one hand, and the government's determination not to let any issue go too far that would seriously threaten its position, on the other. As an example of how the mood and issues shift, the government in 1969 suddenly moved to censor stories on corrupt officials, normally a reasonably accepted area for press activity. *Chosun Ilbo*, Mar. 13, 1969.

43. A good example of the continuing difficulties in this area was the announcement in 1966 by a prominent opponent of the government, in forming a new party, that if he were the president he would initiate an exchange of mail and various personnel visits with North Korea. The man was arrested for violation of the Anti-Communist law, though members of the government and DRP had made similar suggestions at other times. See "Reemergence of Political Oppression," *Tonga Ilbo*, May 27, 1966. See also Chapter 11.

44. *Taehan Ilbo*, Sept. 6, 1965. See Chap. 5, for further discussion of this point.

CHAPTER 4. GROWING ECONOMIC EMPHASIS

1. Park Chung-Hee, *The State, Revolution and I* (Seoul, 1963) pp. 19–43.

2. The disturbances on the campuses in these years, and the political violence such as the labor riots in Taegu in 1946 and Seoul in 1947, were greatly aggravated by the struggles between pro- and anti-Communist leaders and their respective sympathizers. See Allen, *Syngman Rhee*, pp. 84–85; Henderson, *Korea*, pp. 135–147.

3. Allen, *Syngman Rhee*, p. 213.

4. The Interim Government of April–July 1960, e.g., began resurrecting the long-range development plan that the Rhee regime had neglected. The Democratic Government, which succeeded to power in July, announced "Economic Development First" as its theme. And the Military Government cited economic problems as one of the chief justifications for the coup and the introduction of determined and stable leadership. Hahn-Been Lee, *Time, Change and Administration*, pp. 130–131.

5. The economic policy objectives of the Rhee regime are discussed in detail in Chap. 8.

6. New estimates of rice production indicating previous underestimations by as much as 30 percent were issued by the Korean government in 1965, following several years' study and encouragement by both Korean and American experts. See "Revised 1964 Preliminary GNP by New Price Production Data," Bank of Korea bulletin, July 1965.

7. See Chap. 9 below for a discussion of planning in the Rhee period.

8. In the decade following the Korean War, North Korea's national income is estimated to have grown an average of 22.1 percent a year compared to 3.6 percent for South Korea. Figures on North Korea need to be extrapolated and studied from incomplete and uncheckable official sources, but there is little doubt that in the early post-Korean War period North Korea, which suffered damage as great as the South's, made considerable strides in restoring its industrial capacity, raising agricultural production beyond the levels achieved under colonial rule, and achieving a measure of independence from foreign aid. These facts were generally well known in the South, despite the restrictions placed on news and analysis of North Korea by the Rhee and subsequent regimes. See Joseph S. Chung, "Industrial Development of North Korea, 1945–1964: Some Strategic Quantitative Indicators," and Yoon T. Kuark, "Economic Development Contrast Between South and North Korea," in Joseph S. Chung, ed., *Patterns of Economic Development: Korea* (Kalamazoo, Mich.: Korea Research and Publication, Inc., 1966). For a general review of achievements and comments on subsequent economic difficulties in the North, see Byung Chul Koh, *The Foreign Policy of North Korea* (New York: Frederick A. Praeger, 1969), pp. 18–24.

9. Lee Jung-jae, "The Second Five Year Plan and Its Issues," *The Korean Social Science Review* (Feb. 1966), pp. 122–125.

10. See below, Chap. 8, and the comment on avoiding projects incompatible with a unified Korea in the Presidential Message on United States aid, in Lyons, *Military Policy and Economic Aid*, p. 259.

11. See, as one example, the article by Professor Pak Chun-kyu, "Merits and Demerits of Normalization," *Chosun Ilbo*, Feb. 23, 1965, in which the prospects of reunification are seen as dimmed and the opportunity for Japanese hegemony improved by the settlement with Japan. See also below, Chap. 5.

12. Over half the farmers, nearly two-thirds of the businessmen, and 80 percent of the professors in one survey felt that Korean character was bad, either inherently or due to poverty. Sung-Chick Hong, "Values of Korean Farmers, Businessmen and Professors," pp. 797–798.

13. See, for example, the editorial on savings-deposit figures in the *Kyonghyang Sinmun*, Oct. 18, 1965, and the general questioning of statistics on growth in the *Pusan Ilbo*, Aug. 24, 1965.

14. "ROK-Japan Talks and Self-Awakening of People," *Kyonghyang Sinmun*, Mar. 24, 1965. See also the "Declaration of Christian Clergymen and Educators," *Yongnam Ilbo*, July 6, 1965.

15. A purported survey of girls at Korea's most prestigious women's university, Ewha, showed that businessmen—because they would make lots of money—ranked as the girls' first choice for husbands.

16. See editorials in the *Kyonghyang Sinmun*, Dec. 21, 1964, and the *Chonnam Ilbo*, Oct. 1, 1964. The criticism affected the business community itself, which admitted, through the largely big-business-dominated Korean Businessmen's Association, that most large businesses had received preferential treatment. The KBA promised that it would undertake a "self-purge." *Kyonghyang Sinmun*, Dec. 28, 1964.

17. See, as one of many examples, *Kyonghyang Sinmun*, Dec. 30, 1964.

18. An example of many such comments in the press and elsewhere in 1965 can be found in "Korea-Japan Relations—Pro and Con on U.S. Policy," *Tonga Ilbo*, Aug. 5, 1965. Some Koreans reacted against this fear as a distressing example of Korean "flunkeyism." *Hankuk Ilbo*, May 26, 1965. In this vein, see also Pyong-Choon Hahm, "Korea's Mendicant Mentality? A Critique of US Policy," *Foreign Affairs*, 43, no. 1 (Oct. 1964), pp. 165–174.

19. On the positive side, the Military Government's relaxation of import restrictions and granting of export subsidies did have a rather immediate effect, with a 20 percent growth in industrial output in 1962 alone. On the other hand, it did not succeed in capturing the proportion of internal resources it desired for its investment program. Credit expansion and increased budget expenditures were creating a serious inflation that threatened the government's other programs. These problems led to further and, in the case of the currency reform of 1962, often more damaging attempts to achieve a quick change in economic direction. A further blow came in a crop failure of 1962–1963, which led not only to a food crisis in 1963 but to an aggravation of inflationary pressure.

20. These were the Saenara Automobile, Walker Hill, and Stock Market scandals. See Sohn, "The Role of the Military." See also *Korea Annual 1965*, pp. 38–39.

21. The question, seen differently from the respective positions of the Economic Planning Board, Ministry of Foreign Affairs, and the Ministry of Defense, was whether Korea would press for some moderation in the American policy of gradual decline of grant aid or accept that policy and seek only to maximize United States development loans for capital projects. The government in the end chose the latter, in line with its own accelerated development effort and in conjunction with the general trend of United States aid policy. See the summary of the Park-Johnson communique in *Korea Annual 1966*, pp. 79–80, and in the same volume the discussion of United States aid policy, p. 155.

22. See below, Chap. 8.

23. A Joint (United States–Korean) Economic Committee had been established under the Rhee government to review and advise on stabilization and other economic measures. The Military Government had allowed it to lapse. Agreement to restore it came in July 1963 with the visit of the Foreign Minister to Washington. *Korea Annual 1964*, pp. 188–189.

24. Editorials predicting both a decline in fertilizer purchases and a rise in business failures were prevalent throughout the closing months of 1964, some of them on the business question obviously inspired by firms seeking relaxation of credit restrictions. The credit squeeze of that year was hard on many businesses, particularly those that had traditionally operated with a heavy dependence on credit, relying both on credit extensions from the banks and on inflation to make such operations profitable. On the fertilizer question, see *Kyonghyang Sinmun*, Oct. 7, 1964, and n. 38 below. On business failures, see *Kyonghyang Sinmun*, Sept. 25, 1964; *Seoul Kyongje Sinmun*, Oct. 7, 1964; *Pusan Ilbo*, Dec. 23, 1964.

25. The Federal Republic of Germany had already committed aid and

credits to the Military Government in 1961. In early 1965, it agreed to furnish an additional $13.5 million in government loans and $26 million in commercial credits. *Korea Annual 1965,* p. 68.

26. *Korea Annual 1966,* p. 33.

27. See Chap. 9.

28. This was one of the issues between the Korean Businessmen's Association, representing big business, and the Chamber of Commerce, representing small and medium firms. *Kyonghyang Sinmun,* Dec. 21, 28, 1964.

29. Fertilizer targets were set by the government and achieved through the quasi-governmental National Agricultural Cooperatives Federation, which enforced the targets through its monopoly of fertilizer sales and its control of government low-cost agricultural credit. Land development plans were set by the central government and targets parceled out to each province. But there was an attempt to move away from the heavy emphasis on subsidy in the Military Government's agriculture policy and toward more emphasis on market prices and cash crops. Incentives were provided through price programs and occasionally through export promotion of major agricultural products. However, the desired transition in agriculture involved painful readjustment, as much if not more than lucrative incentives. It was not until 1966, therefore, that the administration began to relax some of its centralized controls over the rural sector and to give a freer rein to market activity and private incentives. For a fairly comprehensive review and analysis of Korean agricultural policies and achievements since the Korean War, but with emphasis on the 1960s, see United States Operations Mission to Korea, *Rural Development Program Evaluation Report,* 1967.

30. Ibid., pp. 54–58, Appendix D, pp. 2–3.

31. Ibid., pp. 289–290. In a year-long survey of rural change in several communities undertaken in 1966, Professor Moon Seung-gyu of Chunpuk University found that, of the many different types of government officials, the extension agent was regarded by farmers as their "friend and teacher." Other data in the survey indicated that the extension agent was one of the most effective agents of change. "Annual Report: An Evaluation of Community Development Programs in Rural Korea" (Research Project Jointly Supported by the Agriculture Development Council and North Carolina State University), Jan. 26, 1967, pp. 2–3.

32. For details of some of these efforts, see below Chaps. 8, 9, 10. Perhaps not by chance, the appeals to patriotism and the efforts to set, and then surpass, original targets in the spirit of nationalist zeal, especially concerning the Second Five-Year Plan issued in 1966, were not dissimilar from the type of successful nationalist appeals in support of development featured in North Korea in the late 1950s and early 1960s. See Koh, *Foreign Policy of North Korea,* pp. 19–20.

33. On trade liberalization, for example, see the *Kukche Sinbo,* Aug. 10, 1965; and *Kangwon Ilbo,* Aug. 11, 1965. On the interest reform, see *Sanop Kyongje Sinmun,* Dec. 26, 1964; *Chosun Ilbo,* Sept. 30, 1965.

34. For a review of corruption in the period 1948–1960, see *Chosun Ilbo,* Feb. 16, 1965. See also Henderson, *Korea,* pp. 197–198.

35. See below, Chap. 11.

36. *Korea Annual 1965*, p. 25.

37. These two themes, with great importance placed on the economic, were present in nearly every major pronouncement by the president and the DRP from 1965 onward. See, for example, DRP keynote speech, *Korea Herald*, Jan. 22, 1966, President's New Year message, *Korea Herald*, Jan. 18, 1967, and the president's Second Inaugural Speech, *Korea Herald*, July 2, 1967.

38. During the summer and fall of 1964, following devaluation in May, the pressure for a farm subsidy to offset the rise in fertilizer prices to farmers, was strong throughout the rural areas, and echoed by all parties in the Assembly. The issue pitted the special interests of the rural sector, which had played so important a role in Park's (and the DRP's) election, against the demands of stabilization. The president compromised in part by agreeing to cover the increased costs for purchases in the summer and fall, but refused to continue the subsidy thereafter. For editorials on this issue, mostly in favor of the subsidy, see *Chosun Ilbo*, Sept. 25, 1964, *Tonga Ilbo*, Oct. 6, 1964, *Pusan Ilbo*, Oct. 1, 1964. For an editorial sympathetic to the president's policy, see *Tonga Ilbo*, Oct. 3, 1964.

The president continued thereafter, against the pressures of some of his own advisors as well as the opposition, to resist demands for excessive price support levels or other uneconomic subsidies of the key crops, rice and barley, the prices for which in Korea had traditionally been pushed out of line with world market prices. In a speech to provincial governors in June 1966, the president stated forcefully that the country must seek to bring its grain prices down to world market levels, one of the first times a Korean government had come out officially for this highly controversial policy. Text of the president's speech reproduced by the United States Operations Mission to Korea, July 10, 1966.

39. Chang Key-young was a notoriously independent operator, who achieved his (and the government's) ends with his own choice of methods, compromises, and balancing of financial and business interests. His accrual of real power during the years of high economic growth offended DRP leaders, who were irritated further by Chang's refusal to join the DRP along with the other cabinet ministers at the end of 1964. See *Tonga Ilbo*, Mar. 24, 1965 and *Korea Annual 1966*, p. 45.

40. For a discussion of party issues involved in 1965, see *Kyonghyang Sinmun*, Aug. 18, 1965; *Chosun Ilbo*, Aug. 17, 1965; *Tonga Ilbo*, Aug. 17, 1965.

41. Henderson, *Korea*, p. 181.

CHAPTER 5. THE CLIMAX OF DISSENT: THE JAPANESE SETTLEMENT

1. Lee, *Politics of Korean Nationalism*, pp. 89–100, 237, 262–266. See also *Korea Annual 1967*, pp. 113–114.

2. See above, Chap. 1.

3. Allen, *Syngman Rhee*, pp. 183–190.

4. The feeling was revived when the Vietnam War intensified. Koreans,

who saw economic opportunities in Vietnam for their country, justified to them as a troop-contributing nation, furiously resented Japan's "once again" profiting most from an Asian war in which it did not take part. See, for example, the editorial "US Purchase of Logistical Supplies for Vietnam from Japan," *Chonnam Ilbo*, July 2, 1965.

5. The causes for breakdown were property claims, with both countries making large claims against the other (1952); remarks by Japanese negotiators on the legality of Korean independence and the beneficial aspects of Japanese colonial rule (1953); and the agreement between Japan and the Red Cross for repatriation of Korean residents in Japan to North Korea (1959). See the account of negotiations and chronology in *Korea Annual 1966*, pp. 111–114. For a brief history of the negotiations emphasizing the intermediary role of the United States, see the article by Yi Pyong-kyu, "Korea-U.S.-Japan Triangular Diplomacy," *Chosun Ilbo*, Feb. 24, 1965.

6. A good summary discussion of these issues can be found in *Korea Annual 1966*, pp. 114–119.

7. This was almost as sensitive an issue in Japan as in South Korea; trade and other nondiplomatic relationships had already been established between Japan and North Korea, and strong feelings existed against having Japan, by exclusive recognition of the South, tie itself to one side in the cold war, as it was manifested in Korea. See text from the Japanese *Yomiuri Shimbun* in *Kyonghyang Sinmun*, Feb. 23, 1965, and a longer account filed on the Japanese position from Tokyo, "Japan's Position on Korea-Japan Treaty—Pros and Cons on Ratification," *Tonga Ilbo*, Sept. 28, 1965.

8. See quotation of Japanese Foreign Minister Estusaburo Shiina in *Korea Annual 1966*, p. 10. For criticism of the final settlement as having "legalized" the period of colonial rule, see the statement of the Council for Safeguarding the Fatherland, in *Chosun Ilbo*, Aug. 6, 1965.

A final issue in this category was sovereignty over Tok-to, a small island off the southeast coast of Korea that both countries claimed. In the final settlement, this issue was left unresolved. *Korea Annual 1966*, p. 120.

9. Reparations, per se, were not applicable in the Korean case because Korea had not been at war with Japan. In addition, Koreans felt that, after 35 years of colonial rule, their claims could not be compared to wartime reparations.

10. *Korea Annual 1965*, pp. 16–17. This category also included the less stormy question of the return of cultural assets taken from Korea by Japan, a seemingly routine problem but complicated by the question of whether assets taken from all of Korea would be returned to South Korea or only those taken from below the 38th parallel. *Tonga Ilbo*, June 23, 1965.

11. The basic agreements relating to each category of issues, and a short summary of the points of dispute, is presented in the *Korea Annual 1966*, pp. 119–122. The full text of the treaty and agreements is in the same volume, pp. 382–397. A summary of the agreements, from a more critical point of view, is presented in two editorials, "Signing Korea-Japan Pacts and National Sentiments," *Tonga Ilbo*, June 22, 1965, and "Normalization Pacts Signed: This Is the Beginning," *Tonga Ilbo*, June 23, 1965. A panorama of criticisms

against the government's negotiating position, in excerpts from campaign speeches against the settlement, can be found in the *Chosun Ilbo*, Mar. 28, 1965.

12. See Chap. 4.

13. The president's initial reaction to the demonstrations, encouraged by anti-Kim forces within the DRP, was to recall Kim from Japan and shortly afterward to send him for an extended visit to the United States. The president also met with student leaders and, to the indignation of the Japanese, showed them the secret Kim-Ohira memorandum. But, as described in Chap. 3, these efforts to placate student concern were largely undone by simultaneous government action to infiltrate and discredit the student movement. The situation was further inflamed by an opposition assemblyman's charge that the president and Kim Chong-pil had received $20 million from the Japanese in election funds and that the government had been advanced $130 million of the property-claims settlement. *Korea Annual 1965*, pp. 16–18.

14. See below, Chap. 10.

15. The United States interest resulted from strategic international considerations, which favored the resolution of differences between its major allies in Asia and a desire to see Korea begin to establish realistic economic relations with neighboring countries. Within the United States there had been growing criticism of the type of grant aid going to countries like Korea, which served primarily as a subsidizing function. Restoring relations with Japan was thus one step toward strengthening Korea's economic base and developmental potential.

16. See below, Chap. 10.

17. Full text of the statement is printed in the *Hankuk Ilbo*, Aug. 26, 1965.

18. See, for example, the advertisement of the DRP following its controversial passing of the consent bill through the Assembly committee, *Tonga Ilbo*, Aug. 12, 1965. See also the speech of the president quoted earlier in *Hankuk Ilbo*, Aug. 26, 1965.

19. See comments of opposition spokesmen in *Chosun Ilbo*, Mar. 28, 1965, and of Mme. Pak Sun-chon, leader of the opposition party, in the *Tonga Ilbo*, June 19, 1965. A similar position is suggested more obliquely, in editorials of the *Tonga Ilbo*, June 21, 1965, and the *Chosun Ilbo*, July 2, 1965. See also comment of the *Taehan Ilbo*, May 1, 1965, on the problem raised by the opposition's supporting a settlement "in principle," while opposing the agreements already signed with Japan by the Park government. The editorial suggested that it would be impossible for the Park government, having signed the agreements, to cancel them, even if ratification were delayed.

20. *Chosun Ilbo*, June 24, 1965.

21. *Chosun Ilbo*, July 24, 1965.

22. Comments of various opposition spokesmen, *Chosun Ilbo*, Mar. 28, 1965.

23. See the reaction of students to Japan in Hong, "Values of Korean College Students," p. 100.

24. "On Property Claims Rights," *Tonga Ilbo*, June 10, 1965.

25. *Seoul Sinmun*, July 29, 1965.

26. "Korea-Japan Relations (7th Installment)—Pro and Con on U.S. Policy," *Tonga Ilbo*, Aug. 5, 1965.

27. Yi Chong-sik, "National Sovereignty and Japanese Wind (3rd Installment)—Political Infiltration," *Chosun Ilbo*, Aug. 19, 1965.

28. "Japan and U.S. Asian Policy," *Tonga Ilbo*, May 1, 1965, and "Japan's Position on Korea-Japan Treaty (4th Installment)—Japan's Attitude toward Red China and North Korea," *Tonga Ilbo*, Sept. 30, 1965.

29. *Chosun Ilbo*, Mar. 28, 1965.

30. See Henderson, *Korea*, pp. 225–269, for an historical analysis of factionalism in Korean political behavior.

31. *Tonga Ilbo*, June 21, 1965, and *Hankuk Ilbo*, Aug. 11, 1965.

32. See editorials of the *Tonga Ilbo*, June 22, 23, 1965, cited in n. 11 above.

33. This was recognized by some critics. See comment in editorial on student demonstrations in *Chosun Ilbo*, July 2, 1965, and that of the *Tonga Ilbo*, June 22, 1965.

34. On the various points mentioned, see *Kyonghyang Sinmun*, Feb. 15, 1965; "ROK-Japan Talks and Self-Awakening of People" (editorial), ibid., Mar. 24, 1965; "National Sovereignty and Japanese Wind (3rd Installment)—Political Infiltration," *Chosun Ilbo*, Aug. 19, 1965.

For a subsequent comment on the influx of Japanese songs, novels, magazines, and movies, and the increase of Japanese language instruction, see "One Year History of Normalized Korea-Japan Relations," *Chosun Ilbo*, Dec. 20, 1966.

35. *Korea Herald*, Mar. 31, 1965.

36. Pak Chun-kyu, "Merits and Demerits of Normalization—Focal Points at Issue," *Chosun Ilbo*, Feb. 23, 1965.

37. *Chosun Ilbo*, Aug. 19, 1965.

38. These sentiments were largely expressed privately in conversations. However, suggestions of these sentiments are found in the editorial of the *Kyonghyang Sinmun*, Mar. 24, 1965.

39. By and large, they were descendents of the two factions of the Democratic party that had split into a new and an old group during the Chang Myon regime of 1960–1961. The party led by Yun Po-sun was called the Civil Rule party. The other, which took the name of the Democratic party, had been deprived by the Political Purification Law of its natural leader, Chang Myon, and was led by Mme. Pak Sun-chon, a long-time nationalist leader and one of the country's few female political leaders. See "Opposition Parties—20-year Lineage of Opposition Parties," *Tonga Ilbo*, Feb. 2, 1965, for a description of ideological differences, mainly in terms of the moderate (Democratic party) faction's greater identification with the urban intellectuals. For a criticism of their "sameness," see "Inaugural Declaration of People's party," *Taegu Ilbo*, May 4, 1965.

40. See "Opposition Parties (3rd Installment)," *Tonga Ilbo*, Feb. 3, 1965.

41. On these points of total opposition and personal control, Yun had fought with and finally expelled an important faction of his own Civil Rule party in 1964. *Kyonghyang Sinmun*, Sept. 23, 1964. His determination to be the presidential candidate of any single opposition party was one of the most

difficult points facing negotiators of a final opposition merger in 1965. "Opposition Parties (4th Installment)—Obstacles to Merger Move," *Tonga Ilbo,* Feb. 4, 1965.

42. "People's Party," *Kyonghyang Sinmun,* May 5, 1965. Mme. Pak also, in contrast to Yun, was not considered a likely candidate for President, making her leadership less controversial among her followers.

43. The parties were also being pushed hard in this direction by the press which had never ceased to criticize the opposition for splitting in 1963. See, for example, editorials of the *Taehan Ilbo,* Sept. 26, 1964, *Chosun Ilbo,* Feb. 11, 1965, *Taegu Ilbo,* May 4, 1965.

44. As a preliminary move, while political obstacles still remained for a full merger, opposition politicians of both parties, plus other public figures, joined in a Pan National Struggle Committee against Humiliating Diplomacy toward Japan. In speeches around the country for the Committee, one of Yun's chief lieutenants charged that the Park regime should not have been allowed to negotiate with Japan, since from its inception in 1961 it had proved itself "proficient only in cheating and lying to the people," while Yun predicted the treaty would never reach the Assembly for ratification and that, if it did, "very grave consequences would occur." *Chosun Ilbo,* Mar. 28, 1965.

45. "Election of Representative Supreme Commissioner of People's Party," *Tonga Ilbo,* June 15, 1965, "Promises Made on Eve of PP's Convention," *Kyonghyang Sinmun,* June 15, 1965, and "Future Course of People's Party," *Seoul Sinmun,* June 15, 1965.

46. For example, one of the other two commissioners of the new party was So Min-ho, who had fought long and hard against Syngman Rhee and now stood in equally adamant opposition to what he felt was another basically autocratic government. "Troika of People's Party," *Kyonghyang Sinmun,* June 15, 1965. See also "Interview with So Min-ho," *Tonga Ilbo,* Sept. 7, 1965. Other "adamants" were also represented in the ranks of party officers. See "Ten PP 'Adamants' Issue Statement Demanding Dissolution of Party," *Tonga Ilbo,* July 23, 1965.

47. *Tonga Ilbo,* June 19, 1965.

48. *Korea Annual 1966,* p. 10.

49. The moderates in the opposition had been prepared to offer their resignation en masse from the Assembly should the treaty be ratified. But as the moderates well knew, that resignation could be rejected by the DRP Assembly members, and thus could leave the way open, after such a protest was duly registered, for their return to the Assembly at a later date. However, a quirk in the Korean election law, aimed at reducing the number of independents in Korean politics, stipulated that if an assemblyman resigned from his *party,* he automatically lost his Assembly seat. The adamants, therefore, urged that all opposition members pledge to resign as well from the party, which would make their resignations from the Assembly automatic. "People's Party and Assembly Ratification of Normalization Treaty," *Tonga Ilbo,* July 20, 1965. See also *Tonga Ilbo,* Aug. 9, 1965.

50. *Tonga Ilbo,* July 20, 1965. The call for new general elections was made by Yun as early as June, *Chosun Ilbo,* June 29, 1965, and became a

major issue in late summer when the parliamentary crisis became critical, *Tonga Ilbo*, Sept. 3, 6, 1965. See also "Are Constitutional Amendment and General Elections Feasible?" *Chosun Ilbo*, Sept. 2, 1965.

51. "Assembly Session of August 11 As Seen from Press Box," *Hankuk Ilbo*, Aug. 11, 1965.

52. *Tonga Ilbo*, July 20, 1965. It was reported that the president promised during this meeting not to take "extreme measures" such as proclamation of martial law. *Kyonghyang Sinmun*, July 21, 1965. This was the first such "summit" meeting between political leaders since 1963.

53. *Chosun Ilbo*, July 29, 1965. In August, he made it official by sending the resignation to his local chapter as required by law, *Tonga Ilbo*, Aug. 4, 1965. By this time, the moderates were being hard pressed by the party functionaries and lower officers, who generally sided with the adamants. In early August, the Central Standing Committee of the party, mostly nonassemblymen, passed a resolution in favor of dissolving the party. The moderates barely managed to reverse the decision at a party caucus a few days later. *Kyonghyang Sinmun*, Aug. 5, 9, 1965.

54. Statements of opposing positions can be found in "Dissolution of Party Helping the Enemy?" *Kyonghyang Sinmun*, July 16, 1965, "10 Adamants Issue Statement Demanding Dissolution of Party," *Tonga Ilbo*, July 23, 1965, and "Advertisement: By PP Moderates against Dissolution of Party," *Tonga Ilbo*, Aug. 23, 1965.

55. *Chosun Ilbo*, Aug. 12, 1965.

56. *Korea Annual 1966*, p. 18. The DRP also passed, in the same fashion at this time, the consent bill for dispatch of a Korean combat division to Vietnam. The Vietnam troop issue of that year became caught up in the struggle over the Japanese treaty and became subject, as a result, to the same kind of political tactics, though the debates were less aroused. See Princeton Lyman, "Korea's Involvement in Vietnam," *Orbis*, 12, no. 2 (Summer 1968), 566–567.

The moderates in the opposition, while resigning from the Assembly, did not resign from the party, laying the basis for their later return to the chores of parliamentary opposition. See n.49.

57. See Chap. 3.

58. "Signing Korea-Japan Pacts and National Sentiments," *Tonga Ilbo*, June 22, 1965.

59. The press even congratulated itself on its restraint, commenting "Pressdom could not have cooperated more with the Government with respect to the normalization talks," ibid. For a sharp criticism of the press for not coming out more forcefully against the treaty and in support of the opposition, see Professor Kim Chin-man, "Tokyo Pacts and Our Reflection (4th Installment)—Mass Communications Media," *Chosun Ilbo*, July 1, 1965.

60. In addition to editorials already cited, see "Opposition Dispute," *Tonga Ilbo*, July 24, 1965, "Declaration of Christian Clergymen and Educators," *Yongnam Ilbo*, July 6, 1965, and "PP: Consolidate Your Opinion toward General Elections," *Maeil Sinmun*, Aug. 24, 1965.

61. "Avoidance of Collapse," *Tonga Ilbo*, Aug. 14, 1965.

62. "To Overcome Crisis," *Tonga Ilbo*, Sept. 3, 1965.

63. See editorials of the *Chosun Ilbo*, Sept. 2, 15, 1965, *Chungang Ilbo*, Sept. 30, 1965, *Kukche Sinbo* (Pusan), Sept. 13, 1965, and *Hankuk Ilbo*, Sept. 15, 1965. There had been some pressure for new national elections, but when the government proved impervious to the idea, it was dropped.

64. *Chosun Ilbo*, Oct. 2, 1965.

65. *Hankuk Ilbo*, Oct. 19, 1965; ibid., Jan. 23, 1966.

66. The opposition members walked out of the Assembly in Mar. 1966 on the vote approving the administration's proposal for use of the first year's increment of Japanese funds. *Korea Annual 1967*, p. 9. For a review of issues, see "One-Year History of Normalized Korea-Japan Relations," *Chosun Ilbo*, Dec. 12, 1966.

67. See account in *Korea Annual 1967*, pp. 7–10. The issue led to an explosive incident within the Assembly, when one critic of the government dumped a five-gallon-can of human waste on the Cabinet, summoned for interpellation. In retrospect, the uproar over that incident probably drew attention away from the smuggling issue itself.

68. "What is Japan?" *Tonga Ilbo*, July 8, 1965.

69. Allen, *Syngman Rhee*, pp. 174–181, 199–201.

70. "High Waves on Korean Straits," *Tonga Ilbo*, June 28, 1965.

71. See account of business interests in *Tonga Ilbo*, Aug. 12, 1965.

72. See comments in "On Student Demonstrations," *Tonga Ilbo*, July 2, 1965 and "Lift Closedown Order on University Classes," *Taehan Ilbo*, Sept. 6, 1965.

73. A revealing conversation is reported between a military officer and a student, with the former asserting his determined opposition to the demonstrations in 1965 in contrast to his attitude toward those of Apr. 1960, in Richard Kim, "O, My Korea!," *Atlantic Monthly*, 217, no. 2 (Feb. 1966) 113–114. There was, in 1965, a minor coup attempt by some young officers. The issue, however, seemed to be military promotions rather than national politics, and the rebellious officers did not appear to have widespread support in the military. See *Tonga Ilbo*, May 25, 1965.

CHAPTER 6. THE DIMENSIONS OF ECONOMIC GROWTH AND STRUCTURAL CHANGE

1. See Jerome B. Cohen, *Japan's Economy in War and Reconstruction* (Minneapolis: University of Minnesota Press, 1949), p. 37.

2. Lance J. Taylor, *Aggregate Structural Change: Recent Time Series and Cross-Section Evidence* (Cambridge, Mass.: Project for Quantitative Research on Economic Development, Harvard University, 1967). A number of other studies of this type made in recent years, are cited in n.3 to the Introduction.

3. Economic Planning Board, Republic of Korea, *Overall Resources Budget*: 1968, 1969 (Seoul, 1967, 1968).

4. It should be noted that government consumption as defined here and

in official statistics excludes the value of military assistance from the United States which, as shown in Chap. 8, pp. 380–382, has averaged about 7 percent of GNP from 1959 through 1967.

5. Again, if the value of military assistance is included, the government consumption share would be substantially higher and all the other percentages would be somewhat reduced, because the level of national expenditure would have to be increased by the amount of the military assistance.

6. The capital-goods import shares in 1957–1959 and 1960–1962 are somewhat understated because miscellaneous imports, which include sizable amounts of unclassified items brought in through the foreign assistance programs, undoubtedly include some capital goods.

CHAPTER 7. THE CAUSES OF ECONOMIC GROWTH

1. Frederick Harbison and Charles A. Myers, *Education, Manpower and Economic Growth* (New York: McGraw-Hill, 1964), pp. 31–48.

2. This can be illustrated by comparing "normal" patterns of selected human resource indices, based on a cross section of countries, with the Korean ratios, in the Table below. In 1958–1959 Korea stood fairly close to the normal

Comparison of Korean and Normal Relations of
Human Resource Development and Economic Development[a]

	Normal patterns associated with various levels of per capital GNP			Korean patterns[b]	
				1960	1965
GNP per capita U.S. dollars	$84	$130	$380	$90	$107
Percent of active population in agriculture	83	74	52	61	52
Teachers (1st and 2nd levels) per 10,000 population	17	28	53	34.6	39
First level enrollment ratio	.22	.32	.62	.59	.82
First and second level enrollment adjusted	.20	.33	.66	.62	.72
Second level	.027	.07	.27	.265	.27
Third level	.0015	.0085	.05	.057	.064
Composite human resource index	3	12	50	55	59

Sources: Normal patterns and the Korean pattern for 1960 are from Harbison and Myers, *Education, Manpower and Economic Growth*, pp. 38, 47. The Korean Pattern for 1965 is derived from: Republic of Korea, Ministry of Education, *Education in Korea 1965–66* (Seoul, July 1966). Exceptions noted in note *b*.

[a] Harbison and Myers do not claim that the various measures of human resource development are a function of GNP per capita, or vice versa. They do

find a close association (a correlation coefficient of .888) between their composite human resource index (which is simply a weighted sum of the second- and third-level education ratios) and per capita GNP. They then rank and group countries by the composite index and calculate mean values of the various human resource indicators and per capita GNP for four groups of countries. The Level I countries, which they term Underdeveloped, had a mean per capita GNP of $84. The Level II, or Partially Developed countries a mean per capita GNP of $182. We have interpolated a $130 per capita GNP level to approximate the Korean conditions in 1965. The Level III, or semi-advanced, countries had mean per capita GNP of $380 and human resource patterns roughly comparable to Korea's in 1960. Harbison and Myers include Korea in the Level III countries in their analysis.

   b The figure on percent of active population in agriculture for Korea in 1960 is taken from the 1960 Census, reported in Economic Planning Board, *Korea Statistical Yearbook, 1965* (Seoul, 1965). This is much lower than the figure in Harbison and Myers of 75 percent. The 1965 estimate of active population in agriculture is from Economic Planning Board, *Major Economic Indicators 1957–1966* (Seoul, Mar. 1967).

pattern of human resource development for a country with mean per capita GNP of nearly $200. Only in the ratio of teachers to population was Korea significantly below the norm for that income level. By 1965 this ratio was still somewhat low, but all the ratios of student enrollment were well above the $380 norm. If the comparison is made with countries near Korea's level of per capita income in 1965 (i.e. $107), then the Korean ratios and composite index of human resource development are exceptionally high.

   3. Edgar C. McVoy, "Manpower Development and Utilization in Korea," unpublished paper, May 7, 1965.

   4. Economic Planning Board, Republic of Korea, *Annual Report on the Economically Active Population, 1968* (Seoul, 1969).

   5. See, for example, John W. Mellor, "Toward a Theory of Agricultural Development," in Herman M. Southworth and Bruce F. Johnston, eds., *Agricultural Development and Economic Growth* (Ithaca, N.Y.: Cornell University Press, 1967), pp. 48–50.

   6. United States Operations Mission to Korea, *Rural Development Program Evaluation Report* (Seoul, 1967), pp. 86–88.

   7. "An Evaluation of USOM/Korea's Rural Development Program," report of a team of experts contained in the United States Operations Mission to Korea, *Rural Development Program Evaluation Report*, p. 34.

   8. Raj Krishna, "Agricultural Price Policy and Economic Development," in Southworth and Johnston, eds., *Agricultural Development and Economic Growth*, pp. 504–508.

   9. There were severe shortages of electric power throughout this period, which caused many factories to include power-generating equipment as part of their normal capital equipment to be used on a standby or regular basis. Such power was not very efficient and increased the costs of production, but these costs could be passed on in higher prices in a protected market.

10. Economic Research Center of Korea, *Industrial Structure of Korea, Vol. I, Manufacturing Industries.*

11. Economic Planning Board, Republic of Korea, *Economic Survey, 1963* (Seoul, 1963), p. 50.

12. Ministry of Reconstruction, Republic of Korea, *Economic Survey, 1959, Economic Survey, 1962,* and Economic Research Center of Korea, *Industrial Structure of Korea,* 2 vols.

13. W. D. Reeve, *The Republic of Korea, A Political and Economic Study,* (London: Oxford University Press, 1961) pp. 120, 122, 134–135.

14. Republic of Korea, *Summary of the First Five-Year Economic Plan 1962–1966* (Seoul, 1962).

CHAPTER 8. THE PATTERNS OF ECONOMIC POLICY

1. See Hahn-Been Lee, *Time, Change and Administration,* pp. 130–132.

2. See below, Chap. 10, for a discussion of the debate and the attitude taken during the 1967 election campaign on the issue of growth maximization vs. income distribution.

3. Reeve, *The Republic of Korea, A Political and Economic Study,* p. 120.

4. If the military assistance were included in these various accounting systems, it would give a clearer picture of the economy's scale of operations. We have not tried to incorporate such adjustments in the accounts, other than here in the budget, however, because of the valuation problems and the fact that it would make our statistics different from all the published series. But the reader should at least be aware of the fact that such assistance is omitted and have some idea of its magnitude.

5. Colin D. Campbell and Ahn Chang-Shick, "Kyes and Mujins: Financial Intermediaries in South Korea," *Economic Development and Cultural Change,* 11, no. 1 (Oct. 1962) 55–68; Lee Chang-Nyol, *Mobilization of Domestic Capital* (Seoul, Feb. 1965); Hugh Patrick and E. S. Shaw, "Finance and Development in Korea" (Seoul, Mar. 26, 1965); John H. Gurley, Hugh Patrick, and E. S. Shaw, *Financial Development in Korea* (Seoul: United States Operations Mission to Korea, Aug. 1965).

6. Campbell and Ahn, "Kyes and Mujins."

7. Lee Chang-Nyol, *Mobilization of Domestic Capital,* and Kwang-Suk Kim, *The Unofficial Money Market in Korea* (Seoul: United States Operations Mission to Korea, 1964).

8. The Korean Development Institute, *Analyses of Capital Cost, Selected Industrial Establishments* (Seoul, 1967) provides an interesting analysis of the sources of business finance in Korea in the mid-1960s.

9. See n. 5.

10. Gurley, Patrick, and Shaw, *Financial Development in Korea,* who supported the reform, concluded that tax reform would have to shoulder an even larger burden than financial reform to raise the ratio of domestic saving to national income within the next few years. The consultant on taxation con-

curred "that public savings must carry the major weight during the earlier phases of the [Second Five-Year] plan, with private savings assuming a greater share later on." Musgrave, *Revenue Policy for Korea's Economic Development*, p. 5.

11. Kwang-Suk Kim, *An Appraisal of the High Interest Rate Strategy of Korea* (paper prepared at Williams College, Williamstown, Mass.: 1967), p. 13.

12. On the basis of regressions relating money savings in 1965 prices (Sm) and gross domestic saving in 1965 prices (S) to GNP in 1965 prices (Y), the ceiling rate of interest on time deposits in banks minus the annual percent change in the wholesale price index ($R - \Delta P$), and the change in inventories (Ii), Kim found the following relations:

$$Sm = -124.36 + .21Y + 1.10\ (R - \Delta P), R^2 = .9763,$$
$$\quad\quad\quad\quad (.03)\quad (.37)$$
$$S = -190.76 + .32Y + .23Ii + .30\ (R - \Delta P), R^2 = .9945,$$
$$\quad\quad\quad\quad (.01)\quad (.17)\quad (.14)$$

The first equation shows the strong influence of the real interest rate on money savings, while the second one, with a high .32 marginal propensity to save out of income, has a less strong, but still significant, interest rate effect. Kwang-Suk Kim, *An Appraisal of the High Interest Rate Strategy of Korea*.

13. Ibid., p. 28.

14. The Medium and Small Industry Bank, a government bank, which mixes short and longer-term financing for smaller enterprises, did go along with the interest rate changes on deposits and on its short-term loans. The volume of its loans more than doubled between the end of 1965 and 1967. See Bank of Korea, *Monthly Statistical Review* (Feb. 1967).

15. Economic Planning Board, Republic of Korea, *Economic Survey, 1963* (Seoul, 1963), p. 39.

16. See Chaps. 1 and 4.

17. For the previous election in 1963, the DRP leaders had obtained fantastic amounts from manipulation of the little stock exchange in Seoul by bidding up the prices of the stock of the Stock Exchange Company. That the public was enticed into this speculation is one of the more mysterious aspects of Korea's recent economic history. At least in connection with raising funds for the 1967 election the country did benefit from the inflow of some real resources.

18. C. P. Kindleberger, "Liberal Policies vs. Controls in the Foreign Trade of Developing Countries," Agency for International Development Discussion Paper no. 14 (Apr. 1967).

19. Ronald McKinnon, *Tariff, Special Customs Duty, and Excise Tax Reform* (Seoul: United States Operations Mission to Korea, 1966), has argued that Korean tariff protection was too narrowly focused so that it discouraged domestic production of intermediate goods which were inputs to the protected industries.

20. Kee-Chun Han, "Export Promotion Measures in Korea," p. 116.

21. Detailed descriptions of the export incentives as of 1965 are contained

in P. B. Musgrave, *Trade Targets and Policies in Korea's Economic Development* (Seoul: United States Operations Mission to Korea, Aug. 1965), and Kee-Chun Han, "Export Promotion Measures in Korea."

22. The Bank of Korea actually covered the negative interest rates, since it paid in foreign exchange against the import letters of credit when the commodities were shipped by the foreign exporter and received payment from the domestic producer-exporter only when he shipped the finished commodities. Also, the Bank of Korea rediscounted the commercial Banks' 6.5 percent loans to domestic exporters at a 3.5 percent rediscount rate, thus giving the commercial banks a 3 percent spread.

CHAPTER 9. THE SIGNIFICANCE OF ECONOMIC PLANNING

1. This chapter is based in large part on a paper entitled "The Pattern and Significance of Planning in Korea" written by David Cole with Nam Young-Woo and published in Irma Adelman, ed. *Practical Approaches to Development Planning.*

2. Robert R. Nathan and Associates, *An Economic Programme for Korean Reconstruction,* prepared for the United Nations Korean Reconstruction Agency, Mar. 1954.

3. Joe-Won Lee, "Planning Efforts for Economic Development," in Joseph S. Chung, ed. *Patterns of Economic Development: Korea,* pp. 1–11.

4. Lee, ibid., has appropriately labeled the Three-Year Plan, 1960–1963; and this first version of the Five-Year Plan, 1962–1966, as the "abortive plans."

5. The Oregon Advisory Group in Korea, *A Report on the University of Oregon Advisory Mission to the Korean Economic Development Council, 1959–1961* (School of Business Administration, University of Oregon, Eugene, 1961). This report contains a summary of the Three-Year Economic Development Plan, issued by the Economic Development Council, Jan. 25, 1960.

6. Arthur D. Little, Inc., "Economic Development Planning in Korea, Report of the Arthur D. Little Reconnaissance Survey" (Cambridge, Mass., May 1962).

7. These experts included, in approximate chronological order, Edward S. Shaw, John G. Gurley, and Hugh T. Patrick on the development of financial institutions and policies; Irma Adelman on planning models and conceptual approaches to planning; Richard A. Musgrave on tax and fiscal policy; Peggy B. Musgrave on foreign trade policy; Edward Hollander and Edgar McVoy on manpower planning; and Alan Strout on planning models.

8. Korea Electric Co., *Korea Electric Power Survey,* 2 vols., prepared in 1965 by the Electric Power Industry Team; and Ministry of Transportation, *Korea Transportation Survey,* draft report (Korea, 1966).

9. No private enterprise representatives were included in these industry committees (as had been the pattern in France) because it was feared by the government that they would frequently take advantage of privileged information that they might obtain from the deliberations of the industry committees.

10. These included Professor Han Kee-Chun's study of "The Predicative

Ability of the Korean Input-Output Tables," and the Korean Development Association's long-term projections in "Korean Economy in the 1980's."

11. W. Arthur Lewis, *Development Planning, The Essentials of Economic Policy* (New York: Harper, 1966), p. 26.

12. Economic Planning Board, *Overall Resources Budget*, 1968 (July 1967).

13. This assessment is reported in the Arthur D. Little draft report, "*Economic Development Planning in Korea*," pp. iv–1.

14. *Summary of the First Five-Year Economic Plan, 1962–1966* (Republic of Korea, 1962), p. 29.

15. Fei and Ranis, "Toward a Long-Run Development Strategy for Korea," p. 39.

16. World Bank experts, as late as the summer of 1966, were still suggesting that a $400 million target for 1971 was more reasonable.

17. Economic Planning Board, *Overall Resources Budget: 1968* (Aug. 1967), p. 13.

18. See Peggy Musgrave, "Trade Targets and Policies in Korea's Economic Development," p. 15.

19. Charles Wolf, Jr., "Economic Planning in Korea," p. 235; and Duck Woo Nam, "Korea's Experience with Planning," in Sang-eun Lee, ed., *Report of International Conference on the Problem of Modernization in Asia* (Seoul: Asiatic Research Center, 1966), pp. 520–523.

20. Sung-Chick Hong, *The Intellectual and Modernization*, pp. 99–101.

CHAPTER 10. EMERGENCE OF A NEW CONSENSUS

1. By the end of 1966, 184 projects worth $832 million had already been proposed for private Japanese credits. Moreover, the loans appeared to be directed to small and medium, as well as large, industries of Korea. The mean amount for these projects was $2.2 million, and about one-third were for under $1 million. Republic of Korea, Economic Planning Board, *Foreign Investment Projects—Sector Listing as of the End of 1966*, Apr. 1967.

2. See Chap. 7 and *Seoul Kyongje Sinmun* (an economic daily), May 13, 1969.

3. Aaron B. Horwitz, *Evaluation of Planning and Development in Seoul* (Seoul, United States Operations Mission to Korea, 1966), p. 24; see also *Chosun Ilbo*, May 7, 1967. At one time the vice-mayor of Seoul remarked, quite likely an exaggeration, that projects were being slowed down for lack of labor, and that he had had to recruit more labor from the countryside.

4. In a city with fairly severe traffic problems, traffic deaths were cut nearly in half from 1965 to 1966 because of newly constructed bridges and underpasses. The mayor also opened "neighborhood city halls" as part of a program to provide more rapid and responsive service on daily needs. Horwitz, *Evaluation of Planning and Development*, p. 24.

5. Land development and other food-for-work programs were rather consciously divided among all the provinces for political reasons. On food shortages and land development, see the speech of President Park Chung-Hee to the Provincial Governor's Conference, Dec. 1966. For a discussion of some of the differences in rural and urban changes in this period, see *Rural Development Program Evaluation Report*, pp. 304–305, and Felix Moos, *Some Observations on Korean Cultural Change 1966–67*.

6. At the beginning of the intensive land development program in 1964, about 90 percent of the individual projects had been selected and planned by the central administration and only 10 percent by provincial and county officials. Under pressure from United States advisors and provincial governors, these proportions had, by and large, been reversed by 1967. Also in 1967, the government established a quasi-governmental corporation to promote agro-industry with investment from abroad. Another proposal to help modernize agriculture has been for the removal of the limit on owner-cultivated paddy land. This was discussed frequently after 1965 but not promulgated. It has serious consequences for tenure conditions. The justification, however, is to encourage the more enterprising farmers to expand, some of whom have long been buying extra land under other names and through similar subterfuges. See *Korea Week* 2, no. 21 (Washington, D.C.), Nov. 20, 1969, p. 2.

7. In the two years of the Military Government, diplomatic representation was tripled; economic aid agreements were reached with Germany (West), France, Italy, and other European countries; trade missions were sent throughout Southeast Asia and Europe; and application was made to the Colombo Plan, GATT, and other international organizations. *Korea Annual 1964*, pp. 129–131.

8. One source of frustration was Korea's own "Hallstein doctrine," by which it refused to have diplomatic relations with any country recognizing North Korea. In 1964 and again in 1966, South Korea broke off relations with countries on this basis. *Taehan Ilbo*, Jan. 15, 1966. For a variety of reasons, moreover, the efforts were not bearing as much fruit in the United Nations as had been hoped. In 1965 and again in 1966, voting in the United Nations on the Korean question proved to be a difficult ordeal and at one point almost went against South Korea. *Chosun Ilbo*, Dec. 11, 1966. There was some questioning of whether the whole effort toward neutrals was worthwhile. "Diplomacy toward Nonaligned Countries Needs Review," *Chungang Ilbo*, Dec. 23, 1966.

9. Some critical comments can be found in *Chosun Ilbo*, Jan. 6, 1967; *Hankuk Ilbo*, Jan. 8, 1967. For a positive reaction, see *Korea Times*, Aug. 12, 1967.

10. Lyman, "Korea's Involvement in Vietnam," pp. 565–570.

11. *Seoul Sinmun*, Jan. 18, 1966; *Chonnam Ilbo*, Mar. 10, 1967; *Taehan Ilbo*, Apr. 22, 1967.

12. *Chosun Ilbo*, Mar. 27, 1965; *Hankuk Ilbo*, Mar. 28, 1965.

13. *Korea Annual* 1967, pp. 63, 94–95.

14. The slogan was advanced in a government broadcast, quoted in the *Maeil Sinmun*, Mar. 19, 1966. President Park twice traveled to Southeast

Asia in 1966. In the same year, Korea was a prime mover in the convening of the first "troop contributor nations' conference" in Manila. *Korea Annual 1967*, p. 98.

15. Seung-Kuhn Rhee, "Achievements of the ASPAC Ministerial Meeting in Seoul," *Koreana Quarterly*, 1, no. 3 (Autumn 1966) 18.

16. When the Asian Development Bank was inaugurated in 1966, Korea pledged three times the minimum required capitalization, so that with a pooling of South Vietnam's and Taiwan's vote with South Korea's, Korea obtained a seat on the Executive Board. The same pooling of votes by the three was extended to the World Bank and the IMF. In 1966, Korea began negotiating with Taiwan on respective investments in production and marketing of petrochemicals, resulting in a precedent-setting international agreement in 1968 to avoid competitive national development plans. See Statement by Park Choong-hoon, Deputy Prime Minister, to the International Economic Consultative Group on Korea, May 13, 1968, p. 4.

17. *Tonga Ilbo*, Dec. 30, 1966.

18. *Tonga Ilbo*, May 20, 1965; *Taehan Ilbo*, Dec. 30, 1966.

19. *New York Times*, Jan. 19, 1968, p. 6. Beyond individual earnings, Korean construction firms began to bid on overseas contracts and won several, not only in Vietnam but in Thailand.

20. For an indication of some of the Government's hopes for the future role of Korean diplomacy, see *Korean Herald* (special anniversary issue), Aug. 14, 1966, p. 8.

21. *Chosun Ilbo*, Jan. 22, 1966. For an analysis of the philosophy of "mass capitalism," see *Seoul Sinmun*, Jan. 26, 1966.

22. *Korea Annual 1967*, pp. 1–20, 49–51. Even during protests over the election rigging of June 1967, leading newspapers cautioned the opposition not to go down the path of "no return" as in 1965. *Chosun Ilbo*, June 14, 1967, *Tonga Ilbo*, June 16, 1967.

23. A case in which an author was accused of coming too close to North Korean criticisms of the United States is reviewed in *Tonga Ilbo*, Jan. 2, 1967; *Chosun Ilbo*, May 26, 1967; *Kangwon Ilbo*, May 26, 1967.

24. *Yongnam Ilbo*, May 19, 1966.

25. The coup leaders had presented no new proposals or directions in this area at the time they assumed power. The break with the past was suggested by General Park later in 1963, when he eschewed the idea that reunification could be brought about by "external forces," an apparent rejection of Rhee's continued call for a new outbreak of international hostilities in Korea. There was also at that time a fairly frank appraisal of the slim likelihood that the United Nations would be in a position to supervise general elections in all of Korea, as dutifully called for in the annual UN resolution on the subject, which South Korea supported. But references to alternative strategies were quite vague. Park Chung-Hee, *Country, Revolution and I*, pp. 163–168.

26. State of the Union address, *Taegu Ilbo*, Feb. 1, 1966. In June President Park told a press conference that he felt that unification could not be positively discussed until the late 1970s. *Korea Annual 1964*, p. 12.

27. See particularly his remarks upon returning from West Germany in 1964, *Tonga Ilbo,* Dec. 24 and 29, 1964.

28. For presentation and debate of the government's position, see *Chosun Ilbo,* Aug. 14, 1966. See also *Tonga Ilbo,* Dec. 19, 1966.

29. The 1966 debate ended after a long bipartisan Assembly study produced a White Paper reviewing the question and recommending that a special Territorial Unification Board be established to study the question on a permanent basis. Press reaction to this tepid product was not overly critical. See *Hankuk Ilbo,* Feb. 1, 1967, *Chonnam Ilbo,* Feb. 3, 1967, and, for a more critical comment, *Tonga Ilbo,* Feb. 1, 1967.

30. *Chosun Ilbo,* Aug. 14, 1966.

31. See copy of indictment, *Chosun Ilbo,* July 12, 1966. So was indicted also for his remarks criticizing the troop commitment in Vietnam. But the arrest seemed to have been prompted by his election pledge, as head of a new party, to meet the North Korean premier face to face if he were elected president.

32. *Taehan Ilbo,* Dec. 30, 1966.

33. The party succeeded in recruiting several prominent nonaligned public figures into its ranks during 1966. *Tonga Ilbo,* July 13 and 20, 1966. The candidate chosen was Yu Chin-o, a prominent educator, novelist, lawyer, and former university president. Yu was not a strong figure and had limited governmental, and no political, experience. But he was expected to rally intellectual and other urban support and to give the moderates' candidacy some needed prestige. For a review of Yu's career, see *Chonnam Ilbo,* Oct. 19, 1966.

34. See *Korea Herald,* Feb. 8, 1967, and *Chosun Ilbo,* May 5, 1967.

35. For an analysis, though somewhat sharply critical, of opposition philosophy and appeal, see the series on political parties written by four professors in the *Chosun Ilbo,* Jan. 1, 5, 6, 11, 1967.

36. The platform is reviewed in *Chosun Ilbo,* Sept. 22, 1966.

37. See "Controversial Democratic Socialist Party and its Future," *Chosun Ilbo,* May 20, 1966. When some former student leaders were asked by one of the authors of this book why So's appeal, particularly on reunification, had attracted so little student support, they replied that the students considered So "an opportunist."

38. *Chosun Ilbo,* Apr. 29, 1967.

39. *Korea Annual 1964,* pp. 144–145.

40. *Korea Times,* Apr. 16, 1967.

41. *Tonga Ilbo,* Apr. 1, 1967.

42. See *Hankuk Ilbo,* Jan. 24 and Mar. 30, 1967. A good overall review of contrasting party appeals can be found in the *Taehan Ilbo,* Mar. 30, 1967. A more detailed examination of issues and platform pledges is in the series "Mutual Criticisms of Election Pledges," *Tonga Ilbo,* Apr. 1, 4, 6, 11, 18, 22, 25, 1967.

43. *Chosun Ilbo,* Jan. 6, 1967; *Tonga Ilbo,* Apr. 6, 1967.

44. See above, Chap. 4, on agricultural policies. The loss of the Chollas was also likely due to charges of the opposition that the Cholla provinces were

discriminated against in the selection of industrial sites, a charge to which the Chollas would be sensitive. On the other hand, Park gained back the northern province of Kangwon, which has a large military vote, which he had lost in 1963. Looked at regionally, whereas in 1963 Park had lost the north and won in the south, in 1967 he won all the eastern provinces and lost all the western ones. Regional ties and regional sensitivities figured to some degree in this new division. For voting results, see *Chosun Ilbo*, May 5 and 7, 1967. For an analysis of 1963 results by comparison, see Chong-Sik Lee, "Korea: In Search of Stability," pp. 659–660. It is interesting that, while the overall voting turnout was down from 89 percent to 84 percent from 1963, Seoul's turnout dropped from 78 percent to 67 percent.

45. See editorials in the *Tonga Ilbo* and *Kyonghyang Sinmun*, Jan. 23, 1967.

46. *Tonga Ilbo*, Jan. 25, 1967.

47. *Hankuk Ilbo*, May 5, 1967.

48. One should not overlook in the results the advantages of the Democratic Republican party in funds and organization. But as much as this hurt the New Democratic party in campaigning, it also reflected on its image in comparison with the DRP. See the analysis of results, *Tonga Ilbo*, May 5, 1967.

CHAPTER 11. LINGERING CONSTRAINTS

1. The atmosphere of the campaign for Assembly seats can be gleaned from two series depicting the contests in selected districts around the country, one in the *Chosun Ilbo* and the other in the *Taehan Ilbo*, running through May and early June 1967. See also the results of a candidate survey in *Hankuk Ilbo*, June 18, 20, 1967.

2. *Chosun Ilbo*, June 8, 1967.

3. Though not always, both parties followed generally the practice of nominating the local district party chief as the Assembly candidate. Stiff competition for the district party positions in 1966 and early 1967 had thus preceded the competition for the actual Assembly nominations.

4. *Tonga Ilbo*, June 9, 1967; *Chosun Ilbo*, June 10, 11, 1967. Even DRP officials, like Kim Chong-pil, joined in the criticisms.

5. See the analysis of results in the *Chosun Ilbo* series, June 10, 11, 15, 22, 1967.

6. Ibid., June 10, 1967.

7. This point was underlined by schisms within the Democratic Republican party in 1968 and 1969, largely related to plans for 1971, which led to Chairman Kim Chong-pil's temporary resignation from the party in 1968 and his retirement from politics in 1969. See *Korea Times*, June 10, 1968; *Chungang Ilbo*, May 6, 1969; *Korea Annual 1969*, pp. 23–26.

8. See *Tonga Ilbo*, May 19, 1966, and *Chosun Ilbo* and *Taehan Ilbo* series cited in n.1.

9. In response to the outcry, the president and the Democratic Republican party agreed almost immediately to expel eight DRP members, but this

still left the DRP with more than a two-thirds majority. Compromise was finally reached for the opposition's return to the Assembly around a number of budget and tax bills, passed during the boycott and therefore denounced by the opposition, and with agreement on a joint election investigation team. *Korea Times,* Dec. 2, 28, 29, 30, 1967. Controversy continued around these issues, nevertheless. During 1968, the Supreme Court ruled that three districts would have to have new elections; a group of DRP members formed an "independent" bloc in the Assembly, officially lowering DRP membership just below the two-thirds number; and the Assembly passed amendments to the election law to close some of the possibilities for fraud. *Korea Annual 1969,* pp. 89–90.

10. A valuable ten-part series evaluating the organization, functioning and achievements of the Sixth Assembly (1963–1967) can be found in the *Chosun Ilbo,* during Sept. 1966.

11. The administration acted on only 5 out of 46 such proposals during the period from 1963 to 1967. Ibid., Sept. 29, 1966.

12. Nearly one-third of the Assembly's time 1963–1967 was spent questioning cabinet ministers on political issues. The administration complained of the tremendous loss of time to do its work and threatened to seek legislation limiting the Assembly's prerogative. Ibid., Sept. 13, 1966.

13. See, for example, Henderson, *Korea,* pp. 368–372, who argues for it in the context of a general increase in pluralistic institutions and more multifunctional and multicentered society. It is also advocated strongly by the opposition.

14. See *Tonga Ilbo,* Mar. 13, 1969, *Chungang Ilbo,* May 6, 1969.

15. In this case, the DRP sent the referendum proposal from committee to the president rather than through the plenary session. Opposition members were not informed of the session in which the action was taken. *Sina Ilbo,* Aug. 28, 1969.

16. There was evidence in 1969 of a buildup of praise around the personality of Park that would have seemed almost inconceivable in the first years of his administration. See, for example, the editorial in the semigovernmental journal *Seoul Sinmun,* July 1, 1969, and the statement of the DRP chairman, *Sina Ilbo,* July 16, 1969. There was also evidence of an orchestrated campaign behind a third term for Park, reminiscent of Liberal party days under Rhee. See, for example, editorials in the *Hankuk Ilbo,* Mar. 15, 1969; *Maeil Sinmun,* Aug. 22, 1969.

17. Just after the presidential election, about 28 persons, including 2 minor party presidential candidates and 1 principal campaigner for the NDP, were arrested for violations of the election laws. *Hankuk Ilbo,* May 9, 1967.

18. *Taehan Ilbo,* July 5, 1969; *Hankuk Ilbo,* July 5, 6, 1969. About 30,000 students demonstrated between June 27 and July 5. Another round of demonstrations occurred in August.

19. In reading the editorials of the various papers throughout the summer of 1969—with student demonstrations, violent debate in the Assembly, and even an acid attack on one opposition leader taking place—one cannot help but notice an unusually subdued tone and almost a nonreporting character

to the press, contrasted to that of such stormy periods as 1964, 1965, or even 1966. An allusion to censorship in the coverage of demonstrations is in *Tonga Ilbo*, July 3, 1969. Discussion of police measures to restrict press coverage of corruption among public officials is found in *Chosun Ilbo*, Mar. 13, 1969.

20. Henderson, *Korea*, p. 180.

21. See *Korea Annual 1969*, pp. 254–259, and *Tonga Ilbo*, Aug. 28, 1969. Labor unions were a principal battleground of political forces in the 1945–1948 period, but were placed under government control afterward by the Rhee government, and later the Park government. The most active unions have for some time been those dealing with foreigners, for example, with the United States military, whose successes resulted in increased foreign exchange earnings rather than taxed Korean businessmen. An anomaly of the labor situation is that the laws governing labor are quite generous—so generous that like many laws in the social field they serve more as ideals than regulations and are violated by most Korean if not foreign firms. *Tonga Ilbo*, Mar. 10, 1969. Cf. Pyong-Choon Hahm, *The Korean Political Tradition and Law*.

22. The government has been continually wary of intellectuals for precisely this reason. Intellectuals were the target of many of the special trials under the Military Government and the subject of two sensational spy cases in 1967 and 1968. *Korea Annual 1969*, pp. 17–20, 30.

23. Hahn-Been Lee has noted the emergence of a professionally oriented bureaucracy and a growing body of senior civilian administrators of general, rather than partisan, prestige as one of the main elements of institutionalization of the new emphases on development and performance in the 1960s and a source of support to any regime in the future that desires to maintain a constructive development effort.

24. Both the Rhee and Chang Myon governments faced problems with the military on this issue. Sohn, "The Role of the Military." It may become an issue again soon when the Vietnam war ends, and two divisions, now largely funded by United States aid related to Vietnam, return home. Another source for aggravating this issue would be further reductions in United States military aid (hardware), which in contrast to the reduction in United States economic aid would pose a direct charge on Korean foreign exchange if Korea were to try to make up the difference.

25. Lyman, "Korea's Involvement in Vietnam," pp. 575–577. One symbol of nationalism that might be affected is the United Nations Command structure in Korea, which has placed all South Korean forces under the operational command of an American general since the Korean War. The first Korean commander in Vietnam has pointed with pride to his resisting a similar arrangement for his troops in Vietnam and his determination to prove the tactical superiority of his troops under independent Korean command. *Weekly Hankuk*, Apr. 27, 1969.

26 *New York Times*, Feb. 29, 1968; *Korea Times*, Mar. 21, 1968.

27. The law covering the referendum campaign greatly restricted opponents and favored the government, e.g., the bulletin issued to all voters only gave the government's side. *Tonga Ilbo*, Aug. 16, 1969.

28. *Korea Week*, Dec. 18, 1969, p. 2.

Selected Bibliography

Adelman, Irma, ed. *Practical Approaches to Development Planning: Korea's Second Five-Year Plan,* Baltimore, The Johns Hopkins Press, 1969.

Allen, Richard C. *Syngman Rhee: An Unauthorized Portrait,* Rutland, Vt., Charles E. Tuttle Co., 1960.

Bank of Korea. *Background Material for 1966 International Monetary Fund Consultations,* Korea, 1966.

Bank of Korea. *Economic Statistics Yearbook, 1967,* Korea, 1967.

Bank of Korea. *Monthly Statistical Review 1965–66.*

Bank of Korea. *Review of Korean Economy in 1964,* Korea, 1965.

Bank of Korea. *Review of Korean Economy in 1965,* Korea, 1966.

Bank of Korea. *Revision of National Accounts 1953–62 and Actual Estimates for 1963,* Korea, 1965.

Bank of Korea. *Seventeenth Annual Report—1966,* Seoul, Korea, The Bank of Korea, 1967.

Chung, Bom Mo. *An Image of Education in Korea: A Critique,* Seoul National University, 1966.

Chung, Joseph S., ed. *Patterns of Economic Development: Korea,* Kalamazoo, Korea Research and Publication, Inc., 1966.

Chung-Ang University. *Income Distribution and Consumption Structure in Korea,* United States Overseas Mission–Economic Planning Board Research Project, Korea, 1966.

Economic Planning Board. *First Five-Year Economic Plan 1962–1966* (first draft), Korea, 1961.

Economic Planning Board. *First Five-Year Plan for Technical Development,* Supplement to First Five-Year Economic Plan, Seoul, 1962.

Economic Planning Board. *Foreign Investment Projects—Sector Listing* (as of the end of 1966), Seoul, 1967.

Economic Planning Board. *Korea's Statistical Yearbook, 1965,* Korea, 1965.

Economic Planning Board. *Korea's Statistical Yearbook, 1967,* Seoul, 1967.

Economic Planning Board. *Major Economic Indicators 1955–1964,* Korea, 1965.

307

Economic Planning Board. *Major Economic Indicators 1957–1966*, Korea, 1967.

Economic Planning Board. *Overall Resources Budget: 1968*, Second Five-Year Economic Development Plan, 1967–1971, Korea, 1967.

Economic Planning Board. *Population and Employment*, Korea, 1965.

Economic Planning Board. "Progress and Prospects of the Korean Economy," A report of the delegation of the Republic of Korea to the preliminary meeting of the Proposed Consultative Group for Korea, May 19, 1966, London and Korea, 1966.

Economic Planning Board, *Summary of the First Five-Year Economic Plan 1962–1966*, Korea, 1962.

Economic Planning Bureau. Economic Planning Board, *Nathan Products Series I*, Korea, 1965.

Economic Planning Bureau. Economic Planning Board, *Nathan Products Series II*, Korea, 1965.

Economic Research Center of Korea. *Industrial Structure of Korea, vol. 1, Manufacturing Industries*, Seoul: Korean Traders Association and American-Korean Foundation, 1962.

Economic Survey, Korea: Economic Planning Board, 1959–1966.

Fei, J. C. H. and Ranis, Gustav. "Toward a Long-Run Development Strategy for Korea," 1964.

Government of the Republic of Korea. *The Second Five-Year Economic Development Plan 1967–1971*, Seoul, Korea, 1960.

Government of the Republic of Korea. *The Korean Sectoral Plan 1967–1971* (Annex to the Second Five-Year Economic Development Plan), Korea, 1966.

Grajdanzev, Andrew J. *Modern Korea*, New York, Institute of Pacific Relations, 1944.

Gurley, John H., Patrick, Hugh T., and Shaw, E. S., *Financial Development in Korea*, Seoul, United States Operations Mission to Korea, 1965.

Hahm, Pyong-Choon. *The Korean Political Tradition and Law: Essays in Korean Law and Legal History*, Korea, Royal Asiatic Society, 1967.

Han, Kee-Chun. "Export Promotion Measures in Korea," *Yonsei Business Review I*, vol. 3, no. 1, Korea, 1965; *II*, 3, no. 2, Korea, 1965.

Henderson, Gregory. *Korea: The Politics of the Vortex*, Cambridge, Mass., Harvard University Press, 1968.

Hollander, Edward D. " The Role of Manpower in Korean Economic Development," Korea, United States Operations Mission to Korea, 1966.

Hong, Sung-Chick. *The Intellectual and Modernization: A Study of Korean Attitudes*, Korea, Social Research Institute, Korea University, 1967.

Hong, Sung-Chick. "Values of Korean College Students," *The Journal of Asiatic Studies*, Korea University, May 1963.

Hun, Ryu. *Study of North Korea*, Korea, 1966.

International Bank for Reconstruction and Development, International Development Association. *The Current Economic Position and Prospects of the Republic of Korea*, Washington, D.C., 1964.

Johnson, Robert H. "Profits of Commercial Banks in Korea: An Analysis and Recommendations," Korea, 1966.

Johnson, Rossall J., McKeen, Dale L., Mears, Leon A. *Business Environment in an Emerging Nation: Profiles of Indonesian Economy*, Evanston, Ill., Northwestern University Press, 1966.

Kim, Byong-Kuk, "Central Banking Experiment in a Developing Economy: Case Study of Korea," *The Korean Studies Series*, vol. 12 (finance), Korea, 1965.

Kim, C. I. Eugene. "The South Korean Military Coup of May 1961: Its Causes and the Social Characteristics of Its Leaders," Prepared for the International Sociological Association Meetings, Evian, France, Sept. 1966.

Kim, Kwang-Suk. "The Unofficial Money Market in Korea," United States Operations Mission to Korea, 1964 (preliminary).

Kim, Kyu-Taik and Ho, Hahn-Bae. "Korean Political Leaders (1953–1962): Their Social Origins and Skills," *Asian Survey*, 3, no. 7 (July 1963).

Kim, Kyu-whan. "The Role of Intellectuals in the Process of Modernization through Mass Communication Activities" (reprint).

Kim, Mahn-Je and Norton, Roger D. "A Stabilization Model for Korea," paper presented at the Second Far Eastern Meeting of the Econometric Society, Tokyo, June 29–July 1, 1967.

Korea (New York: Chase Manhattan Bank, 1967).

Korea Electric Company. Electric Power Industry Survey Team, *Korea Electric Power Survey*, vols. 1 and 2, Korea, 1965.

Korea Electric Company. "Long Range Load Forecast: 1967–1976," Korea, 1966.

Korea Institute of Agricultural Economics. *A Study on Food Grains Policy in Korea: 1965*, Korea, 1965.

Korea Land Economics Research Center. *A Study of Land Tenure System of Korea*, Korea, 1966.

Korea University, College of Agriculture, International Agricultural Resource Research Institute. *A Study of the Regional Characteristics of Korean Agriculture*, Korea, 1967.

Korea University. *International Conference on the Problems of Modernization in Asia: June 28–July 7, 1965*, Korea, Korea University Asiatic Research Center, 1965.

Korea University. *Report on Survey of Business Failure in Korea*, Korea, Korea University, Business Management Research Center, 1966.

Korean Annual, volumes 1964–1969. Seoul, Korea, Hapdong News Agency, 1964–1969.

Korean Development Association. *A Study of Internal Consumption Tax Burden by Income Class in Korea*, Korea, 1966.

Korean Development Association. "A Study of Regional Planning by Using Regional Input-Output Model," Korea, 1967.

Korean Development Association. *A Study on Construction Demand and Construction Capacity during the Second Five-Year Plan Period*, Korea, 1968.

Korean Development Association. "A Study on Transport Demand during the Second Five-Year Plan Period," Korea, 1968.

Korean Development Association. *Effective Protective Rates of Korean Industries,* Korea, 1967.

Korean Development Association. *Korean Economy in 1980's,* Korea, 1966.

Korean Social Science Research Institute. *Report on Critical Analysis of Existing Housing Programs: A Pilot Study for Urban Development,* Korea, 1965.

Kwon, Cha-Byung, et al. *Analysis of Korea's Import Substitution Industries,* Seoul National University, 1967.

Lee, Chang-Nyol. *Mobilization of Domestic Capital,* Korea, 1965.

Lee, Chang-Nyol. *The Unorganized Money Market and Interest Rates in Korea,* Korea, 1965.

Lee, Chong-Sik. "Korea in Search of Stability," *Asian Survey,* 4, no. 1, Jan. 1964.

Lee, Chong-Sik. *The Politics of Korean Nationalism,* Berkeley, University of California Press, 1963.

Lee, Chong-Sik, and Hong, Sung-Chick, eds. *Politics and Society in Korea* (expected date of publication, 1971).

Lee, Hahn-Been. "From Ecology to Time: A Time Orientation Approach to the Study of Public Administration," prepared for the International Review of Administrative Sciences, Korea, Seoul National University, 1967.

Lee, Hahn-Been. *Time, Change and Administration,* Honolulu, East-West Center Press, University of Hawaii, 1968.

Lee, Won-Sul. "Impact of U.S. Occupation Policy on the Socio-Political Structure of South Korea 1945–1948," unpublished Ph.D. dissertation, Cleveland, Ohio, Western Reserve University, 1961.

Lyman, Princeton N. "Areas of Research in Political Science in Korea," United States Operations Mission to Korea, 1966.

Lyman, Princeton N. "Economic Development in South Korea: Prospects and Problems," *Asian Survey,* 6, no. 7, July 1966.

Lyman, Princeton N. "Korea's Involvement in Vietnam," *Orbis,* 12, no. 2, Summer 1968.

Lyman, Princeton N. "Students and Politics in Indonesia and Korea," *Pacific Affairs,* 38, nos. 3 and 4, Fall and Winter (Canada) 1965–1966.

Lyons, Gene. *Military Policy and Economic Aid, the Korean Case, 1950–1953,* Columbus, Ohio State University Press, 1961.

McVoy, Edgar C. "Manpower Development and Utilization in Korea," United States Department of Labor, 1965.

Ministry of Agriculture and Forestry. "Food Increased Production Plan: Summary 1965–1971," Korea, 1964.

Ministry of Construction. *Monthly Construction Statistics,* vol. 1, no. 1, Korea, 1968.

Ministry of Education. *Education in Korea: 1965–1966,* Korea, 1966.

Ministry of Finance. *Foreign Trade of Korea, 1966,* Korea, 1967.

Ministry of Finance. *Yearbook of Foreign Trade Statistics 1964,* Korea, 1965.

Ministry of Finance. *Yearbook of Foreign Trade Statistics 1965,* Korea, 1966.

Ministry of National Construction. *Maps of Selected Social and Economic Characters of Korea,* Korea, 1968.

Ministry of Reconstruction. *Aid Requirements for Korean Economy*, Korea, 1959.

Ministry of Reconstruction, Republic of Korea. *Development of the Korean Economy*, Korea, 1958.

Ministry of Transportation, Republic of Korea. *Korea Transportation Survey: Draft Report*, Korea, 1966.

Moos, Felix. *Social Science Factors and Considerations in Korean Rural Development*, Korea: United States Operations Mission to Korea, 1965.

Moos, Felix. "Some Observations on Korean Cultural Change 1966–1967," Korea: United States Operations Mission to Korea, 1967.

Musgrave, Peggy B. "Trade Targets and Policies in Korea's Economic Development," Korea: United States Operations Mission to Korea, 1965.

Musgrave, R. A. "Revenue Policy for Korea's Economic Development," Korea: United States Operations Mission to Korea, 1965.

Nam, Duck-Woo; Lee, Seung-Yun; Kim, Byong Kuk. *Determinants of Money Supply and The Scope of Monetary Policy: 1954–1964*, Korea, Research Institute for Economics and Business, Sogang College, 1965.

National Agricultural Cooperatives Federation. *Agricultural Yearbook: 1966*, Korea, 1966.

National Agricultural Cooperatives Federation. *Problems and Means of Improvement of Agricultural Credit System in Korea, 1965*, Korea, 1965.

National Agricultural Cooperatives Federation. *Rural Credit Survey in Korea, 1965*, Korea, 1965.

Norton, Kathryn. "Research Related to Social Problems in Urban Korea," Korea, United States Operations Mission to Korea, 1967.

Oh, Byung-Hun. "University Students and Politics in Korea," paper prepared for a conference on students and politics, sponsored by the Center for International Affairs, Harvard University, and the University of Puerto Rico, Mar. 27–Apr. 1, 1967, Korea, Sung Kyun Kwan University, 1967.

Oh, John Kie-Chiang. "Korean Democratization and the United States," prepared for delivery at the 20th annual meeting of the Association for Asian Studies, Philadelphia, March 22–24, 1968.

Oh, John Kie-Chiang. *Korea: Democracy on Trial*, Ithaca, N. Y., Cornell University Press, 1968.

Osgood, Cornelius. *The Koreans and Their Culture*, New York, Ronald Press, 1951.

Overseas Technical Cooperation Group. "Survey Report on Korean Steel Industry," Tokyo, 1965.

Park, Jay-Soo. *An Evaluation Study for the Accuracy of the 1960 Population and Housing Census of Korea*, Korea, Bureau of Statistics, Economic Planning Board, 1966 (volume in the 1960 Census Monograph Series).

Parsons, Kenneth H. "Issues in Land Tenure Policy for Korea," Seoul, United States Operations Mission to Korea, 1965.

Reeve, W. D. *The Republic of Korea, A Political and Economic Study*, London, Oxford University Press, 1961.

Research Institute for Economics and Business, Sogang College. "An Economic

Model of the Korean Economy: 1956–66" (preliminary draft), Korea, 1968.

Rhee, June-Il. "Student Demonstrations in 1964 and Government Measures," *The Political Science Review*, Seoul National University, vol. 5, 1967.

Royal Asiatic Society. *Transactions of the Korea Branch*, Korea, 1966.

Shaw, Edward S. "Financial Patterns and Policies in Korea," Korea, United States Operations Mission to Korea, 1967.

Sohn, Jae-Souck. "The Role of the Military in the Republic of Korea," paper prepared for the International Sociological Association Meetings, Evian, France, 1966.

Suh, Dae-Sook. *The Korean Communist Movement 1918–48*, Princeton, N.J., Princeton University Press, 1967.

Supreme Council for National Reconstruction (Republic of Korea). "Overall Economic Reconstruction Plan" (draft), Appendix, Korea, 1961. Korea, 1961.

Supreme Council for National Reconstruction (Republic of Korea). *Explanatory Note for Five-Year Economic Reconstruction Plan*, Korea, 1961.

Surveys and Research Corporation. "The Korea Statistics Project: Apr. 23, 1958–May 31, 1963," final report to the government of the Republic of Korea and the Agency for International Development, Washington, D.C., 1963.

Taxation Bureau, Ministry of Finance. *National Tax Reforms 1960–1964*, Korea, 1965.

United Nations. "Rehabilitation and Development of Agriculture, Forestry, and Fisheries in South Korea," report prepared for the United Nations Korean Reconstruction Agency by a mission selected by the Food and Agriculture Organization of the United Nations, New York, 1954.

United States Mission Operations to Korea. *Evaluation of Planning and Development in Seoul*, Korea, 1967.

United States Mission Operations to Korea. Public Services Division. *Organization and Functions of the Government of the Republic of Korea*, Korea, 1966.

United States Mission Operations to Korea. Public Services Division. *Personal Statistics of the Government of the Republic of Korea*, Korea, 1965.

United States Mission Operations to Korea. Rural Development Division. *Revised Foodgrain Production and Consumption (1962–64)* and Projections to 1971, Korea, 1965.

United States Mission Operations to Korea. *Rural Development Program Evaluation Report*, Korea, 1967.

United States Operations Mission to Korea. *Summary of U.S. Economic Aid to Korea* (FY 1954 through FY 1965 as of June 30, 1965), United States Operations Mission to Korea, 1965.

Wolf, Charles, Jr. "Economic Planning in Korea," *Korean Affairs*, 3, no. 2, July 1964.

Yearbook of Foreign Trade Statistics, Korea, Ministry of Finance, 1964–1965.

Index